PRAISE FOR JOE FRIEL AND
THE CYCLIST'S TRAINING BIBLE

"Joe Friel is arguably the most experienced personal cycling coach in the U.S., and his book *The Cyclist's Training Bible* has become, well . . . the Bible of the sport." —*BICYCLING*

"Joe Friel is one of the world's foremost experts on endurance sports." —*OUTSIDE*

"*The Cyclist's Training Bible* will have you systematically training just as world-class cyclists do. If you scrupulously follow its guidelines, I'm confident your racing performance will dramatically improve." —*TUDOR BOMPA, PHD*

"To say that Joe Friel knows a thing or two about how to ride a bicycle and stay fast would be a severe understatement." —*ROAD BIKE ACTION*

"I find Friel's book a treasure of information for cyclists of all levels." —*ANDY HAMPSTEN, 1988 GIRO D'ITALIA WINNER, 1992 TOUR DE FRANCE STAGE WINNER AT ALPE D'HUEZ*

"Nothing else comes close to *The Cyclist's Training Bible's* comprehensive approach to planning out a season, creating a training schedule, and incorporating diet and resistance training to an overall plan." —*BIKERUMOR.COM*

"Packed with worksheets, charts, visuals, and a dense index and references for further reading, *The Cyclist's Training Bible* is an arsenal of encyclopedic information for ambitious riders." —*DAILYPELOTON.COM*

"*The Cyclist's Training Bible* has become a cyclist's best chance at achieving their goals. This is the ultimate manual for growth as a cyclist." —*BICYCLESMILE.COM*

THE CYCLIST'S
TRAINING
BIBLE

5th EDITION

THE CYCLIST'S
TRAINING
BIBLE

THE WORLD'S MOST COMPREHENSIVE TRAINING GUIDE

5th EDITION

JOE FRIEL

▼velopress®

4745 Walnut Street, Unit A
Boulder, CO 80301–2587

VeloPress is the leading publisher of books on endurance sports. Focused on cycling, triathlon,
running, swimming, and nutrition/diet, VeloPress books help athletes achieve their goals of
going faster and farther. Preview books and contact us at velopress.com.

Distributed in the United States and Canada by Ingram Publisher Services

Library of Congress Cataloging-in-Publication Data
Name: Friel, Joe, author.
Title: The cyclist's training bible: the world's most comprehensive training guide / Joe Friel.
Description: Fifth edition. | Boulder, CO: VeloPress Books, [2018] |
    Includes bibliographical references and index. |
Identifiers: LCCN 2018002047 (print) | LCCN 2018004222 (ebook) | ISBN
    9781948006040 | ISBN 9781937715823 (pbk.: alk. paper)
Subjects: LCSH: Cycling—Training.
Classification: LCC GV1048 (ebook) | LCC GV1048 .F75 2018 (print) | DDC
    796.6—dc23
LC record available at https://lccn.loc.gov/2018002047

This paper meets the requirements of ANSI/NISO Z39.48-1992 (Permanence of Paper).

Art direction by Vicki Hopewell
Cover photograph by Benjamin H. Kristy / Dominion Cycling Photography
Illustrations by Charlie Layton
Composition by Erin Farrell / Factor E Creative

Text set in DIN and Warnock

19 20 / 10 9 8 7 6 5 4 3

To Dirk: My friend, my training partner, my mentor, my pupil, my son

CONTENTS

PROLOGUE

The Cyclist's Training Bible was the first book I ever wrote. That was more than 20 years ago. My interest at the time didn't lie in selling books. In fact, I figured it would sell only a few copies and within a handful of years would be long gone. My motivation then was to see if I could describe the training philosophy and methodology I had developed over the previous 20 years as an athlete, student, and coach. I never dreamed this book would become the best-selling book on training for cycling, or that it would play a role in changing how so many riders prepare to race.

This latest edition of the all-new *Cyclist's Training Bible* is, indeed, all new. When I decided it was time to rewrite it, I threw away the old manuscript and started with a blank page. The only thing that remains similar is the table of contents.

The project took me a year. That's partly because the content had nearly doubled in 20 years, from 70,000 to 130,000 words. Whew! But it also took me a year because before writing each chapter, I went back to the research to see exactly what had changed in the past two decades. While that certainly added to the project's writing time, the research was crucial in helping me describe the advanced and updated training concepts you'll find here.

I'm pleased with how it turned out. But more important, I think you'll find it beneficial to your training. That's been my motivation with every edition.

Writing a book for a broad spectrum of riders is a challenge. I know that some who will read this book are novices who are in their first year in the sport. Everything here will be new for them. Other readers will be intermediates in their second and third years who are still developing their basic fitness and learning about training. Then there will be the advanced riders who have been in the sport for more than three years, who read a previous edition, and who have developed a sound understanding of training and many of its nuances. At the highest level will be elite athletes who have not only been in the sport for several years but also have the ability to perform at a winning level in their race categories. They generally have a deep knowledge of training and sports science.

Regardless of the group you belong to, I've tried to address your needs. By following the training guidelines proposed here, you will advance to the next level of performance.

In fact, competitive performance is what this book is all about. My hope is that you will learn new ways of training to help you grow as an athlete and see better race results. Of course, I don't suggest that reading this book will magically transform you into a professional Grand Tour rider, but it's certainly possible to take your riding to the next level of performance and achieve goals that you previously didn't think were attainable. I've seen this happen many times with the athletes I've coached over the years. I'm certain you can also do it by applying the principles you'll read about in the following chapters.

The purpose of this book is to help you become fitter, ride faster, and achieve high goals. Collectively, these outcomes make up what may be called "high performance." I'll use that phrase a lot in the following chapters. I intend it to mean achieving those three outcomes—fitness, speed, and goals—but high performance goes well beyond your results. It's as much an attitude as an indicator of how well you race. In fact, attitude comes before race results—way before. It is living in a way that makes the achievement of high goals possible: how consistently you train; how disciplined you are about training; what, when, and how much you eat; who you hang out with; how you think about yourself; and much more. A high-performance attitude is a life that is pointed directly at your goal, a goal you relentlessly pursue. Chapters 1 and 2 will touch on many of these matters.

Attitude and lifestyle, however, play only supporting roles in this book. There are other works by sports psychologists that can help you achieve mental high performance. Our focus is primarily on developing your physical high performance, so after introducing the mental component in Part I, we will get to work on your fitness, form, and plan for success.

In many ways, cycling is a different sport than it was 20 years ago. Perhaps the biggest change has been the acceptance of the power meter. Very few riders in the 1990s had them, even though the technology was developed in the late 1980s. Power meters were simply too expensive—about a month's salary for the average person—and too mysterious. Back then, we gauged intensity with heart rate monitors, which had been around for 20 years and were relatively inexpensive. Before that, riders determined training intensity strictly from perceived exertion: how they felt. With power meter prices coming down dramatically in the past several years, training with power has become common and heart rate monitoring and perceived exertion appear to be fading away. But as you'll see in the chapters that follow, while the workouts rely heavily on power metrics, heart rate continues to play an important role and perceived exertion remains critically important for high performance.

There have been many other changes unrelated to equipment since the original book was released. At the time of the first edition, training periodization was largely an unknown concept for the average rider. It was a closely guarded training secret of Eastern Bloc countries throughout the 1950s and 1960s, and remained an enigma in the West into the early 1980s. Before periodization took hold, most riders simply trained however they felt and decided what to do for a workout as they rolled out of the driveway. Saddle time was considered to be the best predictor of performance. When I introduced the annual training plan based on periodization in the first edition, in order to keep it simple I described only one seasonal planning method: classic periodization. In this edition, though, I've expanded considerably on the topic of seasonal planning by introducing several methods in addition to classic periodization. It's all found in Chapters 7, 8, and 9, and created using the annual training plan template in Appendix A. I've also helped you decide which method is best for you. I consider this to be the hub of the book. The chapters that come before and after are intended to enhance your individual training plan.

In the previous four editions of *The Cyclist's Training Bible*, I also offered only one simple way to train for all riders, regardless of their unique physical attributes. Cyclists have become much more knowledgeable about training since then. This edition allows for individualization by considering the reader's particular cycling phenotype—his or her sport-related strength—in recommending how to train. This comes down to your personal racing characteristics as a climber, sprinter, time trialist, or all-rounder. Every rider fits into one of these categories, and so the training methodologies you'll find here are built around this concept, as described in Chapter 2.

The science of training has also grown considerably in the last 20 years, most notably with the development of the Training Stress Score (TSS). As you'll see, using TSS is a much more effective way to gauge training load than simply adding up hours, miles, or kilometers spent on the saddle each week. Learning to train with TSS is one of the smallest and yet most effective changes you can make to increase fitness and race faster. That may sound far fetched, but I know it works. It will focus your training on what's important for high performance. In Chapter 4, I'll teach you what TSS is and how you can use it effectively.

One topic that remains much the same as in the first edition is individualized training based on abilities and limiters. You'll find this explained in Chapter 6. In many ways, this simple concept is at the core of successful training for endurance sports, and it is closely related to your goals and objectives, and even to the workouts found in Appendix B.

An area of study that has seen a lot of research since the first edition is the stress of training and how best to recover from it. It's been well established that you must frequently flirt with overtraining in order to approach your potential as an athlete. This is a challenge for most riders, as the repeated fatigue of such training has an impact not only on subsequent workouts but also on daily life. Managing fatigue is a balancing act, and the timing of the stress-adaptation-performance loop is dependent on how effectively you recover following hard rides. The challenge is to keep the time you need to accomplish this progression as brief as possible without shortchanging adaptation. This is the dilemma of short-term recovery and is explored in Chapters 10 and 11.

Long-term recovery from cumulative fatigue also drives high performance. This is especially evident in tapering for your most important races of the season. Achieving a peak of fitness *at the right time* is not well understood by most riders. Tapering is a complex undertaking that removes fatigue while maintaining fitness. The result is called "form." It's another balancing act related to recovery. Chapter 3 introduces this three-part concept, while the full explanation is held until Chapter 13 so that you fully understand all of the training methodologies of the intermediate chapters before delving into this multifaceted topic.

The strength program you'll find in Chapter 12 is also greatly updated to provide more options for developing the muscular force necessary to produce high power. If you are time constrained, as many riders are, you'll learn in this chapter that not all strength training needs to be done in the gym. You can do it on your bike with no need to lift weights. Should you decide to follow a more traditional gym-based strength program, however, the weight lifting exercises have been updated to provide maximum benefits for time invested, along with additional exercise alternatives when time and energy allow for them.

There wasn't much in the way of training analysis in the first edition. Now that we have more precise ways of measuring training and racing performance, in Chapter 14 I'll help you effectively measure progress toward your performance goals, which were initially explored in Chapters 1 and 5. Training analysis is crucial for continued improvement. We'll explore new ways of looking at training information, with an emphasis on examining only critical data. This will save you time while also improving your performance level.

If you read and closely studied the original book, you'll find some contradictions in this one. What I've written here sometimes disagrees with what I said earlier. That brings us back to where we started: Things change. The sport has changed. Sports science has changed. And I have changed. The evolution of all of this will continue.

And that's a good thing. My hope is that you also evolve as an athlete after reading this book.

Training to become a high-performance cyclist is not easy. I suppose that's partly the reason we do it. Growth in any challenging area of interest is rewarding in many ways. It's not just standing on a podium that makes you successful. The huge challenge of bike racing—and racing well—produces habits and an outlook on life that are good for you in many ways, though not easily formed. You'll become not only a better cyclist but also a better person for accepting the challenge. It's not easy because it takes time, energy, purpose, dedication, and discipline. But that's what makes the challenge rewarding. The benefits come later and are mostly recognizable only to the rider. It is my hope that this book will help you realize all of this.

ACKNOWLEDGMENTS

This book would not have been possible without the contributions of several others.

My philosophy and methodology of training as described here and in all of my Training Bible books grew out of decades of studying many others' works. There are several coaches and sports scientists who stand out; among the especially instrumental are Tudor Bompa, PhD; Eddie Borysewicz; Ed Burke, PhD; Loren Cordain, PhD; David Costill, PhD; Arthur Lydiard; Iñigo Mujika, PhD; and Tim Noakes, PhD. I am deeply indebted to each of you for the role you played in the development of what is found in this book. Thank you all.

Throughout this book, I frequently discuss power-based training and often refer to related metrics the reader may use in training and racing. Nearly all of these metrics come from the mind of Andrew Coggan, PhD. Thanks, Andy, for revolutionizing the way we think about training and for your contribution to my development as a coach.

There were many who assisted with specific topics discussed in the book. Nate Koch of Endurance Rehabilitation reviewed and offered suggestions on my physical therapy discussions in Chapters 1 and 5. Tim Cusick, the developer of WKO software, provided and helped explain Figure 2.1 in Chapter 2. Ben Pryhoda of Training Peaks assisted me in identifying tools for measuring fatigue and provided his thoughts on how to use the information for Chapter 11. And my son, Dirk Friel, a former pro cyclist and general manager of TrainingPeaks, reviewed Chapter 14 and offered his insights for analyzing training. Thank you.

Ted Costantino of VeloPress offered tremendous support for my idea of completely revising a well-established book that had been around for two decades. Thanks, Ted.

The readability you find here comes largely from the professional editing of Ted and his staff. Charlie Layton took my rough sketches and turned them into the figures you find throughout this book. Thank you all.

I would be remiss if I didn't also acknowledge the many athletes I've coached over more than 30 years who trusted me to tinker with their training, racing, and even their lifestyles. You helped shape my understanding of training through your comments and questions. I remain in contact with many of you and always enjoy hearing about your continued athletic successes. Thank you.

And finally, I want to thank my supportive and loving wife, Joyce, who managed other projects around our home while I worked on this book for more than a year. I'm very appreciative of your continued encouragement, Joyce, despite my 4:00 a.m. messing about as I study and write of things I find fascinating.

PART I

MIND AND BODY

You are fully capable of racing at a higher level. You may not believe that yet, but I have no doubts about it. Every athlete I've ever coached could improve. And whether you know it or not, your performance is certainly being held back by your mind, the most common impediment to high performance. It's highly likely that you are also constrained physically—you haven't reached your body's full potential.

Not knowing how to train effectively for competition is quite common. If your mind is not focused and ready for more, you won't achieve more. Being uncertain about the best methods for physical training is also a widespread problem. That's why we're here. I am confident that if you read this book and apply its program to your training, you will become a faster, smarter, more capable, and more accomplished competitor.

In Part I, therefore, we examine the two critical components of high-performance racing—mind and body—starting in Chapter 1 with what needs to happen in your mind. You may be thinking that physical training should be your sole focus as you try to improve, but I want to show you several contributors to what in sport is commonly called "mental toughness." As an athlete, you already have some measure of this skill. It only needs to be further developed. As we examine the concept, new ways of thinking about yourself as an athlete will emerge. That is the basis of mental toughness.

Chapter 2 starts the discussion of how to prepare your body for high-performance racing, beginning with the mental perspective and then progressing to the philosophy and methodology of training I use with the athletes I coach. I've seen this work for so many athletes over the years that I feel certain your performance will also improve by adopting it. The chapters that follow will continue to expand on this topic.

By the end of Part I, you will be ready to move on to the finer points of physical training that hold the potential for helping you become a high-performance cyclist.

1

MENTAL PERFORMANCE

THIS BOOK IS ALL ABOUT high-performance cycling. We bike racers usually think of high performance in terms of training and race results—how physically fit we are and how many podiums we've been on. But there's more to it than that. High performance also has a mental component. High performance is as much a way of thinking and behaving—an attitude—as it is a race result. Get the attitude right, and the physical part, as well as the race results, take care of themselves.

If your mental attitude lags behind your physical performance, you will never reach your full potential. In fact, if anything is holding you back right now as you work to become a winning cyclist, it's probably the mental part of high performance. How can this be? Quite simply, if you have any doubt in your mind about your ability to accomplish anything—if you doubt you can win a race—you probably will fail, no matter how many hours of training you've put in. To win, you need to develop and maintain a winning attitude.

At the core of your attitude about cycling are the hundreds of thoughts and small decisions that define who you are every day. These have at least as great an impact on your race performance as your on-the-bike training.

What are these thoughts and small decisions? Here are a few examples of internal questions that you ask and resolve daily with little or no deliberation: How will I use my time today? What race am I training for? How do I think I'll do in it? Will I work out today? What workout will I do? Will I push my limits or go easy? When will I work out? What will I eat and drink? What do I think about? Will I read or watch TV? Who will I hang out with? Who will I ride with? How do I think about myself? What's my self-talk like? Am I a strong rider? What do others think about me? How do I talk to others? What's most important to me? When will I go to bed? How and when will I wake up?

These performance-defining questions are just the tip of the iceberg. There are many, many more. The overarching question that must precede every one of them, though, is this: Are you making decisions that promote high performance or not? Is your mind in line with your ambitions for the sport?

Every day, the seemingly small and insignificant decisions you make impact who you are and what your athletic performance will be. Individually, these decisions can seem insignificant, leaving no lasting impression and having little effect on your performance. But as similar decisions accumulate over days, weeks, months, and years, they ultimately determine who you become and how you perform as a cyclist—and in every other aspect of your life. As determiners of performance, all of these small decisions and thoughts go well beyond how hard your ride was today.

True high-performance athletes are not only physically fit, they're also mentally fit. They're not perfect, but when it comes to the things that impact performance, they are likely to take advantage of nearly every thought and decision to create opportunities for success. Their daily lives are about high performance. In fact, they are obsessed with success.

Is that good or bad? The answer depends on a lot of variables. But I can tell you that you will never achieve the highest levels of performance without some degree of obsession. The top athletes in the world are highly committed to their goals. That's a requirement for achieving success at anything in life that's difficult to attain.

In this chapter, I touch on only a few mental opportunities for success that will help you perform at a higher level. But the topic of mental fitness is much deeper than I can cover here, so once you have mastered the techniques in this chapter and throughout this book, I encourage

you to become a student of the mental side of high performance by reading other books on the subject and talking with successful people from all walks of life. If you embrace daily improvement in your mental approach to cycling, your training and racing will benefit greatly.

MOTIVATION

High performance is rooted in motivation. Competitive cycling demands an inner drive to excel in order to cope with the mental and physical stresses of training and racing. Motivation starts with a commitment to your goal. It also requires a lifestyle that aligns with the demands of your goal. The higher your goal, the more your daily actions must contribute to achieving that goal. At the highest level, *everything* in your life—from food to friends and beyond—must be focused on the goal.

Everything you must do to achieve high performance leads back to motivation. It's what gets you out of bed early to fit a workout into your day. It's what causes you to make healthy food choices instead of eating sugary junk foods. It's what keeps you going when a workout is so hard it hurts. It's what leads you, after an exhausting three-hour training ride, to spend another 20 minutes analyzing your session training data.

Motivation is also at the heart of setting a high goal. The extraordinary motivation to commit to the demands of focused training and a high-performance lifestyle must be intrinsic. There's nothing I can say to motivate you. I can only offer suggestions and perspective. Your level of motivation is entirely of your own making. You're motivated to excel because you love the sport. There's little else in the world that turns you on

Every day, the seemingly small decisions you make impact what your athletic performance will be.

True high-performance athletes are not only physically fit, they're also mentally fit.

so much. You love how you feel after a race or hard workout. You read about cycling, watch it on TV, hang out with other riders, talk about the sport with friends, and think about it throughout the day. You define yourself as a cyclist. You have an unshakable love for the sport. And so you have a strong desire to push your limits and see how far you can go as a competitive cyclist.

Motivation like this ultimately comes only from within, but being around other motivated riders can also be contagious. This is where your team can contribute a lot to your desire to excel at the sport. Once you master the motivation and knowledge necessary for a high level of success as a cyclist, your rise through the ranks of the sport will be astounding. So while I can't provide you with motivation, I can tell you how to use it to set achievable goals and perform at a higher level. That's where we are headed next on this journey to high performance.

DREAMS, GOALS, AND MISSIONS

High performance always starts with a dream. This is something I've learned from consulting with and coaching athletes who were professionals, represented their countries at the Olympic Games, won national championships, and broke national and course records. The dream was in their minds for a long time before it ever became a goal. All of these athletes came from what otherwise would be considered normal backgrounds, and prior to their dream they never saw themselves as capable of achieving such remarkable accomplishments. They simply had a dream. It persisted and wouldn't go away. At some point, they made the decision to go for it—to make their

dream a goal. They took the first step, which led to many more steps.

Making their dreams into goals meant making changes. This is the hard part and requires some deep thinking. Dreamers must ask themselves, Am I willing to take the first steps toward the goal? What should I change about my life to improve the possibility of success? Can I commit to the changes? How great will the sacrifices be? Am I willing to make them for this goal? What if I fail? What if I succeed?

Excellence is rare. Too many athletes have only wishes—vague stuff they'd like to see happen but that they never truly define as or, much less, pursue as a goal. If you have a lingering dream and gradually give it shape and substance over time, you will eventually come up with that goal. What must come next is the will to pursue the goal—a mission. This requires a change in mindset. There is a purposeful attitude about a person on a mission. Such an athlete will find a way to make a goal happen, regardless of the inevitable obstacles and setbacks.

To help you get started down this path to cycling excellence, there are several questions I'd like for you to consider about your dreams and goals for the sport. Read Sidebar 1.1, "Dreams and Goals," and answer the questions there. There's no need to write down your answers. Just think your way through them while being frank and honest.

After reading the sidebar, did you learn anything new about your dreams, goals, and attitude? You may not have—yet. Sometimes a dream has to percolate for a long time before you decide to take action. But the sooner you do, the better.

Never stop dreaming. For the remainder of this book, I'd like you to keep your dream uppermost in your mind. What would you most

High performance always starts with a dream.

SIDEBAR 1.1 Dreams and Goals

To create a framework for taking action on your goals, answer the following questions as frankly and honestly as you can:

Why do you race?

Why not do something else instead?

Do you have other important hobbies or activities in your life besides cycling?

What would you most like to achieve in the sport this season?

What is the most important thing you must accomplish to achieve that goal?

What stands between you and success this season?

How confident are you that you can achieve your goal?

What was your biggest goal last season? Did you achieve it?

What obstacles did you overcome to achieve last year's goal? Or, why did you not achieve it?

If you don't achieve your goal this season, will you try again?

Were there other people who supported your goal last year? If so, who were they?

Do you commonly start workouts and races too fast and then fade?

How often do you miss workouts, and for what reasons?

Do you prefer to train with others or alone?

How often do you train with other athletes?

How supportive of your cycling goals are your family and friends?

---

like to accomplish as a cyclist? Eventually you will take your dream to the next level by setting a goal (we'll get into the details of goal setting in Chapter 5). For now, your dream may be far off in the future. That's OK. The bigger the dream and the higher the goal, the longer it takes to realize. Once you commit and have a goal, it must become your mission. The more challenging the mission, the more you must focus your life around it. It must be your purpose every day in every decision you make.

Believe to Achieve

There are bound to be setbacks in your race preparation, but they must be taken only as minor roadblocks on the path to success. All successful athletes at every level experience setbacks. When they occur, you must remain confident, be patient, and continue to be mentally tough. Anything less leads to failure.

The key to commitment when setbacks occur is self-confidence. You won't achieve your goal if you don't believe you can. You must believe to achieve. Can you do it? Do you really believe in yourself? Are you confident even when things aren't going well? Self-confidence is that wispy, soft-spoken voice in the back of your head that says, "I can do this." Unfortunately, that positive voice isn't always there when you need it. You're more likely to hear a negative voice in your head, one that always speaks to you as an angry authoritarian, saying loudly, "You *can't* do it!" You'll hear that stern voice often as you prepare for your races, especially on race day, when everything is on the line. You need confidence at these times to remain focused and determined.

You were born to be confident. As a child you did lots of risky things because you were sure you could do them. Why would you think otherwise? In fact, risk was fun. Unfortunately, along the road of life most people lose their self-confidence. Early failures magnified by especially negative people drain it out of them. The good news is that you can overcome this. Here are two easy things I've often had athletes do when they needed to build confidence. You must do these daily, without exception. Every day.

Saving successes. To promote self-confidence, open a savings account of successes. It's easy. Every night when you go to bed, after you've turned out the lights, you experience the only time in the day when there are no external interruptions. Take advantage of this to run a quick check of how training went that day. Review your workouts. Find one thing you did well. It may not seem like a big deal. Maybe you climbed one hill well or had one good interval. Or you finished a hard workout. Or maybe you had one of the best workouts of the season. Relive that day's successful moment repeatedly until you fall asleep. You just made a deposit into your success savings account.

Some of the deposits will be big; some will be small. But your account needs to grow every day. You can make a withdrawal whenever the negative, angry voice speaks to you. The week of a race is an especially good time to make withdrawals, as you begin to question your readiness.

When you feel a bit of anxiety about the upcoming race, go back and pull up one of those memories of success from your savings account. Relive it vividly. When the authoritarian voice in your head says, "You can't," make another withdrawal immediately. Drown out the voice with a success. When someone casually expresses doubt about your chances of success, make a withdrawal. When you step to the starting line, make a withdrawal. At these critical times, pull up the biggest successes in your account. Say to yourself, "Remember that time when I . . ."

Never deposit the bad experiences or unwelcome moments in training. Never. Let them go. They're rubbish. Don't relive them. Stay focused only on the positive experiences. Deposit only those experiences in your account. Withdraw only those. It works.

Fake it 'til you make it. The second thing you can do to boost confidence is to "act as if." That means always assuming the posture and disposition of a confident athlete. Always. Act as if you are confident even if you don't feel that way. You'll be amazed at what that does for your self-perception.

So how does a confident athlete act? Look around at a race or group workout and find athletes who exude confidence. How do *they* act? Study them. What you will probably find is that they stand tall and proud. Their heads are up. They look people in the eyes when talking. They don't denigrate others in order to elevate their own self-esteem. They move adeptly and fluidly—as good athletes always do. They aren't anxious or nervous looking. They're calm. It's obvious they are confident; their demeanor shows it.

Now you may not feel that way all of the time, especially on race day, but act confident anyway.

To promote self-confidence, open a savings account of successes.

Fake it 'til you make it. It's remarkable how taking on the posture and demeanor of confidence breeds confidence even initially, when you're not feeling that way inside. It's not possible to be confident with a slumping posture and defeated demeanor. It's like saying no while shaking your head yes. The two don't go together. Simply "acting as if" will get you through those moments when your confidence is waning. Try it.

MENTAL TOUGHNESS

There comes a time in every race when success and failure are on the line. You sense that you are at your limit. Fatigue is setting in. Your mind is willing to accept compromises: Perhaps the goal that you've worked toward for so long isn't really that important. This is the key moment of the entire race. The fully committed rider will get through it. Others will let go of their goal and settle for something less. Their passion will fade.

Commitment is simply passion for your goal. While it's obvious on race day, it must be there every other day too.

What are the details? What is it that committed athletes have that the others don't?

A few years ago, Graham Jones, PhD, a professor of elite performance psychology, published a paper in the *Harvard Business Review*. He had studied Olympic athletes in order to learn what sets those who medaled apart psychologically from the athletes who didn't medal. Dr. Jones discovered that in comparison with the non-medalists, the Olympic podium-placers:

- Paid meticulous attention to their goals
- Had a strong inner drive to stay ahead of the competition

Commitment is simply passion for your goal.

- Concentrated on excellence
- Were not distracted by other people or athletes
- Shrugged off their own failures
- Rebounded from defeat easily
- Never self-flagellated
- Celebrated their wins
- Analyzed the reasons for their success
- Were very confident of their abilities

There were other findings in Dr. Jones's study, but these give us a good idea of what it takes to be mentally tough. They are some of the same things we've been discussing throughout this chapter: motivation, excellence, big dreams, goals, a mission, commitment, dedication, discipline, and confidence.

As you can tell from the above list, mental toughness isn't just something that mysteriously appears on race day in the lucky few. It's an everyday state of mind as you prepare for your race. It's every thought you have; it's everything you do day in and day out. Mental toughness just happens to show up during hard races.

You need one more thing to be mentally tough that Dr. Jones alluded to in his paper but didn't precisely address: patience.

PATIENCE

Success won't come quickly. Just because you have a dream, a goal, and commitment doesn't mean success is imminent. Cycling is a patience sport. And the longer your race, the more patience it takes. For example, a time trial is not so much a race as it is a test of your patience. I go to several time trials every year. It never ceases to amaze me that there are always athletes who are obviously anaerobic—they're breathing hard—only 1 mile into the race. And they still have 24 miles to go! What are they thinking?

It takes supreme patience to be a good cyclist not only in your races but also in your approach to training. Achieving true peak performance requires months and years, not hours and days. Patience is necessary. You must be ready for a long uphill battle.

How patient you are is evident even in your workouts. An impatient athlete starts a workout or a set of intervals much too fast and then fades as the session continues, finishing weakly. In a race, the impatient athlete does the same thing—starts much too fast, with unnecessary attacks, and then limps to a whimpering finish. This is often the result of being on a passionate mission—the very thing you must do to succeed. Only in this case, your dedication and determination are working against you.

Commitment must be held in check by patience if you are to succeed. You won't accomplish your high goal in the first few minutes of a key workout session or race. The first interval won't be where you achieve your goal. It's what happens late in the workout, interval set, or race that makes the difference. This is when success occurs. It takes patience to hold yourself in check and save your energy for when it really matters: later on. We usually call this "pacing," but it's actually emotion control. Patience means controlling your emotions in the early stages of anything you do.

How do you become patient? There is no easy fix. It's just something you must do every day with everything in your life. When I coach athletes who show signs of impatience, such as doing the first interval too fast, I have them repeat the workout again and again until they get it right. If they start a race too aggressively and then fade, we have a long conversation afterward about the reason why they didn't achieve what they were capable of accomplishing. Helping an athlete learn patience is the hardest thing I have to do as a coach.

You must learn to be your own coach. Be aware of your impatience. Keep it in check. Remind yourself before a hard workout or race that you must contain your emotions early on in order to finish strong. Remind yourself at the start of the season that patience means making small gains toward your goal every day and that the process will take months. If you can learn to do all of this, you can become patient. And patience will lead to success. It's that simple.

COMMITMENT AND TENACITY

For your mission to succeed in the face of setbacks, which always happen, you must have two more things: commitment and tenacity.

There's a moment in every race when fatigue says, "Stop." Your legs are on fire, your heart is pounding fast and hard, and it hurts to breathe. Riders are coming off the back. They've accepted defeat. Their determination, evident early in the race, is gone. To stop the pain, thoughts about giving up creep in to your own mind. "Is this race really that important to me?" you ask yourself. "Why am I doing this?" This moment is the measure of who you are as a cyclist. This moment demands unyielding determination. The fully committed and tenacious rider finds a way to keep going a little bit longer.

While commitment to a goal may be quite obvious on race day, it must also be there on

Patience leads to success.

every training ride. In fact, it's on training days when you're riding hard and feeling fatigued that you become prepared for similar situations in a race. That's why you train—to prepare for those crucial moments that test you. Training isn't only about preparing the body; it's also what prepares the mind. Just as on race day, you must have commitment and tenacity to successfully complete a hard workout that pushes your limits. This is what drives you to do several 2-minute intervals at your top-end power with minimal recovery and make the last one the hardest. That tenacity prepares you for the race-day suffering.

What is tenacity? It's sometimes called mental toughness, and many people seem to think that you either have tenacity and mental toughness or you don't. It's not that way. Athletes have varying degrees of tenacity. Whether during a race or a workout, some riders are capable of coping with extreme suffering. They have a tremendous commitment to succeed and a high level of tenacity. Others are more sensitive to suffering and are unable to hang on for very long when it gets really tough. Even though they have the physical fitness to make it, they mentally give up. They lack a strong commitment. Then there are those who throw in the towel almost immediately at the first sign of suffering. They never had commitment. They were unprepared.

Tenacity can be improved. It's cultivated by race-like training. To grow as a cyclist, your workouts need to occasionally test your limits by challenging you to keep going for just a few seconds longer. That's often all it takes. You know the scenario: Everyone is suffering. A truly motivated rider up front is driving the pace. But that rider will last only a few seconds longer. Then things will calm down. Hanging on for only a few more

agonizing seconds often determines the podium contenders, but hanging on takes tenacity.

Racing is all about managing suffering. Road race outcomes are determined by highly intense episodes that only last from a few seconds to a couple of minutes. Time trials are all about maintaining a high level of intensity on the threshold of extreme suffering for a very long time. Both have to do with fatigue. According to research done by South Africa's Tim Noakes, PhD, the fatigue you experience actually occurs in the brain. He calls this the "central governor theory." His theory is that the brain is constantly monitoring all of the signals from the body, and it decides when it's time to pull the plug. He considers it a self-protection mechanism. It prevents you from doing damage to yourself.

Overcoming the brain's reluctance to continue when you are experiencing extreme fatigue is very difficult. It takes a tremendous commitment and a will to excel bordering on survival on a battlefield. I believe such tenacity is trainable for the highly committed rider. Workouts intended to produce suffering must prepare the mind as much as, if not more than, the body. In later chapters, I'll introduce workouts and training methods that will help you do this.

How is your tenacity? Are you fully committed to your goals and dedicated to excellence in all you do? Do you remain positive even in the face of failure, accepting defeat graciously and then moving on? Do you challenge your mind to continue on for a few more seconds or minutes in the face of extreme fatigue and suffering? That's a tall order. But you already know that racing isn't easy. Being fully committed to excellence is what gives some riders a high level of mental toughness. Tenacity doesn't just mysteriously appear

Training isn't only about preparing the body; it's also what prepares the mind.

Tenacity is cultivated by race-like training.

on race day in some riders. It must be worked on continuously. It's an every-single-day attitude. It's the result of hard workouts. It's every thought you have; it's everything you do. In the end, full commitment will produce a tenacious, high-performance attitude.

At the most basic level, being fully committed to your goal means you *must* train consistently. Without consistent training, there is no commitment and tenacity never develops. Missed workouts are the first sign that a rider lacks commitment. The starting point for high-performance commitment is following standard training routines. The foundation of commitment is training consistency.

CONSISTENCY AND ROUTINES

Your mind and body like routines. You're more likely to train consistently when you have regular and standard schedules in your daily life. You're also more likely to achieve your goal when things happen in a predictable manner instead of occurring at random. An example of this is something you are probably already doing: following a set pre-race routine. You may have found that you are more relaxed and mentally ready to compete if what you do before a race stays much the same from one race to the next. Your pre-race routine probably includes the food and drink you commonly consume, the timing of meals, the music you listen to, a warm-up routine, mental rehearsal, time spent talking with teammates about strategy, and myriad other thoughts and actions. The purpose of all of this is to prepare your body and mind for what is to follow: hard racing.

Having a daily routine that leads up to a workout prepares your mind and body for what's ahead. This may involve a standard time of day for training sessions, the types of workouts you do on certain days in a weekly pattern, the food and drink you take in prior to the workout, your training partners for some workouts, cycling courses unique to certain types of workouts, and lots more. Just as with racing, the purpose of weekly and daily routines is to prepare you for the stresses of training, especially on hard workout days.

When all aspects of daily workouts are random, you are likely to find that your training suffers. To overcome this, you need a weekly training plan, which is covered in Chapter 8. Your daily lifestyle routine, on the other hand, is something I can't suggest for you, as there are simply too many variables: sleep patterns; career, work, or school responsibilities; family life; time spent with friends; and any number of other things that make up your day. I strongly suggest that you give some thought to how all of these affect your training and how you can best organize them to foster excellence.

Your lifestyle routine comes down to priorities. Everything can't be top priority. Most serious riders put time spent with their family and friends first, followed by career responsibilities, and they often fit in training at the third level on their priority list. If there are more than two higher-priority activities that come before training, though, you'll frequently miss workouts. This is the commitment part of training that is so critical to achieving your goal.

Of course, only you can decide how great your commitment is to training and racing. But I can tell you this with great certainty: The higher

The foundation of commitment is training consistency.

your goal, the greater your commitment must be, and therefore the more exacting your daily routine must also be. If you read the biographies of the sport's best high-performance athletes, you will quickly see that their lives revolved around training throughout their careers. Of course they experienced interruptions in their routines, much as you will. Things happen. As a high-performance athlete, you must roll with the punches and continually make adjustments. That's just part of life.

The most crucial take-home message is that you need a standard weekly and daily routine that allows you to fit everything important into your life in the order that reflects your priorities. You've got some level of responsibility to other people, including immediate family, relatives, employers, teachers, coworkers, classmates, friends, teammates, and others. Fitting only these responsibilities into your life is difficult. Also fitting in training that meets the demands of your goal makes establishing a daily routine extremely challenging. So your goal must be realistic with regard to your life. And the higher the goal, the more important it is that you have a standard lifestyle routine in order to produce the desired result.

YOUR HIGH-PERFORMANCE TEAM

Let's shift gears. So far we've been examining what thoughts and actions *you* can take to race successfully. It's time to include others. The more supportive people you have in your corner, the greater the odds of your success. One of the keys for meeting the needs of all of the other people in your life is to ask them to be a part of your high-performance team. Those close to you more than likely want to help (just as, I hope, you want to help them). Asking them to be a part of your personal support team greatly increases your commitment and motivation because you then share a sense of responsibility for the outcome with others. The feelings are mutual for everyone involved, and everyone around you takes on the mission.

Start with your family and friends. Make them aware of your goal and ask for their support and help in achieving it. At the very least, they can attend your races. With a little thought and imagination, I'm sure you can come up with many other ways they can support and assist you. Having those closest to you on your side when it comes to training and racing is a powerful motivator.

Next, include your cycling team. The camaraderie and backing of a good team is critical to your goal achievement. It goes well beyond racing. If they are aware of your goal, you will have the support of a like-minded group of riders who can help you achieve it. They can train with you, offer workout suggestions, provide encouragement, give psychological support when things aren't going well, and much more. And, of course, you should do the same for them. Having your team 100 percent behind you—and being 100 percent behind your team—goes a long way toward achieving your goal.

There are others you can include in your personal high-performance team. One of the smartest moves you can make is to enlist the help of a coach or knowledgeable mentor who can guide you as you prepare for your season. This person can often be the difference between success and failure. The higher your goal, the more important it is to have someone you completely trust pro-

> You must create a routine that reflects your priorities.

viding guidance. It's ideal if your coach or mentor lives nearby, but with today's technology that is not a necessity.

I also suggest including on your team a physical therapist, a sports medicine doctor, a masseuse, a mechanic, and a bike fitter. Additional professionals to consider including are a personal trainer for gym workouts, a nutritionist, a chiropractor, and a sports psychologist. The more experts you have in your corner, the greater the likelihood of goal success.

The higher your goal, the greater the benefit of having such a team behind you. Because of their unique ways of assisting, each will help you successfully navigate the many challenges you'll face in your racing career. Tell each member of the team about your goal and how they can help you achieve it. You may never actually use some of them, such as a doctor if you don't experience any physical breakdowns during the season. But knowing that they are ready to help will boost your confidence and get you through rough patches when something isn't going right.

In addition to their unique contributions to your success as an athlete, each member of your team must also be a happy, positive, and successful person whom you like. If any of them don't fit that description, find someone who does. Surround yourself only with people who believe in and fully support you. Always avoid those who don't.

SUMMARY: MENTAL PERFORMANCE

As a coach, I've learned that all athletes are limited more by their minds than by their bodies. Mental fitness is at least as critical to an athlete's success as physical fitness. If the mental limiter is great enough, the chances of success are severely restricted. So when interviewing an athlete who has asked for coaching, I am mostly concerned with what's going on in their minds. If the athlete has the right attitude, I know that together, we can achieve very high goals. Without at least a spark of that attitude, I've found that success is unlikely. Mental fitness can be developed if the proper attitude is present. That attitude is difficult to define and even more challenging to improve.

In this chapter I described what I look for in the mental makeup of an athlete. The first is the motivation to succeed. This has to be more than a spark because there is little a coach can do to foster motivation. It's got to come from within the athlete. The other stuff I can help the athlete foster. But not motivation.

Second, I listen for a dream. It doesn't have to be a big earth-changing dream, but there must be something there that repeatedly shows up in our initial conversation. Vague wishes don't hack it. The rider has to have been dreaming of accomplishing something for some time. It will excite and drive the athlete to excel. Lacking this, neither one of us will be motivated.

Is the rider willing to make a strong commitment to make the dream happen? This is often hard to discern, so we talk about other challenges the rider has had in any aspect of his or her life and how he or she went about pursuing them. This brings up the important characteristic of tenacity. How hard did the athlete work at pursuing the goal? How long did it take? Did he or she give up or keep going after it with a can-do attitude for a long time? Without committing to a goal and then tenaciously pursuing it, all is lost. There's no hope.

If the athlete has the right attitude, we can achieve very high goals.

Vague wishes don't hack it.

Next, I look at the athlete's lifestyle. Is it random or structured? Is there a discernible pattern to the activities of daily life such as work or school, meals, sleep, and training? Is there consistency in training, or does the athlete miss lots of workouts? Generally, good athletes lead what many would consider boring lives. They do the same sorts of things every day. If they're consistent, I have no doubt they can follow a long-term plan. This doesn't mean that someone who has a chaotic lifestyle can't succeed, but it definitely decreases the odds.

I also want to know what the athlete's family and friends think about his or her training. Are they supportive? I've seen athletes fail primarily because those around them could not have cared less, or they may even have worked against their goal achievement. It's much more difficult to succeed when others think what you are doing is a waste of time.

When it comes to building out a high-performance team of professionals, I can help a lot. If the rider doesn't already have knowledgeable people to depend on, I will provide them. But that comes only after everything else has met my standards.

Then we set about giving shape to and defining the dream. Now the physical side of performance begins.

PHYSICAL PERFORMANCE

IN CHAPTER 1, you read about the importance of your mental approach to high-performance racing. Starting in Chapter 3, you'll be reading only about the physical aspects of preparing to race. While the physical side of training is the primary focus of this book, I can't emphasize enough how important your attitude and thoughts are. How you perceive yourself as an athlete has a lot to do with how well you train and race.

This chapter bridges the gap between the mental and the physical determiners of performance by attempting to establish your potential as a cyclist. Determining the answer to this common concern is no small task. To do it, we need to understand what it takes to race well. Then we'll examine what it takes to achieve your potential, again with only a small shift from the mental side of performance, by considering which philosophy and methodology of training is most likely to bring success. By the end of this chapter, you should have a good understanding of the com-

mitment and resources you'll need to become a high-performance rider.

THE RIGHT STUFF

What are you capable of achieving as a bike racer? The answer can be found not by using a crystal ball to peer into the future but rather by looking backward. For example, if you've been racing for several years while following a well-designed training program such as the one I describe here and in previous editions of *The Cyclist's Training Bible*, then you may not have much room left to grow as a rider. You're probably quite near your potential already. That's not to say you can't improve. I'm sure you can. It's just that the gains you make will be relatively small. A handful of percentage points is about all you can expect.

On the other hand, if you've been in the sport for a short time, if your training has been random, or if you've commonly missed lots of workouts, then your potential for improvement is quite high, as in double-digit percentage points. You only need to follow the principles and training guidelines described in the remainder of this book and you will progressively improve as a rider.

If you're not sure you can do what's necessary to closely follow the training principles in this book, another remedy is to purchase a generic training plan on the Internet written by someone who understands bike racing. It will provide structure, although you will still need to be dedicated to following it. A better solution would be to hire a coach, someone who has been around the sport for several years and has had success producing competitive riders. This can be an expensive way to go, but if your goals are high, it is more likely you will achieve them with expert guidance than without.

More than likely, however, you fall somewhere between these two extremes. You've trained regularly, although sometimes without direction. You've done frequent group rides and occasional hard workouts to get race ready. But there have also been times when you missed a string of workouts. You may have raced often throughout the past few seasons, and you may have finished most races deep in the pack. If this comes close to describing your training and racing, then you also have considerable room for improvement in the sport and this book will help you get there. But it will take dedication to achieve your potential.

Of course, it's not possible for me to say what your exact potential is. How much you will improve by following the guidelines described in the following chapters depends on a lot more than how consistently you train and how focused your high-performance attitude is. Your physical potential obviously also plays a significant role in

The predictors of your success are determined largely by your race goals.

Aerobic capacity, anaerobic threshold, and economy determine your potential for different types of races.

your cycling performance. This brings us to the physiology of high performance.

The physical predictors of your success as a road cyclist are determined largely by your race goals. Those goals, in turn, should be tied to certain types of races. The old saying "horses for courses" is true. If your goal calls for doing a very hilly race, you had better have some climbing proficiency. If you are concentrating on criterium racing, a generous helping of top-end power is a necessity. Time trials demand the ability to maintain a relatively high, steady intensity for a long time. Riders who are good at two or three of these basic disciplines—climbing, sprinting, and time trialing—are called "all-rounders." They are respectable in multiple disciplines but do not excel at any of them. This often describes the rider whose goal involves a race series with different types of events over several weeks, or perhaps a weekend stage race. The cycling disciplines themselves are known as "phenotypes."

So what does it take to have the physiological characteristics to be really good at one of these phenotypes? We'll get into this topic much more deeply in Chapter 6, but for now let's look at each road race–specific phenotype in terms of the three markers of endurance fitness: aerobic capacity, anaerobic threshold, and economy. These determine your potential for different types of races. Every rider has a unique mix of these determiners. Here is a brief explanation of each.

Aerobic capacity, also called "VO₂max," is a measure of how much oxygen you are capable of using when riding at a maximal effort for a few minutes. The more oxygen you can process to produce energy, the greater your aerobic capacity.

Anaerobic threshold (sometimes called "lactate threshold," although physiologically these are not exactly the same thing) is the percentage of your aerobic capacity that you are capable of sustaining for a long time, such as 40 to 70 minutes. The higher the percentage, the greater your anaerobic threshold fitness.

Economy is tied to all metrics of performance in that it has to do with how much energy you waste while riding. Economy is largely determined by your physical structure, but it also includes your pedaling style, position on the bike, and bike-handling skills. The less energy you waste, the better your economy.

Given all of this, what is your potential for success as a cyclist? In other words, can you predict your goal outcome with what you know about yourself, the demands of your goal race, and the physical improvements you'll need to make to bring those into agreement? Knowing the answer to that last question has a lot to do with how you should train—and perhaps even how you should adjust different aspects of your lifestyle such as nutrition, emotional stress, and sleep. In Chapter 6, we'll also examine a concept called "limiters." Limiters, as you will learn there, have a lot to do with the specific details of how you train relative to your goal. But for now let's look only at the big picture. What are the physical demands of climbing, sprinting, and time trialing? What does it take to prepare for each of the three race disciplines? Knowing this helps you understand your potential and what it will take to realize your goal.

Power-Duration Curve and Phenotype

Figure 2.1 illustrates typical power-duration curves for climbers, sprinters, time trialists, and all-rounders. I'll orient you to it. To the left end

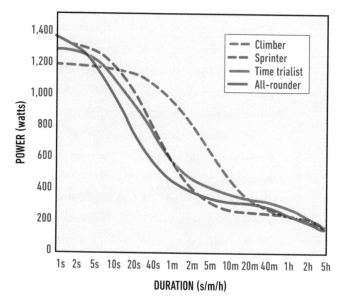

FIGURE 2.1 Typical power-duration curves for a climber, sprinter, time trialist, and an all-rounder

of the horizontal axis are the shorter durations in seconds ("s"). As you move to the right, the durations become minutes ("m") and then hours ("h"). The vertical axis represents very high-power outputs for short durations at the top, with decreasing power as the durations become longer. The curved lines represent how much power a rider in each phenotype is capable of producing for a given duration. The power outputs are not meant to be definitive for each phenotype, but rather they are intended as examples using fairly common elite-rider power data.

Climber. When the climber's power-duration curve is compared with the sprinter's, it is obvious that the left end power isn't nearly as great for the climber. The climber's slope is considerably flatter, yet the climber maintains comparatively higher power outputs as duration increases. To maintain power over time, the climber must have a very high aerobic capacity, a high anaerobic threshold, and excellent economy when climbing a hill. That's why climbing is such a challenge—it places the greatest total demands on the rider's physiology. And there's even more to it than that.

In climbing a hill on a bike, one of the best predictors of performance is the rider's power-to-weight ratio. This is commonly referred to as "watts per kilogram" (W/kg). High power and low weight give the rider a lot of potential when gravity is the primary environmental obstacle to performance.

Sprinter. In the sprinter's curve in Figure 2.1, the left side of the power curve is quite high, with a steep downward slope as the duration increases. This is typical of pure sprinters. They can produce tremendously high power for several seconds but are unable to sustain moderate power for long durations. Their great short-burst power requires excellent economy that in this case means great aerodynamics both in and out of the saddle, along with excellent pedaling and bike-handling skills.

Of course, this is an oversimplification of the physical demands on the sprinter. In order to be in contention at the finish line, the sprinter must first get to the last kilometer of the race with the leaders. That requires a somewhat high level of aerobic capacity and anaerobic threshold. But sprinters are still unlikely to be good at climbing; the race courses best for them are relatively flat. Time trialing talent is also usually lacking, as the power-duration curve is rather low for the durations that are common to time trials.

Time trialist. Power at anaerobic threshold is the best predictor of time trial performance. This is commonly called "functional threshold power"

(FTP) and is discussed in greater detail in later chapters. While a high FTP is critical for all riders regardless of goals, it is especially important for the time trialist.

Most time trial courses are relatively flat, and on these courses body weight is not a factor in the outcome. That's because the greatest environmental impediment to performance on flat terrain is aerodynamic drag, not gravity. In fact, good time trialists are often relatively big riders since the determining factor is high, sustainable power in order to drive the body and bike through the air. A big rider means big muscles. While the combined bike and body weight difference between a small and a large rider is significant on climbs (when overcoming gravity), size is much less important when aerodynamics is the principal constraint. The drag a big rider produces when in an aerodynamic position is not significantly greater than that of a small rider. So time trial results usually come down to who can generate the most absolute power for the duration of the race.

All-rounder. The all-round rider is generally someone who does not excel at climbing, sprinting, or time trialing but is pretty good in at least two of the disciplines. These riders are often in contention when course conditions don't favor the specialists, such as an uphill sprint or a somewhat hilly time trial. The uniqueness of the power-duration curve for this rider is not as apparent as that of the other three. It varies among all-round riders based on their individual blend of climbing, sprinting, and time trialing talents.

Does your goal involve being a climber, sprinter, time trialist, or all-rounder? Is your physical

---

One of the best predictors of performance is power-to-weight ratio.

Pure sprinters can produce tremendously high power for several seconds.

makeup compatible with that goal? If not, what must you focus on to achieve your goal? Your training (and perhaps lifestyle) will be defined by the size of the gap between what is required and where you are physically now. A small gap means your potential for success is high. A large gap will require extraordinary motivation, commitment, tenacity, and training consistency in order to accomplish your race goal.

This discussion of climbers, sprinters, time trialists, and all-rounders is a generalization in order to drive home the point that performance can be predicted from metrics—things you can measure, such as body mass and power production relative to duration. It surely won't surprise you to learn, though, that there is much more to it than this. Training to race is a rather complex task with lots of variables that go beyond these simple metrics. It's not so complex, however, that you can't learn to master and apply it to your unique physiology and goals. The remainder of this book is intended to help you accomplish this. All we've got now is a rough starting point when it comes to horses for courses. There's a lot more to be learned. For example, your philosophy of training—what you believe to be the best way to train—also plays a great part in your goal success.

TRAINING BELIEFS

Training is a research study with one subject: you. If you read sports science research, as I've been doing for the past four decades, you soon learn that while a study may show some measure of performance improvement among the research subjects who have followed a prescribed training method, the study result is merely an arithmetic mean. By digging a little deeper into

the research paper, you will find that not all of the subjects in the study improved by a precise and equal amount. Instead, any gain in the study is an average gain. Some study subjects obviously improved their outcomes more than the average, some less. There may even have been subjects who had a negative change in performance: Their performance declined by following the protocol. That's because the subjects were humans, not robots. Since you are also a human, I can't promise that you'll achieve personal greatness solely by following the guidelines laid out here. You should be prepared to make adjustments based on what you learn works for you.

Training for high-performance racing is also an act of faith. There is no promise that just because you follow a certain methodology by doing given types of workouts that you will absolutely reap great performance improvements. You may have faith that you will—we all do—but there are no guarantees. Nevertheless, you must believe that you are going down the right path in preparing to race or all is lost. You need to maintain faith in your program and follow it beginning to end.

There is a fair amount of physiological difference between each of us regardless of what the training methodology may be. For example, we know that some athletes will respond at a snail's pace when following a certain training method. They are "slow responders." It may take them months to match the gains of the "fast responders," who reap the physical benefits in a few weeks or even days while training in exactly the same way. Why is that so? No one knows for sure. It could be largely genetic, but there are lots of variables in a human's life.

Then there are muscle types. Some endurance athletes are blessed with lots of slow-twitch

You must maintain faith in your training program from beginning to end.

muscles, which have been shown to aid endurance performance. Others, who would like to be good endurance athletes, are instead endowed with plenty of fast-twitch muscles, which primarily benefit performance in power sports such as football.

Since I don't know where you are on the bell-shaped curve for each of the possible variables, I can't say with any degree of certainty that you should train in a given way. I can only make suggestions based on what the research suggests and what I've found to work for *most* of the athletes I've coached. You'll have to make adjustments to these suggestions based largely on personal knowledge in areas that you already know about. You may need to put up with some trial and error to find the best direction for your training.

You must also understand that training is a moving target. What worked for you last season may not produce the same results—or even close to the same results—this season. Your body and mind are always in a state of flux. Things change. Sometimes rapidly. You must always be prepared to make adjustments to how you work out, which brings us back to your training being a research study with only one subject. And you're the only one that matters. It doesn't make any difference how something works for everyone else if it doesn't work for you.

FOUR STEPS TO TRAINING WITH A PURPOSE

In sports science, the principle of individuality says that there is no one-size-fits-all way of training. Athletes differ too much for it to be otherwise. We'll explore this further in the next chapter, but for now you should know the other

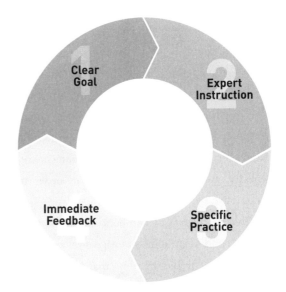

FIGURE 2.2 The process of purposeful training

side of this: that despite the need for individualization, there are also a few general methods that do work for the vast majority of athletes. One of these is having a focused purpose in your training. If you want to race at a high level, you must know exactly where it is you want to go and precisely how you'll get there. That's what purposeful training is all about. It means there is a reason for everything you do in training. As a coach, I have used a four-step progression, as illustrated in Figure 2.2, for many years that I know works well for most athletes in producing high performance. I highly encourage you to give it a try.

Step 1: Clear Goal

The starting point for purposeful training is having a well-defined goal. Your goal describes the outcome you are seeking—the reason you train. A vague, poorly defined goal makes the entire process of purposeful training pointless. For the goal to be well-defined, it must meet several criteria. I'm not going to get into these now, but we

> If you want to race at a high level, you must know exactly where it is you want to go and precisely how you'll get there.

will return to them in Chapter 5. By then, you should be ready to clearly state your season's goal or goals.

It isn't only the seasonal goal that's important. There are many subgoals that lead to your seasonal goal. At the most granular level, every workout should also have a goal. I call the workout goal a "purpose" so that the two types of goals don't become confused (in Chapter 5, I'll introduce a third goal level between these two). The workout's purpose could be something such as, "Do 2 intervals of 20 minutes each at the power sweet spot for muscular endurance with a 5-minute recovery between them" or "Complete a long ride of 3 hours, including 2 hours of steady aerobic endurance." Another common workout purpose is "Ride easy in zone 1 for 1 hour for recovery." So the purpose doesn't always have to be hard-core training. From time to time, it could even be something such as, "Ride with friends just to have fun." After all, fun is probably why you started riding in the first place.

The primary reason to set a workout purpose is to avoid haphazard training, which is all too common among self-coached riders. Heading out the door with no idea of what you will do is a sure way to accomplish little and show up at races unprepared. A steady diet of training without a workout purpose ultimately produces mediocre performance.

Before you start any training session, always ask yourself this key question: What is the purpose of this workout? Don't turn a pedal until you can answer it.

Step 2: Expert Instruction

Your workout purposes, when combined, should ultimately point to your season's goal. In fact, your goal performance is nothing more than the accumulation of daily purposes achieved over the course of many weeks. Your training purposes should follow a progression that leads from where you are at the start of the season to your eventual goal achievement.

Planning this progression can be complex, as it involves understanding a lot about the science of training (which we will get into in Chapter 3). For planning, it helps to engage an expert to give you clear directions on what workouts to do and when to do them. That expert could be a coach, a trusted mentor, or a training partner who can design or suggest a training plan for you. Most riders would improve exponentially by having such a person in their corner. Or, as another option, you could simply purchase a training plan online and follow it. Realize, however, that such generic plans are not designed specifically for you but for a rather large category of athletes who have similar characteristics and desired outcomes. If those characteristics and outcomes happen to match yours, then the purchased training plan may be your "expert."

The expert could also be you, especially if you're a student of training. In fact, teaching you the aspects and components of training is the purpose of this book. This isn't for everyone; many riders don't have the time or inclination to study sports science the way a good coach does. And it is true that self-coached athletes are prone to making lots of rookie mistakes. The learning curve is quite steep and often results in a shallow performance-progression curve due to poor decisions and frequent setbacks. But this is not to say you can't be your own coach. It can be done. I've known many good self-coached athletes. That's why we're here.

The primary reason to set a workout purpose is to avoid haphazard training.

It's important that you know exactly what to do in any given workout.

Realistically, however, without expert instruction your chances for success in achieving your seasonal goal are greatly diminished. With this book as a guide to what to look for, you will find that putting an expert in your corner makes you much more likely to succeed. Your expert should have a good understanding of what you want to achieve and then offer specific guidelines for getting there. The daily guidance you need throughout the season is for such specific questions as how long intervals should be, how to vary the intensities within a workout to develop the various energy systems, how to move to improve skills, when strength workouts should be scheduled relative to on-bike sessions, and on and on. Of course, if you're new to the sport almost anything you do will bring rapid improvement. But for experienced riders preparing for high-performance racing, training requires more than simply suffering during group rides.

Who will be your knowledgeable expert for the coming season: you, a generic training plan, a mentor, your training partner, or a coach?

Step 3: Specific Practice

Once you know the workout's purpose and supporting details provided by the expert (you or your coach) for a given session, everything you do must be specific to both. You must stay focused on doing the workout as planned. The exception comes on those occasions when you decide to make a session easier because you discover you aren't ready for it (perhaps you need more recovery time or the timing isn't right for some other reason). This is something you can do on the fly.

What you do in any workout must be specific to the intended purpose of that workout.

Going the other way—making the workout harder than its intended purpose—requires first consulting with the expert who designed it. There

could very well be a reason for its seemingly low level of difficulty. I tell the athletes I coach that if they feel the need to make the workout easier, they can always make that decision and tell me about it later. But they should not make the session more challenging without talking with me beforehand.

It's important that you know exactly what to do in any given workout. If the workout is fairly complex, write it on a scrap of paper and tape it to your handlebar stem or upload it to your handlebar power device so you can check it from time to time to make sure you're doing the session as intended.

Perhaps the greatest impairment to purposeful practice is the presence of other athletes during a workout. For most workouts, it's very difficult to specifically follow the session's purpose and details if your training partner wants to do something different. In fact, you are better off training on your own if the other athlete is unwilling to follow the plan. So make it a practice to talk about the purpose of your session before heading onto the road. Compromising the session's purpose in order to ride together violates the basic premise of purposeful training. The same goes for those times when you happen to encounter other riders on the road while doing your workout. The inevitable tendency is to turn the workout into a gradually accelerating race. When you sense this happening, the best option is to turn and get away from the other riders so you can do your intended workout exactly as you planned.

The bottom line is that what you do in any given workout must be specific to the intended purpose of that workout if you are to reap the planned benefits.

Step 4: Immediate Feedback

Without doubt, the most effective way to make progress is to have your expert with you while training. That way, you can get immediate feedback if things are not going as they should or you discover a concern about the workout. Feedback even one day later is better than never at all. The same goes for an analysis of how well you performed the planned session. Workout data reviewed as it happens or right afterward is much more effective than data ignored and unanalyzed for several days. It's vital for the expert to immediately examine your performance and offer feedback while the workout is still fresh in your mind. The sooner you get the feedback, the better.

Unless you are the expert, however, it's unlikely that your expert will be able to attend all of your workouts. Usually the expert's feedback will be delayed. But the sooner you can get it, the faster your progression will occur. This feedback can be face to face or via emails or text messages. Beyond that, a weekly conversation to discuss how training is going is a perfect opportunity to ask questions of the expert to make sure you are achieving the intended workout purposes and to help you see the bigger picture as you work toward your goal.

If you are self-coached, you need to stay mentally engaged with how you feel during workouts. If your mind drifts while working on pedaling skills or doing intervals, it's just like the coach has left. The self-coached athlete must always be scrutinizing what is happening. And that continues into the post-workout analysis. You should analyze the data files from whatever devices you are using as soon as possible following each session. The key question you should always seek to answer is, did I accomplish the purpose of the workout? The answer comes from the expert—you.

Once you've followed all four steps for the workout, you are ready for the next session and should return to Step 1 again. But before finalizing the purpose for the next workout, you need to assess your progress to date relative to your seasonal goal. If you're coming along as planned, continue on to the next workout. But if the long-term trend says otherwise, you may need to reconsider your goal and adjust your training strategy appropriately.

SUMMARY: PHYSICAL PERFORMANCE

In this chapter, we examined your potential for high-performance racing by looking back at how you've trained in the past. You then read about the three determiners of fitness for endurance athletes: aerobic capacity, anaerobic threshold, and economy. We also looked at how these determiners blend with the other cycling-specific aspects of your physical makeup, resulting in what is commonly called "talent." You are physically gifted to be good at either climbing, sprinting, time trialing, or as an all-rounder. You may not think so, however, which means our task is to first shift your self-perception toward the recognition of your natural talent and, second, teach you how to go about realizing it.

Realizing a high-performance goal is no small task. It requires having a purpose for your training. Unfortunately, most riders don't. Their workouts are random, lacking clear purpose and direction. Whatever the group ride does

Realizing a high-performance goal requires having a purpose for your training.

that day is their training methodology. In this chapter, I proposed a systematic way of training that I have found to be very effective for most athletes. It starts with having a clear and well-defined goal so you understand exactly what it is you want to achieve.

Then you must have expert instruction on what is necessary to achieve that goal. A personal coach can really pay off. But the expert could also be an experienced and well-informed training partner, a training program purchased online, or even yourself—if you are an avid student of training. It is with the tendency toward self-coaching that the training system often breaks down. Self-coached riders who are well intentioned but have little understanding of what it takes to succeed in the sport often make bad decisions. That ultimately leads to poor race performance. You must have expert guidance if you are to race to your potential.

The third step in purposeful training is specific practice: following the plan to the letter. The workout now has a purpose that is intended to take you one step closer to your goal. It's no longer a random workout that came to mind as you rolled out of the driveway. By closely following the plan day after day, you steadily move toward high-performance racing.

The last element of purposeful training is immediate feedback from the expert on how the workout went. Did you achieve the workout's purpose? If yes, you are closer to meeting your goal. If no, then the expert corrects course to get back on track. The expert opinion should come as soon after the ride as possible. Feedback results from an analysis of the workout data. Knowing what to look for and how to interpret it is critical to this step. We'll examine workout analysis in greater detail in Chapter 14.

I hope Part I has given you a better understanding of what it takes to succeed as a high-performance cyclist from both the mental and physical points of view. Now we need to improve your knowledge of the basics of sports science so that you can become your own expert for more purposeful training.

TRAINING FUNDAMENTALS

In Part II, we examine the training fundamentals that play an important role in coaching, whether with an expert or on your own. We start in Chapter 3 with an explanation of the fundamental sports science concepts of training for endurance sports. You may already have a good understanding of these concepts and may even apply them appropriately in your training. But I urge you to read this section anyway, because I need you to fully grasp their importance to your race preparation and performance. We start with the basic, but often misunderstood, training principles and carefully work our way up to somewhat more advanced concepts such as the interactions of fitness, fatigue, and form.

Then, in Chapter 4, we get into the topic of training intensity. It is a concept that most riders accept at face value but seldom come to completely comprehend, even though intensity is perhaps the single most important contributor to race performance. We start with how to measure intensity and explain why all of the three common methods contribute to your performance. We also delve into the poorly understood topic of intensity distribution over time, and we finish by coming to grips with the Training Stress Score, which has the potential to change your way of training.

By the end of Part II you should have a thorough grasp of some of the most influential aspects of training and be ready to start developing your preparation for the race season ahead in Part III.

BASIC TRAINING CONCEPTS

FOR ALL of the variables among us, athletes have a great deal in common. We're all *Homo sapiens*, and much of our physiology is quite similar. We may not all respond to a training program in exactly the same way, but we can expect many things to be much the same. At the same time, while this book describes common ways to train, the training methods it lays out may not always work for you. I'm well aware of this from coaching hundreds of endurance athletes over more than 30 years. There's no doubt that each athlete I coached was unique and therefore required a training program that was also unique. And while there were many similarities among these athletes, what worked for most did not work for all. The goal of this chapter, therefore, will be to give you the perspective you need to adjust the concepts of this book to your own specific situation. By examining and absorbing the basics of what is currently known about the science of training, you'll be better prepared to create a training plan—the primary focus of this book—that supports your unique personal characteristics with a foundation of well-established scientific principles.

Each of the topics we'll explore has grown from an understanding of how the human body operates, especially in endurance sports. Most of what you will read here will probably make a lot of sense to you. You may already understand many of these concepts, but since they are so basic, you may never have given them much thought. They are so critical to your success, however, that I want to make sure you have a handle of each of them before getting into the critical details on your training program. You'll learn here what they are about, and in later chapters I'll show you how to apply them so your training produces the desired results. You will greatly improve your fitness and race performances if you understand how to use these concepts in the real world of training.

TRAINING PRINCIPLES

Let's start by examining four concepts that form the core of training for sport. Follow these training principles, and you're certain to be headed in the right direction. Violate one of them, as I sometimes see self-coached athletes do, and you greatly decrease your chances of success in racing. They are usually obvious to most advanced athletes who have been around the sport for some time, but even experienced athletes occasionally disregard one. Much of what you will read about in the rest of this book is ultimately based on these four principles, so take your time to make sure you thoroughly understand them.

The Principle of Progressive Overload

This first principle is obvious to anyone who exercises, even if he or she isn't really serious about fitness. It basically states that in order to increase fitness, you must gradually and steadily increase the amount of training you do. In other words, if you want to increase your fitness, you must make your training plan progressively harder.

How much harder? In general terms, the workload needs to exceed the current level of adaptation by stressing the body beyond what it did before. Without stress, fitness cannot improve. Physical stress is evident when you are fatigued after a hard workout or after several days of hard training. That means your body has been overloaded and will respond positively if the overload wasn't too great. If it is too great, it's called "overtraining." Basically, that's an overload that is too great for adaptation to occur, instead causing a breakdown in some way. Later in this chapter you will read about certain concepts related to overtraining and how fitness and fatigue are closely related.

Of course, you shouldn't take this principle to mean that training should become harder every day and every week to progressively increase the stress. There are times when you must reduce the workload in order to recover. Without frequent recoveries built into your weekly, monthly, and annual training, you will most certainly never achieve a high level of fitness.

The Principle of Specificity

There are two broad physiological categories of changes that take place in your body when you exercise. Sports scientists refer to one category as "central" and the other as "peripheral." *Central* changes primarily occur in the heart, lungs, and blood. It doesn't make much difference which endurance sport you participate in for these changes to happen. The heart, for example, doesn't know the difference between running and cycling. It simply pumps oxygen-rich blood regardless of what type of exercise is being done. Running, in this case, has to do with crosstraining, which is beneficial for the central systems.

But if all you do is run, you'll never even come close to achieving your potential as a bike racer. That's because of the necessity to also build *peripheral* fitness. This mostly has to do with muscles. You can't fool the quadriceps muscle in your thigh. It knows the difference between running and riding a bike. Although it's used in both, the way in which it's used in these two sports is completely different. If you only run, your quads will never become highly fit for cycling. It's the same for all of the other muscles that contribute to powering a bike. Swimming, hiking, skiing, or

In order to increase fitness, you must gradually and steadily increase the amount of training you do.

doing anything else that isn't *very* similar to riding a bike will not train them to be fit for riding a bike. To train your muscles for riding, you have to ride.

In light of this principle, crosstraining is largely ineffective for the muscles. The possible exceptions are strength training with weights and other forms of gym exercises, such as plyometrics, to increase the power of the cycling-specific muscles. But even here the exercise movements in the gym must closely mimic the way the muscle is used in the sport. It isn't enough to simply load a working muscle with a lot of weight; you must move it under this load in a way that is very specific to the way the muscle is used when riding. You'll see how this principle is applied to muscular development in Chapter 12.

So which is more important: central fitness or peripheral fitness? We can't separate or distinguish them in the athlete's performance. Both are critical. You'll never be a high-performance cyclist without both systems being well trained. Traditionally, training season starts with an emphasis on the central systems and then gradually shifts toward an emphasis on the peripheral systems. So we might say that the closer you get to your most important race, the more your training emphasis should be placed on peripheral fitness, which therefore means increasing training specificity. In other words, crosstrain very early in the training year, but then as the season progresses make the bike the focus of your training.

The Principle of Reversibility

Reversibility has to do with losing fitness. Whenever you record a zero in your training diary, you have lost fitness. You may not agree with me on this. Many athletes think they gain fitness by taking a day off because they may train or race really well the next day. What they are actually experiencing, however, is something called "form," which we'll return to soon in this chapter. Fact is, you can't gain fitness by resting. Only by working out do you become more fit. A day off means a loss of fitness. To be sure, it's a very small loss—so small, in fact, that it couldn't be measured in an exercise physiology lab. After several such days off from training, however, the loss would become great enough that it could be measured. That's reversibility. Use it or lose it.

This shouldn't be taken to mean that you should never have a day off. There are certainly times when that is warranted. You need to take a day off when you are greatly fatigued. For some athletes, especially those with low levels of fitness—which could describe you early in the season—a day or more off every week may be necessary. Without a complete break from training, riders with a low level of fitness are likely to experience an excessively large training overload that could eventually lead to overtraining. The highly fit athlete, on the other hand, may not need a day fully off to recover. A light training day will perhaps provide all the recovery such a rider needs. This will be explained more thoroughly in Chapter 11.

Reduced training also results in reversibility. When the training load is reduced for several consecutive days, for whatever reason, there is a loss of fitness. But, you may ask, isn't that what we do when we taper for an important race? Yes, and that tapering process—what I call "peaking"—is necessary if you want to race at a high level. This, once again, has to do with form. If you spend a lot of valuable training time tapering and peaking for races throughout the season, then you lose too much fitness and race perfor-

The closer you get to your most important race, the more you should emphasize specificity.

mance declines. That's also related to how many highest-priority races you do in a season. We'll come back to this topic of form and the related topics several times in the coming chapters, with much greater detail in Chapter 13.

The most common and significant loss of fitness, assuming you aren't injured or sick for several days at a time, comes at the end of your season when you take a long—and necessary—break from focused training. We'll get into that in greater detail in Chapter 7.

The basic idea here is that fitness is always changing—sometimes positively and sometimes negatively. You have complete control over the direction.

Fitness is always changing. You have complete control over the direction.

The Principle of Individuality

The principle of individuality simply means that as an athlete, you are unique in many ways. Sometimes your uniqueness means it is best that you train in a certain manner. That's often not evident and must usually be discovered through trial and error, but there are also some obvious signs of your uniqueness. You may be a very good sprinter but poor at climbing and time trialing. Your thighbone relative to your total leg length may be longer than most other riders', a condition that's been associated with powerful and economical pedaling. You may gain strength and muscle mass quite easily, while others following the same program experience only slight changes. You may deal with the heat well or suffer more than most when it's hot.

Since you are unique, your training must also be unique.

Since you are unique, it therefore follows that your training must also be unique. You can't do what your training partner does and expect the same results. Even though your favorite pro rider may do a certain workout, that doesn't mean it's a good one for you. The training program you follow must match *your* distinctiveness if you are to achieve your potential. Starting in Chapter 5, you will determine your unique characteristics, and in Chapters 7, 8, and 9, you'll learn how to design a training plan that is effective for *you.*

DURATION, INTENSITY, AND FREQUENCY

Regardless of your competition level, there are only two factors to consider when designing a workout plan: how long each workout will last and how hard each workout will be. The first is duration, and the second is intensity. With these two factors, you can come up with all sorts of workouts, from intervals to tempo rides to recovery spins.

There's only one more variable to consider: frequency. How often will you train? You can, for example, work out once a day in a week for a frequency of seven, or you can ride every day and lift weights twice a week for a frequency of nine.

Duration

Throughout this book, I'll describe training in terms of duration, not distance. Time is the more critical element in training and racing. Your body reacts to how long you maintain a high intensity, not to how many miles or kilometers you cover. Even though you may cover the same distance when riding into a headwind as you do on a calm day, the durations are different, and each requires a unique amount of power. The power-duration curves you read about in Chapter 2 illustrate this relationship between intensity and time.

Let's look at an example to better understand this concept. Let's say you have trained for a

40 km time trial and you've determined from what you know about the course and your fitness that you can finish in about 55 minutes. That will require a certain power output, and so you've prepared for that in your workouts. However, on race day there is a very strong headwind on the point-to-point course and reports are that riders of your ability are taking around 10 minutes longer to finish than planned. So you can expect it to take you about 65 minutes. Should you race at the originally planned power or change it? Since it's duration and not distance that determines the intensity of the race, you must reduce your planned power. If you don't do that, you will likely blow up in the last few minutes of the race and limp to the finish line.

The underlying concept here is that intensity is *inversely* related to duration. This means that as one increases, the other decreases. As the time of a race or workout gets longer, the intensity you are capable of maintaining is reduced.

Intensity

All you need to measure duration is a clock. But measuring intensity isn't so simple. It's a much more complex metric that can be calculated using a speedometer, a heart rate monitor, a power meter, a lactate analyzer, or any number of other methods including perceived exertion, which is simply your informed assessment of how hard you are working. Some of these tools, such as a speedometer, are very simple and easy to understand. Others, such as a power meter, are not so easily understood and, in addition, can be quite expensive to purchase. The higher your goal and the more experienced you are as a cyclist, the more likely you are to benefit from using a power meter. In Chapter 2 I introduced

one way in which power may be used to gauge your intensity: the power-duration curve in Figure 2.1. The power meter is a tool I highly recommend all serious riders use.

I should also point out, however, that if you are in the first two or three years of training for bike racing, a power meter isn't all that important. In year one, you are primarily focused on changing your lifestyle and building a strong base, so your primary goal is to get out the door and ride often. Frequency is therefore the key to your progression at this stage.

For the intermediate cyclist in years two and three of racing, the common key to continued success is increasing the duration of rides. That builds aerobic endurance and takes a couple of years to accomplish.

The experienced athlete's focus, however, must be on intensity. If training frequency and duration are still not well established, then the advanced rider will not make progress. But once these are mastered, intensity must be the focus for the rider to advance. This doesn't mean that every workout should be at a high intensity—recovery sessions are a necessity, and the topic of recovery will be discussed frequently throughout the remainder of this book. But the intensity of your key workouts will largely determine your success in racing.

Measuring intensity is crucial to your success and progression in the sport. This doesn't mean that frequency and duration are unimportant to the experienced rider. You can't train infrequently for short durations for weeks on end and expect to race at a high level. But at the highest level of competitiveness, these metrics are simply somewhat less important for measuring and ensuring training progress. With rare exceptions,

> The experienced athlete's focus must be on intensity.

intensity must be the primary training focus for the advanced cyclist.

Unfortunately, many advanced athletes continue to believe that long-duration workouts are the key to their racing success. In part, that's because duration is easy and cheap to measure and they spent the early years of their training focused on it with good results at lower levels of racing. As a result, they became hooked on duration early in their sports career.

Accurate intensity measurement is neither easy nor cheap. Moreover, it requires study to become good at using it. In Chapter 4, we'll take an in-depth look at intensity, especially power, and how with proper use, it can help you become a high-performance cyclist.

Frequency

How often do you train? How many workouts do you do in a week? The answer probably depends more on your lifestyle than on what you'd like to do. Most riders tell me that they would like to ride more frequently but are limited by responsibilities related to career, family, and other matters. That makes getting the most from their limited training time critical to performance. This in turn implies being smart about planning training and designing workouts. The serious rider must do the right workouts at the right times. There is no room for sloppy, aimless training. Every training session must count for something. That's why I strongly suggest having a detailed training plan. I know that planning doesn't sound like fun, but it's necessary if you want to reach your high-performance race potential. Smart planning to create a great individual training plan is what this book is all about. In Part IV, we'll get into the details of planning.

VOLUME AND INTENSITY

Volume is the combination of frequency and duration. Simply add up your hours for the week, and you have volume. If you do 7 workouts in a week and each is 2 hours long, your weekly volume is 14 hours. Most athletes measure their training progress this way because it's easy to measure. But for the seasoned athlete, intensity is the most likely key to success.

This does not mean volume is unimportant to the advanced rider. It's usually just less important than intensity. For the typically experienced high-performance rider, volume accounts for roughly 40 percent of race-day fitness while intensity is the reason for the remaining 60 percent.

It's probable, then, that if you've been seriously training in the sport for a few years, your focus should primarily be on workout intensity. Again, this doesn't mean that your rides must be at the highest possible intensity. There are varying degrees of intensity that we call "zones." We'll address that topic in the next chapter. Regardless of whether you primarily train with a power meter or heart rate monitor, you'll use all of the zones in training. How much time you spend in each zone depends on the event for which you are training, your individual needs, and the current seasonal period. We'll come back to this concept several times in the remaining chapters since it's so critical to your success.

DOSE AND DENSITY

To get the most from your training, it's important that you get the mix of volume and intensity right. That brings us to the closely related concepts of dose and density.

Dose has to do with how relatively hard a workout is in terms of either duration or intensity. A hard workout is "high dose," and an easy one is "low dose." A high-dose workout could be a very long ride, a highly intense session such as intervals or a group ride, or some combination of both long duration and high intensity. On the other hand, a low-dose workout is typically of short duration and low intensity.

Density is a measure of how closely spaced the high-dose workouts are. High-density training means that your hardest workouts are very close to each other—perhaps separated by only one day or even done on back-to-back days. In contrast, low-density training would mean there are several low-dose days between the hardest sessions.

Dose and density aren't the same for all athletes. Given the principle of individuality, they are unique to your specific needs and capabilities, with the added variable of your seasonal fitness. At the start of a new season, following weeks of recovery, both dose and density need to be low to allow for a beneficial adaptive process. As the training year progresses, dose and density increase so that by your first high-priority race of the season, you are race ready. That progression can't be overly aggressive or you are likely to break down in some way. In the same way, as you progress from novice to intermediate to advanced, both dose and density should typically increase.

The dose of each workout must be chosen based on your current situation. From time to time, all advanced athletes must do high-dose workouts that are specific to their goal race. The durations and intensities of those workouts will vary based on the type of race. Criterium riders usually do low-duration workouts with very brief

but high-intensity intervals in the last few weeks before the race. For multi-hour road races, the workout durations are often greater, with somewhat lower-intensity but longer intervals. Within those race-specific parameters, the dose is quite similar regardless of the athlete.

Density, however, varies considerably between athletes training for the same types of events. Typically, younger and fitter riders train with high density—their hard workouts are closely spaced. However, at the extremes of aging—juniors and aging seniors—the density of training is usually much lower. They will have more easy, low-dose workouts between the high-dose sessions.

Dose and density may be new to you, but if you've been around the sport and have been training seriously for a few years, you should readily understand these concepts because you've undoubtedly used them to train. Perhaps you've simply never thought about your training this way. Later on, when we get into training periodization, you'll give dose and density considerable thought, as they ultimately have a lot to do with how fit you become.

TRAINING LOAD

The combination of volume and intensity is called "training load." Some riders are able to manage a very high training load of more than 20 hours per week, including a lot of high dose and high density. Others must be more conservative in their approach to training, with a much lower training load. The reason, again, often has to do with the individuality principle. This, of course, includes not only your capacity for training but also how much training time is available given your lifestyle.

Dose and density aren't the same for all athletes.

Since it appears to be difficult to define the intensity of a single workout with an appropriate number, let alone define the intensity of a week of combined workouts, training load is not well understood by most athletes. They have vague notions and use time to measure it—in other words, how many hours they spent training in a week. This dismisses the importance of intensity in the training load and leads to an overemphasis on combined durations. In Chapter 4, I'll introduce a way of combining volume and intensity into a single number: the Training Stress Score (TSS). Once you have a good understanding of this concept, you'll be much more aware of how training load is a volume *and* intensity metric. Then, in Part IV, I'll teach you how to plan your season by using either TSS or time.

SUPERCOMPENSATION

Your training load should be high at times. The consequence of this is that you will often be tired. That's why we include rest and recovery days between hard workouts. It's during these easy days that the body actually becomes more fit. That's because a high-dose workout only produces the *potential* for fitness. Fitness is realized in the following hours of rest and recovery, especially when sleeping.

Low-dose workouts usually follow high-dose workouts in order to prevent breakdowns of various types. This process of alternating stress and rest is necessary to some degree in order to become more fit. If you only apply high-dose and high-density stress and do not recover adequately, you will likely experience overtraining (see Chapter 10). Overtraining is a condition far beyond fatigue. It's much like

having a severe illness, such as Lyme disease, mononucleosis, or chronic fatigue syndrome. You must avoid it. I've seen it end otherwise successful racing careers.

The physical adaptation of increased fitness resulting from alternating stress and rest is called "supercompensation." The human body is an amazing organism that can be molded through wise and consistent training to achieve remarkable performance outcomes. Supercompensation can't be forced on the body. You cannot make it happen at a faster rate than nature intends. Nature has endowed some lucky individuals with a fast response time. Others respond slowly. This is just the principle of individuality showing up yet again. The difference between a slow and a fast responder is likely genetic in origin. This is why in order to avoid overtraining while trying to improve fitness you must pay close attention to how your body is responding and not try to artificially speed up the process.

FITNESS, FATIGUE, AND FORM

I've been using the words "fit" and "fitness" a lot when referring to the benefits of training. I'm sure these words are common in your vocabulary, and it's likely you understand what they mean, at least conversationally. But for now, I propose you think of fitness as "race readiness." In this section, I will introduce a way of thinking about race readiness that may seem unusual to you, and I'll also introduce two additional concepts that are directly related to race readiness: fatigue and form. As we go along, you will find the more sports-specific definition of these terms useful in your training.

Your training load should be high at times. The consequence is that you will often be tired.

Fitness

Athletes use four common ways to determine changes in their race readiness. The one we are most interested in has to do with race results. That's the ultimate measure for the serious athlete. Did you achieve your race goal? If so, then you were very fit on race day and we can deduce that your training prior to the race must have gone quite well. Race results don't lie.

While results may be the ultimate gauge of race readiness, however, they come a bit late. By that time, you're looking in the rearview mirror. You would sleep better the night before the race if there were indicators during the previous weeks that your fitness was progressing. So how do you do that? Here are three other common ways of determining fitness.

As you prepare for a race, you will frequently take note of how your workouts are going and how you feel while doing them. This information will often indicate the direction of your fitness: increasing, stable, or decreasing. But it's quite subjective. Judging how fit you are feeling is hardly foolproof. Sure, it's good information about your progress, but you can't take it to the bank, because there's nothing solid to confirm it. You may think you're are doing well in training and then find out on race day that you weren't.

If you want to get *objective* feedback about your fitness progress, you can go to a clinic for testing. The technician will hook you up to high-tech equipment and put you through your paces on an ergometer for several increasingly grueling minutes. And when it's all over, you'll get a printout with a set of numbers that tell how fit you are. This is good data; if you do it a few times in a season, it will reveal your fitness progress as you prepare for the race. While such testing is an excellent and objective way of actually measuring fitness, it can become rather expensive when doing multiple tests over a period of a few weeks.

A fourth way is to measure your daily training load and determine its progress over time. This method is kind of like applying numbers to the how-you-feel method described above. As explained earlier, training load is the combination of volume and intensity. If your training load increases over time, your fitness also increases because you're able to handle a greater dose and also perhaps a higher density. A training load that's increasing is an indirect measure of improving fitness. If your fitness wasn't progressing, you wouldn't be able to handle greater training loads. So measuring and tracking your training load over time reveals a great deal about how fit you are becoming in a somewhat roundabout but fairly accurate and inexpensive way. You may be able to judge it by feel, but then again, you may not.

The problem, of course, is combining workout duration, which is easy to measure using a clock, with intensity, which is much more challenging to put a number on. And even if you could easily measure intensity, how would you combine it with duration? One way that has been around for a several decades involves the use of an intensity-measuring device such as a heart rate monitor or power meter, a clock, and software compatible with your device to produce a workout score every day. The daily scores are added together at the end of the week to produce a training load number. You can then compare that training load number with past weekly training loads. If the training load is increasing, you can assume that your fitness is improving because you're now capable of handling more physical stress than

Training load is the combination of volume and intensity.

TABLE 3.1 Example of a 120-Minute Workout Score Based on Time in Each Training Zone

A. ZONE WEIGHT	B. TIME IN ZONE (TO NEAREST MINUTE)	C. ZONE SCORE (COLUMN A MULTIPLIED BY COLUMN B)
1	60	60
2	16	32
3	10	30
4	30	120
5	4	20
	Total Time: 120 minutes	Total Workout Score: 262

Multiply zone weight (column A) by time in zone (column B) to produce a zone score (column C).

you could earlier in the season. You're becoming increasingly race ready.

Here's a simple way of looking at how this method works using either a heart rate monitor or a power meter. At the end of a workout, you download your device's data to its accompanying software. Your software should already be set up to show how much time you spent in each training zone (Chapter 4 will guide you in setting up zones). A numeric weight is then assigned to each zone. For example, assuming you use the common five-zone system, zone 1 is assigned a weight of "1" and zone 5 gets a "5." The other in-between zones are assigned weights of 2, 3, and 4, respectively. Then you multiply each zone's weight by the time spent in that zone in minutes. Add up the resulting numbers, and you have the workout's score. Table 3.1 provides an example of how a workout may be scored using this system.

So the rider's 2-hour workout shown in Table 3.1 produced a total workout score of 262. In the same way, each workout would be scored over the course of a week and then, at the end of the week, all of the individual workout scores would be added together, resulting in the week's training load.

Keeping track of your training load week after week gives you a good idea of how fit you are becoming.

In the example in Table 3.1, notice that both durations and intensities were used to establish the total workout score. While this way of producing a training load number is simple, it is tedious and time-consuming to compile.

An easier way is to use software that calculates a workout score for you after you've downloaded the data from your heart rate monitor or power meter. Perhaps the most ingenious such system was developed by sports scientist Andrew Coggan, PhD, and is found on the website TrainingPeaks.com. His system is based on the Training Stress Score mentioned above and is widely used by athletes in many endurance sports. The software does all of the number crunching for you.

Keeping track of your training load week after week through such a scoring system gives you a good idea of how fit you are becoming. If you are able to progressively overload your body over time, you can deduce that supercompensation is under way and you are becoming more fit.

The TrainingPeaks website provides another tool, the Performance Management Chart, which shows your training load progress over the course of the season. In a similar way, this chart also reveals another simple concept that is difficult to quantify: fatigue.

Fatigue

I hope you now understand that your capacity for increasing your training load over the course of a few weeks indirectly indicates that your fitness is improving. If your fitness were not getting better, you couldn't physically manage more volume or more intensity. That's supercompensation at work.

How useful is keeping track of your training load for measuring fitness? Well, it probably isn't as accurate as a lab test. Nor is it as good as the ultimate measure: a race result. It's only a mathematical model for estimating changes in a physiological phenomenon. It's by no means foolproof, but it can be very helpful in judging how your fitness is progressing. If your weekly training load is steadily increasing over several weeks, you can bet that you're gaining fitness. If your training load is decreasing, the opposite is happening: You are losing fitness.

If your weekly training load is increasing, we can also assume something else with a fairly high degree of certainty: You are becoming tired. Whenever you push your limits with more volume and intensity, you experience fatigue. There's no way around it. It's simply the nature of hard training. And just as with fitness, if your weekly training load is decreasing, then not only your fitness is diminishing but also your fatigue. You're recovering.

This brings us to an interesting conclusion: Fitness and fatigue trend in the same direction. If fitness is increasing, fatigue is also increasing. That leads us to assume that in order to become fitter, you must become fatigued. In this regard, fatigue is your friend. Conversely, you are losing fitness if you don't become fatigued frequently. When one is rising, the other is also rising. When one declines, the other also falls.

Fatigue always appears before fitness. If you do a hard workout today, you will be tired tomorrow. It will be quite evident by the way you feel. But we won't be able to measure a change in fitness tomorrow. Fitness changes very slowly—in weeks, not days—while fatigue changes rapidly—in hours and days. This is a good thing and something you will learn to use as you taper for an important race. The purpose of your pre-race taper is to produce form on race day. We'll get into this in depth in Chapter 11, but let's look at form briefly now.

Form

If you watch Grand Tours such as the Tour de France on TV, you may hear an announcer saying that a certain athlete is "on form" or that another rider is "lacking form." What exactly does "form" mean?

The concept of form in sport is thought to have originated in the late 1800s with horse racing in Europe. If you went to a race and wanted to place a bet, you would find a bookie—a bookmaker who keeps the records on bets. The bookie would provide a sheet of paper—a form—with a list of all of the horses racing that day and how they had performed recently. You would then pick one to put your money on because *on the form* that horse appeared to be racing well. Bike racing, which started at about the same time in Europe, also was a betting sport, with similar forms. So bike racing adopted the word. Over the next century, other sports also began to talk about form. Now it seems that every sport, from bike racing to bowling, uses that word to describe athletes' event readiness.

But let's return to the central question: What exactly does "form" mean in cycling? From the

Fitness and fatigue trend in the same direction.

above you can tell that it has a lot to do with racing well. That can also be taken to mean that the rider is fresh. A great deal of fatigue has recently been shed, with only a slight loss of fitness. The rider has rested enough to get rid of fatigue while maintaining a relatively high level of fitness. A rider who is fatigued can't be on form, no matter how great the fitness, since form consists first and foremost of freshness. A significant level of fatigue will always limit performance. The only way to be fresh on race day is to rest in the preceding days by doing what we commonly call a "taper" in order to become fresh. This is a tricky time in the season that will be addressed in greater detail in Chapter 13.

I want to make sure you understand what is going on here. It's very important for high-performance racing. Recall that I explained above that fitness and fatigue trend in the same direction. When one is rising, the other is also rising. And when one falls, the other falls too. So if fatigue is falling during a taper, what is happening to fitness? It's also falling. I know that sounds scary in light of the fact that you will be tapering before a race. I can sense your deep concern: If my fitness drops, how will I race well? The key to understanding this conundrum is also found above: Fatigue changes more rapidly than fitness when resting. So while a pre-race taper will shed a lot of fatigue quickly, fitness will be lost very slowly. If done right, on race day you will *feel* as if you gained fitness, even though that feeling is actually the result of having less fatigue. In other words, you'll be *on form*. Later, I'll show you how to pull this off so that you lose only a small amount of fitness while getting rid of nearly all of the fatigue. Understanding and applying this is one the key concepts in training to race.

A significant level of fatigue will always limit performance.

Fatigue changes more rapidly than fitness when resting.

SUMMARY: BASIC TRAINING CONCEPTS

We covered a lot of basic training concepts in this chapter, starting with an introduction to the four principles of training: progressive overload, specificity, reversibility, and individuality. You undoubtedly already knew about the facts of these, as they simply make sense from an athlete's common thoughts and experiences. My point in reviewing them with you was to make sure you understand how critical each is to your success. Sometimes we forget or overlook the basics when it comes to learning new ways of training. But the simple summary is that to become race ready, you must progressively increase your training load and train in a way that is specific to the demands of the race.

We also examined frequency, duration, and intensity. When frequency and duration are combined, that's called volume. While volume is important, remember that intensity is most likely the key to better performance for the advanced rider who has been in the sport for several years. You can measure intensity in several ways, but currently the most common ways are heart rate and power.

When a workout has a high duration or is highly intense—or both—it is said to be a high dose. The workout dose must vary so that there are occasional high-dose workouts matched with frequent low-dose sessions. How closely these workouts are spaced determines how great the density of training is. Athletes who manage high-density training—meaning their high-dose workouts are closely spaced—are typically young high-performance racers. Juniors and aging seniors are more likely to train with a lower density.

Training load is the combination of volume and intensity. If either of these increases while the other remains constant, or if both increase simultaneously, then the training load is increasing and the result will be greater fitness and increased fatigue. If rest is mixed in with a rising training load, then supercompensation is more than likely to occur, since it's during rest and recovery that the body adapts and becomes race ready. Rest and recovery also contribute to form.

This chapter contained a lot of what you probably thought of before as pretty simple training ideas. But we examined them from a different perspective than you've likely used in the past. My point in this chapter was to make sure that you are ready to move on to more subtly nuanced topics such as the distribution and measurement of training intensity. That's where we are headed next. Tighten your seat belt, as it may get a little bumpier now!

TRAINING INTENSITY

AS YOU READ in Chapter 3, there are only three workout components you can manipulate to produce fitness: frequency, duration, and intensity. For the advanced rider who has been in the sport for about three years or more, the first two should be a given. If how often and how long you ride—your volume—make up the central focus of your training, you have not yet reached the summit of "advanced" rider, even though you may have been training for several years. Frequency and duration should be, respectively, the central workout concerns for those novice and intermediate riders who are still relatively new to road racing. For the advanced athlete, however, intensity determines peak race performance, not volume.

Consequently, this chapter will explore some essential details of training intensity. I'll guide you in learning how intensity can help you become a more accomplished, fitter, and faster rider by examining ways to measure and apply it in training.

TRAINING WITH EFFORT, HEART RATE, AND POWER

Notice that the header here is *not* "Training with Effort *or* Heart Rate *or* Power." If you truly want to be a high-performance cyclist, it's beneficial to use all three of these common intensity measurements, not just one. If you are an advanced rider, I can say with a high level of certainty that you will become much more race ready by becoming proficient with all three.

Of course, while these are the most common measures of intensity for cycling, they are not the only ways to know how hard you are riding in a workout. The ultimate measure of performance is speed. I've never seen a race in which the first person across the finish line was not the winner. The fastest rider always wins, and it's always good to be fast. The problem with using speed to gauge cycling workout intensity, however, is that it's highly sensitive to wind and hills. If you are riding against the wind, your speed won't agree with the effort you are making. Zipping along with a tailwind on a training ride doesn't mean you will be fast when racing. Even a slight wind or a low-grade hill can have a tremendous impact on how fast you are riding. The bottom line is that using speed is not a good way to measure training on the bike relative to using intensity.

This brings us to the topic of effort—how hard it feels when you ride. When we put a number on the effort you are experiencing at any given moment in a ride, it is referred to as a Rating of Perceived Exertion (RPE). You can determine and express work intensity—how hard you think you're going—using a scale of 0 to 10. Table 4.1 illustrates this.

A Rating of Perceived Exertion is probably the most basic way to express the intensity you experience during a ride, and yet for all its simplicity, it has great value. I would encourage you to become good at monitoring your RPE, because it keeps you in touch with your total body. When you use it, you aren't just focused on external numbers. Road racing requires having a good sense of how hard you are working from a purely subjective point of view. In a mass start race, you are seldom able to make decisions at critical times based on power or heart rate. Should you go hard or not? The answer depends largely on how you feel at the time. Being familiar with RPE gives you a good gauge of what's actually happening in the race and how you should respond.

In the days before heart rate monitors and power meters, RPE was the way all riders gauged the intensity of a race or a workout. Granted, they seldom used this scale. They more commonly used descriptive words along the lines of what is in the right-hand column of Table 4.1 (sometimes with a few more colorful terms that

For all its simplicity, a Rating of Perceived Exertion has great value.

TABLE 4.1 The Borg 10-Point Scale for Rating of Perceived Exertion

RATING	PERCEIVED EXERTION
0	Nothing at all
1	Very light
2	Light
3	Moderate
4	Somewhat hard
5–6	Hard
7–8	Very hard
9	Very, very hard (almost maximal)
10	Maximal

are still in use today). The numeric-rating scale was something sports scientists dreamed up later on to make this system a somewhat more precise intensity measurement. You can do it either way, and I'm sure you do when telling others how hard you rode. That's common. But learning the numeric ratings does make it somewhat more exact and more useful in conjunction with your training plan, as you'll see later on.

Becoming skilled at using this scale is an art learned through frequent use. While riding, give some thought to how hard the effort feels at the moment and assign a numeric rating using the RPE scale. Do this frequently throughout workouts, especially those that have a lot of intensity variability, such as intervals or group rides. If you do it on every ride, you'll eventually become good at using RPE. That will help you make split-second decisions during races.

You'll probably discover when doing a group ride, race, or even simply training with a buddy that the ranking of your effort is lower than it would be if you were riding alone at the same power or heart rate. It's common for athletes to assign a lower RPE to any given level of intensity when in a group. In other words, we seem to be capable of working harder with a lower level of perceived exertion when we're with others. That undoubtedly has to do with motivation. We'll return to this phenomenon later on when we talk about workouts in preparation for mass start races.

RPE is entirely subjective—it's your opinion of how you feel at the time you're riding. To make it more accurate, you may use intensity-measuring tools that are objective. Presently, the most common ones for cyclists are the heart rate monitor and power meter. Accurately measuring intensity is so important that I require the riders I coach to have both of these tools. Later in this chapter, I'll give you a quick tutorial on how to set training zones for each of them. Each measures intensity in a unique way, providing information that is not available from the other two methods.

The heart rate monitor was the first tool for accurately measuring intensity. It was invented in the late 1970s in Finland for Nordic skiers. Heart rate measurement gradually became popular in the 1980s, but it wasn't until the early 1990s that the tipping point was reached for its common usage by nearly all endurance athletes across a broad spectrum of sports. Now it seems that almost every athlete wears one, from beginner to Grand Tour rider.

Heart rate tells us how intensely you are working. It does not say anything about performance. The last finisher in a race can have the same average heart rate as the winner. There are no podium positions for high heart rate. It doesn't tell you how fast you are going; it only tells you how much effort is going into the workout. In that regard, it is similar to RPE, but it's more precise. In fact, it's the best tool we have to accurately measure *effort*.

Ten years after the heart rate monitor, the mobile power meter was invented by Uli Schoberer, a German engineer turned cyclist. The power meter was designed to accurately measure *intensity*. It took about 20 years for cyclists to widely adopt it, and it transformed cycling from one of the least technical endurance sports to one of the most technical. Prior to the power meter, cyclists focused on volume when training. That made the sport rather unsophisticated and hung up on very old ideas about how training should be conducted. The power meter changed all that, and it revolutionized training.

A bike power meter directly measures only two things: the force that's applied to the pedal and the speed at which the pedals are turned. Pedal force is called "torque." Pedal speed is called "cadence." The combination of torque and cadence is expressed in watts. While it's beyond the scope of this book to get into every detail of power meter usage, it should be clear that a power meter has the potential to greatly improve your training and racing. I'll show you in this book how to incorporate the power meter into your training plan, but for complete information on how power meters work and how to train with them, please refer to *The Power Meter Handbook*, which I wrote to cover these fantastic tools in the depth they deserve.

INTENSITY REFERENCE POINTS

Let's take a brief and simplified look at intensity from a quasi-scientific point of view. There's no doubt that what I'm about to describe would start a heated debate if I proposed it to a group of sports scientists. They would see it as overly simplified and therefore inaccurate. My purpose

The combination of torque and cadence is expressed in watts.

There are three
broad categories
of intensity:
below the AeT,
above the AnT,
and between the
two thresholds.

in writing this book, however, is not to be precisely scientific but rather to explain ways for you to see the world of training so you can race faster in the real world. That sometimes requires glossing over the "how many angels can dance on the head of a pin" details that define the scientific method. With this in mind, let me set about helping you understand training with measurable intensity in the real world of cycling.

Sports scientists frequently ask subjects in research studies to express what they are experiencing during the test protocol using RPE. But scientists also like to use more precise physiological markers of intensity as reference points for athletes' exertion levels. Two of the most commonly used physiological markers are called "aerobic threshold" (AeT) and "anaerobic threshold" (AnT). I'll often refer to these markers in the following chapters, and they will also have a lot to do with the workouts in Appendix B. For now, we'll take a general, high-altitude view to get an overall idea of what they mean. Later on, we'll dig into them more deeply.

Let's start with Figure 4.1 to compare AeT and AnT with RPE as expressed in Table 4.1 to give you an idea of the intensity of each of these reference points. With this figure you should be able to see how these two intensity reference points may be used to categorize the intensity of

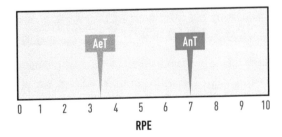

FIGURE 4.1 The intensity reference points compared with RPE

a ride. Note that there are three broad categories of intensity when viewing it from this perspective: below the AeT, above the AnT, and between the two thresholds.

Aerobic Threshold

Sports scientists have various ways in a lab to accurately measure intensity during exercise. A common way is to capture a drop of the athlete's blood by pinpricking a finger or earlobe and then analyzing the blood in a machine designed for this purpose. The drop of blood contains something you've undoubtedly heard of: lactate. Lactate by itself is not the problem child we've commonly been told it is. It is not the direct cause of either fatigue or muscle soreness. It is, however, a good predictor of how intensely the athlete is exercising. The more lactate in the blood, the greater the exertion. Scientists measure lactate in millimoles per liter (mmol/L). During resting (0 RPE), lactate is about 1 mmol/L. This is a very tiny amount—a drop in the bucket. As exercise intensity increases to around 3 or 4 RPE and lactate in the drop of blood correspondingly rises to 2 mmol/L, the athlete is often said to be at aerobic threshold (AeT).

AeT can also be determined in other ways. In the lab, another common tool is to measure the oxygen and carbon dioxide the athlete breathes in and out during exercise while wearing a face mask hooked up to a measuring device and computer. This gas analysis method approximates changes in lactate levels. It's noninvasive—no blood is drawn. But it still requires an expensive test.

You don't really have to understand all of this or have a lab test to find your AeT. For a much simpler and far less expensive method, although not as precise, you can simply calculate your heart rate at about 65 percent of maximum heart rate. Another method doesn't even require your max heart rate; it simply places your AeT at roughly 20 to 40 beats per minute (bpm) below your anaerobic threshold. We'll come back to that reference point next. Short of going to a lab to be tested, you could use your heart rate monitor while exercising and assume that you are quite close to your aerobic threshold at 30 bpm below AnT. For the average-fitness rider, this simple method seems to work well.

Later on I'll teach you how to use this critical AeT intensity reference point in training to fully develop your aerobic system. It makes for a great workout that, as you'll see, I suggest you do frequently.

Anaerobic Threshold

Note in Figure 4.1 that the anaerobic threshold (AnT), at about 7 RPE ("very hard"), is a somewhat more intense effort than the AeT reference point, at about 3.5 ("moderate") on the scale. At around this RPE of 7, you begin to redline during exercise. When you reach this level of exertion in a ride, you're working hard and realize that you won't be able to maintain it for very long; your suffering is just beginning. And the suffering continually increases above 7. The 7 RPE is also sometimes referred to as the "lactate threshold." From a sports scientist's perspective, the lactate and anaerobic thresholds aren't exactly the same thing, since one is determined using a gas analysis test (anaerobic threshold) while the other is determined by measuring the lactate in a drop of blood (lactate threshold). But for our purposes, we'll use the terms as meaning something quite similar: an RPE of 7. You read above that when lactate reaches a level of 2 mmol/L in the blood you are at or quite near your AeT. When it reaches

about 4 mmol/L, you're at the higher of the two thresholds: AnT. At AeT, the body removes the lactate-associated acid flooding the muscles as quickly as it enters them. But at 4 mmol/L and higher, the acid, comprised of hydrogen ions and other chemicals, begins to accumulate in the blood and so restricts muscle contraction. The body can't remove all of the acid unless you slow down considerably. That's why you start to suffer and can only maintain this level of intensity for a limited amount of time. An athlete in exceptionally good physical condition can maintain an intensity at AnT for roughly an hour—with a lot of suffering—whereas AeT can be sustained for several hours without agony.

With the right type of training, you can raise your anaerobic threshold so that you ride faster with higher power before you hit AnT. But note that your heart rate will remain about the same when at AnT, despite changes in fitness. That's an important lesson we'll examine more closely later in this chapter. This phenomenon plays a role in what we call "fitness."

Road racers spend most their race time between AeT and AnT. But race outcomes are almost always determined by what happens at and above AnT. That's why advanced riders must be focused on high-intensity training. The podium placers and finish results often have to do with very brief episodes throughout the race that last for a few seconds to a few minutes. This involves sprinting, climbing, forming a breakaway, closing a gap, "guttering" opponents, and all of the tactical methods used to cause or react to separations when racing. That's what sets variably paced events such as road races apart from the more steadily paced time trial. Time trial results are usually determined by who has

An athlete in exceptionally good physical condition can maintain an intensity at AnT for roughly an hour whereas AeT can be sustained for several hours.

the highest speed and power when near the AnT. In this case, constant surging for a few seconds or minutes is generally not a good idea. We'll come back to this in Chapter 6 when getting into how to train for different types of road races and for time trialing.

INTENSITY DISTRIBUTION

If race outcomes are determined by how well you handle intensities above the AnT, it would seem wise to spend well over half of your training at that level of intensity. But that creates an obvious problem in terms of training density. If you were to do anaerobic workouts day after day, four to five times each week, you'd likely be extremely fatigued all of the time and at risk of overtraining. Even if you weren't physically whipped, your fatigue would certainly be high enough that these hard workouts would be unproductive. You simply couldn't push yourself through such training day after day. As the high-intensity workouts took their toll, your heart rate and power would likely be low despite a high RPE. That's a serious situation sure to result in lackluster training, poor fitness, and mediocre race results.

In fact, I suggest that your distribution of training intensity should be just the opposite. Most of your training time should be at a very low intensity. Over the course of a season, the total time you spend at or below your AeT should be around 70 to 80 percent. The remaining 20 to 30 percent should be above the AeT, with a sizable chunk of that above the AnT. Training like this will mean that when you come to a high-intensity workout you will be fresh enough to ensure it's a good session—one that produces the fitness needed for those brief episodes on race day. In other words, you'll be able to produce high intensities because you will be physically ready for a hard workout.

The bottom line here is that the easier your easy workouts, the harder your hard workouts can be. It's all too common for riders to overdo the middle-intensity region between AeT and AnT, thinking that this will increase the average intensity of their training and therefore performance. But it has just the opposite effect because the high-intensity sessions—the ones that actually determine race outcomes—are compromised due to fatigue. You simply aren't ready for the above-AnT sessions. Anaerobic fitness is not as well developed when the focus is on the intensity between the thresholds. The single biggest mistake in training is to make easy workouts moderately hard (between AeT and AnT), thus decreasing recovery. You need lots and lots of easy riding if you are to perform at a high level. I know that seems contradictory, but it works.

Figure 4.2 illustrates this suggested intensity distribution, which is often referred to as "polarized training."

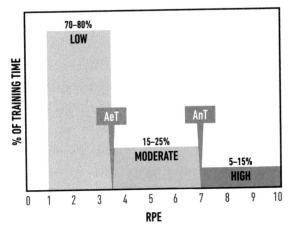

FIGURE 4.2 The suggested distribution of intensities over the course of a season when following a polarized training method

Most of your training time should be at a very low intensity.

This concept of polarized intensity distribution brings us to the topic of seasonal planning. For most advanced riders, it's a good idea to vary the balance of low- and high-intensity workouts throughout season. Varying your workouts decreases the risk of burnout and overtraining, and you are also less likely to get stuck in a fitness plateau. Changing your training intensity distribution periodically can be highly beneficial. That implies distributing intensity in a variety of ways throughout the season. When you examine your overall seasonal distribution, it should be polarized, as shown in Figure 4.2. We'll get into this whole matter of annual planning, especially in regard to intensity distribution, in Part IV.

FUNCTIONAL THRESHOLD

Training with consideration for how intense your workouts are relative to the two thresholds—AeT and AnT—is important to your race preparation. When it comes to specific race preparation, workouts done above the anaerobic threshold determine results. This doesn't mean that aerobic threshold workouts do not contribute to race performance. They do, but in a different way. You may think of AeT fitness as what gets you to the point in the race where above-AnT fitness kicks in: during a hard climb, attack, or sprint. Both are critical. But for now, let's concentrate on AnT and how you can know when you are at or above it, since it ultimately determines race outcomes.

In the description of AnT above, I mentioned that it could be determined by going to a lab or clinic and doing a test involving gradual increases in intensity while measuring blood lactate or the gases that you breathe in and out. The technician administering the test can determine your lactate or anaerobic threshold in terms of heart rate

and power. That's valuable information; knowing when you are at or above the AnT has a lot to do with race performance. Successful training also has to do with knowing where your AnT is. While lab testing may be quite accurate for this, there's a problem: It requires frequent testing, especially if you use a power meter, because as fitness changes so does your power at AnT. Heart rate, however, changes very little with changes in fitness. We'll return to this phenomenon later in this chapter.

Frequent testing is not only inconvenient, it is also expensive. Fortunately, there's an alternative method for finding your AnT that is inexpensive and easily administered. In the early 2000s, Andrew Coggan, PhD, an exercise physiologist and cyclist, came up with a field test for AnT that anyone can do at any time. It's simple and free. But it's not easy.

Coggan's field test improves upon the concept that a fit athlete can sustain his or her AnT for roughly an hour. According to that guideline, instead of going to a lab to find your AnT, you can instead just do a 1-hour ride at a maximal effort and then assume the average heart rate and power for that hour represent your AnT. Brilliant! The problem, of course, is that riding solo as hard as possible for an hour is so grueling that your heart rate and power numbers are likely to come out well below your actual AnT. Now, if the hour-long effort occurred during a race, such as a 40 km time trial or 1-hour criterium, motivation would likely be high and the results would be more indicative of your actual AnT. The problem is that you don't always have races during the season when you need to check AnT to see how fitness is progressing.

Dr. Coggan had a simple solution. Instead of requiring a 1-hour effort, he proposed doing

When it comes to specific race preparation, workouts done above the anaerobic threshold determine results.

a 20-minute test and then subtracting 5 percent from the test results. The result would be an estimate of one's AnT. Since it's not an actual measure of one's lactate or anaerobic threshold, and since it is done in a field test, he called the resulting measure a "functional threshold." The other important products of his 20-minute test are functional threshold heart rate (FTHR) and functional threshold power (FTP).

There are other ways to determine your functional threshold besides a 1-hour race or a 20-minute test. I've had riders do a 30-minute test, for example, since at that duration we tend to slow down just enough when riding alone to be near the results of a 1-hour race. I find the average numbers over 30 minutes closely match the FTHR and FTP results of the 20-minute test minus 5 percent. Another way to get an estimate of functional threshold is an all-out effort for 8 minutes with 10 percent subtracted from the average power. I've even used a 5-minute test, subtracting 15 percent. (Be aware that tests shorter than 20 minutes will not accurately predict FTHR.) There are many other ways as well, but the point is that with race results, 30-minute, 20-minute, 8-minute, and 5-minute tests, you will be able to determine FTP pretty easily.

While all of these methods are useful, they are unlikely to produce the exact same FTP. Some aerobically gifted riders get better results by doing the longer tests, while others who have a lot of anaerobic fitness may get more impressive numbers when doing the short tests. But even though there may be some variability in the results, the numbers produced should be close—probably within a 5 percent range above or below the actual threshold as found in a lab test.

Of course, your functional threshold varies a bit from day to day anyway due to fatigue and many other lifestyle factors. It even varies within the same ride, again due to fatigue. The bottom line here is that the heart rate and power numbers you come up with will never be precise to the exact beat per minute or watt. But that's OK. You only need a number that is close—a ballpark figure in a pretty small yard (think Fenway Park, not Dodger Stadium). The more frequently you test, especially for power, the more likely you are to have accurate numbers. I recommend testing with one of the methods described above every 3 to 4 weeks throughout the season. That will ensure your upper reference point is accurate. And, in turn, that will also mean your intensity-training zones are set correctly.

SETTING TRAINING ZONES

Once you have your FTHR and FTP, you can set your training zones. These zones are crucial to your training because they are used to determine the intensity of workouts. That's why I recommend testing every 3 to 4 weeks. Let's take a closer look at how to do that.

Heart Rate Zones

To set heart rate zones, we go back to Dr. Coggan's 20-minute test. Before getting into the details of this, however, I want to make a point about not using formulas to set your heart rate training zones. If you search the Internet, you will find many formulas that rely on personal data such as age, gender, and perhaps other variables to determine your maximum heart rate. Once you have that number, you're often told to take a percentage of it and call that your AnT or some

> The more frequently you test, especially for power, the more likely you are to have accurate numbers.

other name that refers to the upper threshold. The most common of these formulas for finding max heart rate is 220 minus age. There are some others, but you should steer clear of all of them because they are unlikely to work.

The formulas don't universally work because athletes are unique individuals (remember the principle of individuality from Chapter 3?). A formula may work for a few athletes, but not for most. When *actual* max heart rates are measured in a lab or clinic for a large group of people—all of the riders on the start line of big race, for example—they produce a bell-shaped curve. For those in the middle of the curve, a formula such as 220 minus age can produce a result that is quite accurate. But for those to the left or right of the curve's middle, the formula provides increasingly inaccurate results. And since you don't where you are on the curve, the zones you come up with are likely to be off by quite a bit—perhaps by as much as 20 bpm—either high or low. That's a 40 bpm range! You may as well just guess your max heart rate as do it this way. So *don't use a formula*. Do a field test to accurately estimate your FTHR.

How do you accurately find your FTHR? I'll walk you through Dr. Coggan's 20-minute test. The method for the other test durations mentioned above, from 30 to 5 minutes, is the same as described here. Note, though, that while the 8- and 5-minute tests can be useful for determining FTP, they aren't very accurate when it comes to heart rate. For that, I strongly recommend doing the 20- or 30-minute test. While I also mention the shorter tests in the following discussion, keep in mind that they are intended only for power measurement.

The venue you choose for the test is critical to getting good data. A good test course can be difficult to find. First, it should be a course that you can come back to for future tests. Second, it should be a stretch of road with a bike lane, light traffic, no stop signs, and few intersections and corners. It is best if it's flat to slightly uphill (with a 3 percent or less grade). You will probably need 5 to 10 miles (8 to 16 kilometers) of a route like this, depending on the course gradient and how fast you are.

Having a safe course is critical. Keep your head up so you can see ahead throughout the test while being especially mindful of traffic. Do not take risks to get good data. Of course, you should always be cautious whenever you are riding in traffic, but it is especially important when doing an all-out test such as this. Don't become so focused on the test that you forget to pay attention to what's going on around you.

To ensure that you get good data, do the test on a day when you are well rested. Treat it much as you would a race by backing off from your training for the two or three days prior. A good time for testing is at the end of a rest and recovery week, as described in Chapter 11.

Warm up well before starting the test. For most athletes, the warm-up should last at least 20 minutes, starting at a low intensity and steadily riding faster and harder. In the last 5 to 10 minutes of the warm-up, do progressively shorter and increasingly intensive accelerations at and well above RPE 7 (see Table 4.1). These might start at 2 minutes and gradually become 10 seconds, with nearly complete recoveries after each high effort. Following these accelerations, recover for about 5 minutes at a very low RPE and then start the 20-minute test.

Begin the 20-minute test at a high but somewhat conservative effort. In other words, you

To ensure that you get good data, do the test on a day when you are well rested.

should feel like you could go much faster. The most common mistake riders make when doing this test is starting out too fast, since it feels so easy for the first few minutes, and then slowing considerably in the last few minutes. This produces highly questionable data. The more of these tests you do, the better you will become at pacing them. The key is making the first 5 minutes feel relatively easy—around a 7 RPE. After every 5-minute portion, decide whether you should go somewhat faster or slower for the next 5 minutes. These 5-minute changes in RPE should be very slight. Of course, if you are doing the shorter 8-minute or 5-minute test, the starting intensity will be considerably greater, such as 8 or 9 RPE. For shorter test durations, make a pacing decision every minute.

At the end of the 20-minute test, begin an easy cooldown, allowing your heart rate and breathing to return to resting levels. After you have recovered from the exertion and finished the ride, you are ready for the fun part: analyzing the data.

Upload your heart rate monitor to your favorite software and find your average heart rate for the 20-minute test. Subtract 5 percent, and you have a good estimate of your functional threshold heart rate. If you did a 30-minute test, your average heart rate for the entire test is considered your FTHR with no calculation needed. Once you determine your FTHR, use Table 4.2 to compute your training zones. You can use this table regardless of whether you used the 20- or 30-minute field test to determine FTHR.

Power Zones

If you have a power meter on your bike, or if you have an indoor trainer with a built-in power meter, you can determine your power training zones by doing a functional threshold power test. In fact, if you do the 20- or 30-minute test for FTHR described above, you can find your FTP in the same test data. There's no need to do a separate test. The 8- and 5-minute tests may also be used for a somewhat less accurate estimate of FTP.

If you've used the 20-minute test, subtract 5 percent from your average power (not "normalized" power) for a good estimate of your FTP. If you did a 30-minute test, your average power for the entire 30 minutes is a good approximation of

TABLE 4.2 **How to Determine Heart Rate Zones**

HEART RATE ZONES	MULTIPLY YOUR FTHR BY	YOUR HEART RATE ZONES
Zone 1	81%	Lower than _____
Zone 2	82%–89%	_____ - _____
Zone 3	90%–93%	_____ - _____
Zone 4	94%–99%	_____ - _____
Zone 5a	100%–102%	_____ - _____
Zone 5b	103%–106%	_____ - _____
Zone 5c	107%	Higher than _____

Use the percentages of functional threshold heart rate in the middle column to set your training zones as determined by a field test.

TABLE 4.3 **How to Determine Power Zones**

BIKE POWER ZONES	MULTIPLY YOUR FTP BY	YOUR BIKE POWER ZONES
Zone 1	55%	Lower than _____
Zone 2	55%–74%	_____ – _____
Zone 3	75%–89%	_____ – _____
Zone 4	90%–104%	_____ – _____
Zone 5	105%–120%	_____ – _____
Zone 6	120%	_____ – _____
Zone 7	150%	Higher than _____

To find your bike power training zones, use the percentages shown of FTP as determined by a 20-minute field test.

Source: Adapted from Allen and Coggan, *Training and Racing with a Power Meter.*

FTP. For the 8-minute test, subtract 10 percent from your average power. For the 5-minute test, subtract 12 percent.

Once FTP is determined, use Table 4.3 to set your power training zones. As with FTHR testing, the more times you do this test, the more accurate the results will become, since there is a learning curve associated with pacing such a solo race-like effort.

Zone Agreement

If you train with both a heart rate monitor and a power meter, it will quickly become apparent that the two sets of zones don't always agree. You may be riding in heart rate zone 2 but notice that power is in zone 3. Many riders take this to mean there's something wrong with the zones or even with their hearts. Don't be concerned. This is common and to be expected. In fact, it is actually a good thing.

For advanced athletes, heart rate zones change very little, if at all, throughout the season, since FTHR is quite stable. Just as with effort, it's always about the same. You may notice small changes—

a few beats per minute difference—between your FTHRs in one test compared with another. That's probably mostly due to diet, emotional stress, fatigue, or excitement rather than fitness changes. Novice riders, however, are likely to see their heart rate zones change as they develop basic fitness.

On the other hand, power zones may change significantly throughout the season. Your FTP rises as you get in better shape. You're becoming more powerful on the bike. That's a good thing. This, of course, means that your power zones also rise, since they're based on FTP. When fitness decreases, your FTP also decreases and down come your zones. But all the while, heart rate zones remain constant. Heart rate is a proxy for how easy or hard the ride feels; power relates to how fast you are actually going. So there may well be large and small zone overlaps as FTP changes over the course of a season—or no overlaps at all at some times in the year.

Why does this happen? Look at it this way: If your power zones didn't change, you'd never get any faster at given heart rates. There would be no change in fitness. As you'll see later, riding

Power zones may change significantly throughout the season.

with increasingly higher power outputs at a given heart rate is a key to measuring improvements in aerobic fitness. As Greg LeMond once said in a different context, "It never gets easier, you just go faster."

TRAINING STRESS SCORE

I can't emphasize the central theme of this chapter enough: Training intensity is the key to success for the advanced rider. I continue to harp on this because so many athletes believe that volume—how many hours, miles, or kilometers they ride in a week—is the primary producer of their race-day fitness. Only intermediate athletes—those who have been in the sport for a couple of years—should primarily be focused on volume. Such newcomers to the sport will quickly develop at this stage of their racing careers if they simply increase weekly volume. But that can take a rider only so far, and then performance will plateau. Research studies in a variety of endurance sports have repeatedly shown that for the advanced athlete—someone who has been training for a few years—high performance is a result of *how hard* rather than *how much*.

Why is it that we tend to get bogged down in how much rather than how hard? I believe it has to do with the difficulty of measuring and expressing the intensity of training over the course of a week. It's not easy to come up with a number that says how hard the cumulative training has been. On the other hand, hours, miles, and kilometers are easy to total up for a week. It's so easy to measure volume, in fact, that we come to think of it as the most important metric. The foundation for that belief is developed during the early intermediate stage of training, when we find

that volume equates to performance. After reading this chapter on the importance of intensity, I hope you now understand that as you advance in your training, *how hard* becomes more heavily weighted than *how much*.

While the intensity of training is critical for the advanced rider, this does not mean that volume is unimportant. It only means that volume becomes less important as fitness increases. If I had to assign numbers that describe their relative balance, I'd propose that training intensity accounts for 60 percent of race-day fitness and volume is the remaining 40 percent. Can I prove that? Is there research that backs this up? No, there isn't. This is only my opinion based on more than 30 years of training athletes of all abilities. The bottom line is that training intensity is the key to successful training if you have been around the sport for a few years.

Dr. Coggan came to the same conclusion in the early 2000s. He then developed a simple way to combine volume and intensity into a single training load number with a slight emphasis given to intensity. He called this the Training Stress Score (TSS). In its first iteration, TSS required a power meter to measure intensity. Now it can also be determined from a heart rate monitor, although power is usually a somewhat more accurate measurement.

Dr. Coggan's formula for determining workout TSS is based on the workout's normalized power, intensity factor, and duration in seconds along with the rider's FTP. The resulting TSS number describes the workout's stress level by considering both its duration and intensity relative to what the rider is capable of doing. (It's not the purpose of this book to dig into these terms and the details of how they are determined. For a greater under-

Training intensity is the key to success for the advanced rider.

standing of it all, I recommend Coggan's book *Training and Racing with a Power Meter* or my book *The Power Meter Handbook,* which has a simpler breakdown of power meter usage.)

The bottom line is that thinking in terms of TSS instead of volume changes your way of seeing the world of training for bicycle racing. With your training load based on TSS instead of volume, you'll begin to focus on exactly what produces race readiness: the combination of volume and intensity, with the latter being the primary determiner. That shift in thinking will change both your training and your racing for the better.

In Part IV, I'll put numbers to TSS and show you how to plan your season, weeks, and workouts using TSS. Then your personal TSS training system will become much clearer. For now, I am only introducing the concept since we are discussing the importance of intensity to training.

SUMMARY: TRAINING INTENSITY

This chapter was all about the importance of focusing on training intensity for the advanced rider. We first examined the common ways you can gauge training intensity while riding. The most conventional ways are subjectively rating effort on a 0 to 10 perceived exertion scale, or based on heart rate or power. There are times when each of these is useful to high-performance athletes when they are training and racing. The real-time intensity of a road race is best measured based on perceived exertion. Whether or not to make a move in the heat of battle must come from how you feel, not what your heart rate or power numbers are. But when you prepare for a race, heart rate and power are critical determin-

ers of how hard you are working and what you are accomplishing as a result. The ability to understand and apply each of these three measures of intensity is valuable in developing race readiness.

Next we examined two key levels of intensity—the aerobic and anaerobic thresholds—and how they may be used as reference points in training. The aerobic threshold is the lower of the two, with a Rating of Perceived Exertion typically around 3 to 4 on a 0 to 10 scale. Lactate production, a common way of measuring intensity in the lab, is low when riding at the aerobic threshold (as compared to the anaerobic threshold). An aerobically fit rider should be capable of continuously riding at this lower intensity for several hours. At this intensity, the body is capable of removing lactate as quickly as it's produced. It is a valuable intensity level for training, as it increases aerobic endurance fitness.

At anaerobic threshold, a rider can typically ride for around 45 minutes to just over an hour, depending on endurance fitness. The Rating of Perceived Exertion here is typically around 7, as lactate is produced faster than it can be removed by the body. That creates an increasingly acidic environment for the muscles and makes it difficult to maintain the effort for a long duration.

Knowing these two reference points helps you to optimally distribute training intensities in your workouts and over the course of the season. The bulk of your training should be at or below the aerobic threshold. Research has shown that spending 70 to 80 percent of training time in this low range, with the remainder above the aerobic threshold, produces greater fitness and race readiness than with other distributions. I've found that self-coached riders typically do around half their training above the aerobic threshold, with

Spending 70 to 80 percent of training time below the aerobic threshold produces greater fitness and race readiness.

most of that being between the two thresholds, in the belief that this will raise the average training intensity. While that indeed may be the case, it also means that when it's time to do the workouts that determine race outcomes—above the anaerobic threshold—the rider is a bit too tired to perform as needed. Hence, the race-critical workouts are underemphasized.

To determine a simple and cheap proxy for the important upper reference point—the anaerobic threshold—Andrew Coggan came up with the functional threshold concept that is based on a field test. It simply involves doing a 20-minute maximal effort on a flat to slightly uphill grade and then subtracting 5 percent from the resulting average power and heart rate. Once you determine your functional threshold, you can set up your training zones for both heart rate and power.

It's important to understand that once power and heart rate zones are set, they won't always agree. That's a good thing. Heart rate zones change little if at all throughout the season for an advanced rider. But power zones change considerably to reflect changes in endurance fitness. This means that at the start of the season, your heart rate and power zones may overlap considerably during a ride, but as the season progresses and your fitness improves, they will begin to

separate. For example, when riding in heart rate zone 2 early in the year, your power is likely to also be in zone 2. But later in the season, zone 2 heart rate may produce zone 3 power. In other words, you are going faster at the same effort.

Another purpose of this chapter was to convince the advanced rider that the key to race preparedness lies in the intensity of training, not duration or volume. Both are important, but intensity is more critical. To make it possible to express workout duration in conjunction with intensity, Dr. Coggan came up with the concept of the Training Stress Score. After uploading either your heart rate or power devices to TrainingPeaks.com following a workout, the software calculates TSS. This number reflects how stressful the workout was in terms of intensity and duration. By adding individual workout Training Stress Scores for a period of time, such as a week, you'll get a number representing training load. Part IV will give you numbers for TSS to help you develop a deeper understanding of it as we examine how to plan your training.

Having read the last two chapters, you should now have a solid working knowledge of the fundamentals of training. That means it's time to move on to applying all of this so you can train with purpose.

PART III

PURPOSEFUL TRAINING

Having a purpose when training separates the best from the rest. Purpose starts with having a compelling goal—in this case, where you want to go with your racing in the season ahead. The first step toward your goal is a personal assessment. Where are you now relative to where you want to be? How big is the gap between that goal and your current status, both physically and mentally? Do you have the tools necessary to measure progress toward your goal? We'll seek the answers to these questions in Chapter 5.

Chapter 6 addresses the physical markers of fitness that commonly define endurance performance. It provides a basic concept for understanding how you can use ability-based training to increase your fitness. The remaining chapters in the book will often refer to these abilities and how they are used in making daily decisions about workouts, so pay close attention to them here.

The purposeful training covered in Chapter 6 has to do with determining what's currently standing in the way of your goal success: your "limiters." Knowing your limiters relative to your abilities is what sets the stage for making your training purposeful. Understanding this concept is critical to that purpose.

The decisions you make while reading these next two chapters will give purpose to your workouts and ultimately lead to goal success.

GETTING STARTED

THE START OF a new season is much more important than you may think. While you may not be building significant fitness yet, you are making a series of important decisions and checking off a number of small tasks, and all of them affect how you will train and how beneficial that training will be for the remainder of the year. A well-designed start-up process is so important to how the season plays out that I have athletes repeat the formula in this chapter every year as they start back into training. I consider each of the activities that follow as more than mere suggestions. They are as important to your race preparation and performance as your on-bike training. You will be tempted to skip some of what follows because it seems trivial. But achieving many small tasks makes a big difference, and what you do at the start of your season is often the key to success.

What if you come to this chapter when it's *not* the start of the season? Perhaps you're already well into it. What should you do if you have already started serious training and you've got eight weeks until the next important race? In that case, I strongly suggest you restart your season by following the guidelines that follow. While they will take some time to fit in, they won't significantly interfere with your race preparation. It will be time well spent. On the other hand, if you are currently in the midst of your race season, you should delay all of the suggested start-up procedures that follow until you have a break of several weeks before your next high-priority race.

Regardless of where you currently are in your season, I strongly suggest that you figure out a way to eventually incorporate the seasonal start-up steps in this chapter. They will get you started down the right path, and as a result, you will make substantial gains in performance later on.

TRAINING TOOLS

There's no doubt that you want to ride a good bike with fast wheels, quick and easy gear changes, and responsive brakes because it's obvious they'll improve your training and racing. That's a given. Just as your bike and its components are tools that can make you faster, there are training tools out there that also have the potential to improve your performance to a higher level. What I'm going to propose is that using some of those training tools will improve your racing engine.

I require everyone I coach to use two tools when they ride: a heart rate monitor and a power meter. Why? Because they provide accurate data, and reliable information is the most critical component for making training decisions. That which is measured improves. Heart rate monitors and power meters provide precise measurement of what's happening on a ride—how the engine is running. Without them, you are merely guessing about your engine.

The mere mention of technology ruffles some riders' feathers. There have always been those who adamantly oppose any new technology in sport, and cycling is no different. When rear derailleurs were introduced in the early 20th century, the Tour de France banned them. It preferred to see racers change gears by dismounting at the start of a climb and reversing the rear wheel, which had a single gear of a different size on each side. When bicycle speedometers were introduced, many opposed them. They saw no reason to be so precise about velocity. Aerodynamic handlebars for time trialing were invented in the mid-1980s but were not adopted by road cyclists until 1989, when Greg LeMond used them to win the Tour de France by 8 seconds. In the early 1990s, clipless pedals were introduced and soon began replacing the century-old toe clips and leather straps. Many saw them as an unnecessary change from what worked well (I was one of those!).

Whenever new technology is introduced, someone will always be against it. Such naysayers see themselves as purists who maintain the spirit of the sport and dislike gizmos, especially numbers, getting in the way of "real-world" riding.

And, to be perfectly honest, heart rate monitors and power meters are not necessary for everyone. Novices to the sport who are in their first year of training will get little benefit from them. The biggest challenge those riders face isn't measuring workout intensity but rather simply getting on their bikes regularly. Not all experienced athletes need these tools either, if they are good at sensing how hard they are riding in a workout. They may have an excellent feel for intensity. And if they are self-coached, not having such technology may not hold back their progress significantly.

But if you would like to have better results, training technology can help you build a powerful engine. Training technology costs money, but when you become serious about your racing career, you'll soon find it more important than having nice wheels.

Intensity-measuring equipment such as a heart rate monitor and power meter can help you analyze workouts, spot trends, and design future workouts, even if you never even glance at them during a workout or race. There's a lot to be learned by looking at their data after a workout. Is your functional threshold power (FTP) improving? Are you becoming more aerobically fit? How are you doing compared with this same time last year? Are you getting enough race-like intensity in your training? How many matches did you burn in the race, and how can you train to produce more? A heart rate monitor and power meter help answer such questions by

That which is measured improves.

If you would like to have better results, training technology can help you build a powerful engine.

eliminating reliance on memory and guesswork. With this technology, training becomes more precise and there is a corresponding improvement in race results.

Yes, cycling is an expensive sport and purchasing such equipment adds to the cost. But the price of a heart rate monitor isn't too great, and prices for power meters are dropping steadily. And you don't need to spend a small fortune on the very best power meter. Even the least expensive of the devices reliably provides what you most need: intensity measurement. If you are on a tight budget, check around with bike shops and cycling clubs for used equipment. Athletes often upgrade to new technology at the start of a season and sell their old stuff, which works perfectly well.

Of course, heart rate monitors and power meters are not magic. You also need to invest time in learning how to use them. This book will get you started on that, but to more fully understand the subtle nuances of data analysis you'll need to read books and websites devoted to the topic. This is when having a knowledgeable coach makes life so much easier.

In addition to learning how to use this equipment, there are other concerns. Safety, for example. It's possible to become too focused on device numbers, especially when the equipment is brand new and you're still learning how to use it. Riding in traffic while looking at numbers displayed on your handlebar device is not safe.

There can also be a loss of "feel" for the athlete who becomes overly dedicated to numbers. You may recall the discussion in Chapter 4 about the importance of perceived exertion for bike racing. You can't be an accomplished competitor by watching numbers change during a race. You must be in tune with your body then. The

purpose of the heart rate monitor and power meter is to improve your training and therefore your racing by allowing you to measure how you are progressing and get intensity right for workouts. Your feel will also benefit from that. When it comes to racing, feel is still the key.

The bottom line is that you need a heart rate monitor and a power meter for training if you want to produce better race results. To get your season started right, I strongly suggest that you purchase and learn to use them.

SEASONAL GOALS

Once you have the fundamental tools for serious training, your next step is to define your goal or goals for the season. Perhaps there is only one, such as a podium at the national championship. You've raced at nationals before and come close a couple of times. So you may have been dreaming of this for some time. And now you've decided it's time to turn that dream into a goal. There's only one thing that's absolutely required to make a dream into a goal: a plan. Planning to achieve your goal is what we'll address in Part IV.

Or it may be that you have several goals you want to accomplish in the coming season. In that case, I recommend limiting them to three. As seasonal goals proliferate, it becomes increasingly difficult to manage all of the components that must be developed in training to achieve them. Multiple goals may even be contradictory. For example, if your goal is to podium in a series of several criterium races over the course of a few weeks and you also want to set a personal best in a 40 km time trial that occurs during that same period, there may well be a training conflict. Training for crits and time trials is

> You need a heart rate monitor and a power meter if you want to produce better race results.

significantly different. It's a great challenge to become physically accomplished at both. Two such goals means that your limited weekly training time would be divided between two different and somewhat contradictory physiological outcomes, with one involving a great deal of anaerobic fitness and the other requiring extremely high aerobic fitness. The human body is not capable of fully adapting to divergent demands. It would be best to focus on one goal at a time, and to separate them sufficiently over the season.

There are a few guidelines to keep in mind as you set your goals. To begin with, your goals must be specific, measurable, difficult (but attainable), and have a definite timeline. You must also review your progress frequently. These guidelines are mostly obvious, but I'll touch on a couple of them that often need clarification.

In keeping with my previously mentioned coaching philosophy of "that which is measured improves," I want to emphasize how important it is that you are able to accurately determine progress toward your goal. A goal of "breaking 1 hour for a 40 km time trial on September 10" is measurable, specific, and has a timeline. You can easily measure your progress toward its achievement. But a goal of "ride faster this year" is too vague to be measurable. How fast is faster? Ride faster for what duration? And when? How would you gauge your progress toward this goal? This is the sort of goal that on the surface sounds good, but ultimately has little or no value. It's a weak attempt at goal setting and unlikely to produce a memorable season.

Setting measureless goals is a common mistake in sport because they sound good when you're talking about your season. Another mistake is setting unrealistic ones. For example, a novice cyclist's goal to "win the masters national road race on June 2" is both specific and measurable, but it's probably not going to happen. While it's something that may come true in a few years, it is really only a dream right now. Shooting for the stars with the hope of making it to the moon does not motivate because down deep the athlete knows the goal is unachievable. The training that follows will have no purpose, nor will the rider be motivated to work hard.

A goal can also be too easy. If there is no question at all about your potential for success, then the goal isn't going to challenge you. Your training will have little purpose, and the outcome will be empty. Instead, your goals should challenge you to become a more competitive cyclist by being just beyond your reach.

Training Objectives

Here's the big question when you finally decide on a tough but realistic goal: Why can't you achieve it now? If you did indeed achieve it right now—as the season is getting started—you'd call it an accomplishment rather than a goal. There would be no feeling of achievement. There would be no challenge. It would be no big deal. But since there is some doubt whether you can accomplish it, you obviously lack something. That something standing between you and success is what I call a *limiter*. The primary purpose of your training is to "fix" this performance limiter. The subgoals that define what's needed to fix your limiters are called *training objectives*. In Chapter 6, we will dig more deeply into this concept to figure out your unique limiters, therefore setting the stage for deciding exactly how to train in Part IV.

For now, the take-home message to absorb is that a training objective is a short-term goal to

Your goals must be specific, measurable, difficult, and have a definite timeline.

Your goals should challenge you to become a more competitive cyclist.

be accomplished during the preparation for your most important races in order to achieve your overarching season goal. You will likely achieve these objective outcomes—limiter fixes—in workouts. That will show that you are definitely making progress toward goal accomplishment. If the objective can be measured in some way, all the better. An objective may be, for example, a power output for a given duration that you achieve in specific workouts or in a test as you prepare for your goal race. That could be a goal FTP needed to race at a higher level. The objective could also address lifestyle matters or even mental roadblocks that limit your performance. We'll come back to such topics in the next chapter.

So far, we have a seasonal goal followed by one or more training objectives that are necessary accomplishments needed to fix a limiter in order to achieve the goal. That brings us to the most granular level of high-performance training: daily purposes.

Daily Purposes

If your goal is truly challenging, you'll need determination, hard work, and patience to fix your limiters. You'll need to work on them in some way every day. Such persistent dedication is what ultimately leads to goal achievement. Workout after workout provides the progress to get you there. It isn't easy, but your body gradually adapts to the increasingly difficult training and you eventually are capable of achieving what was beyond your reach just a few weeks earlier.

The process of steady improvement means that every workout must have a purpose. Your daily workouts simply can't be random with the hope that something positive happens and somehow the goal is achieved. Each workout, each day, must focus on something that will produce greater race readiness. Consequently, each workout must have a purpose. Your focus for any given day could be something quite challenging, such as improving power or developing greater endurance. Or it could be something quite undemanding, such as an easy ride—or even a day off—so you can recover from the previous day's hard workout. While hard workouts create the potential for greater fitness, it's during recovery when the body adapts and becomes stronger. This is the patience part of training that is so critical for goal attainment. Whatever the workout may call for, you should start by knowing exactly what you'll do that day to move one tiny step closer to a training objective and your goal, and how you will recover from the workout to build fitness. High performance requires daily action and daily planning. The more challenging your goal, the more important each day's workout purpose becomes.

Purposeful training leads to small daily gains that eventually produce the accomplishment of season goals. And as your goals become more challenging, every decision in your daily life becomes more important, even when you aren't on the bike. This includes daily choices ranging from what you eat, to how long you sleep, to who you train with, and even to such seemingly insignificant stuff as what you think about. Everything matters if the goal is high. A goal that you know will be difficult to achieve demands the focus of everything in your life.

If you are now at the start of a new training year, I hope you have been dreaming about the coming season. What do you want to accomplish? What are your dreams? It's from your dreams that your goals, objectives, and daily

While hard workouts create the potential for greater fitness, it's during recovery when the body adapts and becomes stronger.

purposes will become apparent. In Chapter 7, I'll ask you to put your seasonal goal and supporting objectives in writing. Then we'll get into your daily purposes in Chapter 8, when we get to the nuts and bolts of how to plan a training week.

ASSESSMENT

If you are reading this at the start the new season, you're probably fresh and ready to go. You may be champing at the bit to get started. Your enthusiasm should be tempered, however, by a study of what it takes to restart serious training properly. Training now with too much aggression often results in what I call "Christmas stars"—riders who are in the best shape of the season even though it's only midwinter. By the time the race season actually starts, these stars are often burnt out.

A proper return to training has a couple of stages. The first stage is to determine your current status. The key question to ask is, "Physically and mentally, where am I now?" The answer has three parts: physical soundness for training, mental readiness to go after a high goal, and current cycling fitness. What follows is how I go about determining the athlete's physical, mental, and fitness status. I highly recommend you follow this process and accomplish it fully within the first four weeks of your return to training for the new season. Your race performance for the year ahead will greatly benefit.

Physical Assessment and Bike Fit

In Chapter 1, I suggested that your personal high-performance team should include a physical therapist who works with endurance athletes, especially cyclists. The start of a new season is the time to schedule an appointment with this PT for a physical assessment. It's something I have riders I coach do every season to help avoid injuries and also to prepare them for a bike fit. These two parts of the early season process fit together perfectly.

The PT should do a head-to-toe examination, looking at posture, strength, range of joint motion, muscular balance, dynamic function, and whatever structural idiosyncrasies and asymmetries may affect physical health and training consistency. The purpose is to determine your unique risk for injury to avoid physical breakdowns in the coming season. The bike fitter will also use the resulting information to ensure that your bike and body match up to optimize performance and reduce the risk of injury.

If the therapist unearths any risks for breakdown from your individual physical characteristics, he or she should design a corrective exercise program for you that may involve functional strengthening and mobility exercises. Also ask for equipment and bike position suggestions to pass along to your bike fitter. The therapist may also have suggestions for you and your coach, if you have one, regarding the types of workouts that may prove structurally beneficial, as well as exercises and movements that are best avoided, at least in the short term until physical corrections have taken hold.

The injury-prevention program your PT designs for you is as important as your bike workouts, and you should follow it with great care. A physical therapist who is used to working with endurance athletes will understand that you have limited time, and he or she should streamline the corrective exercise program so that it provides optimal benefit in a reasonable amount of time.

The injury-prevention program your PT designs for you is as important as your bike workouts, and you should follow it with great care.

If the therapist discovers severe structural weaknesses, it's a good idea to schedule a follow-up exam to gauge progress and make adjustments to your exercise routine. Predicting future injury sites and reducing injury risk through a thorough physical assessment often makes the difference between a successful race season and a season of frustration.

Following the physical assessment, see a professional bike fitter to get your bicycle set up properly. Don't ask your spouse, friend, or training partner to do it for you. And don't do it by yourself. Bike fit is too important to your season. It has the potential to make a substantial improvement in your race performance. I've seen riders raise their FTP by more than 10 percent after simply having their bikes adjusted to their bodies. And those improvements were made for riders who thought their position on the bike was already perfect and didn't need adjusting. Every rider believes that. How much training would it take to accomplish a 10 percent power increase? Several weeks. Don't skip this; it's too important to your performance.

You should have a bike fit every season, even if you are riding the same bike you were properly fitted to last season. Things change. You gain or lose muscle strength, flexibility, or mass, and your range of motion changes due to aging, strength training, and changes in training workloads. Or you may have changed your saddle, handlebar stem, pedals, shoes, or something else from the previous season. Or the types of races you're doing this coming season are different from last year's. Or you have minor but niggling knee tenderness. So get a pro to set you up on your bike each year, and if you have road and time trial bikes, have both set up properly. A bike position

adjustment by a professional fitter is a must-do if you really want to race at your potential.

The best professional cycling teams in the world insist on physical assessments and bike fits for their riders at the start of every season because they know how critical they are to their success. They're no less important for you.

Mental Assessment

Just as your physical readiness to train and race is critical to goal achievement, your mental readiness is also important to racing success. In Chapter 1, you read about the importance of mental fitness when it comes to high performance as an athlete. The start of a new season is the time to assess your mental readiness. Sidebar 5.1, Mental Skills Assessment, will help you determine personal mental strengths and weaknesses. Be completely honest as you answer each of the questions. No one else is going to see your results (unless you decide to share them), so there is no reason to embellish your true feelings. When you're done, return to reading this section. I'll wait for you.

Now let's take a look at your Mental Skills Assessment ratings. Since you're reading this book, you probably scored high (4 or 5) for motivation. In general, serious athletes are highly motivated people, at least when it comes to their sports. While being highly motivated to train and race is commonly accepted as a positive characteristic, it also has a dark side. This becomes apparent when the athlete doesn't reduce training in order to rest after a hard training period or refuses to back off from training when tapering before an important race. This is the sort of person who must have a coach pulling back the reins. I've known self-coached athletes who were

You should have a bike fit every season, even if you are riding the same bike.

SIDEBAR 5.1 Mental Skills Assessment

Read the statements below and choose an appropriate response for each from the following:

1 = NEVER   2 = RARELY   3 = SOMETIMES   4 = FREQUENTLY   5 = USUALLY   6 = ALWAYS

____ 1. I believe in my potential as a competitive cyclist.

____ 2. I train consistently and eagerly.

____ 3. I stay positive when things don't go well in a race.

____ 4. Before races, I can imagine myself doing well.

____ 5. Before races, I remain positive and upbeat.

____ 6. I think of myself as a successful cyclist.

____ 7. Before races, I have no self-doubt about my ability.

____ 8. The morning of a race, I awake nervous but eager to start.

____ 9. I learn something from a race when I don't do well.

____ 10. In my mind's eye, I can see myself handling tough race situations.

____ 11. I believe my ability as a cyclist is quite high.

____ 12. I can easily picture myself in key situations before a race.

____ 13. Staying focused during long races is easy for me.

____ 14. I am always aware of my exertion levels in races.

____ 15. I mentally rehearse what's expected of me before races.

____ 16. I'm good at concentrating on what's important as a race progresses.

____ 17. I'm willing to make sacrifices to attain my goals.

____ 18. Before an important race, I anticipate and can visualize my race tactics.

____ 19. I look forward to doing very hard workouts.

____ 20. When I visualize myself in a race, it almost feels real.

____ 21. I think of myself as having great potential as a cyclist.

____ 22. In races, I can tune out distractions.

____ 23. I set high race goals for myself.

____ 24. I like the mental challenge of a hard race.

____ 25. The harder the race, the better I concentrate.

____ 26. I am mentally tough when racing.

____ 27. I can relax and stay loose before races.

____ 28. I remain positive despite making a mistake in a race.

____ 29. My confidence remains high after a poor race performance.

____ 30. I work hard at being the best athlete I can be.

SCORING: Add up the numerical responses you gave for each of the above statements according to the sets below and then determine your rating for each by using the scale at the bottom of the page.

MENTAL SKILL	STATEMENTS	TOTAL	RATING
Motivation	2, 8, 17, 19, 23, 30	_____	_____
Confidence	1, 6, 11, 21, 26, 29	_____	_____
Thought habits	3, 5, 9, 24, 27, 28	_____	_____
Focus	7, 13, 14, 16, 22, 25	_____	_____
Visualization	4, 10, 12, 15, 18, 20	_____	_____

How to determine rating:

IF "TOTAL" IS . . .	THEN "RATING" IS . . .
32–36	5
27–31	4
21–26	3
16–20	2
6–15	1

so motivated that they avoided rest and recovery unless forced to yield to them because of overwhelming fatigue. Overtraining is likely with such a mindset. Very few athletes fully understand how devastating overtraining is. This topic will be discussed in greater detail in Chapter 10, but for now I'll just say that you must manage your enthusiasm for training and high achievement in order to race at the highest possible level.

Your confidence, thought habits, ability to focus, and visualization skills also play key roles in training and racing. A low score (1, 2, or 3) for any of these categories indicates a need to improve that mental skill. The most effective way, if also the most expensive, is to work with a sports psychologist. A coach who is well grounded in the mental aspects of sport is a good alternative. An inexpensive option is to read books written by sports psychologists. Such books (as of this writing) that you may consider reading are found in Sidebar 5.2.

Fitness Assessment

I've said it a couple of times in this chapter, but please let me say it once more: That which is measured improves. Want more money in your bank account? The starting point is seeing how much you have now and then looking at your bank statement frequently. Would you like to get your body weight down a few pounds? Start now by weighing yourself and then step on the scales periodically to see how you're doing. When you repeatedly measure something that is important, you begin to focus on it. It stays in the forefront of your daily thoughts. Daily decisions begin reflecting your goal. Without measurement, goals are merely hopes and wishes—nothing more.

> ### SIDEBAR 5.2 Recommended Sports Psychology Books
>
> Afremow, Jim. *The Champion's Comeback: How Great Athletes Recover, Reflect, and Reignite.*
>
> Afremow, Jim. *The Champion's Mind: How Great Athletes Think, Train, and Thrive.*
>
> Bell, Jonny. *Sports Psychology: Inside the Athlete's Mind.*
>
> Cox, Richard. *Sport Psychology: Concepts and Applications.*
>
> Fitzgerald, Matt. *How Bad Do You Want It?: Mastering the Psychology of Mind over Muscle.*
>
> Gonzalez, D. C. *The Art of Mental Training: A Guide to Performance Excellence.*
>
> Grover, Tim S. *Relentless: From Good to Great to Unstoppable.*
>
> LeUnes, Arnold. *Sport Psychology.*
>
> Lynch, Jerry. *Spirit of the Dancing Warrior: Asian Wisdom for Peak Performance in Athletics and Life.*
>
> Mack, Gary, and David Casstevens. *Mind Gym: An Athlete's Guide to Inner Excellence.*
>
> Orlick, Terry. *In Pursuit of Excellence.*
>
> Smith, Leif, and Todd M. Kays. *Sports Psychology for Dummies.*
>
> Weinberg, Robert, and Daniel Gould. *Foundations of Sport and Exercise Psychology with Web Study Guide.*

The achievement of race fitness works with this measure-to-improve model quite nicely—provided you can measure fitness. And you can measure it if you have a heart rate monitor and power meter. What I will show you now is how to use these tools in field tests that reflect progress toward your race fitness goals. A field test is a way of measuring fitness without going to a lab or clinic for expensive testing. Before the power meter came along, you plunked down a couple hundred bucks, rode a stationary bike during an increasingly painful ordeal, and got your numbers from the technician after you finished. You didn't want to do this too often for obvious reasons: It was expensive and it wasn't even a real-world test. Races are not done indoors on ergometers while wearing a gas mask and having your finger pricked repeatedly to draw blood.

A heart rate monitor and a power meter let you measure your fitness with a field test. You can do your field test whenever you like, and you can do it exactly as you race—on the road, riding a moving bike.

The downside of a field test is that there is a possibility for error. In the clinic, the technician will see to it that variables such as equipment choices and warm-up are the same from one test to the next. Athletes are less likely to do that in a field test, and so they may introduce variables that could interfere with outcomes. These variables often result in improvements in the range of 1 to 3 percent from one test to the next. Such small gains (or losses) in performance can be influenced by some uncontrolled variable such as equipment selection, weather, nutrition (even something as minor as pre-test caffeine), warm-up procedure, or course selection. When you do a field test, you must minimize all such variations from one test to the next.

There are other considerations. Following a clinical test, the technician gives you lots of details about how your body works and therefore what you can do in training to possibly improve performance. A field test, on the other hand, is more of a "black box" test: You simply put in a hard effort and see what the resulting performance number is. How that number is interpreted is up to you—unless you have a coach who can help you draw conclusions.

When you do a field test, you must minimize variations from one test to the next.

Both clinical tests and field tests are valuable in their own ways. I use both with the athletes I coach in order to get a broad view of our seasonal starting point. Clinical testing requires considerable scheduling (and cash outlay), while following up with field tests is easy to fit in (and inexpensive).

So what will you measure in a field test? There are a few metrics that serve as good markers of current fitness and can help gauge how your race preparation is coming along. For now, these field tests will help to put numbers on your fitness as the season is just beginning. You will come back to these tests periodically throughout the season to measure progress. There's more on this seasonal progression in Part IV.

Two of the field tests, functional threshold power (FTP) and functional threshold heart rate (FTHR), were also described in Chapter 4. They are briefly explained in Sidebar 5.3 again and are also in Appendix B. Besides the FTP and FTHR tests, there are two others described here: functional aerobic capacity and sprint power.

SUMMARY: GETTING STARTED

The purpose of this chapter is to get you started on a new season in such a way that the likelihood of success is greatly increased. I took you step by step through the process I use every year in getting an athlete started. The start of a new year is by far the best time in the entire season to take a close look at everything that is likely to affect your training and racing. I strongly recommend that you return to this chapter every year. For those riders I've coached, what

SIDEBAR 5.3 **Field Tests for Assessing Fitness**

Warm up well before starting any of the tests that follow. For most athletes, the warm-up should last at least 20 minutes. Start your warm-up with a low intensity, and steadily ride faster and harder. In the last 5 to 10 minutes of the warm-up, do progressively shorter and increasingly intensive accelerations at and well above RPE 7 (see Table 4.1). These might start at 2 minutes and gradually become 10 seconds with nearly complete recoveries after each high effort. Following these accelerations, recover for about 5 minutes at a very low RPE. Then start the selected test.

Functional Aerobic Threshold (FAeT) Test

The purpose of this test is to measure trends in aerobic endurance fitness over the course of your season. It is best done after a few days of reduced training load to allow for rest and recovery. It may also be done as a workout to maintain or build aerobic endurance at any time in the season (see workout AE2 in Appendix B). You need both a heart rate monitor and a power meter for this test.

Following the warm-up, ride steadily on a flat to gently rolling course or indoor trainer for 1 to 3 hours. The longer your race, the longer the test. If your goal race is a criterium or time trial, ride for 1 hour. If your goal race is a 3-hour road course, ride for 3 hours. Use a heart rate monitor to maintain your AeT heart rate throughout the steady test portion. You can determine your AeT heart rate in a clinic or lab test, or you may estimate it. It is likely to occur at 20 to 40 beats per minute below your FTHR (see below). In the absence of clinic or lab data, use a heart rate range that is 30 bpm below your FTHR plus and minus 2 bpm. For example, if your FTHR is 152, your estimated AeT heart rate range for this test is 120 to 124.

Following the session, consult your power meter data. Divide your normalized power (NP) for the AeT portion of the ride by your average heart rate for the same portion to determine your current efficiency factor (EF). Your EF value will increase as aerobic fitness improves over time. During a period of greatly reduced training, as at the end of the season, you should expect your EF to decrease, indicating a loss of aerobic fitness. That is normal and to be expected as fitness declines at certain times of the year. This test should be done year-round, at least every 3 to 4 weeks. If possible, use the same course every time.

FTP and FTHR Test

The purpose of this 20-minute test is to determine your FTP and FTHR as described in Chapter 4. You must use a power meter to determine FTP, and you must use a heart rate monitor to determine FTHR. Do this test following 3 to 5 days of active rest and recovery. Warm up well before starting the test portion, then do the following test ride on a stretch of road that is flat to slightly uphill (3 percent grade or less) with a wide bike lane, light traffic, no stop signs, and few intersections and corners. You will probably need 5 to 10 miles (8 to 16 km), depending on how fast you are and whether the course is flat or uphill. A safe course is critical. Throughout the test, keep your head up so you can see ahead. (You may also do this on an indoor trainer.)

→

For the test, ride your test course as if you are doing a time trial that lasts 20 minutes. Hold back slightly in the first 5 minutes (most athletes start much too fast). At the end of every 5-minute portion, decide whether to go slightly faster or slower for the next 5 minutes.

After the workout, find your average heart rate from the 20-minute test portion. Subtract 5 percent, and you have an estimate of your FTHR. Then use Table 4.2 to compute your heart rate training zones.

To determine FTP from the same test, subtract 5 percent from your average power (not "normalized" power), and you have a good estimate of FTP. Then use Table 4.3 to set your power training zones.

As described in Chapter 4, you may also determine FTP by using 5-, 8-, and 30-minute tests, although the 20-minute test described here is preferred. See Chapter 4 for these alternative tests.

Functional Aerobic Capacity Test

This test is done to determine your functional aerobic capacity power. Aerobic capacity, as determined in a clinic or lab, is called "VO_2max." This field test requires a power meter. It is best done following reduced training for 3 to 5 days. The course you use for the test should be safe. That means light traffic, no stop signs, few intersections, no turns, and a wide bike lane. For safety, you should look ahead throughout the test. Do *not* ride with your head down. The selected test course should also be a flat to slightly uphill (3 percent grade or less) section of road that you can use every time you do this test. (You may also do this on an indoor trainer, but only if it is very stable, as the test typically involves a lot of forceful side-to-side rocking.)

Following the warm-up, ride a steady all-out effort for 5 minutes on your test course. Your average power for the 5-minute test portion is a good predictor of your power at aerobic capacity.

Sprint Power Test

The purpose of this test is to gauge the progress of your sprint. A power meter is required. Do it following a couple of days of reduced training load. You will need a flat to slightly uphill section of road that is roughly 50 to 100 yards long, depending on how fast your sprint is and the gradient. The road section used for the test should have light traffic, a wide bike lane, no intersections, and no stop signs.

Following a thorough warm-up, from a rolling start pedal as forcefully and quickly as you can counting 8 right- or left-side pedal strokes (16 total strokes) in your preferred sprint posture—standing or sitting with your hands on the hoods or in the drops. Your average power output for the 8 strokes is a measure of your sprint power.

is described above became what they expected to do annually. They also learned how it paid off later with better training and racing. I guarantee it will do the same for you.

In the following chapters, I'll frequently refer to field-test progress and to analyzing workout and race data in order to make decisions to perform better. To do both of these requires reliable data. Guessing about how you are progressing is a sure way to have a mediocre season. The measurable data needed comes from two devices: a heart rate monitor and a power meter. You must have both if you want to race at the highest level possible. Throughout this book you will get tips on how to use these tools, but I'd highly recommend that you read books devoted to the topic. Two of my books that I'd recommend are *Total Heart Rate Training* and *The Power Meter Handbook*.

Getting started on a new race season begins with dreams, goals, and objectives. Eventually these will lead to the daily purposes of your workouts. In later chapters I will give more structure for each of these steps and help you blend them into an annual training plan for the season ahead. For now, I just want you thinking about the season ahead. What have you dreamed of accom-

plishing as a cyclist? What performance goals do you most want to achieve in the coming months?

To accomplish those goals you need to get started down the path that leads to success. That involves an assessment of your physical and mental strengths and weaknesses as an athlete and a plan to make your weaknesses stronger. An hour spent with a physical therapist followed by an appointment with a professional bike fitter has great potential for better race results. By strengthening both your mental and physical weaknesses you will start the season with greater potential for success than ever before.

Next comes an assessment of your fitness. That involves field tests to establish baselines for aerobic threshold efficiency, threshold power, aerobic capacity power, and sprint power. In the coming season you should repeat these field tests regularly to measure progress. We'll come back to this topic later.

That's it. You're ready to start the new season. As you look back at the end of this coming year, you'll realize how much the suggestions in this chapter did for your racing. Now it's time to get started building fitness for the coming season. That's where we are headed in Chapter 6.

PREPARING TO RACE

THIS BOOK is about training for road races and time trials. But the basic principles of preparing to race may be applied to any endurance cycling event, including mountain bike, cyclocross, gravel grinders, gran fondos, century rides, some track races, multisport, and ultradistance cycling. While there is a lot of similarity between these events (each involves riding a bike, after all), specific races generally require specific training. The primary training differences between these races come down to each sport's distinctive emphasis on duration and intensity. In this regard, each cycling event requires a distinct way of preparing in order to be fit on race day.

So how do you prepare for a road race or time trial? You start by developing the fitness required to meet the duration and intensity demands of the event. For example, what is the expected duration of the race? A 20-minute time trial, a 45-minute criterium, and a 3-hour road race obviously require different workout durations.

That's reflected in the preparation, and it's fairly easy to figure out.

When it comes to intensity, the differences are more intricate. Bicycle road racing is unique in the world of endurance sports because the race outcomes are determined by intermittent episodes of very high intensity that last a few seconds to a few minutes. What average and peak intensities do you expect? How long will the peak intensities last? How do you build those expectations into your training plan? Fitness for a road race requires an entirely different way of training than, for example, running a marathon. On the other hand, time trial fitness is based, in part, on how steadily and how long the rider can sustain a relatively high intensity. In that regard, a time trial is somewhat similar to running a marathon.

For the advanced rider, manipulating training intensity is the key to effective race preparation. Is the race pacing steady, or is it highly variable? Predicting intensity and duration lie at the heart of designing a training program. The training for a road race or a time trial must reflect how the race will be conducted in regard to these two variables. Therein lies a dilemma. Training concurrently for both a road race and a time trial places difficult and often contradictory demands on the rider. It's difficult to be a peak performer in both at the same time. Not only are there time constraints when it comes to determining workouts, there are also adaptive constraints. The body has a limited capacity for becoming maximally fit for both long, steady intensity and brief, highly variable intensity. That's why Grand Tour winners are so exceptional. They typically have multiple talents that contribute to their race readiness, and they can perform at a high level in terms of both duration and intensity.

All of this is what makes the sport of cycling so challenging. When we get to Chapter 8, which addresses weekly and daily workout planning, you may be faced with the dilemma of how to be fit for such contradictory outcomes. Before we attack that problem, however, let's first concern ourselves with a broader view of endurance fitness by coming to understand it from a purely physiological perspective. In this regard, fitness and race preparation are much less complex.

WHAT IS FITNESS?

So far I've used the word "fitness" a lot and assumed that you understand what it means. You undoubtedly do in the broad sense that it reflects a readiness to race. But there's a lot more to fitness than that. Understanding what's happening inside of your body when you train gives you a deeper understanding of what training is about.

You're not simply doing hard workouts with the hope that race readiness will somehow happen. You're preparing your body for the specific stresses of race day by pre-stressing it in workouts in ways that produce deep physiological changes to biological systems. With an understanding of these systems, workouts become more meaningful, as they are closely related to physical outcomes that can be measured with the field or lab tests described in Chapter 5.

Regardless of whether you are a world-class rider preparing for a Grand Tour or an accomplished rider who mostly does local criteriums, there are only three physical metrics of endurance fitness that must be developed through training. That's it. Only three. They are aerobic capacity, anaerobic threshold, and economy. As humans, we're all the same when it comes to these three indicators of endurance fitness. All that varies is how well developed each of them is. Every rider has a unique blend of fitness when it comes to these indicators. Let's take a brief look at them and how you can develop each one with specific types of training. In later chapters, we'll dig deeper into the details of training them.

Aerobic Capacity

Also referred to as "VO$_2$max," aerobic capacity is your physiological proficiency for using the oxygen you inhale to produce energy. It's your maximal volume of oxygen. The more oxygen your body is capable of processing, the more energy it produces and the greater your power output becomes.

It's common to find that the fastest athletes also have the highest aerobic capacities. Their massive power outputs are closely tied to their capacities for converting oxygen into watts. But

The three physical metrics of endurance fitness to develop are aerobic capacity, anaerobic threshold, and economy.

don't take this to mean that your VO_2max tells you how well you will do compared with others in your race category. The order of finish in a race is a reflection of more than one's aerobic capacity. The two other physiological factors—anaerobic threshold and economy—also play a major role in race outcomes. One of these three by itself does not constitute all it takes to race fast. And of course, this doesn't include other critical race determiners such as strategy, tactics, pacing, nutrition, heat adaptation, and lots more.

Aerobic capacity, however, is the "ticket to the club." If you aspire to be a world-class rider, you have to have high aerobic capacity. It does not by itself determine race outcomes, as all the top riders are likewise blessed. Much of this blessing is inherited. This physiological winning lottery ticket was passed along to top riders by their parents. But that ticket only gives them the potential for winning. They must nourish their unique opportunity to excel in endurance sport. Their lifestyles, including training, have a lot to do with realizing their potential. Your potential for producing energy from inhaled oxygen was also given to you by your parents. But training is necessary for it to play a role in your race outcomes.

Your VO_2max starts with your heart. Changes in aerobic capacity largely have to do with how much oxygen-carrying blood your heart pumps to your working muscles with every beat. This per-beat measurement is called "stroke volume" and has a lot to do with how great your aerobic capacity is. One purpose of training is to increase your stroke volume. There are two ways to do this.

The first is to increase stroke volume with long-duration workouts and high volume. The heart responds positively to lots of saddle time spent at elevated intensity—above about 50 percent of VO_2max—by becoming more efficient and effective, which ultimately means a greater stroke volume.

The second way to improve aerobic capacity is by doing high-intensity intervals, especially when you do them near the power associated with your VO_2max, which you can determine with the functional aerobic capacity power field test (see Appendix B). At that intensity, your heart approaches its maximum pumping rate. These very hard efforts will produce a higher stroke volume more quickly and completely than doing lots of long-duration rides. Most seasoned athletes employ both training strategies by doing long-duration workouts and high-intensity workouts. In Part IV, you'll learn how to incorporate both into your training.

Besides stroke volume, there are other physiological contributors to aerobic capacity such as aerobic enzymes found in the muscles, blood vessel diameter and ability to dilate, blood volume, and hematocrit, or red blood cell count. All of these have to do with delivering massive amounts of oxygen to your muscles when you put the pedal to the metal. Each has both inherited and trained characteristics.

Body weight also has a lot to do with aerobic capacity. The formula for determining VO_2max is expressed in terms of milliliters of oxygen consumed per kilogram of body weight per minute. What this means is that as you lose body weight, especially excessive fat as opposed to cycling-specific muscle, your VO_2max increases. You have undoubtedly experienced this phenomenon at both ends of your normal weight range. When you have gained weight, you ride a bike uphill more slowly even though the power output stays

Aerobic capacity is the "ticket to the club."

the same. It's what you would expect to happen if you rode wearing a heavy weight vest. Conversely, when your body weight is low, you can increase the speed of riding up a hill at any given power output. This is clearly the effect of body weight on aerobic capacity. Of course, when gravity is not an issue, for example when doing a flat ride, body weight is not a disadvantage. That's why big riders with huge aerobic capacities do so well in flat races but are quickly dropped when the course turns uphill.

Anaerobic Threshold

In Chapter 4 I told you about the anaerobic threshold. My point then was to explain the two intensity markers (anaerobic threshold and aerobic threshold) between which you need to distribute your training time. I also showed you how to set training zones using your functional threshold, an easily established substitute for the anaerobic threshold, as the key reference point. It can be determined with a simple field test (this test is described in Appendix B). Now I'll complete that discussion of anaerobic threshold by showing you how it contributes to your race-day fitness.

Time trials are typically raced at about the anaerobic threshold—a little above or a little below based on the duration of the race. To become a good time trialist, you need to build a very high anaerobic threshold using your functional threshold power (FTP) as a marker of progress toward that goal. A great deal of the training for a time trialist will involve workouts done at or near your FTP. As mentioned above, road race outcomes depend largely on brief, high-intensity episodes at well above anaerobic threshold—at or near aerobic capacity and

For the most part, road race results are greatly dependent on what happens above the anaerobic threshold.

higher. How high the intensity is depends, as always, on how long the episode lasts. Creating or responding to a breakaway in a road race usually means riding at or near aerobic capacity for a few minutes. Race-winning sprints that last only a few seconds are done at about anaerobic capacity, which is well above aerobic capacity. But there are times when the anaerobic threshold also plays a determining role in the outcome of a road race. For example, a long, steady, high-intensity climb is often done at or near FTP, much as in a time trial. And once a break is formed, it typically proceeds at around FTP. So having a high FTP is certainly also beneficial for road racing. But for the most part, road race results are greatly dependent on what happens above the anaerobic threshold.

Economy

The last of the big three physiological determiners of race fitness is economy. Sport science understands less about this one than the other two, but it may be the most important. It has to do with how efficiently you use oxygen while riding. Measuring oxygen used is just another way of measuring energy expended. In the human body, the volume of oxygen consumed is directly related to the amount of energy expended when you're riding aerobically. Your cycling economy is much like the economy rating for a car. For a car, it's how many miles it can go per gallon of gas in given conditions. When it comes to the rider's body, it's how many milliliters of oxygen are used per mile at various intensities. Both are measures of the energy being produced, and both provide a measure of economy. For you as a rider, the less oxygen you use to produce a given power output, the more economical you are.

It could be argued that economy becomes more important to the outcome of a race as the race gets longer. This is because in races lasting several hours, a tiny amount of wasted energy during a single pedal stroke is multiplied many times over and can easily result in a tremendous amount of wasted energy. Even a slightly sloppy pedaling technique due to poor skills or an improperly fitted bike can cause unnecessary fatigue in a long race. That's why I place so much emphasis on having a professional bike fit done annually and doing skill-development drills early in every season.

Recall how aerobic capacity is increased? It's boosted by doing high-volume training and also including high-intensity intervals. Such training also can improve economy. But there is a limit to how much economic benefit you get because there are things you can't control. You have control over some factors, such as pedaling skills, but you can do nothing about many determiners of economy. For example, a cyclist with long thighbones relative to total leg length will likely be more economical than a rider with short thighbones. Long thighbones provide better leverage in pedaling. A time trialist with narrow shoulders has an aerodynamic advantage over a rider with broad shoulders. Unfortunately, you can't change your bones (though you should always seek to improve your riding position). Your economy is also improved by having a high percentage of slow-twitch muscle fibers. These are good for endurance, while fast-twitch muscles are better for sprinting. Although muscle types can be changed a small amount through training, they are largely determined by genetics. And there are many other changes to our physiology we would also make if we had control over them, such as increasing the number of mitochondria we have (these are the little powerhouses in the muscle cells that convert oxygen into the energy used for pedaling a bike). These are all things we have little or no control over.

So what things *can* you control to improve your economy in order to use less oxygen as you ride? The most common is technique—how skilled you are at making the movements of the sport. Besides pedaling, this includes how skillfully you corner, climb, sprint, and make other complex movements. Technique can be improved, but it takes time. You must realize that if you decide to go the route of altering your current technique—your pedaling style, for example—there will be a period of time during which you almost certainly become *less* economical. This will show up as a higher than usual heart rate and a higher Rating of Perceived Exertion at any given power output. And it may take weeks, if not months, to make the new technique your normal one. But it will be worth it: At that point, you should have become more economical at the same heart rates as before the change. You'll waste less energy.

Other changes that are beneficial for cycling economy are reducing excess body weight for climbing and using more aerodynamic and lighter equipment. The most notable gear economy improvements are aerobars on your time trial bike, light aero wheels, and an aerodynamic helmet and bike frame. But even if you purchase all of these equipment upgrades, the most likely energy-saving benefit will still come from a professional bike fit.

Intensity and frequency are most likely to improve economy. Training at a high power with

Aerobic capacity is boosted by doing high-volume training and high-intensity intervals.

a high cadence contributes to improved economy at all speeds and power outputs. However, long-duration workouts when you are trying to change pedaling technique to boost economy are often counterproductive. As fatigue sets in, pedaling skills tend to revert to old habits. One of the best ways to improve your technique, and therefore your economy, is to ride frequently for short sessions as you concentrate on skill development. A great time to do this is at the very start of the base period of training, early in the season, when refining skills is often the objective. You'll find pedaling-specific drills under the heading "Speed Skills" in Appendix B.

Plyometric exercises have also been shown to improve economy for cycling. These exercises involve explosive jumping, bounding, and hopping drills. Short, powerful hill repeats are also beneficial for economy. Both improve muscular force and therefore pedal power. There is still a great deal of debate about whether or not traditional weight lifting improves economy. I believe it does, as I have seen so many of the athletes I've coached over the years improve their performances remarkably after a few weeks in the winter devoted to lifting weights. I'll cover the details of power, force, and strength options in Chapter 12.

Training at a high power with a high cadence contributes to improved economy at all speeds and power outputs.

ABILITIES

Now it's time to take all of this science talk about the three determiners of fitness and begin shaping them into common cycling-specific workouts. To do this, I organize all workouts into six categories called "abilities." Each of the abilities is related to aerobic capacity, anaerobic threshold, and economy in some way. The six abilities are divided into basic and advanced, as follows:

Basic abilities
Aerobic endurance
Muscular force
Speed skills

Advanced abilities
Muscular endurance
Anaerobic endurance
Sprint power

You should concentrate on developing the three basic abilities before moving on to training for the last three. The basic abilities are typically developed early in the preparation for a race, and the advanced abilities are the focus of the last few weeks before the race. But sometimes there are exceptions to that rule, which will be addressed in Part IV. For now, let's get a good understanding of the abilities by taking a brief look at each. For the remainder of the book, I will frequently refer to these abilities when discussing training, so having a working knowledge of them is important.

Basic Abilities

In some ways the basic abilities—aerobic endurance, muscular force, and speed skills—are the most important of the six. Just as the foundation of a house ultimately determines how sound the aboveground construction will be, the basic abilities establish the foundation on which your race-specific fitness will be built. The more you develop these abilities, the greater your eventual race performance. If these abilities are weak, the subsequent advanced ability training will be quite limited and you will never achieve your potential as a racer. The basic abilities are generally the ones a cyclist should focus on early in the season (the base period) and return to again for further development after long pre-race tapers and lengthy post-race recoveries. During such low-training load periods, the basic abilities gradually fade away. Figure 6.1 illustrates the basic abilities.

Aerobic endurance. Aerobic endurance is the ability to keep going for a very long time at a low to moderate intensity. It is improved by doing long, somewhat easy, and very steady workouts in zone 2—below RPE 5 (see Figure 4.1). Such workouts have a lot to do with building aerobic capacity since they contribute significantly to the volume of your training (recall that high volume boosts VO_2max). Aerobic endurance training does this by making several positive changes to your physiology. For example, by doing lots of aerobic endurance training, some of your fast-twitch muscles begin to take on the endurance characteristics of slow-twitch muscles. Your blood also becomes better at carrying oxygen to your working muscles. Your body builds more tiny capillaries to deliver the oxygen-rich blood to your muscles. The muscle cells make more enzymes to produce energy using the delivered oxygen. And that's just a partial list of the many benefits of aerobic endurance workouts. Aerobic endurance training is the single most important of the six abilities for a cyclist because as an endurance athlete, you must first of all be aerobically fit. Poor aerobic endurance is a game-stopper.

In Sidebar 5.3, you read about the functional aerobic threshold field test that allows you to measure aerobic endurance changes throughout the season and gauge your progress (also see Appendix B for this test). As you will see later on, we'll use this simple test frequently throughout the season to see how your aerobic endurance is progressing.

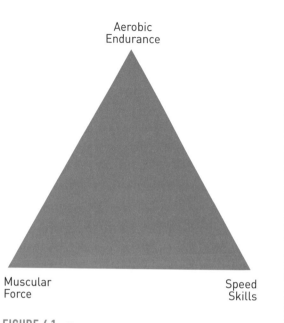

FIGURE 6.1   The basic abilities of training

Muscular force. This is the ability to use your cycling-specific muscles to overcome resistance. It certainly benefits all three fitness markers, but it's most closely related to economy. Propelling your body and bike through the air causes resistance to forward movement. If there is a headwind, the resistance is even greater. And gravity produces tremendous resistance when riding uphill. The better you are at overcoming such resistance, the faster you can ride in such situations. Muscular force workouts thus contribute to improved performance in many ways.

The key to this ability is your muscular system, especially the primary mover muscles for the sport. These are mostly in the legs, although torso stability also plays an important role in powering the pedals. If all of these muscles are strong yet not bulky, then you will excel in overcoming the negative effects of air, wind, and gravity. If your muscles are weak, you will always be slow no matter how aerobically fit you are. If

Aerobic endurance is the ability to keep going for a very long time at a low to moderate intensity.

you can easily overcome resistance, then you are quite economical under certain conditions.

Muscular force is improved by training against resistance—overcoming gravity by weight lifting and climbing hills, and by riding into the wind. While training this ability early in the base period, you will come to see how such workouts greatly boost performance. The training is simple—but not easy. Muscular force workouts are typically repetitions done at a very high intensity with one of the above types of resistance. For the very early stages of your annual training, this could be the weight lifting that is discussed in Chapter 12. But having muscular force in the weight room is not enough. This ability needs to be transferred to the road, where it becomes specific to riding a bike.

Speed skills. Skill is the ability to make the movements of the sport in an efficient and effective manner. As explained above, skill development is one of the best ways to improve economy and therefore boost fitness and performance. The movements of some sports, such as tennis and golf, are complex and challenging to learn, while others are relatively simple. Pedaling a bike appears to be a rather simple skill, but that is misleading. Effective pedaling skills are quite complex, with a lot of both big and small muscles firing and relaxing in a pattern that ultimately determines how economical you are. Master the skills of riding a bike and your fitness and race performance will improve as you become better at using and, more importantly, conserving energy. As with aerobic endurance and muscular force, the critical time to develop your skills is early in the base period. Doing long endurance rides or muscular force training on the road with

poor skills is a waste of time. So speed skills need early season development. And the newer you are to the sport, the more critical this is.

I call this ability "speed skills" because the purpose of such training is to make the movements, no matter how complex, at a speed that is necessary when racing. Here I'm *not* referring to bike speed—as in how fast you are moving down the road—but rather to your leg speed when pedaling. The high cadences at which you ride in a race must be done skillfully so as not to waste energy. It's easy to master a skill if you do it slowly enough. In fact, that's the way pedaling skills are typically introduced—at a slow cadence. When the demands of the workout or race require a high cadence, your skills must remain economical. If you become sloppy at high cadences, you'll waste energy and your fitness will be poor. Appendix B provides a list of drills for improving pedaling speed skills.

There are other skills to master, including the skills for cornering, sprinting, and climbing. These are somewhat less complex than pedaling skills and will be developed when doing specific-ability rides that fall into these categories.

Advanced Abilities

As the basic abilities are rounding into shape early in the season, training gradually shifts toward the three advanced abilities: muscular endurance, anaerobic endurance, and sprint power. These are the keys to high-performance racing. The basic abilities should be well developed after a few weeks of training. It seems there's always room for a bit more improvement, but at some point you must shift the focus of training toward the more race-specific advanced abilities.

> Muscular force is improved by training against resistance.

> Speed skills need early season development.

How do you decide when the time is right? There may be physical indications based on testing, or even on how you feel when riding. Building the basics may take 8 to 12 weeks. It's never wrong, however, to extend basic ability training for a few more weeks if you have time relative to your next high-priority race. The more basic ability fitness you have, the greater your eventual race fitness will be due to having a sound foundation to build on.

The advanced abilities differ in this regard. It can be counterproductive to extend training at that level beyond about 8 to 12 weeks. This is especially true for the anaerobic endurance ability, as the stress it places on the body far exceeds the stress of the other abilities. It's quite possible to do too much and become burned out, injured, or sick.

It is possible, however, to cautiously insert minimal amounts of advanced ability training throughout the early season base period, even while the basic abilities are still the primary focus of training. Doing so can be beneficial, as it may stimulate slight physical adaptations and make the transition from early to late season race preparation less stressful for the body. The key to doing this is keeping advanced ability portions of workouts short, with long recoveries between the high-intensity repetitions.

For example, you may have a muscular force workout on the bike planned in the base period. Following the muscular force repetitions, you could include 3 or 4 intervals of 20-second duration done at anaerobic endurance intensity with 20-second recoveries. Such a workout is best done only by veteran riders with many years of racing experience, an exceptional ability to monitor their bodies, and a good working knowledge

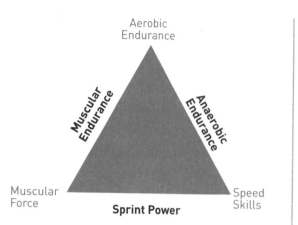

FIGURE 6.2 The advanced abilities of training

of effective training. It's easy to do too much high intensity early in the year and wreck the entire season.

Most riders would be better advised to separate the basic and advanced abilities with an overlap of only 2 to 3 weeks in training. We'll describe this more conservative approach to training in Part IV when we talk about periodization. Highly experienced advanced riders may consider adopting a somewhat more liberal approach to training at that point.

With all of this in mind, let's dig a little deeper into the advanced abilities and their role in preparing to race. These abilities are illustrated in Figure 6.2. Be sure to note the two basic abilities that form the adjoining corners for each advanced ability side of the triangle. These two basic abilities are the base fitness foundation for the advanced ability between them.

Muscular endurance. Muscular endurance is the ability to ride for a *moderately* long time at a *moderately* high effort, as in time trialing. Muscular endurance workouts have a lot to do with your anaerobic threshold fitness, as discussed above. This is often the ability that delivers you to those brief, very high-intensity episodes that determine the outcome of a road race. It's also the single most important ability for time trialing. And, as mentioned earlier, it is often the ability that gets you up a long climb at a steady effort.

Muscular endurance results from having well-developed fitness in the basic abilities that form the two corners of the triangle closest to that side in Figure 6.2: aerobic endurance and muscular force. If either of these is poorly developed, then muscular endurance will also be poor. This is why base training is so important to race fitness.

Workout durations to build muscular endurance are moderate because they are shorter than what you do for aerobic endurance workouts. But the intensity (around 7 RPE) is much greater than that of aerobic endurance training. However, the effort is moderate because it's less intense than muscular force repetitions. When training this ability, you will be near your anaerobic threshold heart rate and power.

Muscular endurance is improved by doing long (6- to 12-minute) repeats with short (90-second to 4-minute) recoveries, or long (20- to 40-minute) steady efforts in heart rate or power zones 3 and 4 or RPE 5 to 7. These are grueling workouts, but they pay off with greatly improved fitness. One of the best markers of improvement from such training is an increased FTP as measured by the functional threshold power field test described in Chapter 5 (and also in Appendix B). By following the suggested training guidelines in later chapters, you will do a considerable amount of this type of training in the late base period and also throughout the entire build period.

Anaerobic endurance. Once your basic abilities are well honed, building fitness by training anaerobic endurance is one of the most effective things you can do to perform well in road races. That's because anaerobic endurance training is the single best type of workout for improving your aerobic capacity fitness. I know the terms "anaerobic endurance" and "aerobic capacity" may sound contradictory and somewhat confusing; that confusion stems from what is somewhat of a scientific misnomer dating back to the 1960s in exercise physiology. I'll try to explain.

Whenever you are exercising above the anaerobic threshold, you are, by definition, *anaerobic*. As described in the anaerobic threshold discussion in Chapter 4, at this intensity acidic hydrogen ions are accumulating in the muscles and blood vessels, accompanied by other cellular changes that ultimately contribute to short-term fatigue (fatigue is *not* caused by lactic acid). But whenever you are using oxygen to produce energy, as you are when doing anaerobic endurance intervals, you are by definition *aerobic*. You are using oxygen. And that is still happening when you are at your aerobic capacity, even though the term "anaerobic" means "without oxygen." So when you are doing anaerobic endurance workouts, you are accumulating muscle fatigue very rapidly, but you are still, to a small extent, using oxygen to produce energy. Even though the term "anaerobic" is somewhat inaccurate, I'm afraid it's here to stay.

The anaerobic endurance workout calls for short—a few seconds to a handful of minutes—highly intense intervals done in zone 5 or about RPE 9, with equal to somewhat shorter recovery breaks between them (see Appendix B for details). Anaerobic endurance training should be done sparingly and with great caution. It is very strong medicine. It's not candy. In the periodiza-

Muscular endurance results from having well-developed fitness in the basic abilities: aerobic endurance and muscular force.

tion planning guidelines in Part IV, you will see how I emphasize these workouts at only a few select times throughout the season. This workout must always be treated with caution. Whenever a workout has the potential to produce a high reward, it also presents a high risk. Always closely monitor your body during and immediately following an anaerobic endurance session to get a proper balance between stress and recovery.

Sprint power. As the name implies, this is the advanced ability for sprinting at very high power outputs for a few seconds. It's improved with very short (less than 20-second) maximum-effort intervals with long (several-minute) recoveries. It's an ability that is particularly important for some races, such as criteriums and flat road courses, especially for riders who are sprinters. Notice that this advanced ability is primarily the product of the basic speed skills and muscular force abilities. Fully developing these basic abilities in the base period will pay off with greatly improved sprint power in the following build period.

In the Chapter 5 explanation of training sub-goals—what I call *objectives*—I introduced the concept of limiters. A limiter is a goal-specific weakness that stands between you and the successful accomplishment of a seasonal goal. Why is it a *goal-specific* weakness? That's because not all of your weaknesses are race-performance limiters. For example, an athlete may not be very good at climbing hills. That's definitely a weakness. But if the most important races of that athlete's season are flat criteriums, then this weak-

ness is not a limiter. It's not standing in the way of goal success. That's why limiters are goal-specific. The concept may be thought of as a mismatch between your weaknesses and the demands of the event for which you are training.

Every athlete has limiters, even the pros. It's just that for some athletes the limiters are more obvious than for others because their weaknesses are greater. That's usually the case for those who are relatively new to the sport. Riders who have been training seriously for several years still have weaknesses and limiters, but they just aren't as obvious. The advanced rider knows what his or her weaknesses are, but the limiters are subtle.

The common way of thinking about road cycling weaknesses is in terms of climbing, time trialing, and sprinting. Figure 2.1 illustrated the power-duration differences between riders who have well-established strengths in each of these disciplines. No one, not even the best all-rounders, is great at all three of these. Everyone has weaknesses in at least one of them. A weakness in two is much more common. If you've been in the sport for at least a couple of years, then you undoubtedly know which is your strength and which are your weaknesses. Once you know your weaknesses, you need to compare them with the demands of the most important races in your upcoming season. You have a limiter whenever you have a weakness that matches up with a demand of the event. For example, if the course is quite hilly and climbing is your weakness, then that's a limiter. If the race is a criterium that is likely to come down to a finish line sprint and sprinting is your weakness, then that is your limiter.

You are unlikely to become as good at your limiters as you are at your strengths, even if you

TABLE 6.1 The Abilities to Focus on in Training for Given Limiters

LIMITER	ABILITY
Climbing	Anaerobic endurance or muscular endurance
Time trialing	Muscular endurance
Sprinting	Sprint power

train expressly for them. But you can close the gap and improve them through serious training. The smart rider also seeks to employ race tactics in order to get a slight advantage when limiters—even those you've improved considerably with training—are challenged. If you're not a great climber, for example, you might start at the front of the pack on a climb and then drift back so that by the top you are still in the group. Or you could use your race knowledge to decide whose wheel to sit on when the sprint is about to start. For time trialing, unfortunately there's not much you can do tactically to hide your limiter. That's why the time trial is known as the race of truth. It's just you and the clock.

What is your highest priority race of the season? What is your limiter for that race? As you plan your new season, these are perhaps the most important questions you'll need to answer. Your training will focus on this limiter. That doesn't mean you should neglect your strength. You have to maintain it, and fortunately maintenance is much easier and less demanding than remedial training. In fact, the greater your limiter, the more you must ensure that your racing strength remains strong in order to counterbalance it. The simplest application of this rule is to select races that emphasize your strengths. A strong climber is wise to pick a race that requires a lot of climbing. That would counterbalance a sprinting limiter if the race were flat.

The strong time trialist and sprinter may also make race choices that emphasize their particular strengths.

Of course, as we all know, choosing races that match our strengths is not always possible. If you're a climber doing a race series that involves some criteriums, you'll need to prepare for races that are a mismatch for your strength. What do you do then? How do you strengthen a limiter?

This question brings us back to the abilities discussion above. Once you know your limiter, strengthening it comes down to knowing which workout types, based on abilities, are required to bring improvement. Table 6.1 suggests workouts to focus on in order to strengthen a limiter.

Climbing is perhaps the most common limiter for road cyclists. As suggested in Table 6.1, it requires a high level of either anaerobic endurance or muscular endurance, depending on whether you aspire to be a "power" climber or a time trial climber. The race course may also help to decide this. If the course has a lot of short, steep hills, then power climbing is a must. Anaerobic endurance is then the focus of limiter training. If the climb is long, you may be able to effectively train for it by doing muscular endurance workouts. A long, steady climb done in a manner similar to a time trial is usually the better option for the rider with a climbing limiter.

The advanced ability workouts you do in the last few weeks before the race indicate the need

Select races that emphasize your strengths.

to emphasize a certain mix of workouts in the base period. This again takes us back to Figure 6.2 and the basic ability corners of the triangle that accompany each advanced ability side. For example, aerobic endurance and speed skills are basic abilities to concentrate on in the base period in order to prepare you for anaerobic endurance limiter training in the last few weeks prior to the race. If muscular endurance is your limiter, you'll need to focus your base period training on aerobic endurance and muscular force.

At the same time, as you focus on your advanced ability training, you cannot ignore the other abilities. Instead, you need to distribute your limited training time and energy to optimize your race preparation. All three advanced abilities must still be developed, but the base period training emphasis should be on the limiter-related basic abilities.

Of course, climbing requires a high power-to-weight ratio, regardless of which of the two ability types best suits the course and rider. So another of the rider's climbing limiters may be either power or weight. You'll climb faster if you're carrying less weight uphill—you already know that. Similarly, the greater your power output becomes, the faster you will climb a hill at any given weight. Increasing power while shedding unnecessary weight is the ultimate solution. Comparing functional aerobic capacity power (FACP) and functional threshold power (FTP) with body weight over time provides a good indicator of how well you may be able to climb at any point in the preparation for your race (see Appendix B for field tests that measure these power outputs). FACP is closely associated with anaerobic endurance ability and FTP with muscular endurance ability.

Of course, you may be coming into a season when your two or three most important races place multiple demands on your abilities, thus requiring you to develop two or three abilities concurrently. For example, let's say your first big race of the season is a hilly road race and climbing is a weakness. In this case, you may aspire to become a better climber. But your second big race of the season is a flat criterium, and your limiter for it is sprint power. So how do you manage all of this preparation given that you have limited time to train yet need to develop a great deal of race-specific fitness prior to these two races?

There are many things to consider here. One of the most important is how much time you have between races. Another is how great your limiters are. In other words, how much improving do you have to accomplish and how much time do you have to accomplish it? It is never easy when you have a couple of significant limiters that need attention and very little time between races to work on improving them. In this case, you would need to make some critical decisions. For example, which race is more important to you? Which limiter is greater? If you can't be equally good for both races and both limiters, you're going to need to cut yourself some slack by focusing on what you *can* accomplish rather than what you'd *like* to accomplish.

Determining your limiters in this way is perhaps the most critical decision you'll make as the new season begins. As a coach, I know this decision can make or break an athlete's success, and so it is what I give the most thought to early in the year. It's no less significant for you. I strongly suggest that you carefully consider the demands of your most important races. As a rule, you should have only two or three critical races in a season

You need to distribute your limited training time and energy to optimize your race preparation.

(more on that in Chapter 7). Then carefully consider how your strengths and weaknesses stack up to the anticipated race demands. You'll have a perfect combination if your strengths match the demands of the race. Training will be easy to figure out. But if your weaknesses mismatch the race's demands, you have a limiter and need to start working to fix it. That makes for a much more challenging season.

For novice riders (and even some intermediates), the basic abilities are the typical limiters. Athletes new to the sport should focus their training on them. There is no need to devote much time to the advanced abilities until the basic ones are well established, and establishing them may take one to three years of basic training. For experienced athletes who have devoted several years to improving aerobic endurance, muscular force, and speed skills, the common limiters are the advanced abilities—muscular endurance, anaerobic endurance, and sprint power. But, as you will see when we get to the topic of planning your season in Chapter 7, the experienced athlete should still reestablish the basic abilities each season before progressing to advanced ability training. The basic abilities tend to erode following a reduction in training load, such as during a race taper and following a break from training for whatever reason. At such times, it's a good idea to return to basic ability training to rebuild them.

There are many other possible weaknesses beyond the six abilities in Figure 6.2 that may be limiting your performance. I've already discussed one that typically limits climbing: the power-to-weight ratio. The others mostly have to do with lifestyle and include such matters as training inconsistency, limited time for training, lack of confidence, limited support from family

and friends, poor nutritional choices, insufficient equipment, an inadequate training environment, a propensity to overtrain, frequent illness or injury, inappropriate body composition, insufficient sleep, unusual psychological stress, a physically demanding job, and many more. These must also be addressed if you are to perform anywhere near your potential as a cyclist. I suspect you know which apply to you. We'll touch on them in the chapters to come.

SUMMARY: PREPARING TO RACE

For the endurance cyclist, what is fitness? In this chapter you read that there are three physiological determiners that answer this question: aerobic capacity, anaerobic threshold, and economy.

Aerobic capacity, often referred to as VO$_2$max, has to do with the maximal volume of oxygen your body can process to produce energy. The more oxygen your body is capable of consuming, the faster and more powerfully you can ride. Your potential for aerobic capacity is widely considered to be the result of genetics—who your parents were. Given that inherited upper ceiling, there are two ways to bump your aerobic capacity to a higher level. One way is to ride a lot of hours every week. But the more effective way is to do high-intensity intervals. These intervals are done well above the anaerobic threshold for up to about 5 minutes duration with recoveries that are the same length or somewhat shorter. The very best cyclists all have very high aerobic capacities. Many amateur riders can also process a lot of oxygen, but they may be held back from advancing to a higher level of competition due to excessive body weight. That's the reason pro cyclists are so skinny. Excess weight reduces their aerobic capacity since it's limited by mass. The bigger you are, the more oxygen you need to climb at the peloton's speed.

Another fitness marker, anaerobic threshold, is highly trainable. High-intensity training also plays a role here, as the AnT responds quite nicely to workouts done at or near this threshold. It's expressed as a percentage of your aerobic capacity. The higher the percentage, the greater your capability for fast racing, especially when you're time trialing or steadily climbing a long hill.

The last of the big three determiners of endurance fitness is economy—how much energy is used to produce a given power output. Just as with a car and its economy rating, your body has an economical limit for fuel consumption. Your body's economy, however, can be improved by refining skills, shedding excess weight, and using more aerodynamic equipment and positioning. There are, however, some physical properties of your body that affect economy and can't be changed, such as bone structure. Others can be improved including, once again, your weight, along with training fast-twitch muscle fibers to take on more of the characteristics of slow-twitch fibers by doing lots of aerobic endurance riding.

This chapter also introduced the six abilities that we will look at in terms of workouts for the remainder of the book: aerobic endurance, muscular force, speed skills, muscular endurance, anaerobic endurance, and sprint power. The first three are the basic abilities. These will likely be the focus of your early season training, and you'll return to them at various times during the race season. Together they form the foundation of your training on which the advanced abilities—

muscular endurance, anaerobic endurance, and sprint power—are built. The advanced abilities are much more race specific and will likely be the focus of your training in the last few weeks before your most important races. Each ability category includes workouts that are linked in some way to the three fitness determiners.

Once you understand how all of the abilities are related to race preparation, the next step is to decide which of these, especially from the advanced category, are race-specific weakness areas for you. I call these *limiters*, as they are holding you back from achieving your seasonal goals and objectives. The limiters may be thought of as the three well-understood racing characteristics you're already quite familiar with: climbing, time trialing, and sprinting. If you are weak in any one of these and your goal race demands that you be strong in that area of performance, then it is a limiter. Your training must address this limiter or you will fall short of your goal. Each limiter is associated with one or more of the six workout abilities in Table 6.1. This means that once you've identified a weak ability, it must become a focus of your training in order for you to have a successful race. It's also important that you maintain the abilities that are your strong suits.

The primary purpose of this chapter was to give you a general understanding of preparing to race so that your limited time and energy are used in the most productive way. That means eventually achieving your most important goals for the season. To do this, it's also important that we examine how the ability-associated workouts can be organized to bring you to a peak of fitness on race day. That's the essential goal of training, and it's where we are headed next.

Anaerobic threshold is highly trainable.

PLANNING
YOUR SEASON

consider Part IV to be the heart of this book. It's about planning your season—determining what types of workouts you'll do and when you'll do them. When I started racing back in the 1970s, I began this way because it just seemed logical. I used a calendar to sketch out when I would do certain workouts in preparation for my race schedule. While I didn't know it at the time, I was using a simple periodization model to plan my season.

Periodization is really what these three chapters are about and what I consider to be the foundational model for training. I had never heard of it as a young athlete, but by the 1980s I became aware of the concept from talking with other athletes, coaches, and sports scientists. About that time, I read a book by Tudor Bompa, PhD, titled *Theory and Methodology of Training* (it's still in print today). Bompa, a Canadian, was a recent emigrant from Romania, a Communist Bloc country at the time. He is considered by many to be one the founding fathers of the periodization concept. Later, I came to know Dr. Bompa and spent some time discussing training with him. In 1996 he wrote the foreword to the first edition of this book.

The concept of periodization in sport has its roots in the Soviet Union in the 1950s and 1960s. It was a state secret during the early decades of the Cold War and was used only by Eastern European countries. Western athletes and coaches were unaware of it at the time. Most non–Eastern Bloc athletes trained somewhat randomly then. Cyclists simply trained as their coaches had trained before them. There was little in the way of a scientific method, and certainly no periodization. European distance runners were the first to adopt periodization, starting in the early 1970s, and the secret leaked out to Western athletes at international competitions shortly thereafter.

When I wrote the original version of this book back in 1995, training periodization had only been known in the West for about 20 years, and it was something used by only some elite athletes. I was introducing the concept to nearly all amateur road cyclists, so I kept the discussion simple. I suggested just one way of periodizing a season: the "linear" or "classic" version. This is the oldest and most basic version. It is perhaps the easiest to understand and follow, and the one still used by most athletes around the world today. It works well for most amateurs, and even some pro riders use it. But there are many other variations on this basic model that are used by serious riders.

In Chapter 7, I will describe linear periodization as the starting point for understanding the concept. That will lead into a discussion of planning a week in Chapter 8. Then in Chapter 9, I'll introduce other periodization models, including their common advantages and disadvantages, and help you select the method that best suits your needs.

By the end of Chapter 9, you should have an annual training plan laid out, and you'll be ready to start focused training.

PLANNING OVERVIEW

FRANZ STAMPFL, a now mostly forgotten coach of the 1950s, once said, "Training is principally an act of faith." His point was that there are no guarantees. An athlete must believe in and be fully committed to a way of training, as doubt negatively affects race performance. Regardless of how much science and deep thought you invest in preparing for the season ahead, the bottom line is that you must trust that it will produce the race results you seek. This suggests the need to follow a credible and believable training methodology.

The starting point for any training methodology is its underlying philosophy. As a coach, the philosophy I have used for many years is rather simple: The closer you are to your race, the more your training must be like the race. On the surface this seems obvious, yet I frequently talk with athletes who are confused when it comes to deciding how to train at given times of the season. This training philosophy and its associated methodology are what this chapter is about. They

will broaden your understanding of how to train. If you follow the guidelines here and in the following two chapters, your workouts will steadily morph into races. As your training sessions gradually take on the characteristics of your goal race, you can take comfort in knowing that your chances of success are greatly enhanced. If you've done it in training, you can do it in a race. Faith becomes confidence. The starting place for implementing this philosophy and methodology is your periodization plan.

PERIODIZATION

I'm sure you've heard this term used many times. You probably use it yourself to describe how you organize your season. But do you really know what periodization is? It's merely the application of the philosophy I outlined above with a slight organizational twist: the division of a season into subperiods, with the workouts in each of these periods becoming somewhat more race-like than those of the previous period as you progress toward the race. You will learn how that is done here and in Chapter 8. By the end of Chapter 9, you will have developed a seasonal plan that takes into consideration all you have read about so far while applying this philosophy to your training methodology.

To begin with, you must first accept that training must be a steady and gradual building process. Peak race performance doesn't happen suddenly or mysteriously. Your body must go through a lot of physiological changes while you prepare to race. Each of these changes has a timetable. They cannot be rushed—nature must run its course. You can't force your body to become fit on some sort of artificial schedule in order to fit the race calendar. It must be gently coaxed to a higher level of fitness by allowing for cellular adaptation. This means that despite having a carefully designed periodization plan, you must be willing to make changes to it as needed. A rigidly followed plan that doesn't allow for breaks from training when you are overly tired and doesn't consider the many other lifestyle demands on your time is worse than no plan at all. The plan must be dynamic to be effective. You must take into account how you feel on a daily basis and be willing to modify the plan as needed. Training flexibility is vital to your race success. You *must* be willing to make changes. That almost always comes down to taking a break when needed. Chapter 11 will get into the topic of rest and recovery, including "recovery on demand."

What does it mean for workouts to become increasingly race-like? It's simple. As you get closer to the day of your most important race, your workouts should gradually take on the characteristics of that race based on your goals

Training must be a steady and gradual building process.

for it. For example, if your goal is a 40 km time trial done at an average power of 200 watts, your workouts must involve doing increasingly longer intervals at around 200 watts over the course of your race preparation. Given adequate training time, by race day you will come to realize that you are capable of holding that power for the entire race. Your faith becomes confidence.

If your goal is to podium in a road race and the greatest barrier standing between you and that goal—your limiter—is a long climb, then you must increasingly do workouts involving similar long climbs. When you come to realize in workouts that you are capable of lengthy climbing with a fast group, your faith becomes confidence.

If race day is expected to be so hot that heat will determine the outcome, then you need to frequently train in the heat in the last several weeks pre-race to be fully adapted. Along the way, you must have faith. That and proper training breeds confidence.

Gradually making your workouts like the race simply involves knowing what the demands of the event will be and bringing your strengths and limiters into alignment with those demands. Following this training philosophy is not at all complicated, and it makes you race-day confident and ready to go. There are many such basic details in seasonal planning. Let's take a deeper look at them.

PLANNING

The philosophy of workout progression brings us to a critical concept in periodization: the timing of workouts by ability. Chapter 6 introduced the concept of abilities and divided them into two categories, basic and advanced. Figure 6.2 in the previous chapter shows the relationships of those two categories. In review, the basic abilities are at the corners of the ability triangle: aerobic endurance, muscular force, and speed skills. On the sides are the advanced abilities: muscular endurance, anaerobic endurance, and sprint power. These last three are commonly the race-like abilities that determine how well prepared you are on race day.

The important message from Chapter 6 is that the advanced abilities are the products of the basic abilities. If you want to have good muscular endurance, you must first optimally develop your aerobic endurance and muscular force. In the same way, strong anaerobic endurance results from well-developed aerobic endurance and speed skills. The basic abilities of muscular force and speed skills ultimately produce sprint power.

In this chapter, I'm going to get you started on planning your preparation for the first important race on your calendar. We'll start with what sports scientists call "linear" or "classic" periodization. This was the planning model first used by athletes in the early days of periodization. It's called "linear" because it follows a simple progression of the abilities, from basic to advanced. Not all periodization schemes do that (as you will see in Chapter 9). In linear periodization, we begin the season by focusing on the basic abilities; as training progresses, the emphasis gradually shifts to the advanced abilities. It's not a sudden jump from basic to advanced but rather a gradual transformation involving a considerable overlap of the two categories.

Sports scientists call the early part of the season (when the basic abilities are emphasized) the "general preparation" period. Most athletes call it the "base" period, and so that's what I

will call it. But the "general preparation" title is descriptive of the purpose of the base period—to prepare in a *general* way for the latter part of the season. Essentially, when in the base period, you are training to train. You're doing things that aren't exactly like the race—for example, lifting weights.

Sports scientists call the training progression following the base period the "specific preparation" period. Most athletes call it the "build" period. Again, "specific preparation" is a good name, as it implies that the emphasis of training is on workouts that are specific, or similar, to the race for which you are training. An example would be race-like group rides. While the scientific names are quite descriptive of the training process, we'll use the terms "base" and "build" throughout this book.

In addition to base and build, there are a few other periods that must be understood to fully grasp the big-picture concept of periodization planning. Using common athlete language, the others are the "prep," "peak," "race," and "transition" periods. Table 7.1 lists each of the periods in the order in which they generally occur in linear periodization, along with a description of each.

To prepare your annual training plan, you must have a clear idea of what the focus of your training will be. You need to minimize your limiters while continuing to develop your already well-established ability strengths. All of this was described in Chapter 6 and is crucial to moving on with planning.

You should also have a general understanding of the training periods you will use in your annual training plan, as shown in Table 7.1. With all of this in mind, I will help you create a plan to prepare you to race by developing both ability

Linear periodization follows a simple progression of abilities from basic to advanced.

TABLE 7.1 **The Common Periods in a Linear Periodization Model**

PERIOD	LENGTH	PURPOSE	PRIMARY ABILITY FOCUS
Preparation	1–4 weeks	Prepare to train	Basic abilities
Base	9–12 weeks	Train to train	Basic abilities
Build	6–8 weeks	Train to race	Advanced abilities
Peak	1–2 weeks	Taper for race	Advanced abilities
Race	1–3 weeks	Remove fatigue Sharpen fitness	Advanced abilities
Transition	1–4 weeks	Rest and recover	Basic abilities

categories using the linear model. This will be a big picture, an overview of where you are going and what you should work on along the way in preparation for your race. We'll pull together many of the concepts discussed in the previous chapters in order to provide structure and purpose for your training.

If you are coming to this chapter at the start of a new training season—probably in late fall or winter—then your timing is right on. If, however, you are already well into the season, then applying what is discussed here will mean making adjustments to blend your recent training with a new and probably different training method. That may require considerable adjustment on your part, and it will have so many individual variations that I can't offer detailed general guidance. I can only suggest that you make the changes gradually. Don't change everything you've been doing thus far. Slowly adopt the routines suggested here and in Chapter 8. In either case, by the end of this chapter you will have developed most of your annual training plan in preparation for your next important race.

Once you have a plan for your season, you can use this same method again in the following seasons. Doing so will allow you to masterfully

devise an annual training plan that provides a purpose for each workout and produces race-day readiness. Save the plans you develop and the adjustments you make to them along the way so that you have a record of what was done in the past. These, along with season-ending notes, will help you easily plan for future seasons.

Before we get into the design of your annual training plan, it's important to understand the fine details of how the training of abilities fits into a linear periodization plan. This goes beyond the brief overview in Table 7.1. Figure 7.1 shows all of the periods (called "mesocycles") and breaks them down into weekly subperiods ("microcycles"). Each mesocycle is made up of 1 to 4 microcycles. This figure shows how the basic and advanced abilities are emphasized and blended into a training plan as you prepare for the *first* important race of the season.

Be aware that Figure 7.1 only shows how to prepare for the first important race of your season. For the important races that follow, you don't have to go through the entire periodization process again as shown in Figure 7.1. This is because of the fitness you steadily accumulate over the course of the season. It doesn't need to be entirely redeveloped. But there is certainly a

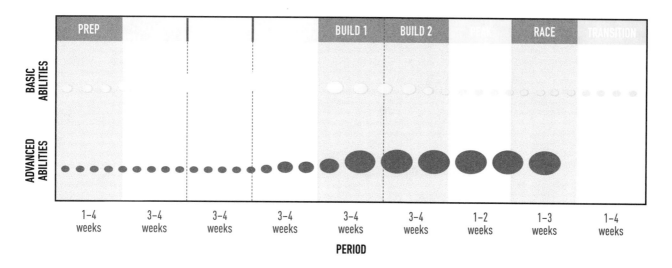

| PREP | | | | BUILD 1 | BUILD 2 | PEAK | RACE | TRANSITION |

| 1–4 weeks | 3–4 weeks | 3–4 weeks | 3–4 weeks | 3–4 weeks | 3–4 weeks | 1–2 weeks | 1–3 weeks | 1–4 weeks |

PERIOD

Overview of linear periodization showing preparation for the first important race of the season

slight to moderate loss of fitness that typically occurs during the peak and transition periods. When you taper for a race during the peak period and recover after the race in the transition period, even if it's only for a few days, your fitness is somewhat compromised, especially the basic abilities. The longer your peak and transition periods, the more fitness you lose.

The fitness you've built prior to the initial race won't, however, be entirely lost when you back off from hard training for just a couple of weeks. But some basic ability fitness will likely be in need of attention before the next important race of the season. Preparation for these races is a bit more complex than it was for the first race of the year. At this point, it all comes down to how much time you have between the first and second races. The more time you have, the easier it is to get ready. In a perfect season, you'd have about 12 to 16 weeks between your major races (with many other less-important races during that time, of course). What this means is that after a short break from serious training in the few days after the first race (the transition

period), you would return to a few days of basic ability–focused workouts, as in base 3, before returning to the build, peak, and race periods with their emphasis on the advanced abilities. In this case, your periodization plan may look similar to Figure 7.2.

It's uncommon in road racing to have more than 12 weeks between important races. So you'll likely have far fewer than 12 weeks separating important races once you're past your first race of the season. The less time you have to prepare, the greater the challenge when it comes to planning and preparing. Figure 7.3 suggests a plan for when there are only 7 to 11 weeks between races.

When there are fewer than 7 weeks until your next important race, there are several difficult decisions to be made. First of all, you will have to decide if you need a transition period. While that period may last a month or more after the last race of the season, post-race recovery is considerably shorter during the season. With fewer than 7 weeks to prepare for the next race, you may only take 2 or 3 days to rest and recover before starting back into serious training. I strongly suggest

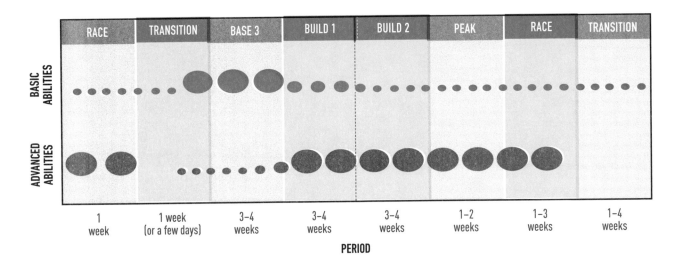

RACE	TRANSITION	BASE 3	BUILD 1	BUILD 2	PEAK	RACE	TRANSITION

BASIC ABILITIES

ADVANCED ABILITIES

1 week	1 week (or a few days)	3–4 weeks	3–4 weeks	3–4 weeks	1–2 weeks	1–3 weeks	1–4 weeks

PERIOD

FIGURE 7.2 A suggested preparation plan for the second and third most important races of the season when there are 12 to 16 weeks to train following the previous race

taking that short break whether you feel like you need it or not. Near the end of the race season, if you didn't take a break earlier you will come to understand why this is important. It's more mental than physical. The break in training allows you to recharge. Without it, you are likely to be burned out in a few weeks. A couple of days off from serious training will be good for you in the long term.

Following the short transition period break, you are ready to return to focused training again. Now you must decide how much time you'll devote to basic and advanced ability training. As mentioned earlier, it's common for the basic abilities to erode slightly when tapering for a race and recovering in the days after. The longer the taper and transition, the more likely you will need to return to a base 3 training program, which emphasizes the basic abilities but also includes some advanced ability work, as illustrated in Figure 7.3. Otherwise, if the taper and the post-race break from training were quite short—perhaps a combined 10 days or fewer—you may

decide, given that you have only a handful of weeks until your next race, to devote your attention to the build period and the advanced abilities. If there are only 4 weeks or fewer remaining, training may be mostly build 2 training, followed by a very short taper. Three to 5 days in the peak period and a shortened race period should do it. Build 2, of course, includes very race-like workouts. This strategy should work fine if your basic ability fitness is still strong.

The key basic ability to consider when deciding how to plan for the few weeks before your next race is aerobic endurance. Doing the functional aerobic threshold (FAeT) test as described in Sidebar 5.3 and also in Appendix B and comparing the results to your last FAeT test will help you decide if a focus on the redevelopment of this basic ability is necessary. If your efficiency factor from the more recent test shows a decrease of more than 10 percent, I would strongly recommend returning to a short base 3, with a heavy emphasis on aerobic threshold training (workout AE2 in Appendix B). Otherwise, it is prob-

It's common for the basic abilities to erode slightly when tapering for a race and recovering in the days after.

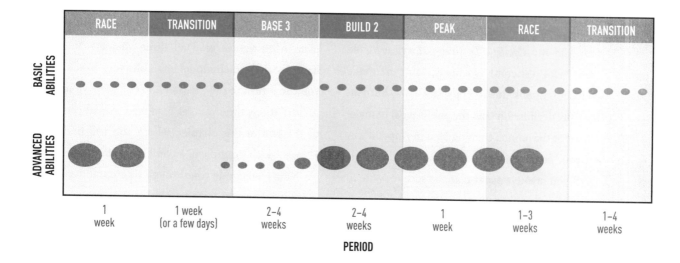

RACE	TRANSITION	BASE 3	BUILD 2	PEAK	RACE	TRANSITION

FIGURE 7.3 A suggested preparation plan for the second or third most important race of the season when there are only 7 to 11 weeks to train following the previous race

ably OK to go directly to build period training, with an emphasis on the advanced abilities. For the highly experienced veteran rider, it may even be possible to blend aerobic endurance workouts with the advanced abilities to produce a hybrid period. This may prove risky, however, as it requires a deep understanding of your body and what it can—and can't—handle.

It should be obvious by now that this discussion has to do with making difficult training decisions once you are well into the race season. How to prepare for the second and third races of the season is not something you can decide while designing your periodization plan prior to the season. While you may tentatively set a mid- and late-season training plan early in the season, the final decisions must be made at the time. I suggest returning to this discussion and rereading it immediately after finishing each important race of the season to decide how to go about preparing for your next race. Figures 7.1, 7.2, and 7.3 will help you prepare your plan for the next stage of the season.

THE ANNUAL TRAINING PLAN

It's time to start designing your annual training plan for the season ahead. As mentioned earlier, the best time to do this is at the start of a new training year, usually in November, December, or January. But you may be coming to this task well into your race season. That's OK. Simply design your plan for the remaining weeks of the year.

There are many ways to prepare your written plan. A simple way is to use a common paper calendar onto which you record all of the details described below. Or you can use an electronic calendar, which is easy to update with quick changes. A variation on this is to use the annual training plan (ATP) feature at TrainingPeaks .com, which is available to subscribers and follows the procedures I explain in this chapter. It will save you a lot of time and thought, as many decisions suggested here are built into the software. Perhaps the most expedient way, and certainly the least expensive, is the paper-based plan

The best time to design an annual training plan is at the start of a new training year.

provided in Appendix A (this ATP format is also found in my *Cyclist's Training Diary*, available from VeloPress.com). Normally, you can't make copies of a book due to copyright laws, but you have my permission (and the publisher's) to make copies of the annual training plan in Appendix A for your personal use.

If you create a paper plan, be sure to write in pencil, as there are certain to be many changes throughout the year. In more than 30 years of coaching, I've never seen an athlete's plan go unaltered for an entire season. There's typically a lot of erasing and revising because of illness, lifestyle interruptions, and unexpected but necessary breaks from training.

Before getting into the details of your plan, let's revisit why I suggest you should prepare a written training plan. It isn't to impress anyone or to simply feel organized (although there's a lot to be said for the confidence that comes with such a feeling), but rather to create a dynamic guide to point you in the right direction as you start a new season and to assist you in making decisions along the way. This is easiest to do at the start of the season, when you have a big-picture perspective, as opposed to when you're in the heat of battle. Before the season starts, you can see the entire forest. After that, trees get in the way. Planning is also best when emotions don't cloud your decision-making.

In the remainder of this chapter, I'm going to take you step by step through the process of laying out your annual training plan for the season ahead. Follow along using whichever format you prefer—paper or electronic. But don't write down your plan details until you have finished reading Chapters 8 and 9. Chapter 9 is especially crucial to your overall plan. It contains alterna-

> Planning is best when emotions don't cloud your decision-making.

> I strongly suggest having no more than three goals for the season.

tive periodization models to this chapter's linear plan. After you've read all three chapters and have decided which model best suits your needs, you can return to this chapter and complete your ATP. If at any time you get confused, skip ahead to the end of this chapter, where you will find Figure 7.4, an example of a completed plan.

Next I will guide you through six steps in laying out an annual training plan for the coming season:

Step 1: Establish Season Goals
Step 2: Determine Training Objectives
Step 3: Set Annual Training Volume
Step 4: Prioritize Races
Step 5: Divide Season into Periods
Step 6: Estimate Weekly Volume

Step 1: Establish Season Goals

At the top of the annual training plan in Appendix A, there is a space to write your season goals. You can see how this is done in the example shown in Figure 7.4. Chapter 5 described how to set your goals for a race season. Here is a quick summary of the key points in writing a goal.

I strongly suggest having no more than three goals for the season. More than that, and you run the risk of diluting your training attention. It's important that you stay focused on the most important race outcomes you want to achieve. Along that same line of reasoning, fewer than three is also good and will give you an even sharper focus.

Write each goal as an intended seasonal outcome. In the coming years, what will you look back on with satisfaction and a feeling of great accomplishment? Don't get involved with the supporting details yet. Set your outcome goals based on what you want your most important achievements to be. Keep in mind that these are not the subgoals you must accomplish in order to achieve your overarching goals. Outcome goals aren't, for example, "lose weight" or "learn to use my power meter." Those are goal-supporting objectives, which we will get to in the next step. An outcome goal will usually be a race result. It could also be something along the lines of "be selected for the national team."

Your goals should be measurable. In road racing, the most common measurement is your position in the race results. For time trialing, it's your finishing time. It could also be the accomplishment of a team strategy goal, such as successfully leading out your team sprinter in an important race. What is it you want to accomplish in the most important races of the season?

Write your goal or goals in the spaces provided at the top of the annual training plan in Appendix A. Be sure to make them measurable and reflective of the most important outcomes you seek to accomplish in the coming season.

Step 2: Determine Training Objectives

Near the top of the annual training plan there are spaces for four training objectives. These are subgoals that address your ability limiters. Chapter 5 described training objectives and how they fit into the big picture of supporting your seasonal goals. Chapter 6 addressed ability limiters. Here's a quick review.

Training objectives are subgoals that provide feedback about how your training is progressing. They aren't at the same level as your season goals, but they are important for goal achievement. If you accomplish these, you can also expect your season goals to be achieved. It's during workouts or low-priority races that training objectives are accomplished.

The underlying purpose of a training objective is to "fix" or strengthen a goal-specific weakness—your limiter—that is preventing the achievement of one or more season goals. In Chapter 6, you determined your ability limiters relative to climbing, sprinting, and time trialing. That assessment led to the determination of your weakest advanced abilities: muscular endurance, anaerobic endurance, and sprint power (see Table 6.1). That, in turn, led to the determination of which basic abilities—aerobic endurance, muscular force, or speed skills—are most in need of your attention. Now it's time to establish subgoals for improving those ability limiters.

A training objective is simply a statement about one of your ability limiters and how you will know when it is corrected. Let's take a look at some basic abilities limiters as training objectives. For example, if climbing is a limiter, Table 6.1 suggests that either anaerobic endurance or muscular endurance is your primary underlying ability limiter, depending on which type of climber you aspire to be. Generally speaking, for the rider whose limiter is climbing, more success is likely to be had by focusing training on the muscular endurance ability. If this is your selected ability limiter, your training objective may be something along the lines of "climb Lee Hill in less than 20 minutes by April 23." This subgoal is something that you would be aiming for in a workout or low-priority race. This also means that during the base period, as you focus on the basic abilities, you would devote a large portion of your training to aerobic endurance and muscular force (see Figure 6.2). Of course, as

A training objective is simply a statement about one of your ability limiters and how you will know when it is corrected.

discussed in Chapter 6, body weight also plays an important role in your climbing ability, regardless of which advanced ability you decide to work on. If weight is your primary limiter, then the training objective may be along the lines of "weigh 154 pounds by April 23."

If your goal-specific limiter is sprinting, then the most important advanced ability that your training must concentrate on is sprint power. For this limiter, you might set a goal along the lines of "average 1000 watts for sprint power test by May 30" (see Sidebar 5.3 for the details of this field test). Figure 6.2 then suggests that if sprint power is your limiter, the basic abilities you should primarily work on are muscular force and speed skills. Of course, sprint power workouts would play a major role in the build period.

Anaerobic endurance may also be a limiter if you race primarily in short criterium races or are frequently dropped at any race distance during explosive accelerations that last from a few seconds to a few minutes. That advanced ability would then be the primary concentration of your training in the build period, with aerobic endurance and speed skills the primary focus of the base period. In this case, your training objective may be something such as "increase functional aerobic capacity power to 430 watts by August 7" (see Sidebar 5.3 for the functional aerobic capacity test).

For a time trialing limiter, the most likely advanced ability limiter is muscular endurance. So your training objective may be "increase functional threshold power to 280 watts by July 15" (see Sidebar 5.3 for the functional threshold power field test). In the early season base period, training for such a limiter would focus on muscular force and aerobic endurance. In the build

period leading from the base period to the start of the race taper, your workouts would be heavily weighted toward muscular endurance.

There may also be training objectives in the base period. Although you are focused primarily on the basic abilities, your training objectives are always related to the accomplishment of advanced ability objectives. For example, an aerobic endurance objective may be something such as "increase my efficiency factor by 10 percent by March 1" (the efficiency factor is described under "Field Tests" in Appendix B). A muscular force objective may be "leg press 2.5 times my body weight by the end of base 1" (see Chapter 12 for details).

Note the inclusion of a calendar date or deadline for the accomplishment of each of these training objective examples. You have to know when that objective must be accomplished. Deadlines provide motivation. It's best if you accomplish an advanced ability training objective no later than the start of your taper, typically 1 to 3 weeks prior to the race. Basic ability objectives must be achieved before starting the build period. This allows you time to concentrate on accomplishing them throughout the preceding base period. If the basic ability objective isn't achieved by the start of the build period or the advanced ability by the peak period, you will have to reconsider the related seasonal goal.

So how do you know what the power goal for your training objective should be? There is no foolproof way to determine this. The starting point is knowing your current power for the related field test (see Appendix B). A 10 percent increase is probably near the upper limit of what you can expect to achieve. It's a stretch, but doable. Will a 10 percent power improve-

You have to know when an objective must be accomplished. Deadlines provide motivation.

ment be enough to realize your training objective? The answer may lie in knowing what other riders who are accomplished climbers, sprinters, or time trialists are doing as far as power output. Setting your training objective is often somewhat of a crapshoot. To improve the odds of getting it right, you need lots of power data. Talk with other riders and coaches. Do some Internet research. Websites such as BestBikeSplit.com, Strava.com, and AnalyticCycling.com may prove helpful in setting a training objective. Bear in mind that when it comes to power, body size often plays a role. Big riders generally have an advantage when the time trial course or sprint is flat, while small riders have the advantage on climbs.

Now is the time for you to give some thought to your ability limiters (as determined in Chapter 6) and write training objectives that address them at the top of your annual training plan. Note that you may not have a limiter for every ability. There's a limit to how much you can accomplish in a short time. Narrow it down to four or fewer limiters that are *most* likely to affect race performances for your most important races. If you improve them, your season goals will become achievable.

At the top of the annual training plan there is a space for your annual volume in hours or TSS. Here you will record how many total hours you anticipate training over the course of the season. This includes all of your rides, your strength training, and your crosstraining time. If, however, you use Dr. Coggan's Training Stress Score (TSS) system, as explained in Chapter 4, record your total expected TSS volume for the year here. I encourage you to consider using TSS because it combines training intensity along with time,

whereas annual training hours only considers training time (to learn more about TSS, see my book *The Power Meter Handbook*). As explained in Chapter 4, of the two fitness-producing factors, intensity is more critical for the advanced athlete. That's why TSS is the way to go. Using TSS will change your perceptions of what training is about. It's not simply how many hours (or miles or kilometers) you ride. Rather, it's what you did with those hours. Time in the saddle simply isn't a good predictor of race performance.

If you are coming to this chapter already well into your race season, you should still determine how many hours or TSS you anticipate training for the remainder of this season. Record it on your ATP as training volume.

How do you decide what your annual training hours or TSS should be? One way is to look back at the total volume you did last season. Again, this should include all bike, strength, and crosstraining workouts for the entire year. If that season went well and you think you could manage a somewhat greater training load, which ultimately means greater fitness, consider increasing the volume by up to 10 percent for the season ahead. This is an especially good idea for athletes who are in their first five years in the sport. They probably can handle more. If you are beyond five years, you may want to keep annual hours the same but do more high-intensity workouts in the new season. This will, of course, have no effect on hours but will increase TSS by perhaps 10 percent.

Another way to estimate annual training volume is to determine what your typical average training hours or TSS are for a week. What was your average last season? Multiply that by 50 weeks to estimate total annual hours. If you know

TABLE 7.2 **Volume Guidelines for Cyclists**

CATEGORY	SUGGESTED ANNUAL HOURS	AVERAGE WEEKLY HOURS	SUGGESTED ANNUAL TSS	AVERAGE WEEKLY TSS
1 or 2	700–1,000	14–20	35,000–50,000	700–1,000
3	500–700	10–14	25,000–35,000	500–700
4	350–500	7–10	17,500–25,000	350–500
5 or Juniors	220–350	4–7	11,000–17,500	200–350
Masters	350–650	7–13	17,500–32,500	350–650

This table is a general guide for determining annual training volume in either hours or TSS based on your competitive race category as assigned by your national federation (category 1 is highest). A masters category is also included.

If your training hours are artificially low, the key to improved performance is to emphasize high-intensity training.

you will miss a certain number of weeks due to vacations, career, or other lifestyle issues, factor that in and multiply your anticipated weekly volume by this reduced number. Otherwise, I suggest using 50 weeks instead of 52, as I can almost guarantee you will miss at least two weeks of training in the coming year due to illness, injury, or short-term decisions to take some time off. Let's hope the first two of these won't happen, but they have a way of showing up from time to time.

A third option is to base annual volume on your official federation-assigned racing category using Table 7.2. Let's look especially at the "Suggested Annual TSS" column. While a low-intensity week may produce 45 TSS points per hour, a high-intensity week could result in 55 per hour. A long-term hourly average TSS of 50 is common. This is what is used in Table 7.2 to suggest average TSS per week. Multiplying your anticipated training hours by 45, 50, or 55, depending on how intensely you expect to train, will give you a good estimate of TSS for the year ahead.

Realize that while this table is based on my experience in coaching athletes who race in the standard five competitive amateur categories, category 1 being the most advanced, it doesn't

mean that the suggested volume is right for you. You may have more or less time to train than is indicated here. If your training hours are artificially low—physically you are capable of doing more, but your lifestyle doesn't allow it—the key to improved performance is to emphasize high-intensity training. If you've not trained this way in the past, adopting it will mean that your TSS may increase even though your hours don't.

As you examine Table 7.2, consider the hours you are available to train and whether you will use only that or, instead, do workouts based on TSS. Then record your appropriate planned annual volume in the space provided on the annual training plan.

Step 4: Prioritize Races

Your training for the coming season may start whenever you prefer, so long as you have allowed enough time to prepare for your first race. The start of the new season is usually preceded by the transition period—a short break from focused and serious training (see Table 7.1). Following the transition, you should allow roughly 5 to 6 months to become fully race ready. That's not always possible, so you may need to make some

TABLE 7.3 **How to Determine Your Race Priorities**

RACE PRIORITY	MAXIMUM NUMBER IN A SEASON	RACE IMPORTANCE	SPECIAL RACE-DAY PREPARATION
A	3	Most important. Your season's goals are determined by these.	Include a 1- to 2-week peak period prior to race week.
B	8	Of secondary importance. You want to do well, however.	Reduce training for 2 to 5 days prior to race day.
C	Unlimited	Least important. Use as race tune-ups, tests, hard workouts, social events, or for experience.	No special preparation. Treat these as workouts.

adjustments to what is suggested here. We'll look at the start of the new season next as you set up your annual training plan. If you are already in your race season as you read this, follow the procedure described here for the remainder of your race season.

In the "Week" column on your ATP, the "1" row is the first week of the new season following the transition period. Next to that column is the "Mon." column. Record the date of the season's first Monday here, followed by the dates of all the Mondays for the coming season in the rows that follow. For example, the first Monday of October may be the second day of that month. So under "Mon.," write in 10/2 for October 2. The next row down would then be October 9 and is recorded as 10/9. Do this for the remainder of the season so that every weekly row starts with Monday's date for that week.

After recording all of the Mondays for the season, write down the races you intend to do in the coming season in the column labeled "Race." Place them on the ATP in the appropriate weeks based on their dates. It's quite likely that not all of the dates for your planned races have been announced yet. But you more than likely know when they will occur, so use those expected dates. For example, let's say that you

have an event scheduled for Saturday, May 6 in the coming season. It would be listed in the row that starts with Monday, May 1 and is labeled as "5/1," since that row includes all the dates from May 1 through May 7. If you have two races on the same weekend, list them both in that row.

Once you have listed all of your planned events in the "Races" column, go to the "Pri." column next to the race name and designate the priority of each by writing in "A," "B," or "C." Table 7.3 will help you determine how to rank your upcoming races.

Your season's plan will be designed around the A-priority races. I strongly suggest having no more than three of these (a stage race or two races in the same week count as one race). Why is that? Since you will taper—meaning you will reduce your training—for 1 to 3 weeks prior to the race and then recover for at least a couple of days during the post-race transition period—again with reduced training—you will lose fitness, especially for your basic abilities. Since you're giving up a bit of fitness to gain race form (see Chapter 3 for an explanation of form), there is definitely a downside to these most important races. That means you must be conservative in choosing how many to do in a season. If there are too many, you will be giving up a lot of fitness and running out of time to

Your season's plan will be designed around your A-priority races.

102 THE CYCLIST'S TRAINING BIBLE

get back in shape for the next. Three is about the most that can be managed and still allow time to rebuild fitness and come to peak form before the next A-priority race. The more you can spread out your important races on the calendar, the more fit you are likely to be for each of them, as described in the "Planning" section above, which discussed the spacing between races. There, you may recall, I explained how more than 12 weeks between A races makes planning easy, while fewer than 12 weeks makes planning increasingly complicated.

With regard to race performance in the coming season, there are two basic ways to design your training plan. One way is to do no more than three A-priority races, as suggested above, with a taper for 2 to 3 weeks prior to each. This is highly likely to result in your best possible race performances. You can still do several B-priority races for which you back off of training for 2 to 5 days prior, as shown in Table 7.3. You can think of this as a mini-taper with a resulting small peak in race form. The second way is to not do any A races and instead do lots of B races without a true peak for any of them, but having just a few days of recovery prior. Your performances aren't likely to be the best possible, but this approach may well make your race season more enjoyable. I've known many good riders who enjoy competition so much that their whole season consists of frequent B races. Not scheduling A races preceded by a long taper for each makes that possible—but at the possible cost of performance.

Another possibility is that you may have only one A-priority race scheduled for the entire season. That presents a different kind of puzzle. It takes about 5 or 6 months to progress through the standard periodization process prior to the first A race of the year. With perhaps as much as

6 months until your race, what do you do with the remaining 6 months, when you're likely to have lower-priority races? There are two common solutions. The first, and probably the best, is to designate a second A race about 12 to 16 weeks prior to your most important A race. Train for that first race and include a taper prior and a short transition period after. This will give you a chance to see how well you can perform while testing your training for high-priority races. What you learn from that will undoubtedly add to your performance at the more important race.

The second way to solve the dilemma of only one important race per season is to start your base period training as described in this chapter, but when you complete base 3 do not continue into the build period. Instead repeat base 3 as many times as is needed to leave you about 12 weeks until your most important A-priority race. Then start the build period of training. You can never have enough base fitness, so this second method can prepare you quite well for the specific race-like training that precedes your A race.

Note in Table 7.3 that the C-priority races are treated as workouts, meaning you taper for about the same time period as you would before a hard workout. That usually means a day or two of reduced training load. These events are done strictly as throwaway results, meaning you don't expect to be in top form or even race ready. But you will still race hard. They are typically done as tune-ups before A or B races to get into the mindset and routine of racing. They may also be done as tests of fitness, as hard workouts, for fun, or even as social events done with your training partners or team. For the novice rider, they also provide the experience necessary for growth as a competitive cyclist. When new to the sport, one

C-priority races are treated as workouts, meaning you taper for about the same time period as you would before a hard workout.

of the fastest ways to learn what it is all about is to race, and to race a lot. The first year as a cyclist should be a learning experience. Participating in C races is one of the best things you can do to make the learning curve steep.

Step 5: Divide Season into Periods

The next planning task in completing your ATP is to divide your season into periods. Table 7.4 will help you do that. It expands on Table 7.1 by dividing the seasonal periods into mesocycles,

along with the types of workouts to be done in each. It also defines mesocycle durations based on age, since that is usually closely related to how quickly one recovers after a hard workout or race. We'll come back to that latter point shortly.

The suggested mesocycles described in Table 7.4, "Workout Types, Their Purposes, and Their Durations" are generally the way to do workouts when training for most types of road races and time trials using a classic linear model. But there may well be individual differences in the way

TABLE 7.4 The Mesocycles, Their Purposes, and Their Durations

MESOCYCLES	WORKOUT TYPES, ABILITIES, AND GENERAL PURPOSES	DURATION (UNDER AGE 50 OR QUICK RECOVERY)	DURATION (OVER AGE 50 OR SLOW RECOVERY)	PLANNED REST AND RECOVERY DURATION
Prep	Prepare to train: crosstraining, weights, functional strength, speed skills, general athleticism	1–4 weeks	1–4 weeks	Not needed
Base 1	General training: aerobic endurance, muscular force, speed skills	4 weeks	3 weeks	Last 3–5 days of base 1
Base 2	General training: aerobic endurance, muscular force, speed skills, limited muscular endurance	4 weeks	3 weeks	Last 3–5 days of base 2
Base 3	General training: aerobic endurance, muscular force, speed skills, limited muscular endurance, and anaerobic endurance	4 weeks	3 weeks (repeat base 3)	Last 3–5 days of base 3
Build 1	Specific training: muscular endurance, anaerobic endurance, sprint power; maintain aerobic endurance, muscular force, speed skills	4 weeks	3 weeks	Last 3–5 days of build 1
Build 2	Specific training: muscular endurance, anaerobic endurance, sprint power; maintain aerobic endurance, muscular force, speed skills	4 weeks	3 weeks (repeat build 2)	Last 3–5 days of build 2
Peak	Specific training: simulate a portion of the race every 72–96 hours; otherwise, recovery workouts	1–2 weeks	1–2 weeks	Not needed
Race	Specific training: short intervals at race intensity or greater and decreasing in number daily; rest	1 week	1 week	Not needed
Transition	Rest and active recovery	2 days to 4 weeks	2 days to 4 weeks	Not needed

you train during any given period in the season. For example, when I work with advanced athletes, I may have them do a small amount of the muscular endurance, anaerobic endurance, and sprint power ability training throughout most of the base period to slightly boost specific fitness before starting into the build period, when there is a heavy emphasis on all three of these. The key phrase here is "small amount." For older riders, I would likely have them do very brief anaerobic endurance workouts year-round, as they help to maintain their aerobic capacities (a decline in aerobic capacity is a major issue for aging athletes).

Notice I said these are *brief* workouts. Don't get carried away with doing high-intensity workouts in the base period. That will ultimately be counterproductive. Schedule few such sessions and keep them quite short. Save the longer, very difficult high-intensity workouts for the build, peak, and race periods. Intense workouts are never done in the base period in traditional linear periodization, so this is a suggested variation from the norm. But there may be times when it is appropriate for certain athletes. Should you decide to do them, be cautious; sprinkle them into your training weeks quite lightly.

The bottom line here is that you should feel some freedom to experiment with the linear model suggested in Table 7.4. You may well discover something that works for you that isn't commonly done. The only hard-and-fast rule in periodization that I strongly suggest you adhere to is the philosophy described above: The closer in time you get to your A-priority race, the *more* like the race your training must become. Of course, that also implies that the farther away your A-priority race is, the *less* like the race your train-

ing should be. But other than this timing caveat, training periodization can be quite flexible.

Let's return to the age and mesocycle duration shown in Table 7.4. Actually, the topic of duration has more to do with recovery than age. Age is only a way to simplify this planning, even though age is not always an accurate marker of one's ability to recover quickly. Regardless of age, you need to schedule breaks from focused and serious training every few weeks in order to shed some of the accumulating physical and mental fatigue of training.

Some athletes need these recovery breaks more frequently than others. How often has to do with several physiological variables, of which the most important is hormone production. Anabolic (tissue-building) hormones—growth hormone, testosterone, estrogen, insulin-like growth factor, and others—have a lot to do with how well and how quickly you recover from hard-training sessions. These hormones are known to decrease with age. The less of them you produce, the slower you recover. The slower you recover, the more frequently you need recovery breaks from training. By sometime around age 50, the low production of hormones becomes quite evident; it is obvious that you need more time to recover than you used to. That's why Table 7.4 shows more frequent recovery at several times throughout the season for the over-50 rider. But I've known many over-50 athletes who recover quite quickly. I've also known under-50 athletes who recover slowly. So even though this table implies that age determines period duration, you may well not fit into these two categories neatly based simply on your age. In other words, determine which column, "under age 50" or "over age 50," to use after giving considerable thought to

Don't get carried away with doing high-intensity workouts in the base period.

your capacity for recovery. Base the decision on your past experience with accumulating fatigue. If you're unsure, go ahead and use age to choose a column.

Besides those over 50, novice and intermediate athletes may also need shorter mesocycles, as their capacities for recovery may not yet be fully developed. Building recovery ability typically takes three years or so, so novices and intermediates should use the "over age 50 or slow recovery" column.

In the "Planned Rest and Recovery Duration" column, the "Last 3–5 days" during the base and build periods is a rather broad range. Again, some athletes recover slowly and so may well need most of a week of reduced training before returning to serious training, while others will recover quite quickly and only need 3 or 4 days. Your recovery in one of these short breaks may also vary from one mesocycle to the next, depending on how challenging the training stress was. So this 3- to 5-day range may be considered an "on-demand" decision. If you are still tired after 4 days, take another day—or more—to recover. Recovery is important. Don't neglect it. We'll look at it more thoroughly in Chapter 11.

We've covered a lot of small details so far in this section. Now let's pull back to a bigger overview that is the central focus of this section: periodizing your season.

"Periodizing" means assigning training periods to each week of the year in the "Period" column of your ATP. You'll fill in this column by working up the page or backwards on a calendar starting from your first A-priority race of the season. At the intersection of the "Period" column and the row, or week, of your first A-priority race, write "race" in the "Period" column. That's the title of the race week mesocycle as shown in Table 7.4. Then go up

one more weekly row and write in "peak." Move up the page another row and again write in "peak." Doing this gives you a 3-week taper before your race—2 peak weeks and 1 race week.

Do you need 3 weeks? Maybe not. Some athletes are likely to come into better race-day form with only 2 weeks of tapering. In fact, some research seems to support a 2-week taper for competitive cyclists. Again, this is a part of the individualization you need to consider when designing your plan for the season. There is little I can tell you that will help you determine which way to go other than to say it's based entirely on your experience—what's worked for you in the past. Again, it's OK to experiment with this to determine if a 2- or 3-week taper is better for you. But for now, if in doubt, record 2 peak weeks and 1 race week.

In the weekly row above your first peak week, write in "build 2." Now you must decide if you will allow for 3- or 4-week mesocycles based on the discussion above about recovery, age, and experience level. This is a very important decision. If you're an experienced cyclist confident of your recovery abilities, you can use 4-week mesocycles. Otherwise, you should most likely use 3.

If you're following a 4-week mesocycle, write in "build 2" three more times going up the page so that you have 4 weeks of build 2 above your first peak week. If you're using 3-week mesocycles, write in "build 2" in only three rows. Now do the same thing—3 or 4 weeks each—for the build 1, base 3, base 2, and base 1 mesocycles.

Note that you may decide to use different mesocycle durations—either 3 or 4 weeks—for the base and build periods. Some athletes recover quite quickly when focused primarily on the basic abilities in the base period, but somewhat more

Some athletes are likely to come into better race-day form with only 2 weeks of tapering.

slowly when training the advanced abilities in the build period. Such athletes may opt to use 3-week mesocycles in build and 4 weeks for base. Again, this is a personal decision based on experience. If unsure, keep your base and build mesocycle durations the same, either 3 or 4 weeks as determined by your age, capacity for recovery, or experience level. If you're confused by any of this so far, see Figure 7.4 for an example of how it's done.

In the row above your first base 1 week of the season, write "prep." This may be only 1 week or as many as 4. In fact, there have been times when I've completely omitted it for some athletes when they had only a few training weeks prior to the first A race. I've also extended it beyond 4 weeks when athletes had excessive time until their A-priority event and we decided to delay base training for whatever reason. The most common determining point here is the number of training weeks available before your first A-priority race. It may even come down to how eager you are to start serious preparation for the new season. The prep period is pretty laid-back and mostly a time of not very challenging workouts. Weights and strength training are the exceptions to the workout level. You could shorten the prep period if you're ready to go and then, if timing allows it, lengthen the base 3 mesocycle by repeating it or a portion of it later. As I've said before, you can never have too much base fitness.

What we've accomplished so far is designing your plan to take you to the first race of the season. Now it's time to move on to the following events.

Go back down to the weekly row immediately below your first race week. It's quite possible that you will have one or two more A-priority races in the following one or two weeks. If so, write in "race" for each such week so that you have two or

three consecutive rows labeled "race." While it's common in road racing and time trialing to have multiple A-priority races in consecutive weeks, you may not have any.

Following the last week designated as a race mesocycle, as you progress down the page from your first A race write in "tran" for the week after that race or after the last of your back-to-back A races. As noted in Table 7.4, this transition period may last a couple of days or be as long as 4 weeks. I've even had athletes take up to 6 weeks at the end of the race season if their training year was exceptionally stressful. If this first transition mesocycle comes early in your season, which is likely, then I suggest making it just a 2- or 3-day break from focused training. But it could be 7, depending on lingering mental and physical fatigue from the race or even muscle soreness. After the last A race of the season, you will probably need a much longer break, more on the order of 4 weeks. The thinking here is to give not only your body but also your mind some rest. It's OK to exercise in the transition period, but training is forbidden. The purpose is to rest and rejuvenate by not having a strenuous workout routine. Keep any such exercise low intensity and brief. Crosstraining is a good option.

For the novice athlete, it's generally best to do only the base periods to allow for increased attention to the basic abilities for an entire season. The base 3 mesocycle, while emphasizing the basic abilities, provides enough advanced ability training to develop race fitness. For the novice athlete, base 3 is repeated and replaces all of the build subperiods. A 1-week peak period is also generally the way to go for the novice.

Planning up to the first A-priority race of the season is now complete. That was the easy part.

For the subsequent A races that don't immediately follow your first A race, you have decisions to make and some mesocycles to leave out. For example, when scheduling beyond the first A race, you will not repeat the prep period, and probably not base 1 or base 2 either. However, you should return to base 3 after the first transition period if your basic abilities, especially aerobic endurance, have obviously declined in the last few weeks of tapering for and recovering from the first A race. You may even want to do base 3 twice if there are enough weeks remaining until the next A race. Again, you can't have too much basic ability fitness. Ignoring weakened basic abilities will greatly detract from training and racing for the rest of the season.

If your basic abilities are still strong after the first A race, you may want to start back into training with a build 1 or a build 2 mesocycle, depending mostly on how many weeks separate these races. A note of caution: Don't shortchange the basic abilities in order to do more high-intensity training, thinking that will make you stronger. It won't if your basic abilities have been compromised by tapering. For the details of how to schedule these subsequent weeks, see Figures 7.2 and 7.3 above along with the accompanying discussion.

Of course, if you are doing all this planning in the off-season, you are guessing about what sort of fitness you'll have several months from now. That's another reason why the ATP is likely to change throughout the season. But for now, if you have enough time between races—perhaps 10 weeks or more—include base 3 as the starting point for training after the first transition period of the season.

Complete the "Period" column on the ATP through the end of the season by assigning the appropriate mesocycles that lead to each A-priority race. And remember that for the B-priority races on your schedule, you will include a few days of reduced training in order to be ready for them. The perfect time to have such races is at the end of rest and recovery weeks, but that's not always possible, especially if you are racing frequently. Later on, should you decide that the plan you have isn't right for the subsequent races, you can always make changes (that's why you should record your plan using a pencil or do it electronically). I've never coached an athlete who made it all the way through a season with no ATP adjustments.

Step 6: Estimate Weekly Volume

Most of your plan for the new season is now complete, and you should have a strong sense of how your training will play out, especially before the first race. It should be evident that there is a steady progression from the basic to the advanced abilities as you make the workouts more like races. There are only two steps remaining: estimating weekly volume and assigning the actual workouts. The latter will be the focus of Chapter 8. For now, you need to decide on volume—how many hours or TSS you will do each week—and enter that in your ATP.

If your training will be based on hours, use Table 7.5 to determine weekly volume. If your training will be based on weekly TSS volume, use Table 7.6. Which should you use? As discussed in Chapter 4, I highly recommend TSS-based training because it shifts your purpose away from only how many hours you rode to a combination of hours and workout intensity. And since intensity is considered to be the greater contributor to race performance, using

Don't shortchange the basic abilities in order to do more high-intensity training, thinking that will make you stronger.

TABLE 7.5 **Weekly Training Hours**

PERIOD	WEEK	ANNUAL HOURS																	
		300	350	400	450	500	550	600	650	700	750	800	850	900	950	1000	1050	1100	1150	1200
Prep	All	5.0	6.0	7.0	7.5	8.5	9.0	10.0	11.0	12.0	12.5	13.5	14.5	15.0	16.0	17.0	17.5	18.5	19.5	20.0
Base 1	1	6.0	7.0	8.0	9.0	10.0	11.0	12.0	12.5	14.0	14.5	15.5	16.5	17.5	18.5	19.5	20.5	21.5	22.5	23.5
	2	7.0	8.5	9.5	10.5	12.0	13.0	14.5	15.5	16.5	18.0	19.0	20.0	21.5	22.5	24.0	25.0	26.0	27.5	28.5
	3	8.0	9.5	10.5	12.0	13.5	14.5	16.0	17.5	18.5	20.0	21.5	22.5	24.0	25.5	26.5	28.0	29.5	30.5	32.0
	4	4.0	5.0	5.5	6.5	7.0	8.0	8.5	9.0	10.0	10.5	11.5	12.0	12.5	13.5	14.0	14.5	15.5	16.0	17.0
Base 2	1	6.5	7.5	8.5	9.5	10.5	12.5	12.5	13.0	14.5	16.0	17.0	18.0	19.0	20.0	21.0	22.0	23.0	24.0	25.0
	2	7.5	9.0	10.0	11.5	12.5	14.0	15.0	16.5	17.5	19.0	20.0	21.5	22.5	24.0	25.0	26.5	27.5	29.0	30.0
	3	8.5	10.0	11.0	12.5	14.0	15.5	17.0	18.0	19.5	21.0	22.5	24.0	25.0	26.5	28.0	29.5	31.0	32.0	33.5
	4	4.5	5.0	5.5	6.5	7.0	8.0	8.5	9.0	10.0	10.5	11.5	12.0	12.5	13.5	14.0	15.0	15.5	16.0	17.0
Base 3	1	7.0	8.0	9.0	10.0	11.0	12.5	13.5	14.5	15.5	17.0	18.0	19.0	20.0	21.0	22.5	23.5	25.0	25.5	27.0
	2	8.0	9.5	10.5	12.0	13.5	14.5	16.0	17.0	18.5	20.0	21.5	23.0	24.0	25.0	26.5	28.0	29.5	30.5	32.0
	3	9.0	10.5	11.5	13.0	15.0	16.5	18.0	19.0	20.5	22.0	23.5	25.0	26.5	28.0	29.5	31.0	32.5	33.5	35.0
	4	4.5	5.0	5.5	6.5	7.0	8.0	8.5	9.0	10.0	10.5	11.5	12.0	12.5	13.5	14.0	15.0	15.5	16.0	17.0
Build 1	1	8.0	9.0	10.0	11.5	12.5	14.0	15.5	16.0	17.5	19.0	20.5	21.5	22.5	24.0	25.0	26.5	28.0	29.0	30.0
	2	8.0	9.0	10.0	11.5	12.5	14.0	15.5	16.0	17.5	19.0	20.5	21.5	22.5	24.0	25.0	26.5	28.0	29.0	30.0
	3	8.0	9.0	10.0	11.5	12.5	14.0	15.5	16.0	17.5	19.0	20.5	21.5	22.5	24.0	25.0	26.5	28.0	29.0	30.0
	4	4.5	5.0	5.5	6.5	7.0	8.0	8.5	9.0	10.0	10.5	11.5	12.0	12.5	13.5	14.0	15.0	15.5	16.0	17.0
Build 2	1	7.0	8.5	9.5	10.5	12.0	13.0	14.5	15.5	16.5	18.0	19.0	20.5	21.5	22.5	24.0	25.0	26.5	27.0	28.5
	2	7.0	8.5	9.5	10.5	12.0	13.0	14.5	15.5	16.5	18.0	19.0	20.5	21.5	22.5	24.0	25.0	26.5	27.0	28.5
	3	7.0	8.5	9.5	10.5	12.0	13.0	14.5	15.5	16.5	18.0	19.0	20.5	21.5	22.5	24.0	25.0	26.5	27.0	28.5
	4	4.5	5.0	5.5	6.5	7.0	8.0	8.5	9.0	10.0	10.5	11.5	12.0	12.5	13.5	14.0	15.0	15.5	16.0	17.0
Peak	1	6.5	7.5	8.5	9.5	10.5	11.5	13.0	13.5	14.5	16.0	17.0	18.0	19.0	20.0	21.0	22.0	23.5	24.0	25.0
	2	5.0	6.0	6.5	7.5	8.5	9.5	10.0	11.0	11.5	12.5	13.5	14.5	15.0	16.0	17.0	17.5	18.5	19.0	20.0
Race	All	4.5	5.0	5.5	6.5	7.0	8.0	8.5	9.0	10.0	10.5	11.5	12.0	12.5	13.5	14.0	15.0	15.5	16.0	17.0

If your volume is based on hours, find your annual volume hours in the top row of this table. Then scan down that column to find your weekly hours for each week of each mesocycle in your season.

TSS will shift your training focus away from saddle time to how long you rode plus how intense the ride was.

In the top row of whichever table you decide to use, find your annual hours (Table 7.5) or annual TSS (Table 7.6) as determined by what you recorded at the top of the ATP in the "Hours/TSS" space. By scanning down that column, you can see how much training volume you need each week in each mesocycle. Record these volume numbers in the appropriate weekly rows of the "Hours/TSS" column on your ATP.

Now I need to drive home a critical point. Your weekly volume is not a rigid number that *must* be accomplished. It's only meant to be ballpark guide, albeit a small ballpark. It only *suggests* how

TABLE 7.6 **Weekly TSS**

PERIOD	WEEK	ANNUAL TSS

PERIOD	WEEK	15K	17.5K	20K	22.5K	25K	27.5K	30K	32.5K	35K	37.5K	40K	42.5K	45K	47.5K	50K	52.5K	55K	57.5K	60K
Prep	All	240	280	320	360	400	440	480	520	560	600	640	700	720	760	800	840	880	920	960
Base 1	1	280	330	380	430	480	520	570	620	670	710	760	810	850	900	950	1,000	1,040	1,090	1,140
	2	310	370	420	470	530	580	630	680	730	780	840	890	950	1,000	1,050	1,100	1,150	1,210	1,260
	3	350	400	460	520	580	630	690	750	810	860	920	980	1,030	1,090	1,150	1,210	1,260	1,320	1,380
	4	240	280	320	360	400	440	480	520	560	600	640	700	720	760	800	840	880	920	960
Base 2	1	290	335	380	430	480	520	570	620	670	710	760	810	850	900	950	1,000	1,040	1,090	1,140
	2	330	385	440	500	550	600	660	720	770	820	880	940	990	1,040	1,100	1,150	1,210	1,260	1,320
	3	370	440	500	560	630	690	750	810	880	940	1,000	1,060	1,120	1,190	1,250	1,310	1,370	1,440	1,500
	4	240	280	320	360	400	440	480	520	560	600	640	700	720	760	800	840	880	920	960
Base 3	1	330	385	440	500	550	600	660	720	780	820	880	940	990	1,040	1,100	1,150	1,210	1,260	1,320
	2	370	440	500	560	630	690	750	810	880	940	1,000	1,060	1,120	1,190	1,250	1,310	1,370	1,440	1,510
	3	410	475	540	610	680	740	810	880	950	1,010	1,080	1,150	1,210	1,280	1,350	1,420	1,480	1,550	1,620
	4	240	280	320	360	400	440	480	520	560	600	640	700	720	760	800	840	880	920	960
Build 1	1	370	440	500	560	630	690	750	810	880	940	1,000	1,060	1,120	1,190	1,250	1,310	1,370	1,440	1,510
	2	370	440	500	560	630	690	750	810	880	940	1,000	1,060	1,120	1,190	1,250	1,310	1,370	1,440	1,510
	3	370	440	500	560	630	690	750	810	880	940	1,000	1,060	1,120	1,190	1,250	1,310	1,370	1,440	1,510
	4	240	280	320	360	400	440	480	520	560	600	640	700	720	760	800	840	880	920	960
Build 2	1	410	475	540	610	680	740	810	880	950	1,010	1,080	1,150	1,210	1,280	1,350	1,420	1,480	1,550	1,620
	2	410	475	540	610	680	740	810	880	950	1,010	1,080	1,150	1,210	1,280	1,350	1,420	1,480	1,550	1,620
	3	410	475	540	10.5	680	740	810	880	950	1,010	1,080	1,150	1,210	1,280	1,350	1,420	1,480	1,550	1,620
	4	240	280	320	360	400	440	480	520	560	600	640	700	720	760	800	840	880	920	960
Peak	1	290	335	380	430	480	520	570	620	670	710	760	810	850	900	950	1,000	1,040	1,090	1,140
	2	240	280	320	360	400	440	480	520	560	600	640	700	720	760	800	840	880	920	960
Race	All	240	280	320	360	400	440	480	520	560	600	640	700	720	760	800	840	880	920	960

If your volume is based on TSS, find your annual volume TSS in the top row of this table. Then scan down that column to find your weekly TSS for each week of each mesocycle in your season.

much training you should do in a given week. This number can and should be changed to better suit your situation when you come to that particular week, or any given day, in your season. It's certainly acceptable if you don't achieve that precise volume number each week, but you should be close to it—most of the time.

There undoubtedly will be situations that come up from time to time throughout the season that cause you to miss workouts or shorten them. It could be, for example, unusually bad weather for riding. On the other side of the coin, there may also be weeks when you have additional, unexpected time to ride. So don't feel like these weekly volume numbers are fixed requirements carved in stone. They are recommendations, not hard-and-fast edicts.

In Chapter 8, we'll discuss individual workout duration and TSS to see how they make up the weekly volume numbers recorded for each week of your ATP.

I'm often asked about volume, so it's probably a good idea to again emphasize that weekly volume throughout the season includes saddle time, strength training, and any other aerobic cross-training you may do. It does not include stretching, passive recovery techniques, yoga, meditation, or anything else along those lines. Does it include basketball, tennis, football, and other similar games? That has to be your call, but I suggest strictly limiting what you call a crosstraining workout to common aerobic sports such as running, swimming, off-road riding, snowshoeing, cross-country skiing, and similar endurance activities.

Weekly volume throughout the season includes saddle time, strength training, and any other aerobic crosstraining you may do.

SUMMARY: PLANNING OVERVIEW

I expect this chapter was a rather tedious read for you, especially if you are new to seasonal planning. The process of getting organized is never very exciting—and can even be downright boring. But the payoff later, when the focused training and racing begins, will be immense. The time you invest here will pay dividends by giving your training a sharp focus. Athletes who never plan and make their daily workout decisions as they roll out of their driveways are much less likely to be prepared to race well as compared to those who have planned their training. I can't emphasize enough how important this is to your goal achievement. The higher the goal, the more that planning plays a role in its achievement.

Planning your year gets easier every time you do it. By returning to this chapter at the start of each new season, you'll find that it becomes less tedious and time consuming. You'll breeze through it in future seasons, having done it before. Saving your annual training plans after each season makes it easier to create future plans and also serves as a quick summary of how your season went.

Of course, you'll recall that I suggested you not complete your annual training plan until you have finished reading this and the next two chapters. That's because Chapter 9 introduces alternative periodization models, and you may decide that one of them fits your situation better than the linear model described in this chapter. Linear periodization is the simplest of all the models, and it's also the most commonly used by athletes around the world. After you've finished reading the next two chapters, return to the start of this one and use the tables to help make volume decisions as suggested in Tables 7.2, 7.4, 7.5, and 7.6. And, of course, race prioritization will remain the same (see Table 7.3).

When you have completed your ATP, including what was covered in this chapter, it should look something like Figure 7.4. This example of a training plan is based on the linear model. Note that there are some parts of your ATP that aren't complete yet: the weights and workouts by ability sections. Those all have to do with the finer details of weekly training and will be addressed in the next chapter.

Having a carefully designed annual training plan is much like having a coach. Not only does it provide detailed guidance on a daily basis, it also fosters greater confidence in your training as your workouts become more purposeful. But for it to help you achieve your goals, it must always be viewed as a work in progress, not as something carved in stone that must be followed without question. As a self-coached athlete, you must be able to look in a dispassionate way at where you are now in training and what you need to do in the upcoming days. If you get caught up in your emotions after a poor workout, race, or lackluster week, things are frequently going to be in a state of flux and progress may be reversed. Your training decisions must reflect what is best for you in the long term.

To get that high-altitude view, I strongly suggest sitting down at the end of each week to review and modify your planned workouts for the next week. When you feel some reluctance about getting organized, as everyone does from time to time, remind yourself of the reason you do this. You want to achieve your goals and be the best rider possible. The time you spend planning and updating the plan will pay off. Believe me, it works. I've seen it help hundreds of athletes achieve high goals in 30-plus years of coaching.

Now let's bring all of the pieces together as you take the final planning step: planning the details of the training week. This is where the rubber meets the road, and the purpose of Chapter 8.

ANNUAL TRAINING PLAN

Athlete _Chris_

Hours/TSS _35,000 TSS_

Year _2019_

MOST IMPORTANT WORKOUTS

WEEK	MON.	RACE	PRI.	PERIOD	HOURS / TSS	DETAILS	WEIGHT LIFTING	AEROBIC ENDURANCE	MUSCULAR FORCE	SPEED SKILLS	MUSCULAR ENDURANCE	ANAEROBIC ENDURANCE	SPRINT POWER	TESTING
01	11/5			Tran	—									
02	11/12			Tran	—									
03	11/19			Prep	560									
04	11/26			↓	560	Test FTP								
05	12/3			Base 1	670									
06	12/10				730									
07	12/17				810									
08	12/24			↓	560	Holiday travel								
09	12/31			Base 2	670									
10	1/7				770									
11	1/14				880									
12	1/21	Florence 20 km TT	C	↓	560	Test FTP								
13	1/28			Base 3	780									
14	2/4	Bartlett Lake HC	C		880								ı	
15	2/11	McDowell RR	C		950									
16	2/18	Florence 20 km TT	C	↓	560	Test FTP, FACP								
17	2/25			Build 1	880									
18	3/4	Hungry Dog Crit	C		880									
19	3/11				880									
20	3/18	Tumacacori RR	B	↓	560	Test FACP								
21	3/25			Build 2	950	Off work								
22	4/1	Superior RR	B		715									
23	4/8				950									
24	4/15			↓	560	Test FTP, FACP								
25	4/22			Peak	670									
26	4/29			↓	560									

FIGURE 7.4 Example of an Annual Training Plan

Season Goals

1. Win State TT (sub-61 min. 40 km)
2. Top 10 at Nats. TT (sub-1 hour 40 km)
3. Podium at Nats. RR

Training Objectives

1. Squat 1.3 x body weight by 12/30
2. Raise FTP to 230 W by 2/24
3. Increase functional aerobic cap. power to 260 W by 4/21
4. Achieve sprint power of 800 W by 7/14

WEEK	MON.	RACE	PRI.	PERIOD	HOURS/TSS	DETAILS	WEIGHT LIFTING	AEROBIC ENDURANCE	MUSCULAR FORCE	SPEED SKILLS	MUSCULAR ENDURANCE	ANAEROBIC ENDURANCE	SPRINT POWER	TESTING
27	5/6	State TT Champ	A	Race	560									
28	5/13			Tran	—									
29	5/20	Tucson Crit #1	C	Base 3	730									
30	5/27	Tucson TT #1	B	↓	630	Test SP, FACP								
31	6/3			Build 1	880									
32	6/10	Tucson Crit #2	C		880									
33	6/17	Tucson TT #2	B	↓	560	Test SP, FACP								
34	6/24			Build 2	950									
35	7/1	Tucson RR	B		760									
36	7/8	Tucson TT #3	B	↓	560	Test SP, FACP								
37	7/15			Peak	670									
38	7/22	Masters Nats. RR-TT	A	Race	560									
39	7/29			Tran	—									
40	8/5				—									
41	8/12	Eagle Century	C		—									
42	8/19				—									
43	8/26	Copper Century	C		—									
44	9/2			↓	—									
45	9/9													
46	9/16													
47	9/23													
48	9/30													
49	10/7													
50	10/14													
51	10/21													
52	10/28													

MOST IMPORTANT WORKOUTS

PLANNING A WEEK

IN THIS CHAPTER, we are going to look into what you are probably most interested in—workouts. But let's start by getting oriented to your planning mission. If you are reading this chapter for the first time, I suggest that you only skim it and not make any weekly planning decisions or record anything in your annual training plan yet. Wait until you have read Chapter 9 before doing that. Once you have read these two chapters and have selected the periodization model you intend to use in the coming season, return to Chapter 7 and then to this one to finish off your ATP. If at any time you become confused, refer back to Figure 7.4 or ahead to Figure 8.1 for examples.

Before getting into the details of workouts, let's do a quick review of the key periodization guideline explained in Chapter 7—my proposed training philosophy. As you train for a key race, your workouts should gradually take on the characteristics of the race. If you are training for a time trial, your workouts must increasingly become like a time trial. If your goal event is a criterium, your workouts in the last several weeks prior to that race will be like the race—highly intense. It's no different if you are preparing for a road race or stage race. Workouts always become increasingly race-like as you progress through the season.

Of course, the other side of this philosophy coin is that the farther you are from the race on the calendar, the *less* like the race your workouts should be. For example, as you'll read about briefly in this chapter and dig into much more deeply in Chapter 12, I recommend you do some neuromuscular training. The most common workout type in this category is weight lifting. And yet there is never a time in a bike race when you stop, get off the bike, and lift weights. It's a nonspecific way of training for cycling. In other words, it's general training—not like bike racing. There are less obvious examples of this, such as doing long, steady rides at your aerobic threshold, as we'll get into later. As you also read in Chapter 7, general training makes up the bulk of what you do in the early season mesocycles: the prep and base periods. Although general, these types of workouts greatly contribute to the later development of the basic fitness necessary to do the race-specific workouts in the build, peak, and race mesocycles.

The bottom line for this workout progression over the course of the many weeks of your race preparation is to gradually shift the focus of training from general to specific. Of course, that training philosophy assumes that you are striving to achieve a very high goal in your A-priority races. But if that is not your intent—if you are training instead for low-key cycling events and your only purpose in going to races is to have fun—then all of this planning is of little value. And in that case, I certainly understand not doing it. Planning is a big project and takes a time commitment, especially the first time you do it. But if you are indeed serious about your race goals and laser-focused on achieving them, then what I described in the previous chapter and what will be explained here will help you succeed. All of this planning may seem tedious now, especially if you're doing it for the first time, but I can guarantee you that the payoff later on in the season will be worth all of the time spent now.

What I will help you do next is complete your ATP by explaining how to schedule and record workouts in your plan. By the time you've finished this chapter, your plan will be completed through the first A race on the season. Return here and to Chapter 7 to make planning decisions for subsequent A races in the coming season.

Planning may seem tedious now, especially if you're doing it for the first time, but I can guarantee you that the payoff later on in the season will be worth all of the time spent now.

SCHEDULE WEEKLY WORKOUTS

If you've read Chapter 9, selected a periodization model to use in the coming year, and followed the instructions in Chapter 7, you should have your ATP mostly complete. With annual volume, season goals, training objectives, a calendar of the season by Monday dates for every week ("Mon"), your races and their priorities ("Pri."), a breakdown of the season by period, and your weekly volume filled in, your plan needs only one more thing: workouts. These weekly training sessions will be indicated on the far right side of the ATP, as shown in Figure 8.1.

Note that there are eight categories that make up your workout choices for each week, starting with the "Weight Lifting" category, should you decide to do that in your race preparation (more on this in Chapter 12). To the right of the "Weight Lifting" column are columns for the six abilities discussed in Chapter 6: "Aerobic Endurance (AE)," "Muscular Force (MF)," "Speed Skills (SS)," "Muscular Endurance (ME)," "Anaerobic Endurance (AnE)," and "Sprint Power (SP)." You may recall from the abilities discussion in that chapter that these define the types of workouts you'll do throughout the season. The last workout category on the far right side of the ATP is "Testing (T)." Periodic testing is necessary to gauge progress and to help you make decisions about future training. The suggested tests are described in Sidebar 5.3. All of the ability workouts and field tests are described in detail in Appendix B.

The last step in completing your ATP will be to decide which workouts you will do and when. All of this decision-making comes down to your ability limiters and strengths as discussed in Chapter 6. The purpose of the workouts is to improve limiters while maintaining strengths. We'll start by working out the details of strength training—the "Weight Lifting" column. Then you'll go down through each of the weeks and mark the ability-based workouts you intend to do with an "X." By the time you have your ATP done, it should look something like Figure 8.1.

Weight Lifting Column

In Chapter 12, I will explain why you should *probably* be doing strength training (weight lifting). You may decide not to do it for any number of reasons that will be explained there. For now, let's assume you will be following a periodized strength program in addition to your on-bike training. Your weight lifting routine must change throughout the season just as your bike workouts do. You don't do the same strength workouts week after week for the entire season, just as you don't do the same bike workouts endlessly. That means you will essentially be following two periodization schemes: one for weights and the other for the bike. But they must be in agreement. If too much attention is given to increasing strength at the same time that you are trying to do heavy-duty bike training, both will suffer. So it's a bit of a juggling act to increase strength while also riding. The major concern now is to pair the two programs with a time stagger so they don't cause a conflict. You'll do this by recording the strength phases in the "Weight Lifting" column on your ATP and matching them with the entries already made in the "Period" column. For now, we will look only briefly at each strength period, because Chapter 12 covers all of this in much greater detail.

Start at the top of the ATP in the "Weight Lifting" column and record the abbreviation, as described in the following discussion, for each strength period as you progress down through each week of the season. If you're unsure what to do, see Figure 8.1.

Preparation period. There are two components to the prep period: anatomical adaptation and muscular transition. To get started, in each of the weeks at the beginning of your season already marked as a prep period, write in "AA" in the "Weight Lifting" column. This stands for anatomical adaptation—the strength period in which you become accustomed to the various exercises you will do in the weight room. The purpose here is to master the movements of each exercise with low weight loads and high repetitions. This and all of the other weight lifting phases are explained in much greater detail in Chapter 12.

Most riders need at least 2 weeks of AA with 2 or 3 sessions per week in the weight room. You probably don't need more than 2 weeks in this phase unless you are completely new to weight lifting. Two weeks means doing 4 to 9 AA workouts at the start of the season.

If you have more than 2 weeks planned for your prep period, then you should also write in "MT" for muscular transition for the remaining weeks. This period is when you gradually increase the loads while reducing the repetitions. Serious weight lifting is just beginning. Again, you should have at least 2 weeks and as many as 3 devoted to MT. If you don't have 2 weeks remaining in your prep period, put "MT" into the first part of base 1 so that you complete a minimum of 2 weeks (4 to 6 workouts) of the MT phase before starting the next one.

You will be following two periodization schemes: one for weights and the other for the bike.

ANNUAL TRAINING PLAN

Athlete _Chris_

Hours/TSS _35,000 TSS_

Year _2019_

WEEK	MON.	RACE	PRI.	PERIOD	HOURS/TSS	DETAILS	WEIGHT LIFTING	AEROBIC ENDURANCE	MUSCULAR FORCE	SPEED SKILLS	MUSCULAR ENDURANCE	ANAEROBIC ENDURANCE	SPRINT POWER	TESTING
01	11/5			Tran	—									
02	11/12			Tran	—									
03	11/19			Prep	560		AA	X		X				
04	11/26			↓	560	Test FTP	AA	X		X				
05	12/3			Base 1	670		MT	X		X				
06	12/10				730		MT	X		X				
07	12/17				810		MS	X		X				
08	12/24			↓	560	Holiday travel	MS	X		X				X
09	12/31			Base 2	670		MS	X		X	X			
10	1/7				770		MS	X		X	X			
11	1/14				880		SM	X	X	X	X			
12	1/21	Florence 20 km TT	C	↓	560	Test FTP	SM	X		X				X
13	1/28			Base 3	780		SM	X	X	X	X	X		
14	2/4	Bartlett Lake HC	C		880		SM	X	X	X	X	X		
15	2/11	McDowell RR	C		950		SM	X	X	X	X	X		
16	2/18	Florence 20 km TT	C	↓	560	Test FTP, FACP	SM	X		X				X
17	2/25			Build 1	880		SM	X	X	X	X	X		
18	3/4	Hungry Dog Crit	C		880		SM	X	X	X	X	X		
19	3/11				880		SM	X	X	X	X	X		
20	3/18	Tumacacori RR	B	↓	560	Test FACP	SM	X		X				X
21	3/25			Build 2	950	Off work	SM	X	X	X	X	X		
22	4/1	Superior RR	B		715		SM	X	X	X	X	X		
23	4/8				950		SM	X	X	X	X	X		
24	4/15			↓	560	Test FTP, FACP	SM	X		X				X
25	4/22			Peak	670		SM	X		X	X	X		
26	4/29			↓	560		SM	X		X	X	X		

FIGURE 8.1 Continued example of an Annual Training Plan

Season Goals

1. Win State TT (sub-61 min. 40 km)
2. Top 10 at Nats. TT (sub-1 hour 40 km)
3. Podium at Nats. RR

Training Objectives

1. Squat 1.3 x body weight by 12/30
2. Raise FTP to 230 W by 2/24
3. Increase functional aerobic cap. power to 260 W by 4/21
4. Achieve sprint power of 800 W by 7/14

WEEK	MON.	RACE	PRI.	PERIOD	HOURS/TSS	DETAILS	WEIGHT LIFTING	AEROBIC ENDURANCE	MUSCULAR FORCE	SPEED SKILLS	MUSCULAR ENDURANCE	ANAEROBIC ENDURANCE	SPRINT POWER	TESTING
						MOST IMPORTANT WORKOUTS								
27	5/6	State TT Champ	A	Race	560		—	X		X	X	X		
28	5/13			Tran	—		MS	X		X	X	X	X	
29	5/20	Tucson Crit #1	C	Base 3	730		MS	X		X	X	X	X	
30	5/27	Tucson TT #1	B	↓	630	Test SP, FACP	MS	X		X				X
31	6/3			Build 1	880		SM	X	X	X	X	X	X	
32	6/10	Tucson Crit #2	C	↓	880		SM	X	X	X	X	X	X	
33	6/17	Tucson TT #2	B	↓	560	Test SP, FACP	SM	X		X				X
34	6/24			Build 2	950		SM	X	X	X	X	X	X	
35	7/1	Tucson RR	B	↓	760		SM	X	X	X	X	X	X	
36	7/8	Tucson TT #3	B	↓	560	Test SP, FACP	SM	X		X				X
37	7/15			Peak	670		SM	X		X	X	X	X	
38	7/22	Masters Nats. RR-TT	A	Race	560		—	X		X	X	X	X	
39	7/29			Tran	—		—							
40	8/5			↓	—		—							
41	8/12	Eagle Century	C	↓	—		—							
42	8/19			↓	—		—							
43	8/26	Copper Century	C	↓	—		—							
44	9/2			↓	—		—							
45	9/9													
46	9/16													
47	9/23													
48	9/30													
49	10/7													
50	10/14													
51	10/21													
52	10/28													

Base 1 period. For this period, record 4 consecutive weeks of "MS"—muscular strength, the most challenging strength workouts of the season. If you don't have 4 weeks remaining in base 1, roll the remaining weeks of MS into base 2. You should complete MS before starting the hard bike training sessions of the base 3 period. This is a critical admonition that is often violated by riders. Trying to do very demanding workouts in the weight room and on the bike concurrently will result in excessive fatigue and poor training in both categories. If you have multiple base 3 periods scheduled back to back, as may be the case if you need to fit in extra training weeks for the periodization plan to match the timing of an A-priority race in your schedule, devote no more than 4 back-to-back weeks to MS weight lifting. Once these 4 weeks of heavy-duty lifting are done, the focus of serious training shifts to the bike and weight lifting moves into a maintenance mode.

Base 2, base 3, build 1, build 2, and peak periods. You'll record strength training for all of the remaining periods in the buildup to your first A-priority race of the season as "SM"—strength maintenance. As the name implies, all you are doing in these weight sessions is maintaining the strength gains you made in MS. Whereas in previous weeks you were doing gym workouts 2 or even 3 times each week, now you are only lifting weights 1 time each week. So the strength workouts are now not only less frequent but also much less taxing, thereby allowing you to train hard on the road. Again, what you must avoid are days when both strength training and on-bike training are at high workloads. So in the peak period, the SM workouts should be given a very low priority. Then, the primary focus of training must be

highly specific, with race-like workouts. Weight lifting in the peak period must not conflict in any way with bike workouts. It's not a problem to lift then, but the single weekly workout should be so brief that you can do a hard workout the same day if one's scheduled. Chapter 12 will explain how to do SM workouts to keep them from compromising your readiness for high-quality bike sessions.

Race period. During this period, assuming it only lasts 1 week as suggested in Chapter 7, leave the "Weight Lifting" column blank. There is no need for strength training at this time. But if you have two or three A races in consecutive weeks, then pencil in SM for the second week only. Back-to-back A-priority races make for a very challenging race preparation routine.

Transition period. There is no need to lift weights during this period. In fact, you shouldn't. The primary purpose now is mental and physical recovery. So if your transition period lasts 1 week or more, as it usually should at the end of a complete season, leave the "Weight Lifting" column blank. If, however, your transition period is only 1 or 2 days, as is common *during* the race season, you may return to the MT, MS, or SM weight phase to match what's called for in your on-bike training period plan for after the training break. Such decisions on how to plan for the second and following A races of your season are best made at that time rather than now. So let's examine your options as you move on to the latter part of the season.

You should now have the "Weight Lifting" column of your ATP complete through the first A-priority race of the season. In subsequent periods, as you prepare for your second and third most important races of the season, it could be a good idea to include a few sessions of the MS phase of weights by returning to the base period, even though you may now be in base 3. Of course, there may not be enough time for base training if your A races are separated by only a few weeks. In that case, something has to give and the logical candidate is weights. So I recommend either recording "SM" or leaving the column blank. It all comes down to your available time and limiters. If your limiter is muscular endurance, then a few MS sessions may be beneficial at this time. But if that's not your limiter, return to SM. Obviously there is a limit on how long you can maintain strength as developed in the previous MS phase, even by following the strength maintenance phase without a break in the routine. After a few weeks of SM, strength begins to slowly erode.

You don't have to make this decision now. It can wait until after the first A race. This is one of those times when self-coaching relies heavily on the art of training, as there is no science to tell us exactly what must be done in a given situation. It simply comes down to what you think is best at the time. When in doubt, leave it out. If you are unsure whether you should be weight lifting at this time of the season, then you are probably better off not doing it.

Balancing the physical stresses of strength and on-bike training can be quite confusing. The example shown in Figure 8.1 may help you put together an effective plan. Otherwise, you will need to make decisions based on experience. But, when unsure, especially whenever you are planning for the build, peak, and race periods, put the greater emphasis on bike workouts, not on weights.

Abilities Columns

Now I'm going to show you how to assign bike workouts by ability, as is typical in a linear periodization model. In fact, what we'll get into here will make it clear why this model is called "linear" in the first place. The workouts progress in a straight line from the general, basic abilities to the specific, advanced abilities with a few weeks of gradual conversion between them. You must understand that there are many ways to periodize and plan workouts besides the linear model. These often involve customization and lots of creativity. In Chapter 9, we'll get into some of these other methods.

You'll assign ability-based workouts in your ATP by marking the type of workouts you'll do each week in the appropriate ability columns. Of course, you'll only do this through the first race of the season. At that point, you'll plan for the next race much as you did when you planned out your weight lifting in the "Weight Lifting" column. The abilities, described in Chapter 6, include the basic abilities—aerobic endurance, muscular force, and speed skills—and the advanced abilities—muscular endurance, anaerobic endurance, and sprint power.

Besides the standard six abilities listed as the column headers, there is also a column titled "Testing." I'll tell you more about that in the following section.

The methodical procedure of assigning ability-based workouts for the entire season is simple, but it can be monotonous when done with paper and pencil. Planning with a digital version online makes the task quick and simple. What this task involves is placing an "X" in the ability column for each type of workout you'll do each week. This will help you to make decisions

Self-coaching relies heavily on the art of training, as there is no science to tell us exactly what must be done in a given situation.

when it's time to determine the specifics of your workouts. We'll get into those details shortly. For now, let's designate workouts for each period leading up to your first A race.

Preparation period workouts. As I'm sure you are aware by now, the preparation period is quite low key. Its primary purpose is to move you toward structured training following an extended rest and recovery break during the preceding transition period. The prep period is typically only included at the start of a new season, and it's seldom repeated in a given year unless you've had an exceptionally long break from training. The only serious training during this period is in the weight room, if you elect to do that. Chapter 12 will help you make this call. Your focus should be on becoming accustomed to the strength exercises and, after a few such sessions, gradually moving to heavier loads for each exercise (as described above and in much greater detail in Chapter 12). Strength work essentially takes the place of developing the muscular force ability. But should you decide not to lift weights after reading Chapter 12, then I highly recommend doing another form of neuromuscular workouts as suggested in that chapter.

If you decide not to lift weights but instead to do an optional form of strength development, place an "X" in every weekly "Muscular Force (MF)" column during the prep period. Other than weight lifting or MF, the only other ability-based workouts in the prep period are for aerobic endurance and speed skills, the two remaining basic abilities. But understand that these are still not going to be serious, hard-core sessions. You're starting to get back into an organized training pattern, and weight lifting or MF

is the only thing that even comes close to being serious. Place an "X" in the "Aerobic Endurance (AE)" and "Speed Skills (SS)" columns for every week in your prep period, regardless of how many there may be.

Base 1 period workouts. In this period, the emphasis is very definitely on muscular force training, as you are now lifting weights using heavy loads and low reps or you are doing alternative MF sessions as described in Chapter 12. These are challenging workouts done 2 or 3 times each week, and so the AE and SS workouts remain quite easy in order to balance stress. As with the prep period, place an "X" in the "Aerobic Endurance" and "Speed Skills" columns for each week in this period. Again, should you decide to do MF workouts in place of weight lifting, then also mark every base 1 week with an "X" under "Muscular Force." If you are doing weight lifting and you've indicated the phase in the "Weight Lifting" column, then you are done here.

Leave the last week of your base 1 period unmarked. We will come back to that in a little while.

Base 2 period workouts. By base 2, you should be starting to cut back on weight lifting or your optional MF training, as described in Chapter 12, by introducing a maintenance program with reduced workout stress and only 1 session per week. This will allow more time and energy for workouts intended to improve the speed skills and, especially, aerobic endurance abilities. Your training will now also include the very early stages of an advanced ability, muscular endurance. Mark the "AE," "MF," "SS," and "Muscular Endurance (ME)" columns with an "X" for every

The primary purpose of the prep period is to move you toward structured training.

week in base 2 *except* the last week. Do not, however, mark the MF ability if you are still doing MS strength sessions in the gym. That may be the situation if your prep period was short, resulting in rolling weight lifting over into base 1.

The MF workouts will convert the general strength built by weight lifting, or by doing the suggested alternative MF workouts of the base 1 period, into bike-specific strength workouts that place an emphasis on this ability. The MF bike ability will eventually evolve into power, resulting in increased wattage and faster racing. I'll come back to that later. While MF training in base 2 is now your primary focus, ME is just being introduced. These early season ME workouts are not very difficult, but during the next several weeks they will become an important part of your training.

Base 3 period workouts. This is the period when your workouts start transforming into a somewhat more race-specific type of training. Base 3 might be described as an in-between period. Up until now, it really didn't matter all that much if you were training for a long road race, stage race, criterium, or time trial. Prior to this period, the workouts were quite similar. The only significant difference was workout duration. Typically, long road races and stage races call for longer workouts than do crits and time trials. But now, in base 3, there is the beginning of a substantial shift in workout emphasis from the basic abilities to the more advanced abilities.

Regardless of the type of race for which you are training, mark the base 3 ability columns exactly as you did in base 2, with an "X" in the "Aerobic Endurance," "Muscular Force," "Speed Skills," and "Muscular Endurance" columns. Only this time, also place an "X" in the "Anaerobic

Endurance" column. In base 3, this new ability workout is introduced into your training. As with base 1 and base 2, leave the last week unmarked; we will come back to that shortly.

Build 1 and build 2 period workouts. After several weeks of base training, your general fitness should be coming along quite well. You should realize by the start of build 1 that you are muscularly strong, have improved pedaling and bike-handling skills, and great aerobic endurance. Additionally, you should have established the early stages of muscular endurance and anaerobic endurance. But you aren't ready to race yet. That's where we are headed next. In the build 1 and build 2 periods, the workouts will become increasingly specific to the demands of your first A race. For the next several weeks, you will build fitness to match the demands of that race as closely as possible. While the selected abilities will remain largely the same as in the base 3 period, the workouts will become much more race-like, with an emphasis on intensity.

The workout changes in these build periods are intended to help you become race ready in a few weeks. The next step in this progression is to transition the workouts for aerobic endurance, muscular force, and speed skills into maintenance-only sessions, just as you did with SM weight sessions. That means placing less emphasis on the basic abilities with less frequent and shorter workouts. They simply become portions of the more advanced ability workouts. That means merging the basic ability training into warm-ups, cooldowns, or even including them in recovery rides.

Another change that keeps your total training time manageable—and somewhat lower than it

Long road races and stage races call for longer workouts than do crits and time trials.

was in the base periods—is that multiple abilities are combined into single sessions. We do this to make these workouts more race-like. The typical road race or criterium doesn't demand only one ability. Such races always place multiple demands on you: terrain changes, windy conditions, high and low temperatures, tight corners, pack riding, surges, long accelerations, and sprints, with fatigue accompanying all of these demands. Anaerobic endurance and sprint power are at the heart of build 1 and 2 training for road races and crits, but muscular endurance also plays a big role. Group rides are also critical to your performance at this time.

Stage racers can expect all of these same conditions and situations, compounded by the challenge of recovering between stages. We'll come back to all of this later in this chapter.

Time trialists should be preparing for moderately high-intensity, steady pacing. That means a great emphasis on muscular endurance, but with some anaerobic endurance included to boost aerobic capacity.

You need to prepare for all of the situations you can anticipate in your race.

The bottom line is that you need to prepare for all of the situations you can anticipate in your race. So, based on which of these three race categories your first A race falls into, mark the appropriate ability columns with an "X" for every week except the last in both the build 1 and build 2 periods. Also place an "X" in each of the basic ability columns (AE, SS, and MF) for both periods for every week except the last ones.

Peak period workouts. With your race now only two or three weeks away, your training shifts to peak period workouts and expected race details such as terrain, weather (heat, cold, side winds), strategies, and tactics that closely match the

demands you expect. In the peak period there is an increased emphasis on preparing for the expected intensity of the race as workout duration decreases (more on the tapering routine may be found in Chapter 13). Also eliminated from the training routine are workouts that emphasize the three basic abilities. They should all be quite well established by now. In the peak period, you are either working very hard or recovering. Mark your ATP for all of your peak period weeks with an "X" in the same columns as you marked in the build periods. Do not, however, include the MF ability. SS workouts may still be done as a part of an advanced ability workout. AE sessions are essentially the easy workouts that separate the high-intensity sessions.

Race period workouts. The emphasis of the race week is rest, with workouts that are quite brief but still focused on the anticipated intensities of your race. Mark your race week just as you did for the peak period. Chapter 13 will cover the details of training in the peak and race weeks.

Transition period workouts. As previously mentioned, this is when you take a well-deserved break from race preparation. Depending on where you are in the season, the transition period may last from a couple of days to a few weeks. There are no key workouts, no structured training, and no scheduled volume. The purpose of this period is strictly rest and recovery—both physical and mental. You've just completed an A-priority race preceded by several weeks of challenging training, and so the time away from hard-core workouts will recharge your batteries. Do not mark any abilities in this period. Leave this period in the ATP blank. You can still exercise, but it must be an unplanned, spur-of-the-moment decision and should be short and easy. If exercise seems appropriate, try crosstraining. Otherwise, feel free to take as much time off the bike as you want. Enjoy life. There is more on the transition period in Chapter 11.

Rest and Recovery Weeks

Now we'll return to those last weeks of the base and build periods and mark the planned workouts. Chapter 11 covers the topic of rest and recovery in greater detail, but for now, as you are filling in your ATP, place an "X" in the "Aerobic Endurance" and "Speed Skills" columns for the last weeks in each of your base 1, base 2, base 3, build 1, and build 2 periods. Also place an "X" in the "Testing" column for each of these same weeks.

As you will read about later in much more detail, the rest and recovery break from training typically lasts 3 to 5 days. For this period, the suggested workouts are found in the "Aerobic Endurance" (especially workout AE1) and the "Speed Skills" sections of Appendix B. Immediately following this brief break from training is the time to do field tests to gauge progress and make adjustments to the training zones before starting the next mesocycle. If the break is only 3 or 4 days of easy rides followed by a field test day, you will still have 2 or 3 days remaining in the week. Even with a 5-day rest and recovery followed by a field test, you still have 1 day remaining. In any of these three situations, assuming you recover quickly from the field test, you will start back into serious training with an emphasis on the appropriate abilities associated with the next mesocycle on your ATP. You can't make this decision now; instead, you must wait until you are recovered to see how many days are needed. Again, see Chapter 11 for details.

Planning for Subsequent A Races

If you have decided to train with a linear periodization model and have come back to this chapter after reading Chapter 9, you should now have the easy part of your ATP completed for the season: preparing for the first A race. The hard part is determining how to assign workouts for the remaining A-priority races later in the season. There is an overview of how to do this in Chapter 7, which, along with Figure 7.2, may give you a better understanding of how to periodize those remaining A races on your calendar. The example of an annual training plan in Figure 8.1 may also help with this.

In summary, the biggest question you need to answer after the first A race of the season is how well-maintained your aerobic endurance is. Aerobic endurance is critical to performance in endurance bike racing and is the most important of the basic abilities. There is a strong possibility that you have lost some AE fitness given your emphasis on the advanced abilities in the previous build, peak, and race periods. The transition period also is likely to have compromised your AE fitness. One way to determine if there has been a loss is to repeat the functional aerobic threshold (FAeT) test immediately following your transition period. This will allow you to see how your efficiency factor compares with what it was back in your last base 3 period (this test is explained in Appendix B under "Field Tests"). If it is at about the same level as it was in the base period, you can go straight into a build period in preparation for your next A race. If your efficiency factor, however, is lower by 5 percent or more than the previous base 3 best test result, then I strongly suggest starting back into base 3 training. And, if possible, continue in that period until EF is less than 5 percent lower than it was previously. The emphasis of base 3, if you repeat it, should then be on aerobic endurance.

That's the best-case scenario. But you may not have adequate time to do that given the number of weeks until your next A race. This is when the art of self-coaching comes into play. If the number of training weeks is inadequate to allow a concentration on rebuilding AE, you may have to customize the remaining weeks so that you rebuild AE while also preparing your advanced abilities for the next race. This blending of basic and advanced abilities for a short period of time is not optimal, but it's sometimes necessary.

In the Figure 8.1 ATP example, notice that the rider returned to base 3 for a little more than 2 weeks (4 days in week 28 are also base 3) following the first A race and brief transition period to reestablish not only aerobic endurance but also muscular force (note the MS weight sessions) and speed skills. The last week of this base 3 period includes a B-priority race and then goes straight into 2 back-to-back build periods, 1 peak week, and 1 race week. This is a near-perfect plan when there are ample weeks between races. That's highly likely when there are only two A races in a season. But when there are three, the timing is usually considerably tighter and so planning is more challenging. Again, all of this detail about subsequent A races is discussed in more detail in Chapter 7. Figures 7.2 and 7.3 will help you decide how to plan when you have only a few weeks between races.

Races during this subsequent base period complicate things, but frequent racing is common

in cycling so complications are to be expected. Races at this time, especially if they're C-priority, are considered training sessions, and so they will account for some of the advanced abilities training planned during this time. In Figure 8.1, the athlete could safely assume that a criterium in week 29 will provide adequate stimulation for developing muscular endurance, anaerobic endurance, and sprint power. Otherwise, that week is primarily devoted to the basic abilities.

Following the first A race, after you've determined the periods necessary to best prepare you for the next one, mark the abilities columns as described above based on where you are in the season (that's likely to be base 3, build 1, or build 2) and your race type: road race, stage race, criterium, or time trial. Refer to Figure 8.1 to see how this is done.

Testing Column

Throughout the season, you should regularly test your progress and check your training zones for accuracy as described in Chapters 4 and 5. Your power zones are likely to change every few weeks, but your heart rate zones should stay fairly constant throughout the season. The best time to test is after a rest and recovery break, every third or fourth week of the base and build periods. You should feel fresh following 3 to 5 days of reduced training load, which is exactly what's needed to produce accurate and meaningful test results. The tests are described in Appendix B under the heading "Field Tests." Depending on your personal capacity for hard work, you may decide to do two tests in one day, such as the functional threshold power and functional aerobic capacity tests. If you'd rather not do two tests in a single day, you should have at least 2 days remaining in

Blending basic and advanced abilities for a short period of time is not optimal, but it's sometimes necessary.

You should regularly test your progress and check your training zones for accuracy.

the rest and recovery week that you can use for testing. You will probably need a recovery day following a test day.

WEEKLY AND DAILY TRAINING

Your ATP should now be completed, including annual volume, season goals, and training objectives. Also filled in should be the "Mon.," "Race," "Pri.," "Period," "Hours/TSS," "Details," and workout abilities columns. I haven't mentioned the "Details" column. As you can see from the example in Figure 8.1, this is where you add brief comments about such things as tests to be done in rest and recovery weeks, race comments, planned vacations, travel, other times when you anticipate missed training, and other reminder notes.

Now we're finally down to the part of the planning process that riders find most interesting: determining what the weekly training routine will look like. This is highly individualized based on such important lifestyle commitments as family and career. These can't be compromised just to make room for training. You certainly must have priorities in life, and most riders place family and career in the highest categories. Another lifestyle factor that must be considered is weather. If you live somewhere that commonly experiences seasonal weather patterns so bad that riding is impossible outdoors, then you're going to need to do some workouts on an indoor trainer. This usually means reduced workout durations and weekly volume relative to days and weeks when you can ride on the roads. The weather conundrum may be so significant where you live that it has some bearing on the periodization model you choose to follow. Chapter 9

will assist with that decision. But even if you decide to use the linear model as described in this and the previous chapter, you must be willing to make adjustments from time to time while acknowledging that the perfect application of your training plan isn't possible. Everyone experiences planning setbacks and training interruptions that require plan adjustments. We'll return to the matter of missed workouts later in this chapter. For now, let's dig a little deeper into weekly training routines, volume distribution, and what your typical training week in the base and build periods should look like when weather is not a factor. In Chapter 11, we'll look at the rest and recovery along with transition weeks, and in Chapter 13 at the peak and race weeks.

Near the end of this section, in Tables 8.2, 8.3, and 8.4, you'll find suggested weekly routines. These may or may not work for you given your personal lifestyle, local weather, training load capacity, and other mitigating factors. They represent only one example of distribution options and are not to be taken as the gospel of how to distribute time or TSS. There are many other ways of doing this.

There are several other factors that need to be considered before designing your personalized routine. Let's look at those next.

Base and Build Weekly Routines

Once you've determined a weekly routine, you can usually repeat it for several weeks so long as all of the other important commitments in your life stay much the same. Having a set daily training routine is beneficial both physically and mentally. Your body and mind like it when the pattern of your days stays much the same week after week. Humans function best when life's routine

Everyone experiences planning setbacks and training interruptions that require plan adjustments.

Group rides
can be quite
similar to
what you will
experience in
the event.

is predictable. When a new mesocycle begins, however, there may be a need for a change to the weekly schedule. For example, going from the base to the build period in linear periodization often means a shift of focus from duration to intensity. That is likely to necessitate a change in the weekly training pattern. Otherwise, I suggest keeping the training weeks as much alike as possible throughout the season, as this contributes to successful training.

Using Table 8.1, pencil in the general types of workouts you will do in the base 1 and 2, base 3, and build mesocycles. (Notice that I've separated out base 3 since it is a somewhat transitional period between the early base and build periods.) The starting place for this step is to note what you currently do on each day of the week in each of these periods. Pencil them in by day and mesocycle. Use the categories of group rides, races, breakthrough workouts (hard rides as described below), recovery rides, days off from training, and weight lifting. As you read on, you may come to the conclusion that changes to your training patterns are needed. That's why I suggest doing it in pencil. Later in this chapter I will suggest training patterns based on what I have commonly used when coaching riders.

Let's take a look at your current routine from another perspective and make changes if any are needed. It may not change at all and, in fact, probably won't. To create an effective weekly routine that stays much the same throughout the season, it's necessary to schedule your workouts on the best days based on your lifestyle and unique training needs. The routine also must allow you to get the most fitness possible for the time invested. To do that, we'll dig a little deeper into each of those workout categories and discuss when to schedule them and how best they are arranged relative to each other by mesocycle.

Group rides. Let's start this discussion with the two build periods. In those mesocycles, fast group rides are important to your race preparation if your A-priority event is a road race, stage race, or criterium. That's because group rides can be quite similar to what you will experience in the event, and you probably recall that specificity of training is the purpose of the build mesocycles. For the serious roadie, these group workouts

TABLE 8.1   **Planning Weekly Routines for the Base and Build Mesocycles**

DAY OF THE WEEK	BASE 1	BASE 2	BASE 3	BUILD 1	BUILD 2
Monday					
Tuesday					
Wednesday					
Thursday					
Friday					
Saturday					
Sunday					

Using a pencil, write in the types of workouts you plan to do on given days. These may be group rides, races, breakthrough workouts, recovery rides, days off, and weight lifting.

in the build period are often C-priority races that, according to Table 7.3, are treated as hard-training sessions rather than as races. This doesn't mean you shouldn't give them your best effort, but rather that you shouldn't taper as before an A race or reduce training for a few days prior, as with B-priority races. Treat a C race just as you would treat a hard workout. The day before is usually an easy day, but that's it as far as the pre-race recovery goes.

Your C-priority races probably happen on weekends, just as your group rides do, although in some locales there are also group rides during the week. For the most serious cyclists, two group rides in a week are adequate; that may even be too much for some riders, especially those who recover slowly after very hard rides. Unless you are preparing for a stage race, it's probably best to avoid back-to-back fast group rides on the weekend. One or two group rides in a week leaves enough time and energy to do one or possibly two more hard sessions that week. You are likely to do these solo, but they may be done with a training partner. I would caution you not to become so dependent on group rides for your race preparation that they come to make up nearly all of your hard workouts. That could leave some area of your advanced fitness underdeveloped.

In the two build period columns, pencil in one or two group rides on the days you are likely to do them. More than likely there is no change from what you previously recorded as your normal routine.

I started with the build mesocycles for this category since they are generally the easiest to figure out. The base period takes a little more discussion when it comes to group rides. I'm sure it's obvious to you that in the build periods, it's

pretty much a given that you will do group rides and races. The base periods are different. You are much less likely to be racing and doing fast group rides in base 1 and 2, as they can be detrimental to developing the general fitness that is the purpose of these mesocycles in a traditional linear model. If you do any group rides at all in base 1 and base 2, they are best approached as aerobic endurance workouts—not done with highly anaerobic intensities or race-like riding. Save that for the base 3 and build periods. Too much race-like training in the two early base periods is likely to leave you too tired to do an adequate amount of basic ability training, and it may also lead to an early peak that will detract from race performance later in the season. You must be patient in the early base periods. I call riders who don't have such patience "Christmas stars," as they achieve peak race fitness by midwinter and go downhill from there. By late in the race season they are often burnt out.

Even though you may not plan to do a fast group ride in base 1 or base 2, you may get sucked in when you're passed on the road by a hard-charging group of Christmas stars. You must resist getting caught up in such "racing" when your purpose for the base period workout that day was recovering or developing aerobic endurance, muscular force, or speed skills. The possible exception to this avoidance of anaerobic training and racing is the base 3 period. That is when the fast group ride is first introduced into your training. Even then, it must remain a rather subdued aspect of racing, with only 1 such session per week.

On the weekly training routine plan in Table 8.1, confirm the days when your group rides or races are likely to take place each week in all five periods.

For the most serious cyclists, two group rides in a week are adequate. Unless you are preparing for a stage race, it's probably best to avoid back-to-back fast group rides on the weekend.

Weight lifting. Now you will decide the days for weight lifting workouts. Your primary concern is that your weekly plan be realistic. Does it fit your capacity for training? The most common mistake is making the training week overly hard by scheduling weights along with hard on-bike workouts. You can't mix the most challenging gym workouts with very challenging bike workouts in the same weeks. That will not work. You should either be doing heavy-load weight lifting sessions (the MS phase) or hard bike rides—not both in the same week or on back-to-back days. That's why I suggest scheduling your gym workouts so they reach a high point for physical stress in the base 1 period. This is the time when on-bike sessions are rather low key.

Once the MS strength phase is completed, usually by base 2, you will start the strength maintenance (SM) phase, which is much less stressful. This allows for more focused training on the bike. The only exception to this is if you return to base 3 following your first race of the season and include MS weight workouts. As you can see in the example in Figure 8.1, the rider has done this for weeks 28, 29, and 30. There are also some advanced ability workouts on the bike scheduled for these same weeks. This mix of stressful sessions must be monitored very closely to ensure that you don't overreach or compromise your fitness in either area of training. That may be accomplished by doing only 1 MS session in such weeks, or by greatly reducing the amount of advanced ability, on-bike training that is done then. It isn't as effective to do 1 MS session in a week as it is 2, but by this time in the season bike training must be paramount. Should you decide to do 2 MS in a week, you'll likely need to reduce your advanced ability bike workouts. Such a

decision is an individual call based on your specific limiters.

Which days of the week should be scheduled for weight lifting workouts? There are several things to consider that are discussed in greater detail in Chapter 12. But with the current intent of only producing weekly training routines, let's examine scheduling gym workouts relative to bike sessions and mesocycles. You can make changes to this later, once you have finished reading the entire book.

Although you may be capable of doing more, you probably only need to lift weights 2 times each week in the prep and base 1 periods. The exception might be riders for whom muscular force is the major limiter. If your MS phase extends into part of base 2, which is common when there is no prep period scheduled, then your on-bike workouts must remain low key at these times, when weight lifting is the dominant workout. Once the MS phase is completed and SM begins, you should do only 1 weight lifting session per week. That's when the bike workouts are ramped up. That typically starts in base 2 and is certainly the case for base 3.

During the anatomical adaptation (AA), muscular transition (MT), and MS phases, the 2 weekly sessions should be separated by 2 or 3 days to allow for recovery. That would mean, for example, lifting weights on Monday and Thursday or Monday and Friday. You could also lift on Tuesday and Friday or Tuesday and Saturday. Wednesday and Sunday would also work. On the other hand, Monday and Saturday doesn't work out very well because there is only 1 day for recovery separating Monday from the previous Saturday. You must come into each of the MS sessions rested and ready.

You can't mix the most challenging gym workouts with very challenging bike workouts in the same weeks.

You probably only need to lift weights 2 times each week in the prep and base 1 periods.

Once the MS phase is complete, usually by base 2, you will only be lifting weights 1 time each week, and that single session must not be overly challenging, as you will read in Chapter 12. You can do it on any day of the week that works best for your lifestyle and gym availability. You still may find, however, that even the SM phase requires you to keep the bike session aerobic on the following day. This is an individual matter that has to do with your capacity for this type of training load. Most riders with well-developed muscular force have no trouble at all the day after an SM session and may do any bike workout they want. Others find that they carry some fatigue forward even from such a reduced workload and so must be cautious the following day.

With all of this in mind, make sure your weekly training routine reflects what you have now determined are the best days for you to lift weights in the base 1, base 2, base 3, build 1, and 2 periods. Remember that in base 1 and perhaps in base 2, when doing MS weight lifting, the bike workouts are relatively easy. Once you move beyond MS and go to 1 day per week for weights, you are ready to increase the emphasis on bike workouts. This is when you can start joining group rides—although be sure to keep them rather easy in the base 2 period. If you are uncertain about the best days for all of this, bear with me as I take you through the many considerations of the harder bike sessions in the following discussion. After that, you may need to return to the weight lifting workouts and rearrange them as needed.

Breakthrough workouts. With the group ride and weight lifting sessions now recorded on your weekly routine, you'll next decide when to sched-

ule the breakthrough (BT) training sessions for the week. These are the hard workouts that help you to *break through* to a new level of fitness. Every workout you do that results in physical stress and produces fatigue is a breakthrough workout. The advanced abilities workouts are very effective at this. The basic abilities workouts are somewhat more subtle in producing greater fitness. Regardless of type, if you are tired the day after a workout and feel the need to recover, then you have experienced a breakthrough workout.

The usual concern for breakthrough workouts is that you come to them rested and ready, and then recover for a day or so afterward. But there are exceptions that you'll read about in the "Stage Race Training Routines" section that follows. When you're not preparing for a stage race, your weekly routines by period should reflect this emphasis on rest and recovery both before and after the BT sessions.

The types of BT workouts you do in a given week depend on the mesocycle and your race goals. For example, it's common in the base periods to have BT workouts for the basic abilities, such as aerobic endurance and muscular force. Although the intensity is moderate, the stress of aerobic endurance sessions comes from their long duration (see Appendix B for details). The muscular force workouts done on the bike are stressful due to the heavy loads placed on the muscles (find more on this in Chapter 12). As you read earlier, the build periods in a linear periodization model are focused on the advanced abilities: muscular endurance, anaerobic endurance, and sprint power. These are stressful workouts because of their high intensity. But generalizations like these about when such workouts are done in the season don't always hold true.

The build periods in a linear periodization model are focused on the advanced abilities: muscular endurance, anaerobic endurance, and sprint power.

For example, it's not unusual for advanced riders to do some limited anaerobic endurance training and even group rides in the base 3 period in order to boost aerobic capacity. Later in the build period, these are likely to become the primary focus of training.

Stage race training routines. If you are preparing for a road race, criterium, or time trial, the weekly routines you've laid out using Table 8.1 are almost complete. All that's needed at this point is an understanding of when to schedule rest and recovery days and what the workouts on those days will be.

Preparing for an A event that is a stage race requires a different approach to training. With only a few exceptions, the typical stage races for amateurs last three or four days and include three to five stages. There are a few weeklong stage races, but they are rare. So here we'll examine how to prepare for short stage racing. If you will be doing a greater number of stages, you can follow the procedure described here but you should continue it somewhat longer.

The three primary challenges of such races are being physically and mentally prepared for back-to-back races, managing energy expenditure in daily races, and recovering between stages. We'll examine the preparation for repeated stages here, and then we'll look at the recovery component in the next section. The stage-specific management of energy involves knowing when to work hard in a stage and how to gauge the proper effort at the time. This ultimately comes down to race strategy and tactics, and that is beyond the scope of this book. (I recommend reading *Racing Tactics for Cyclists* by Thomas Prehn for more on this topic.)

The general approach to physically and mentally adapting to repeated daily high stress over several days of racing follows the same methodology as preparing for any other type of racing. You must introduce your body gradually to the anticipated stress and follow that with ample downtime (recovery) for the physical adaptations to take place. Basically, that means doing BT workouts on back-to-back days to simulate what is anticipated in the race and then resting for a day or more. The number of these closely spaced sessions is gradually increased over a few weeks in the build period to foster adaptation. You may, for example, do 2 hard workouts on consecutive days this week and the next. That may be followed by a couple of weeks that include 3 days of consecutive BT sessions each week. And then in the next 2 weeks, do 4 such sessions. The idea is to simulate what is expected in the stages for each of these workouts.

The BT workouts during such a period should replicate the pattern of the stage race you are preparing for. If a three-day stage race is scheduled as a time trial, road race, or criterium, you should use that same pattern in your back-to-back daily training. By spreading these adaptive periods out over several weeks and being sure to include adequate recovery between the workouts and the groupings of BT sessions, your body gradually adapts.

I need to warn you, however, that such training is quite risky, especially for the rider who is not capable of managing high levels of such accumulated stress. It flirts with overtraining. The most vulnerable are novices, juniors, and seniors. There are also some riders who don't fall into one of these categories but simply don't manage such repeated stresses very well. If one of these situa-

Preparing for an A event that is a stage race requires a different approach to training.

If a three-day stage race is scheduled as a time trial, road race, or criterium, you should use that same pattern in your back-to-back daily training.

tions describes you, then you need to first decide if a stage race is right for you and, if it is, be very conservative in following the training regimen described here.

In fact, everyone should be cautious when preparing for a stage race. For most riders, it's probably best to do no more than 4 consecutive days of such training before taking a much-needed break. You may even find that your limit is 3 days. You must not push yourself so hard that you break down with injury, illness, or burnout.

I call this method of closely spaced workouts over several days "crash training." That name is intended to imply a risk. You're likely to crash and burn by doing this. By that, I mean that all sorts of bad things are likely to happen, including overtraining. I'll come back to overtraining in Chapter 10. For now, you must simply realize that crash training has the potential to ruin your season if you become overly dedicated to it.

On the other hand, if done cautiously, crash training has the potential to really boost your fitness. I've seen riders come away from such training, or a stage race followed by a few days of recovery, with fitness far above where it was before the crash period.

The key to crash training is being conservative. This means paying attention to how your body is responding and staying focused on recovery. If you are preparing for a weeklong stage race, after 2 or 3 consecutive days of BTs it's wise to go for an easy ride before doing another 2- or 3-day crash. Regardless of how many stages your race includes, you need to schedule 3 to 5 days of rest and recovery after a crash period. Most advanced riders find 4 days of crashing are about all they can safely and effectively manage without extended recovery.

Rest and recovery days. In Chapter 11, I will cover short-term recovery during hard-training weeks. For now, you only need to give consideration to how you schedule weekly BT workouts in order to allow adequate time to rest and recover before the next BT session. Coming to these workouts exceptionally tired can be counterproductive. You are less likely to experience a breakthrough when fatigue is not relieved within the first 48 hours following a BT workout. Instead, you are likely to experience a poor-quality session when the next BT is scheduled. Recovery workouts are just as critical to your fitness gains and your success on race day as the BT workouts. Replacing a scheduled easy ride or day off with a breakthrough in order to increase fitness gains is counterproductive.

The more experienced you are as a cyclist, the greater your weekly training load can be. That's because you recover faster after several years of focused training. Conversely, those who are new to serious training need to limit the number of BT sessions in a week. They recover more slowly. Age also plays a role; junior and senior athletes need more recovery and fewer BT sessions in a week (for more details on aging and training, see my book *Fast After 50*). The bottom line is that young advanced athletes, especially those in their 20s and early 30s who have been in the sport for a few years, can typically schedule several breakthrough workouts in a week—4 is not uncommon for these riders. But be conservative in making such a decision. The most common mistake athletes make is not allowing enough recovery time between BT workouts. As a result, they go into these sessions a bit tired and subsequently show little progress throughout the season.

The key to crash training is being conservative. This means paying attention to how your body is responding and staying focused on recovery.

Your weekly routines. You now have all of your workout types recorded in Table 8.1. In doing this, you have considered when you will do group rides, weight lifting, breakthrough workouts, recovery rides, and days off from training. What you now have are standard training weeks for each of the base and build periods. These do not, however, include the rest and recovery weeks every third or fourth week at the end of each mesocycle. We'll discuss this in Chapter 11. For now, I'll reiterate the point that it's not possible to create a perfect routine that will work week after week for an entire season without change. You will need to make frequent adjustments on the fly as things pop up in your daily life. But you have a template that will work for most weeks.

Table 8.2 is my suggestion for what the base and build training weeks may look like for the advanced rider. It's only a suggestion, of course, because I don't know your level of proficiency, your age, how well you handle training load, or your lifestyle. What you see here is only an example for a fictitious rider, but it may prove helpful as you're tweaking your weekly plan.

The BT workouts you see in Table 8.2 vary by period and may be very long rides at low intensity, long rides at a moderate intensity, and high-intensity training such as intervals. The exact type of BT workouts *you* decide to do depends on your strengths, limiters, periodization model, and the seasonal period. Note in this linear periodization example that in the base 1 period the athlete does only 3 BT sessions in a week with

TABLE 8.2 An Example of Standard Training Weeks in the Base and Build Periods for an Advanced Rider Using Linear Periodization

DAY OF THE WEEK	BASE 1	BASE 2	BASE 3	BUILD 1	BUILD 2
Monday	Weight lifting (MS) (and optional recovery ride)	Weight lifting (SM) (and optional recovery ride)	Weight lifting (SM) (and optional recovery ride)	Weight lifting (SM) (and optional recovery ride)	Weight lifting (SM) (and optional recovery ride)
Tuesday	Recovery	Breakthrough	Breakthrough	Breakthrough	Breakthrough
Wednesday	Breakthrough	Recovery	Recovery	Recovery	Recovery
Thursday	Recovery	Breakthrough	Breakthrough	Breakthrough (Group ride?)	Breakthrough (Group ride?)
Friday	Weight lifting (MS)	Recovery	Recovery	Recovery	Recovery
Saturday	Group ride (easy)	Group ride	Group ride or race	Group ride or race (may swap Sat.–Sun.)	Group ride or race (may swap Sat.–Sun.)
Sunday	Breakthrough	Recovery	Recovery (or day off)	Recovery (or day off)	Recovery (or day off)

Breakthrough workouts may be long and fully aerobic or short and highly intense, depending on the rider's strengths and limiters and capacity for workload. Recovery workouts are easy rides, days off, speed skill enhancement, or low-intensity aerobic endurance workouts intended to maintain ability gains made earlier in the season.

weight training (MS phase) accounting for 2 of these. But starting in base 2, when weight lifting workouts are reduced, the athlete does 4 BTs for the remainder of the base and build periods. These more challenging sessions are introduced gradually throughout the base period and are common in the build period. Besides short and low-intensity spins, recovery workouts may include a day off, a speed skills workout, or a maintenance session for aerobic endurance.

Weekly Volume Distribution

Before moving on to the next step in designing your training week, let's take a look back at an important training concept from Chapter 3. There I explained the relative importance of workout frequency, duration, and intensity. You may recall reading that for the *novice* rider, the frequency of workouts should be the primary focus. At this level, the beginner is making a significant lifestyle change and so the motivation to simply get on the bike regularly is the greatest obstacle to improvement. Frequent rides indicate success.

For the *intermediate* athlete, a rider in the second or third year of the sport for whom training frequency is no longer a concern, the most important variable is duration: how long the workouts last. Their need is to increase the length of certain rides to boost fitness, especially aerobic endurance.

For the *advanced* rider, a rider who has been training for three or more years, intensity is usually the key to racing performance. This doesn't mean going fast and hard all the time, as Table 8.2 illustrates with its great number of recovery days. Nor does it mean that frequency and duration—called "volume" when combined—is unim-

portant. It's simply less important than intensity for this athlete. Volume is still important, but typically it's not the primary performance limiter at this level.

You may also recall from Chapter 3 that volume commonly has to do with the number of hours an athlete rides in a period of time, such as a day, week, month, mesocycle, or year. Unfortunately, this number—or the number of miles or kilometers covered in that time—is all too often what advanced riders become obsessed with. That's probably because they became so fixated on it in their first three years in the sport that they are unable to see training from any other perspective, even though training hours or distance are not as important to their performance as intensity. That's why I strongly suggest that you use Training Stress Score (TSS) to measure volume. While hours, miles, and kilometers are easy to measure, TSS is a more accurate accounting of how your training is going, since it blends frequency, duration, and intensity into a single number.

Again, all of this doesn't mean that weekly hours are unimportant; it only means that they are less important than intensity for the advanced rider. It is still necessary to get your weekly hours right. Too many weekly hours and the constant fatigue will lead to poor performance in your breakthrough workouts. Too few and you'll be undertrained. Given such a choice, you should take the latter. Being undertrained is far better than being overtrained. But it would be best, of course, if you simply get your weekly hours *and* TSS right. That's where we're headed next.

Hours and TSS distribution. How do you get the weekly training volume right? The answer

> I strongly suggest that you use Training Stress Score (TSS) to measure volume.

is found in Chapter 7, with the details in Tables 7.2, 7.5, and 7.6. These tables helped you project annual volume, which is at the top of your ATP. You then divided that number into weekly volume, which you recorded for each week building up to your first A race. Now we will break down weekly volume into daily workout duration or TSS. By the time you've completed this, your weekly plan will be done through the first race of the season. Let's get started.

Tables 8.3 and 8.4 break down the volume on your ATP into suggested hours or TSS, respectively, for each day of the week. By now you should have decided which of these metrics you will use to measure volume. If you've not yet made that decision, you may want to return to Chapter 4 under the heading "Training Stress Score" to read about the merits of TSS. I highly recommend using TSS because in one number it reflects not only frequency and duration but also intensity. I realize this is likely to be a significant shift in how you view training. It may be a bit difficult to accept at first. But I think you'll find that in the long run it will not only prove to be a more accurate way of measuring progress, it will also change your perspective on training so that you become more focused on what's important.

On your ATP, note your weekly volume for the first week of the season, unless that's a transition period, which won't have a scheduled volume. In the left column of the table you decide to use—Table 8.3 for weekly hours or Table 8.4 for weekly TSS—find that first week number. If you are using TSS, the exact number may not be there, so use the one that comes closest to it. To the right of your weekly volume on the selected table is the suggested division of that first week of your season into hours or TSS for each day.

This is the process that you will be following each week of your season to find your daily volume and plan the week.

Realize that this daily hour or TSS pattern may not exactly match what you have scheduled as your weekly routines for the base and build periods when you filled in Table 8.1. So you may need to rearrange the daily hours to better fit your weekly plan. And it's also possible that you need to schedule a workout that calls for a greater duration or TSS given the type of event you're preparing for. That's OK. The daily numbers from the table are just suggestions.

The time to decide what the daily workout time or TSS will be is at the end of every week as you plan for the coming week. So there's no need to use these tables now. When doing the final planning for the upcoming training week, return to this section to find your planned weekly volume distribution. Once you get into it, you'll find that this weekly planning is quick and easy—as long as your training is progressing as it should. When things aren't going so well, planning becomes difficult.

I'm often asked if weight lifting time or TSS should be included in the "Weekly Volume" column of your ATP. Since this is part of the training load in preparing for a race, it makes sense that it should be. However, while time lifting weights in a workout is easy to determine, it's not very indicative of progress made in gaining strength. For example, if the gym where you lift is busy, you could spend a lot of time simply standing around waiting for a station to open. That does nothing to improve performance. As with on-bike training, TSS is a better indicator of what you accomplished in a weight lifting session. In Chapter 12, I'll explain a method you can use to give a TSS value to your strength workouts.

In one number, TSS reflects not only frequency and duration, but also intensity.

TABLE 8.3 Daily Training Hours

WEEKLY HOURS	MONDAY	TUESDAY	WEDNESDAY	THURSDAY	FRIDAY	SATURDAY	SUNDAY
4:00	0:00	1:00	0:00	1:00	0:00	1:30	0:30
4:30	0:00	1:00	0:00	0:45	0:30	1:30	0:45
5:00	0:00	1:00	0:00	1:00	0:30	1:30	1:00
5:30	0:00	1:00	0:30	1:00	0:30	1:30	1:00
6:00	0:00	1:15	0:30	1:00	0:45	1:30	1:00
6:30	0:00	1:15	0:45	1:00	1:00	1:30	1:00
7:00	0:00	1:30	0:45	1:15	1:00	1:30	1:00
7:30	0:00	1:30	0:45	1:15	1:00	2:00	1:00
8:00	0:00	1:30	1:00	1:15	1:00	2:00	1:15
8:30	0:30	1:30	1:00	1:15	1:00	2:00	1:15
9:00	0:45	1:30	1:00	1:30	1:00	2:00	1:15
9:30	0:45	1:30	1:00	1:30	1:00	2:30	1:15
10:00	0:45	2:00	1:00	1:30	1:00	2:30	1:15
10:30	1:00	2:00	1:00	1:30	1:00	2:30	1:30
11:00	1:00	2:00	1:00	1:30	1:30	2:30	1:30
11:30	1:00	2:00	1:00	1:30	1:30	3:00	1:30
12:00	1:00	2:00	1:00	2:00	1:30	3:00	1:30
12:30	1:00	2:00	1:00	2:00	1:30	3:30	1:30
13:00	1:00	2:30	1:00	2:00	1:30	3:30	1:30
13:30	1:00	2:30	1:00	2:00	1:30	3:30	2:00
14:00	1:00	2:30	1:00	2:00	1:30	4:00	2:00
14:30	1:00	2:30	1:30	2:00	1:30	4:00	2:00
15:00	1:00	2:30	1:30	2:30	1:30	4:00	2:00
15:30	1:00	2:30	1:30	2:30	2:00	4:00	2:00
16:00	1:00	3:00	1:30	2:30	2:00	4:00	2:00
16:30	1:00	3:00	1:30	2:30	2:00	4:00	2:30
17:00	1:00	3:00	2:00	2:30	2:00	4:00	2:30
17:30	1:00	3:00	2:00	2:30	2:00	4:30	2:30
18:00	1:00	3:00	2:00	3:00	2:00	4:30	2:30
18:30	1:00	3:30	2:00	3:00	2:00	4:30	2:30
19:00	1:00	3:30	2:00	3:00	2:30	4:30	2:30
19:30	1:00	3:30	2:00	3:00	2:30	4:30	3:00
20:00	1:00	3:30	2:30	3:00	2:30	4:30	3:00
20:30	1:00	3:30	2:30	3:00	2:30	5:00	3:00
21:00	1:00	3:30	2:30	3:30	2:30	5:00	3:00
21:30	1:00	3:30	2:30	3:30	3:00	5:00	3:00
22:00	1:00	4:00	2:30	3:30	3:00	5:00	3:00
22:30	1:00	4:00	2:30	3:30	3:00	5:00	3:30
23:00	1:30	4:00	2:30	3:30	3:00	5:00	3:30

$\rightarrow$

TABLE 8.3 (continued)

WEEKLY HOURS	MONDAY	TUESDAY	WEDNESDAY	THURSDAY	FRIDAY	SATURDAY	SUNDAY
23:30	1:30	4:00	2:30	3:30	3:00	5:30	3:30
24:00	1:30	4:00	2:30	4:00	3:00	5:30	3:30
24:30	1:30	4:00	2:30	4:00	3:30	5:30	3:30
25:00	1:30	4:30	2:30	4:00	3:30	5:30	3:30
25:30	1:30	4:30	2:30	4:00	3:30	5:30	4:00
26:00	1:30	4:30	2:30	4:00	3:30	6:00	4:00
26:30	1:30	4:30	3:00	4:00	3:30	6:00	4:00
27:00	1:30	4:30	3:00	4:30	3:30	6:00	4:00
27:30	1:30	4:30	3:00	4:30	4:00	6:00	4:00
28:00	1:30	5:00	3:00	4:30	4:00	6:00	4:00
28:30	1:30	5:00	3:00	4:30	4:00	6:00	4:30
29:00	1:30	5:00	3:30	4:30	4:00	6:00	4:30
29:30	2:00	5:00	3:30	4:30	4:00	6:00	4:30
30:00	2:00	5:00	3:30	5:00	4:00	6:00	4:30
30:30	2:00	5:00	3:30	5:00	4:30	6:00	4:30
31:00	2:00	5:30	3:30	5:00	4:30	6:00	4:30
31:30	2:00	5:30	3:30	5:00	4:30	6:00	5:00
32:00	2:00	5:30	4:00	5:00	4:30	6:00	5:00
32:30	2:00	5:30	4:00	5:30	4:30	6:00	5:00
33:00	2:00	5:30	4:00	5:30	5:00	6:00	5:00
33:30	2:00	6:00	4:00	5:30	5:00	6:00	5:00
34:00	2:00	6:00	4:30	5:30	5:00	6:00	5:00
34:30	2:00	6:00	4:30	5:30	5:00	6:00	5:30
35:00	2:00	6:00	5:00	5:30	5:00	6:00	5:30

Find your weekly volume for a given week on your annual training plan in the "Hours/TSS" column. To the right is a suggested distribution of those hours into daily workout time.

MISSED WORKOUTS

You may have noticed that in assigning workouts on your ATP, I assumed the progression would follow a rather standard calendar-based flow. In other words, you are expected to be ready to move on to the next mesocycle every 3 or 4 weeks. That may not always work out for various reasons. The most likely causes of training interruptions have to do with lifestyle, illness, poor weather for rid-

ing, and failure to achieve your performance goals in the previous period as determined by testing. You are likely to have at least one of these disrupt your training plan sometime during the season. Even if you avoid coughing colleagues at works, it's still likely you will have to vary your training to accommodate some interruptions.

When interruptions only mean one to three days away from training, I suggest continuing on with your training plan without any significant

TABLE 8.4 **Daily Training Stress Scores**

WEEKLY TSS	MONDAY	TUESDAY	WEDNESDAY	THURSDAY	FRIDAY	SATURDAY	SUNDAY
240	0	50	0	50	20	80	40
260	0	50	0	60	20	80	50
280	0	50	20	60	20	80	50
300	0	50	30	60	30	80	50
320	0	60	30	60	40	80	50
340	0	60	30	60	50	90	50
360	0	70	40	60	50	90	50
380	0	70	40	60	50	100	60
400	10	70	50	60	50	100	60
420	30	70	50	60	50	100	60
440	40	70	50	70	50	100	60
460	40	70	50	70	50	120	60
480	40	90	50	70	50	120	60
500	50	90	50	70	50	120	70
520	50	90	50	70	70	120	70
540	50	90	50	70	70	140	70
560	50	90	50	90	70	140	70
580	50	90	50	90	70	160	70
600	50	110	50	90	70	160	70
620	50	110	50	90	70	160	90
640	50	110	50	90	70	180	90
660	50	110	70	90	70	180	90
680	50	110	70	110	70	180	90
700	50	110	70	110	90	180	90
720	50	130	70	110	90	180	90
740	50	130	70	110	90	180	110
760	50	130	90	110	90	180	110
780	50	130	90	110	90	200	110
800	50	130	90	130	90	200	110
820	50	150	90	130	90	200	110
840	50	150	90	130	110	200	110
860	50	150	90	130	110	200	130
880	50	150	110	130	110	200	130
900	50	150	110	130	110	220	130
920	50	150	110	150	110	220	130
940	50	150	110	150	130	220	130
960	50	170	110	150	130	220	130
980	50	170	110	150	130	220	150
1,000	70	170	110	150	130	220	150

→

TABLE 8.4 (continued)

WEEKLY TSS	MONDAY	TUESDAY	WEDNESDAY	THURSDAY	FRIDAY	SATURDAY	SUNDAY
1,020	70	170	110	150	130	240	150
1,040	70	170	110	170	130	240	150
1,060	70	170	110	170	150	240	150
1,080	70	190	110	170	150	240	150
1,100	70	190	110	170	150	240	170
1,120	70	190	110	170	150	260	170
1,140	70	190	130	170	150	260	170
1,160	70	190	130	190	150	260	170
1,180	70	190	130	190	170	260	170
1,200	70	210	130	190	170	260	170
1,220	70	210	130	190	170	260	190
1,240	70	210	150	190	170	260	190
1,260	90	210	150	190	170	260	190
1,280	90	210	150	210	170	260	190
1,300	90	210	150	210	190	260	190
1,320	90	230	150	210	190	260	190
1,340	90	230	150	210	190	260	210
1,360	90	230	170	210	190	260	210
1,380	90	230	170	230	190	260	210
1,400	90	230	170	230	210	260	210
1,420	90	250	170	230	210	260	210
1,440	90	250	190	230	210	260	210
1,460	90	250	190	230	210	260	230
1,480	90	250	210	230	210	260	230
1,500	90	250	210	230	210	280	230
1,520	90	270	210	230	210	280	230
1,540	90	270	210	250	210	280	230
1,560	90	270	210	250	210	280	250
1,580	90	270	210	250	210	300	250
1,600	90	290	210	250	210	300	250
1,620	90	290	210	270	210	300	250

Find your weekly volume from your annual training plan in the "Hours/TSS" column for a given week. To the right is a suggested distribution of that TSS into daily TSS.

change. If, however, you missed a BT workout, which is likely, rearrange the remaining workouts in the week so you can fit it back in. Just be careful not to put two BT sessions back to back. You might have to leave one out. Forget about the other missed sessions that weren't BTs.

Of course, longer unplanned breaks from training with more than three workouts missed are also possible. What should you do then? Let's take a look at how to modify your training plan when several sessions are missed regardless of the reason.

Four to Six Missed Workouts

This is often the hardest situation to deal with. It's usually easy to make an adjustment if the lost time was due to a lifestyle interruption. But if it was due to illness, such as a bad cold, sore throat, or flu, you probably won't be ready to return to normal training right away, even if the symptoms are gone. Your body's chemistry has probably changed, which will affect your capacity for exercise. This may show up as low power, a high heart rate, and elevated perceived exertion. If this is what you're experiencing, you will need to treat it as more than six workouts missed, even though you are starting back into training again (see "One or Two Weeks Missed" below).

If the four to six days of missed training were not due to illness but rather a lifestyle interruption such as business travel or family matters, and you are healthy and mentally ready to get started right away, you will need to make some adjustments to the ATP. The first change is to consider the lost training time as a rest and recovery period—what you normally do at the end of a mesocycle. This is necessary but will throw off the training schedule for your A-priority race. Without making a change, your training plan will no longer be synchronized to bring you to a peak of race readiness. You lost too much fitness, so you'll need to make some adjustments.

There are a couple of solutions. The first option, if you are in the base or build period, is to reduce the length of the current period by 1 week. If you still aren't synchronized after making that change, do the same for the following period. For these two options, do *not* eliminate a rest and recovery week, although you may shorten it to 3 or 4 days, since you probably will not accumulate much fatigue given the shortened mesocycle. That will also help you to get back on track.

The second option is to change the peak period if it was planned for 2 weeks; make it only 1. The lost time makes gains in fitness more important than gains in form. Neither of these options is perfect. Both are going to result in reduced race readiness and probably a compromised performance. But that's the reality of missing nearly a week of training. You can't miss several workouts *and* have the same fitness as if no training was missed. Unfortunate, but that's just the way life is sometimes.

Once you are ready to train again, you will need to step back and make up probably 2 or 3 BT workouts that you missed during the downtime. Decide which were the most important ones, given your limiters, and reschedule them. This will likely mean pushing other workouts farther into the future in your plan. Eventually something will have to give. You'll either have to miss a culminating workout planned for later on or decide you are progressing well enough to omit, modify, or combine missed workouts remaining in the plan. There are simply too many variables here for me to be able to tell you exactly how to handle your situation. You'll have to judge the state of your fitness and plan accordingly.

One or Two Weeks Missed

If 7 to 14 days of lost training was due to illness and you were in the build period, start back into training in base 3. If you were in base 2 or 3 at the time of the interruption, return to the previous

You can't miss several workouts and have the same fitness as if no training was missed.

base period or repeat base 1 if that's where you were at the time. Stay with that period for 2 to 4 weeks, or until your aerobic endurance workouts indicate that you are aerobically back to where you left off before the lost training. You will know because your heart rate and power will again match, as they did before you got sick. The efficiency factor calculation as described in workout AE2 will help you determine this (see Appendix B). But when in doubt, give it another day or two before going to the next step.

When your efficiency factor and workout power return to what they were before the break, repeat the last week of hard training you did before the interruption. If that week goes well, begin moving forward with your original training plan. If it doesn't go well, rest for a couple of days and then repeat the previous hard-training week. At some point, you will need to leave out 1 to 3 weeks, or even more, of planned training. That could mean omitting build 2 or perhaps the first week of a 2-week peak period. Make sure you complete the full base period, however.

More Than Two Weeks Missed

If you were in the build period when this long training pause happened, return to base 3 and start over again from there. If you were in the base period, back up one period from where you left off and start training again from that point. As with the previous scenarios, you will have to leave out a significant portion of your plan—at least 2 weeks. The priority for omissions is the first week of peak, build 2, and build 1, in that order. Again, complete all three base periods.

If your 2 weeks of lost training was the peak period, continue on with your race week as if nothing happened. If you lost 2 or 3 weeks of

build 2, repeat as much of build 1 as you can fit in while reducing the peak period to 1 week only. If more than 3 weeks were lost, omit both the build 2 and peak periods, repeat as much of build 1 as is possible, and then go directly into race week training. But in all of these situations, if the lost time was due to illness, be conservative with both workout length and intensity as you start back by doing only short- to medium-duration workouts with intensity primarily in zones 1 and 2 until you are back to feeling normal. Your efficiency factor (see workout AE2 in Appendix B) will help you determine when your aerobic fitness is reestablished. When it is, your training can once again go full bore.

SUMMARY: PLANNING A WEEK

This chapter provided lots of details for planning your season. You may feel somewhat overwhelmed by it all. It's not easy to plan a season that will bring you to peak form and fitness on a given day in the distant future. There's a lot of planning and not a little uncertainty. If you are feeling a bit taken aback by this, I strongly suggest you follow the linear periodization model described in this and the previous chapter. Chapter 9 will take you into even more complex periodization models. If you've been around the sport for several years and what you've read so far seems simple enough, then you may want to consider using one of the more complex models described in Chapter 9 to more closely match your individual training needs.

If you decide to use the linear model, return to Chapter 7 and fill in the details of your annual training plan. If all of what you've read in these last two chapters seems simple enough, then I suggest holding off on completing your ATP until you've read the next chapter. When in doubt, keep it simple: Use the linear model.

The first time you devise an annual training plan for the seasonal big picture—the macrocycle—all the way down to the weekly workouts—the microcycles—is quite tedious and time consuming. But once you have done it and understand the *how* and *why*, it becomes much easier for future seasons. More importantly,

you now have a plan for the upcoming season that can keep you on track to achieve your high-performance goals—if you use it. With a completed seasonal plan, the key to making it work for you is to look it over at the end of each week and make small adjustments as necessary to the coming week's workouts and also your long-term direction. I think you'll find, as most athletes do, that having a plan gives your training a focus while boosting your confidence as race day gets closer.

PLANNING ALTERNATIVES

CHAPTERS 7 AND 8 walked you through the steps of planning your season and weeks using the linear periodization model. That model has been around for more than 50 years and continues to be popular among athletes and coaches, largely due to its simplicity. But despite being rather simple, it's produced high performance at every level of ability, including world records and Olympic medals. Just because it's popular and successful for other athletes, however, doesn't mean it's the best for *you*. While some cyclists may respond quite well to this classic training method, it's possible you could compromise your performance by using it. So in this chapter, I'll suggest a few alternatives.

How will you know which model is best for you? Unfortunately, there's no surefire way to tell, short of trial and error. And, even more unfortunately, what you discover may not stay the same over time. You may find that next season—or even in a few weeks, when you change mesocycles—that what was working well no lon-ger seems as effective. Training is an experiment with only one subject: you!

The only planning details that truly remain constant are the four training principles described in Chapter 3. You must follow them carefully no matter which planning model you use. Let's briefly review these principles before looking at alternatives to the linear model.

The first training principle is *progressive over-load*. This says that the workload must gradually increase over time to improve fitness. If it stalls for too long, fitness plateaus. Something must continually change to boost race readiness. That something is workout frequency, duration, intensity, or some combination of these three.

The second principle is *specificity*. The types of workouts you do must be similar to what you will do in the goal race. If the race is a road race or crit, for example, training must include high intensity and an appropriate workout duration.

Reversibility is the third principle. As the training load decreases, fitness is lost, which is sometimes necessary. This may seem surprising. But losing fitness is necessary to be on form for a race, and likewise to recover from hard training. Those are the only times that reversibility is a good thing. Otherwise, it's to be avoided.

The last principle is *individuality*. Your training demands are unique to you in many ways, both physically and mentally; therefore, your training must reflect your personal needs. These requirements are your strengths and limiters. You'll recall that limiters are race-specific weaknesses that must be the primary focus of training in order to prepare for the demands of the A race. While doing this, your strengths must be maintained. Since it's far easier to maintain a strength than to improve a limiter, this principle has a lot to do with how you use your valuable training time—which is just another way of saying your periodization plan.

And you may also recall another critical dictum that must be considered when training, regardless of the planning model: Your workouts must become *increasingly* like your A-priority race as race day gets closer. That's a bit similar to the specificity principle, only with the inclusion of a timing factor. If, on the other hand, your training gradually (over the course of several weeks) becomes different from the demands of the race, then the reversibility principle kicks in. You will lose race-specific fitness. That might happen if, for example, you gradually reduce your training at goal race intensity and instead start doing something altogether different, such as long, slow distance rides. If so, your fitness for high-intensity performance—a very important element of bike racing—will gradually erode. This means that no matter which periodization model you decide to use, you must always be aware of

how race-specific your workouts are becoming throughout the season. That's the ultimate key to high-performance planning.

As you also learned in Chapter 3, there are only three training variables that can be modified: frequency, duration, and intensity of your workouts. Other than mode (for example, riding a bike as opposed to running), there is nothing else to adjust regardless of your experience, race category, or planning model. Periodization is nothing more than the management of these three variables in order to produce race readiness at the right time.

This chapter will provide periodization alternatives so you can decide how you are going to arrange the three variables throughout the season. You may, however, decide to stay with the linear periodization model described in the previous two chapters. That's the model to use if you've never planned a season before. It's easy to use and likely will produce good results.

If you have tried that system in a previous season and now want to try something different, start with one of the several models described in this chapter. Pick the one that seems to fit your unique needs and is most appealing to you. If you discover that it doesn't meet your needs, then make adjustments until you discover what does. Just be sure to follow the training principles above, regardless of your chosen model.

LINEAR PERIODIZATION ALTERNATIVES

The linear periodization model described in Chapter 7 is called "linear" because it follows a straightforward progression. Its common underlying concept in endurance sports is that

Your training must reflect your personal needs.

Your workouts must become increasingly like your A-priority race as race day gets closer.

the training year begins with an emphasis on workout duration (the base period) and gradually morphs into an emphasis on intensity (the build, peak, and race periods). You don't have to be a sports scientist to understand it. Linear periodization is simple and makes sense even to novices. It's easy to measure progress with the linear model because there are well-defined ability outcomes that are developed independently in each period. While this may seem logical and simple, periodization doesn't have to be structured that way to be called linear.

Throughout the past five decades, several other ways of periodizing training have been introduced by coaches, athletes, and sports scientists to meet unique needs while fixing some of the flaws in the linear system. Many coaches and athletes have had concerns with the linear format. The most common concern is that it sets an upper limit for how many A-priority races an athlete can peak for in a season: typically only two or three. And related to that is the concern that this peak of fitness can be maintained for only about three weeks. Linear periodization is also not generally as effective for highly experienced elite athletes as it is for novices and intermediates. And many athletes find it to be monotonous, since training stays largely the same for weeks at a time with only small changes from week to week.

What can you do about these flaws in linear periodization while maintaining a simple plan that brings you to a peak of fitness on race day? Let's start by looking at ways you can make rather small but important changes to the basic linear model. Then, in the remainder of this chapter, we'll examine some nonlinear periodization models. Along the way, consider how each alter-

native method would work for you given your lifestyle, what's worked for you in the past, and what makes sense to you now.

This is a good time to also point out that a periodization plan is perhaps not needed at all. The alternative is random training—doing what you want when you feel like it. That may seem rather loosey-goosey, but it may not be all that bad for some riders. Somewhat random training actually works quite well for novices who simply need to work out frequently and for whom performance is judged by simply getting to the finish line. Even some highly advanced athletes may appear to be training randomly. While they may not have a written plan and seem to make last-minute decisions about workouts, most have a plan in their heads. They know what's needed and the order in which their abilities are best developed. Such a method is well suited to athletes who have been around the sport for many years and have learned what works best for them. Most of us, however, are better off having a written plan, even if it's only a rough outline, for how training should progress to avoid the many pitfalls on the road to racing.

With all of this in mind, let's a take a look at some common ways you can tweak linear periodization so that it better fits your unique needs.

Slow Recovery and Linear Periodization

In Chapter 11, we'll take an in-depth look at the details of the multiday rest and recovery breaks that come at the end of each base 1, base 2, base 3, build 1, and build 2 period. But for now I want to address a couple of periodization alternatives related to this matter that could have a big impact on the quality of your training.

> Linear periodization is not as effective for highly experienced elite athletes as it is for novices and intermediates.

One of the critical issues in designing a periodization plan, regardless of which type you may use, has to do with how quickly you recover from hard training, especially in the base and build periods. Some athletes recover quickly. These athletes usually do well with a periodization plan based on 4-week base and build mesocycles, as described in Chapter 7 and illustrated in Table 7.4. For the first 3 weeks or so (it is likely be a few more than 21 days—to be explained in Chapter 11) of each 4-week period, the quick-recovery athlete trains with a high training load—either high duration or high intensity or both, depending on the period and goal. This is followed by a rest and recovery break that typically lasts 3 to 5 days.

For the athlete who recovers more slowly, training needs to be organized somewhat differently. These athletes need more frequent rest and recovery periods. They can't train hard for 3 weeks or so before taking a physical and mental break. Slow-recovery riders need the break considerably sooner than fast-recovery athletes, usually after 2 weeks or so (this, again, may be a bit more than 14 days, as will be explained in Chapter 11). Table 7.4 also reflects this.

So how do you know if you are a fast- or slow-recovery athlete? Experience is the best indicator. How tired do you usually feel after 2 weeks of hard training? If you're still eager to go hard another week, then you most likely recover quickly. If you often find yourself fatigued and the quality of your training drops in week three, then you recover slowly.

Two types of athletes who typically recover slowly are novices and riders over the age of 50. This isn't always the case, however. I've coached over-50 and novice athletes who recovered quickly and for whom 3 weeks or so of quality

Athletes who recover slowly need more frequent rest and recovery periods.

TABLE 9.1 Adjustment for Slow-Recovery Athlete

PERIOD	MESOCYCLE WEEKS
Base 1	Week 1
	Week 2
	Week 4
Base 2	Week 1
	Week 2
	Week 4
Base 3	Week 1
	Week 2
	Week 4
Base 3	Week 2
	Week 3
	Week 4
Build 1	Week 1
	Week 2
	Week 4
Build 2	Week 1
	Week 2
	Week 4
Build 2	Week 2
	Week 3
	Week 4

How to adjust the base and build subperiods of the annual training plan for the slow-recovery athlete who uses a classic linear periodization plan.

training before taking a few days of rest and recovery worked just fine. I've also coached advanced and under-50 athletes who recovered slowly. You need to be honest with yourself when evaluating recovery. Doing long or intense workouts in the third consecutive week when you're fatigued is counterproductive. If that frequently happens to you, then I highly suggest going to 3-week subperiods on your annual training plan. That means about 2 weeks of hard training followed by a few days of rest and recovery. If you are a fast-recovery rider, then stay with a 4-week mesocycle plan.

Table 9.1 is based on the pattern in Table 7.4 and shows how slow-recovery riders may alter the number of weeks in a base or build period in order to return to training ready to go. Notice in Table 9.1 that the base and build periods have been reduced to 3 weeks. Also note that the base 3 and build 2 periods have been repeated so that the total training time prior to the race isn't reduced. In fact, it's increased from 8 weeks in the build period for fast-recovery riders to 9 weeks for those who recover more slowly. The base period stays the same, 12 weeks. The weekly volume shown here remains the same as was suggested in Tables 7.5 and 7.6. In other words, for each week listed below, find the weekly volume for that exact week (for example, base 1, week 2) in either Table 7.5 or 7.6, depending on the way you determine volume: either hours or TSS. The number of weeks in the other periods—prep, peak, and race—remain unchanged.

Another way of solving the slow-recovery conundrum is to redefine what a week is. So far I've used the term to mean 7 days. The problem with that for the slow-recovery rider is that it spaces hard-training days too closely if doing 3 such sessions in a week. They are only 48 hours apart, which is pretty tight for a slow-recovery rider. There either isn't enough time to recover

or the athlete must do only 2 hard workouts each week in order to adequately recover. Neither is a good solution. Workouts too closely spaced only add to the cumulative fatigue; workouts too far apart compromise fitness. An alternative solution is to train in 9-day "weeks." A 9-day week includes 2 days for recovery after each hard-training day. This fix means that 6 hard-training days are included in 18 days, whereas a 7-day week with 2 hard-training days per week would yield a total of 5. So the 9-day week allows for more quality training along with more rest and recovery. Table 9.2 provides an example of what a base or build period might look like using 2 back-to-back 9-day training weeks followed by 5 days of rest and recovery. Notice that the last 2 recovery days of the second 9-day week are rolled into the following 5-day rest and recovery break at the end of the mesocycle. This would make for a 21-day mesocycle. Of course, the rest and recovery break doesn't have to be 5 days. You could use a longer or shorter break based on how you feel at the time.

The recovery, or "R," days in Table 9.2 can be changed to customize training to your unique capacity for training load. For example, 1 or more of the second of the 2 back-to-back recovery days may be changed to a moderate workout instead

Workouts too closely spaced only add to the cumulative fatigue; workouts too far apart compromise fitness.

TABLE 9.2 An Example of Base and Build Mesocycles

	DAY 1	DAY 2	DAY 3	DAY 4	DAY 5	DAY 6	DAY 7	DAY 8	DAY 9
Week 1	BT	R	R	BT	R	R	BT	R	R
Week 2	BT	R	R	BT	R	R	BT	R&R	R&R
Week 3	R&R	R&R	R&R	Start of next 9-day week					→

This example uses 9-day weeks followed by 5 days of rest and recovery for a rider who recovers slowly. "BT" indicates a breakthrough workout, "R" means a recovery day, and "R&R" is an extended rest and recovery period. Following the last R&R day, the next 9-day week begins.

of an easy day (or day off) if you find you can handle a bit of an increase in your training load. This could, for example, be an aerobic threshold workout in low zone 2 or even a tempo ride in zone 3 (see Appendix B). Such small changes can be made on the fly if you pay close attention to how you're feeling. Such tweaking allows you to create a training week that precisely fits your needs for stress and rest. As always, if you're unsure, take the more conservative route. It's far better to be slightly undertrained rather than slightly overtrained.

The downside of the 9-day week is that it can be difficult for the athlete whose job or other daily constraints demand a 7-day week. For example, there will be days when a long ride must be done on a workday. Consequently, the 9-day week is best for the athlete who has a very flexible lifestyle. In this regard, it's perfect for the retired athlete. (The 9-day week is more fully described in my book *Fast After 50*.)

Time-Limited Periodization

Let's talk about weekly training volume. As you saw in the previous chapter, Table 8.3 suggests daily workout durations and Table 8.4 does the same for the daily TSS. These can be used each week throughout the season based on the recommended annual volume from Tables 7.2, 7.5, and 7.6. That seems simple enough. However, those numbers may simply not fit your situation. For example, what do you do if you have the physical capacity for managing high daily workout durations, as in those tables, but your lifestyle simply doesn't allow it? Not having enough time to train is perhaps the most common problem for serious riders who want to follow a linear periodization plan. The time constraints set by your career,

family, and other responsibilities may make it impossible for you to train at the prescribed volume Table 7.2 suggests. You'd love to, and physically could do it, but you just don't have the available time. What can you do about this?

Let's look at an example to see how to resolve this common problem. An athlete may decide she is capable of training 600 hours in a year. She's come close to that in the past, so there's reason to believe it is a good number. Based on an annual volume of 600 hours per year, she should be capable of training, on average, about 13 hours per week, with a big week of 18 hours in base 3, week 3 (according to Table 7.5). While that will probably push her to her limit, it seems realistic given her capacity for training. But what if she can't do that many hours because of limited available time for training? Maybe the most she can do, once all of her weekly responsibilities are accounted for, is 15 hours in a week. Table 7.5 suggests there should be 7 weeks greater than 15 hours in preparation for her first race of the season. What does she do?

A simple solution would be to change to an annual volume of 500 hours, but that's not a good idea, even though the biggest week would then be 15 hours and would fit her schedule. Why not? Simply because the training plan would then be too easy for her. While the training load will still adhere to the progressive training principle, it simply won't be great enough in most weeks to produce an increase in fitness. The weekly volume is simply far too low for her throughout much of the season.

Instead, the best option for this athlete is to train to a 600-annual-hour schedule but lop off the weekly volume at 15 hours when she comes to those 7 higher-volume weeks.

It's far better to be slightly undertrained rather than slightly overtrained.

Not having enough time to train is perhaps the most common problem for serious riders who want to follow a linear periodization plan.

Won't that also cause a loss of fitness? She could potentially reach a slightly higher level of fitness by doing those 7 bigger weeks. So what does she do about that? There really aren't too many options. She has no choice but to shorten the longest workouts in those highest-volume weeks. To help make up for that, she may also consider slightly increasing the intensity of some of the workouts in those weeks when training time is reduced. An easy, zone 1 recovery ride may no longer be necessary given the shortened workouts, since it's apparent she could handle more, so she could consider bumping the intensity of that ride up to zone 2. The general rule is that as duration goes down, intensity can go up. I can't tell you exactly which workouts she can do that with—or even if she should do it. It all comes down to the art of self-coaching. She'll have to make some decisions when she comes to those high-volume weeks based on how she is feeling at the time and how her training has been going. My advice to her is to be conservative when increasing the intensity of workouts in those few modified weeks. One additional zone in a given workout is plenty. And it should only be done for a few workouts.

Another fix that may work for her is to move the "excess" hours from a chopped-off week of high volume to a lower-volume week. Using the example from above, this would make nearly all of the weeks in the base period into 15-hour weeks. The same could then be done in the build period so that the volume is also increased across the board. In this way, total training time remains the same as the unaltered plan called for.

These fixes aren't as good as keeping the volume as it was originally called for in Table 7.5, but that isn't an option for the time-limited athlete.

The alternatives suggested above are, however, probably better for the time-crunched athlete than simply training to a lower annual volume. Of course, while I was using hours in this example, the same changes could be made if your training is instead based on TSS, as in Table 7.6.

Inverse Weeks Periodization

You may have noticed in Tables 7.5 and 7.6 that in the base 1, 2, and 3 periods the volume increases somewhat in each subsequent week within a period. For example, Table 7.5 shows a gradual weekly progression in hours in base 3 for the 500-hour column:

Week 1: 11.0
Week 2: 13.5
Week 3: 15.0
Week 4: 7.0

Please understand that these weekly hours (or TSS, if you train that way) don't have to be precise. They are intended to be only ballpark numbers—albeit a small ballpark. But generally, I've found that most athletes come very close to achieving scheduled weekly volumes when following a plan. Toward the right end of Table 7.5, the weekly increases are much larger, on the order of around 4 to 5 hours per week. In Table 7.6, on the right side, the TSS values also increase by large amounts.

Having coached hundreds of athletes over the last three-plus decades, I've run into many who found this way of increasing weekly volume for 3 of the 4 weeks to be overly taxing. By the time they got to the third week, they were often quite tired due to the accumulation of training volume, and yet they faced a third week that was even bigger. Workout quality often declined as the weekly training volume increased. For these athletes, I've found it would often work better if the weekly increase in hours was inverted so that the first week in a 4-week period was the biggest and the third the smallest (before starting a rest and recovery week with 7.0 hours). That way, they were fresh for the first week—the biggest—and mentally relieved that the following 2 weeks each took a step down in terms of volume. So essentially, the weekly volume is turned upside down: It declines from the start to the finish of the period.

I really don't know if this method has a greater physical or psychological effect, but having a decreasing weekly volume seems to improve the capacity for some hard-training athletes. If that is done for the same 500-annual-hours volume in the base 3 example above, the weekly hours progression becomes:

> **Week 1:** 15.0
>
> **Week 2:** 13.5
>
> **Week 3:** 11.0
>
> **Week 4:** 7.0

That may not seem like a big deal, but it could make a difference in how well your training goes as the period progresses. Of course, another option for the athlete who still finds the cumulative volume increase over 3 weeks to be a problem is to change the format from 4 weeks to 3 weeks, with the last several days of the third still dedicated to rest and recovery.

Reverse Linear Periodization

The three suggested periodization modifications above still keep the classic linear periodization model intact. These changes are rather small.

Next we'll take a look at how to make a substantial change to the linear model.

Where we are headed now is a planning model called "reverse linear periodization." While this is still a linear model, it no longer follows the classic format. Basically, it takes much of the classic linear model and turns it upside down. Instead of a base period that emphasizes duration while keeping intensity low followed by a build period that emphasizes higher intensity, reverse periodization turns this pattern around. In reverse linear periodization, the base period is made up of high-intensity but low-duration workouts and the build period includes low intensity with high volume. This way of training is popular with athletes who live where the winters are cold and daylight is limited—in other words, where the weather is not conducive to riding outdoors. By reversing the linear periodization model, the short but intense workouts are done in the winter and the long, less intense sessions in the summer. Problem solved. Maybe.

As is sometimes the case, in solving one problem a new one is created. As I explained in Chapter 3 and above, the key to racing success for the advanced athlete is race-like intensity—not duration. You may recall the discussion about how workouts must become increasingly like the demands of the race, in both duration of the workouts and intensity. The shorter the goal A-priority race, the harder it is for the reverse linear model to make the workouts similar to the race. For a short race, the workouts are becoming increasingly different from the race. So if you are an advanced athlete training for a short-duration race such as a criterium, you'll get faster by focusing on higher intensity in the build period weeks, not on long workout durations.

In reverse linear periodization, the base period is made up of high-intensity but low-duration workouts and the build period includes low intensity with high volume.

If, however, you are training for a long, relatively low-intensity event (at or below the anaerobic threshold) such as a century ride, gran fondo, long time trial, or perhaps even a stage race with many stages, this may prove to be an effective training strategy. Why? Because the intensity in such long races is rather low and the duration is quite high compared with races such as crits and short road races.

Using this reverse linear periodization model, you would do the highest-intensity workouts, especially anaerobic endurance and sprint power sessions (see Appendix B), in the base period, with a more moderate intensity between the aerobic and anaerobic thresholds in the build period. Again, the critical key to this decision is making sure you are doing increasingly race-like workouts in the build period. If your race outcome is dependent on very high-intensity efforts for short periods of time, as most road races are, then reverse linear periodization is probably not the best option for you.

But assuming it is an appropriate planning model for you, how would you do it? For the volume of training, reverse the weekly hours and TSS in Tables 7.5 and 7.6. Swap base 2 and build 1 volumes week for week. In other words, the volume in build 1, week 1 becomes the volume for base 2, week 1. And do the same for weeks 2, 3, and 4. Swap out the base 3 and build 2 weeks in the same way. By doing this, you will decrease the volume in the base 2 and 3 periods while increasing it in the build 1 and 2 periods.

And since weekly volumes have been swapped around, workout intensities are reversed in the same manner. This means adjusting Table 8.1 to be more specific about the types of workouts you plan to do, especially the breakthrough sessions. Again, with reverse linear periodization, the higher-intensity workouts will be scheduled for base 2 and 3 in the early weeks of the season, with the more moderate-intensity workouts in the build 1 and 2 periods later in the season as you get closer to race day.

Note that the prep and base 1 periods remain unchanged when it comes to volume and the method of training. Weight lifting also stays the same as originally suggested, although there may be a need to isolate gym workouts from high-intensity sessions in the modified base 2 period should the MS strength phase spill over into part of that period.

Also remaining unchanged are the peak and race periods. The only change is that the intensity of the workouts for these weeks will be at about the anaerobic threshold (for more on this, see Chapter 13).

Again, you should only use reverse linear periodization if your A-priority race is long and the duration is mostly moderate—between the aerobic and anaerobic thresholds. If that is not the case, your training will violate the rule that training should become increasingly like the race as you get closer to the race.

If you are seriously considering reverse linear periodization due to winter-weather training restrictions and the need to ride indoors despite your goal of a highly intense A-priority road race, you might instead consider using the basic concept suggested above for the time-limited rider. Cut back on the higher-duration rides when you're unable to train outside on the road and instead increase the intensity of the planned workout by one zone. Or you may rearrange the weekly workouts so that you do the shorter workouts when you must be indoors.

If your race outcome is dependent on very high-intensity efforts for short periods of time, as most road races are, then reverse linear periodization is probably not the best option for you.

NONLINEAR PERIODIZATION ALTERNATIVES

There are two other planning models that we should examine: "undulating" periodization and "block" periodization. These are the most popular of the nonlinear options and are used by many successful riders.

*Non*linear periodization means that the plan doesn't follow the simple stair-stepping linear format you've been reading about so far. In the classic linear model, you travel a straight path throughout the season, starting with an emphasis on workouts that steadily get longer and then shifting over to an emphasis on gradually increasing intensity as you approach race day. With a reverse periodization plan, you do it the other way around. Either way, it's always linear, with carefully measured stair steps. The two methods we'll now examine don't follow a straight and simple path. They are a bit more complex, yet all they do is manipulate workout duration and intensity. Regardless of your training model, those are the only two session details that can be changed, and what I'm going to describe in what follows are different ways of doing this.

We'll look first at undulating periodization and then at the block model. Both of these are considerably different from what you've read about so far. But just as with linear periodization, they leave a considerable amount of wiggle room for deciding exactly what you'll do in workouts and how you will lay out a plan for them.

Undulating Periodization

This training method, true to its name, is based on changing things around every few days by undulating the two training variables. It's popular with power sports such as weight lifting. That being the case, why as a bike racer would you want to use this planning model? It could be that you can't devote all of the time needed every week to adequately build fitness using linear periodization. You might also feel the need for more variety in your training. Doing the same workouts on the same days week after week with only small tweaks may be getting a bit tiresome. Frequently changing things around, as undulating periodization does, may boost your enthusiasm and motivation for training. Consequently, your fitness and race performances could improve. There aren't many endurance athletes using this model, but I've seen it work well for a few. So you'll likely be on the cutting edge by training this way. That's not necessarily a bad thing.

Undulating periodization for the cyclist alternates intensity and duration weekly, regardless of the period. The most common way to do this is to make 1 week a base-like week, with high duration and volume, and the following a build-like week, with high intensity. This provides a lot of variety, which may make training more enjoyable. It also means doing both high duration and high intensity throughout most of the year. This suggests that when following a 4-week mesocycle with the last week mostly devoted to rest, recovery, and testing, there will be 2 weeks of either high volume or high intensity and only 1 week of the opposite. I suggest that in the early part of the season—for example the first 12 weeks of what is normally called the base period—that you do 2 weeks of high duration in every 4-week period and 1 week of high intensity. Then in the last 12 weeks or so before the race—the build period—do 2 weeks of high intensity separated by 1 week

TABLE 9.3   An Example of 4-Week Base Period in an Undulating Periodization Model

Base week 1	Emphasize duration
Base week 2	Emphasize intensity
Base week 3	Emphasize duration
Base week 4	Rest, Recovery, and Test (see Chapter 11)

TABLE 9.4   An Example of 4-Week Build Period in an Undulating Periodization Model

Build week 1	Emphasize intensity
Build week 2	Emphasize duration
Build week 3	Emphasize intensity
Build week 4	Rest, Recovery, and Test (see Chapter 11)

of high volume. Tables 9.3 and 9.4 illustrate such a plan for undulating duration and intensity.

Of course, "duration" in Tables 9.3 and 9.4 doesn't mean all of the workouts should be equally long. Some should certainly be longer than others. Your capacity for handling high-volume training determines how long each of the individual workouts should last and how many high-duration sessions you can do in a week. It may be 2, 3, or 4, depending on your capacity for work. The other workouts are recovery rides. The same is true for the "intensity" weeks. In this regard, such training may prove risky for the athlete who believes all workouts must be either very long or very intense. The general rule that balances duration and intensity should be followed: The high-duration sessions should be low intensity, mostly zone 2, while the high-intensity sessions must be low duration. Trying to mix both high duration and high intensity for a given workout throughout an undulating system is likely to lead to injury, burnout, or overtraining.

Block Periodization

This is the newest periodization model. It was devised in the 1980s by Vladimir Issurin, a Russian sports scientist. It was created for truly elite athletes, such as professional cyclists, but has also been used successfully by some who aren't quite at that level of performance, such as

the highest category amateur riders. The reasoning behind it has to do with how close the elite athlete is to his or her potential. The closer one is to racing at an extremely high level relative to the best athletes in the world, the more difficult it becomes to make progress. The fitness gains at this level of performance are hard to come by and can be tiny, and yet they can be significant.

For the elite athlete who mixes several types of workouts in a week, as is commonly done when following a linear periodization plan, the problem of making even tiny fitness improvements is compounded. The physiological stress isn't sufficiently focused on any single ability while trying to develop several at the same time. The training stress is spread too thin. The elite athlete is more likely to make fitness gains by focusing attention on only one type of workout in a mesocycle, which is called a "block" in this model. Attempting to develop more than one ability at a time dilutes the physiological effect of each workout. Repeatedly focusing on the same ability in a block produces positive changes much more quickly for the rider at this top level of performance. For example, in one study in which block and linear periodization methods were used, when the athletes repeated the same workouts for a few weeks before changing to another type of workout—as in block periodization—it took them half as many weeks to achieve

> For the elite athlete who mixes several types of workouts in a week, the problem of making even tiny fitness improvements is compounded.

TABLE 9.5 The Dominant and Maintenance Abilities to Be Developed Using Block Periodization and Their Suggested Order of Progression in the Buildup to an A-Priority Race

BLOCK	WEEKS	DOMINANT ABILITY (FOCUS)	MAINTENANCE ABILITY (FOCUS)
Prep	1–4	(Preparing to train)	Muscular force
Early base	4–6	Muscular force	Speed skills
Late base	4–6	Aerobic endurance	Muscular force
Early build	4	Muscular endurance	Aerobic endurance
Late build	4	Anaerobic endurance	Muscular endurance
Peak	1	(Race-like workouts)	(Recovery between workouts)
Race	1	(Race-intensity sessions)	(Taper volume)
Transition	1–4	(Rest and recover)	Aerobic endurance

the same levels of fitness as when they used the classic linear method.

Why is this method not so great for athletes who aren't quite elite? Pro riders and those who are highly advanced have a base of fitness that typically goes back many years, and they are extremely fit relative to the average advanced athlete. All of their abilities are well developed. How can such an advanced athlete get that last 1 percent of improvement? The closer one is to his or her potential, the more difficult it is to make gains. That isn't the case for intermediate-level athletes, and certainly not for novices. They have plenty of room left to advance their fitness and performance. Training load dilution is not an issue. Highly focused training isn't necessary to make significant gains at this level. Should intermediate or novice athletes focus their training on only one ability in a week for several weeks, as suggested here for highly advanced athletes, the other abilities that are not being maintained will fade quite badly. So this method is definitely not suggested for those who are relatively new to serious training or who are *not* podium contenders at high-level races such as national and world championships.

Block periodization seems to work best when there is a focused workout progression that follows a somewhat linear path. In other words, in the base period, the emphasized workouts are still the basic abilities, and in the build period, they are still the advanced abilities.

Table 9.5 offers a suggested pattern for planning workouts throughout the season using block periodization. Here I'm using the terms "early" and "late" in the "Block" column to describe the seasonal progression since the linear base 1, 2, and 3, and build 1 and 2 patterns aren't readily applied in this method. The athlete progresses to the next block once the focal or "dominant" ability is determined to be well established. The lengths of the blocks (found in the "Weeks" column) are only rough guidelines. Any given athlete may need more or less time to achieve the primary objective of a given block. While the dominant ability is being developed, the secondary ability is maintained, which means there are fewer such workouts. The workouts that maintain an ability can be done about half as frequently as the workouts required to initially produce the same dominant

TABLE 9.6 An Example of a Base or Build Training Week Using the Block Periodization Method

MONDAY	TUESDAY	WEDNESDAY	THURSDAY	FRIDAY	SATURDAY	SUNDAY
Maintenance	Dominant	Recovery	Dominant	Maintenance	Recovery	Dominant

Refer to Table 9.5 for a definition of "dominant" and "maintenance" abilities by period.

ability. What would typically be the prep, peak, race, and transition periods remain the same as described in Chapter 7.

Table 9.6 provides an example of how training may be organized for base and build weeks using block periodization. This is only an example of how such a training week may look for an elite rider and would need to be customized for each individual.

A SIMPLE PLAN

If this is your first time through the book, you may be feeling overwhelmed. I've dumped a ton of information about periodization on you. If your head is swimming and you really don't know what to do about planning your season, then this section is for you. Let's look at a simple way of planning.

Remember this rule from earlier in this chapter? Periodization can be boiled down to one simple sentence: *The closer you get to race day, the more like the race your workouts must become.* For the novice rider, this means gradually increasing the frequency of workouts in a week. For the intermediate athlete, it implies increasing the durations of the workouts. And for the advanced rider, who already has frequency and duration nailed down, making the workouts "more like the race" suggests that workout intensity is the primary focus of training.

If this is all you know about periodization and you adhere to it, you'll do fine. Because when it's all said and done, the most important question is, are you prepared to race? If you can answer that question affirmatively—which you can if your workouts gradually become like the race—then you will do well. If you're not sure, then you haven't made your workouts enough like the race. It's that simple.

Making some of your workouts like the race can certainly be accomplished without a degree in sports science. While it's helpful if you understand the subtle nuances of training, it's certainly not necessary in order to race well. With this in mind, let's take a look at a much simpler solution for planning your season.

The simple solution starts with merely laying out a standard week that fits your lifestyle and then keeping it much the same, with only slight changes as you progress through the season. That's it. Once you have finalized your standard week, all you need to do is repeat it for 2 or 3 consecutive weeks before taking a few days of rest and recovery, which is explained in Chapter 11. As the season progresses, your standard week remains largely the same. All that changes are the details of the workouts as they become increasingly race-like over several weeks.

To make the workouts more race-like, the advanced rider begins the season by increasing workout durations. The workouts become a little longer every few weeks while the intensity remains low—mostly zones 1 and 2. This is when the basic abilities are developed: aerobic

The closer you get to race day, the more like the race your workouts must become.

endurance, muscular force, and speed skills. That's the base period and takes about 10 to 12 weeks to be well established.

In the build period, the next 10 or so weeks, the amount of time at a race-like intensity is increased while the workout durations slightly decrease. Now the advanced abilities are improved: muscular endurance, anaerobic endurance, and sprint power. This period should include fast group rides and races. Slightly decreasing the duration as the intensity increases keeps the workouts from being so hard that recovery is prolonged. You may only do 2 or 3 race-intensity workouts weekly. This comes down to your capacity for work and how quickly you recover.

If you set up a standard week and follow these simple guidelines, all you need to do beyond that is taper your volume in the last 2 or 3 weeks prior to your race. You do this by making your workout durations shorter, as described in Chapter 13. This simplified planning method will improve your fitness, boost your confidence, and bring you to race day ready to go.

SUMMARY: PLANNING ALTERNATIVES

Now that you've read all three chapters in Part IV, you should be ready to decide which periodization model you will use to prepare for your next A-priority race. I've proposed two commonly used model categories: linear and nonlinear. I've also proposed a very simple planning method. Should you decide to use the linear model, return to Chapters 7 and 8 and follow the step-by-step guidelines there to create your plan. If you intend to follow a modified linear plan as described

Once you create a plan, do not consider it final and fixed.

earlier in this chapter, then make adjustments as needed as you reread the previous chapters. Planning with the nonlinear models will be a little more complex, but typically athletes who use these systems are experienced enough to know how to plug them into a plan. If you've never created a training plan before and are brand new to periodization, follow the classic linear pattern that is the focus of the previous two chapters. To keep it really easy, use the simplified method described near the end of this chapter.

As mentioned earlier, once you create a plan, do not consider it final and fixed. You'll need to make changes throughout the season as unexpected demands placed on your time cause you to skip a workout now and then. Of course, race day never changes, so you must make modifications for the coming weeks that will get you back on track. The section in Chapter 8 titled "Missed Workouts" can help you make these decisions.

A good time to preview the coming week's training and make adjustments is on Sunday, after your last ride of the week. After recording your workout, look at the coming week's plan. Will it work as scheduled? If so, you're ready to go again starting tomorrow. If there are doubts, then make adjustments based on how the week you just finished went, your current levels of fitness and fatigue, and known lifestyle activities in the coming week that may require you to make adjustments. This takes a few minutes, but the payoff is an appropriate weekly plan that you can precisely follow.

The bottom line is that your training plan is both a guide to what you will do and also a record of what you have done. Plan ahead, make modifications as necessary, and avoid making last-minute changes as you are rolling out of your driveway to start a ride; they are sure to result in random training and poor race performance. Always keep a written ledger of what you've done in your training diary (see Chapter 14) so that when it comes time to plan the next season you have a record of what has and hasn't worked. A written plan for this season will prove invaluable when it comes time to design your next season. It gets easier every time you do it.

PART V

STRESS AND RECOVERY

What have we accomplished so far? The first six chapters were an overview of the philosophy and methodology of high-performance training. In Chapters 7, 8, and 9, we covered a lot of ground on the periodization of your season. That leads to actually riding your bike. But before delving into some of the proposed workouts, which we'll do in Chapters 12 and 13, let's step back from planning for a moment and set the stage for Chapters 10 and 11 by putting where we are headed into context.

For the high-performance rider, training is everything you do in life. It's not just riding your bike; training also includes your daily routine and obligations. Performance can't be compartmentalization into just what you do on the road. Nothing in life works that way. Everything you do contributes to your race results. For example, if your job is physically demanding, its demands will certainly impact how much energy and enthusiasm you have for riding every day. Even if your work isn't physical, it can leave you dispirited and drained when it's time to ride. It doesn't end there. What you do for work certainly produces stress, but so does what you think, who you spend time with, what you eat, and everything else in your life. Then there are the life-changing events that have a tremendous impact on your level of stress, including changing jobs, moving, getting a divorce, experiencing financial problems, and many more.

You must remove excessive training and lifestyle stress during recovery in order to restore a normal and manageable level of stress to your daily routine. This is usually a physical process, but it can also be mental, for example listening to music or chatting with friends are great ways to unwind mentally.

The next two chapters take a deeper look at the interplay of stress and recovery for the high-performance athlete. We'll start by examining the point at which training stress becomes excessive—in other words, when training stress goes beyond what you are capable of physically handling. That isn't pretty, but I'm sure you've experienced it on more than one occasion.

Of course, stress isn't always a bad thing. Stressing the body beyond its current muscular state is necessary to create the potential for fitness. So we'll look at that, too. Then, in Chapter 11, we'll delve into the other side of training: recovery. That's when the potential created by hard rides results in fitness. The balance between these two opposites, stress and recovery, produces your race results. One without the other is meaningless.

TRAINING STRESS

THERE'S ONE THING that sets exceptionally high-performing riders apart from everyone else: how much physical training stress they can handle. We can measure that stress in many ways. We could talk about how many miles or hours they ride in a week. You've probably seen what the pros do in this regard. Twenty-five hours on a saddle and 500 miles a week is normal at that level. In earlier chapters, we also looked at using the Training Stress Score (TSS) as a much more precise way of measuring your training load, since it includes workout intensity in addition to duration. The pros typically average around 150 TSS per week throughout much of the season. That's a huge number.

I often hear "normal" athletes say that it's as if the pros are from another planet—perhaps Krypton. But then pros may not have all of the other stressors in their lives that you have in yours: a 40-hour-plus job, kids, a mortgage, and many other responsibilities. Managing it all comes down to how much stress, of all kinds, you can handle.

This chapter is about stress, but not all kinds. We'll be looking specifically at the physical stress that results from training. Mental and emotional stress are beyond the scope of this book, but you must certainly take them into consideration. I've known athletes who had to cut way back on training—or even stop—in order to cope with a psychologically stressful event. That's often necessary, because stress doesn't occur in a compartment separate from the rest of our lives. Stress affects the entire person, no matter where or how it originates. The body reacts in much the same way, regardless of the cause.

A mid-20th-century Austro-Hungarian endocrinologist named Hans Selye proposed that there were two types of stress: eustress and distress. Selye defined eustress as healthy stress. In the context of this book, when the training load is manageable and produces increased fitness, it's eustress. On the other hand, excessive training produces distress. Society generally uses the word "stress" to mean "distress," which implies both its mental and emotional aspects. But that's not how Selye described the term.

Selye also proposed that predictable physiological reactions occur when an organism experiences either of these types of stress. Training eustress produces fatigue followed by fitness, as was discussed in Chapter 3. That's very healthy. When training is distressful, it results in excessive fatigue that we call overtraining. Not good.

It's sometimes necessary to flirt with distress in order to produce a high level of performance. In Chapter 8, I explained crash training, a technique used when preparing for a stage race. That would certainly fall into the category of distress. Distressful training is not to be taken lightly. It's serious and can even be dangerous. You'll see how to manage it a little later in this chapter.

How much training stress can you handle without becoming exceedingly distressed? There's only one way to find out: Push your limits. Ride more miles, with more intensity, or both. But be careful. This is dangerous. Test your limits infrequently, and only when your lifestyle stress is very low. A good time might be at a cycling camp or when you're taking a vacation from work. You must pay very close attention to your body during such experiments. More on that later.

The purpose of this chapter is to examine training stress and how you can ensure that it is composed mostly of eustress, with carefully measured amounts of distress, so you can achieve a healthy and high level of fitness. We will start by examining two pairs of related yin and yang topics: risk and reward, and overreaching and overtraining.

> When training is distressful, it results in excessive fatigue that we call overtraining.

> Risk has to do with workouts and training methods that have a high potential for causing breakdowns. Reward is all about getting fitter and faster.

RISK AND REWARD

Do you push yourself so hard that you often break down with an injury or miss workouts due to illness? Do you sometimes feel burned out or have low motivation to train? Or do you find that despite steadily training at a safe workload, you simply can't reach the level of performance you feel you are capable of? These situations have to do with another set of workout opposites: risk and reward.

Risk has to do with workouts and training methods that have a high potential for causing breakdowns because they are so strenuous. If you experience such breakdowns several times each season, then your workouts are either unnecessarily stressful or you are crowding otherwise manageable workouts too closely together. Your training load is too often excessively challenging. That's always the case when someone breaks down.

Sports medicine doctors sometimes refer to these breakdowns as "too much, too soon." Had you been a bit more conservative in your training, the breakdown could have been avoided. When you do too much too often, you break the dose and density concept explained in Chapter 3. The workout dose may be too great, producing distress, or more likely, you messed up the density, with hard workouts too compactly spaced over too short a period of time.

On the other side of this coin, reward refers to the positive outcomes of workouts that are appropriately stressful—in other words, they achieve eustress. Reward is all about getting fitter and faster. To reap workout rewards, the risks of doing periodic hard workouts must be kept at a dose and density that is high but stays just within your physical limits most of the time. That "most of the time" takes us back to crash training, which you'll recall must be done sparingly. While there's no doubt that crash training is risky, it also presents the potential for high reward. The bottom line is that some level of risk is necessary for high performance. In training, seldom does anything good come from the complete avoidance of risk. It's possible to be too conservative.

You can be so conservative in training and so concerned with risk avoidance that you achieve little or no increase in fitness for weeks at a time. Because you're reading this book, though, I suspect that doesn't describe you. You're more likely pushing the limits of risk frequently in order to hasten greater fitness for an upcoming race. That's what high-performance athletes do.

Figure 10.1 illustrates the risk-reward curve. Change the words in the figure a bit, and this could be a guide for investing in the stock market. Wise investors know that a stock with a high potential for monetary reward is accompanied by a high degree of risk. Blue chip stocks, those with a long history of slow but steady growth, are generally low risk. The reward of investing in these stocks is small, but the risk of losing your money is low. The opposite is true if you invest in a new company selling a new technology. You could become wealthy in a short period of time, or you could lose it all. Risk and reward are both high in this case.

So it is with training. When the risk is low, the reward is also low; when risk is high, reward is also high. Just as with a stock market investment, training has the potential to go either way. The key is finding balance. This takes the wisdom of knowing what your body can handle, the patience to stay the course, and a commitment to your plan.

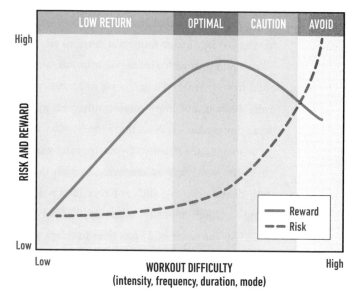

FIGURE 10.1   The risk-reward curve

Frequently, overinvesting in high-risk training through excessive volume or intensity is likely to result in injury, illness, burnout, or overtraining. On the underinvesting side, riders who do mostly short-duration, low-intensity workouts are unlikely to experience training setbacks, but their race results will always be poor. That's what comes of low-risk training. Of course, it's highly unusual for a truly serious rider to undertrain. It's nearly always the other way around.

The way to keep the risk relatively high yet manageable is to be a tad restrained with dose and density. For example, you should not start your weight lifting program at the beginning of a new season with high loads and low reps. Save those for the muscular strength (MS) phase. Jumping immediately into a high-intensity MS workout is very risky. It's much smarter to let your body gradually adapt by starting the season with light loads and high reps and then, over several sessions, increasing the loads while reducing the reps. Given enough time, your body will

The way to keep risk relatively high yet manageable is to be restrained with dose and density.

make adjustments that slowly prepare you for heavier loads. Similarly, interval sessions on the bike should start with a manageable intensity and build from there. You'll gain a bit of fitness with every session, but more importantly, you won't break down after a session that's too hard.

Managing the density of your training works much the same way as managing session dose. High-dose workouts—such as heavy-load weight lifting or high-intensity intervals—should be spaced so that your body has time to adapt and grow stronger between workouts. Adaptation can't be rushed. You may need 48 hours or more of recovery for your body to grow stronger. The change after a single session is miniscule, but given enough small incremental changes, you will make great progress over time—without risking a breakdown.

Please note that I am not saying you should never do high-dose workouts that may also be high density. There's a time and place for such training. But it's certainly not something you should do frequently, and these workouts must be strictly managed. When doing high-dose and high-density training, be patient: It's the key to making steady progress while avoiding setbacks. Allow your body time to adapt before doing another risky workout. If you don't, you greatly increase the risk of overtraining.

AVOIDING OVERTRAINING

The word "overtraining" is batted around rather casually by serious athletes. When asked, most will admit they've trained exceptionally hard at times, and perhaps even continue to do so frequently. As a result, they say, they are often overtrained. That's unlikely. Overtraining, or the "overtraining syndrome," as it's usually referred to

in sports medicine, is a little-understood condition in which the body has become overwhelmed by the stress of training. It's in a state of distress. The word that better describes the experiences of serious athletes who have merely pushed the limits of their training too far is "overreaching." Most self-professed *overtrained* riders are actually *overreached*. Overreaching is an early stage of the progression that can lead to overtraining syndrome.

The difference between overreaching and overtraining is that when you are overreached, despite being very tired, recovery is still adequate, allowing the body to adapt and grow stronger. When you're overtrained, recovery is inadequate and the body experiences a decline in performance—and fitness—despite a high training load.

Truly being overtrained is not something to be taken lightly. It's among the worst physical conditions an athlete can experience. And yet paradoxically, in order to reach a high level of fitness it's something you must always flirt with. It's a risk you must take if you are to perform at a high level. The key is knowing how to reap the rewards while avoiding the breakdowns. Flirting with overtraining is what overreaching is all about. It's at the core of high-performance training. How can you overreach and yet avoid overtraining? Let's explore the answers to that question.

The reason why overtraining syndrome is so poorly understood by those in the sports medicine field is that it's hard to pin down. The symptoms are difficult to define because they are so diverse and vary widely among overtrained athletes. The only symptoms that are common are poor performance and fatigue. But these can occur when an athlete is just overreached and not overtrained.

What we do know is how overtraining occurs. It happens when an athlete ignores fatigue from

High-dose workouts should be spaced so that your body has time to adapt and grow stronger between workouts.

overreaching and continues high-stress training with inadequate rest and recovery. These circumstances greatly increase the possibility of overtraining and a subsequent decline not only in fitness and performance but also in health.

How long one can continue in an overreached state before becoming overtrained depends on a few individual factors. Young riders may press on for several weeks while on the edge of exhaustion before becoming officially overtrained. It could take a month or more for this to occur. Senior riders and those who are relatively new to the sport may become overtrained in less than three weeks. And there may be other individual characteristics that speed up or delay the onset of overtraining.

If an athlete is only overreached, it's possible to shed the accumulated fatigue by resting or training very easily for a few days in order to avoid overtraining. After that, the athlete can return to normal high-stress training. But once overtraining syndrome has fully taken over the body, the fatigue will not go away so easily. Besides the physical indicator of fatigue, the rider generally becomes listless, grumpy, and unmotivated. These common psychological symptoms are usually identified by a spouse or close friend. But there are other indicators that something is wrong.

Table 10.1 lists the common symptoms of overtraining. Not all of these will occur with every athlete. In fact, an overtrained rider or close companion may only be aware of a couple of them. Also notice that several are contradictory, such as "hungrier than normal" and "loss of appetite." This is due to the progression of symptoms and the source of overtraining, such as excessively high workout durations or intensities.

Many of the common symptoms listed here may also occur with diseases such as chronic fatigue syndrome, Lyme disease, or the early stages of infectious mononucleosis. In fact, an athlete who experiences deep and lingering fatigue along with any of the other symptoms listed in Table 10.1 should see a physician to be tested for these and other medical conditions that may present with similar symptoms. The most common way to diagnose overtraining is to eliminate other possible diseases with comparable symptoms.

Frequent training that exceeds what the body is capable of adapting to is common among serious athletes. And, as mentioned above, this is often necessary in order to achieve high levels of performance. But in the absence of timely and adequate recovery, this is a formula for athletic disaster. We'll get into the topic of recovery more fully in Chapter 11.

MANAGING OVERREACHING

I've suggested several times that overreaching among serious athletes is not only common but also necessary from time to time. It's a risk that must be taken in order to reap the rewards. The key to avoiding overtraining while overreaching is frequent recovery. That's why in Chapters 7 and 8 I suggested that you include extended rest and recovery breaks from hard training about every third or fourth week during the base and build periods. These breaks help you shed the accumulated fatigue of the previous period. If you've been overreaching, these R&R breaks will be rejuvenating. Your batteries will be recharged and ready to go again. You'll also find out if you're overtrained, because the fatigue won't go away—even if you go several days with no workouts at all during these breaks. That's unlikely, but it does happen from time to time with extremely motivated riders.

> Overtraining occurs when an athlete ignores fatigue from overreaching and continues high-stress training with inadequate rest and recovery.

TABLE 10.1 **Common Symptoms of Overtraining Syndrome by Category**

CATEGORY	SYMPTOMS
Physical	Resting heart rate higher or lower than usual
	Weight loss
	Hungrier than normal
	Loss of appetite
	Lethargy
	Restless sleep, insomnia
	Chronic fatigue
	Muscle soreness
	Joint soreness
	Slow-healing minor cuts
	Menstrual cycle dysfunction
Performance	Hard workout performance greatly reduced
	Bike power low at a given heart rate
	Unable to complete workouts
	Decreased muscular strength
	Poor muscular coordination
	Mediocre bike-handling skills
	Deterioration of skills
Psychological	Moody, grumpy, and emotional
	Apathetic
	Low motivation to train
	Poor concentration
	Decreased self-esteem
	Very high race anxiety
	Loss of competitiveness
	Depression
Physiological	Low peak lactate level
	Heart rate low at a high power or pace
	High heart rate at low to moderate power intensities
	Perceived exertion high at a given power output
	Low heart rate variability
	Increased oxygen consumption during submaximal exercise
	Reduced maximal exercise capacity
Immunological	Increased susceptibility to colds, flu, and allergies
	Swollen lymph glands
	Bacterial infection
	Abnormal white blood cell differentials
Biochemical	Reduced muscle glycogen concentration
	Elevated serum cortisol
	Decreased serum ferritin
	Decreased bone mineral density

Essentially, overreaching is managed over-training. Management has to do with training at a high workload while constantly paying attention to how you are responding to the stress. The single most important question to ask is, how do I feel today? If you answer, "I feel tired" for several days in a row, then you need to recover—regardless of where you are in your plan. It doesn't matter if you're in a base or build period, or even if your race is just around the corner on your calendar; you need to stop and rest up now. The downside of the resulting tiny fitness loss is not worth the potential huge loss of fitness that would occur should you become overtrained.

We might call this managed approach to stressful training "deliberate overreaching." It's achieved by paying close attention to both stress and rest. That's why I've placed so much emphasis on periodization in this book. The purpose is to emphasize recovery and adaptation. The latter is what happens when you train hard and then recover. With periodized training, you lay out a plan that alternates hard training days with recovery days. The reason for including all of these breaks from serious training should now be obvious. It's to make sure you don't push yourself into an overtrained condition. If your training is appropriately hard, the preplanned breaks should come at about the right times.

Table 10.2 summarizes this discussion by showing the common progression from deliberate, performance-enhancing overreaching to negative, performance-degrading overtraining.

TABLE 10.2 The Common Progression from Moderate Overreaching to Overtraining Syndrome

PROGRESSION	STAGE	COMMON SYMPTOMS
1	Moderate overreaching	High perceived fatigue Minimal change in performance 24–36 hours of rest restores training capacity Performance improves following 1–2 days of rest
2	Functional overreaching	Very high perceived fatigue Performance decline is possible Several days of rest required to resume normal training Performance improves following a few days of recovery
3	Nonfunctional overreaching	Very high perceived fatigue Performance decline is obvious Several days of rest required to resume normal training Performance is not improved after a few days of recovery
4	Overtraining syndrome	Very heavy perceived fatigue Performance decline is obvious More than 1 month of rest needed to shed fatigue and resume training Performance greatly diminished after adequate recovery time Competitive season is over

SUMMARY: TRAINING STRESS

As much as I hate to say it, in training, greed is the greatest emotional challenge for advanced athletes. Our insatiable desire for fitness often pushes us to the edge of what the human body can safely handle. This creates massive fatigue. The fatigue is so great that it is generally enough to stop most of us from forging ahead. But some athletes are so highly motivated that they push beyond the fatigue boundaries that nature commonly uses to tell them, "That's enough." This creates a deep physiological imbalance. But the body has the final say. It responds by developing what's known in sports medicine as overtraining syndrome. There are many symptoms for this condition (see Table 10.1). The most common are fatigue and a decline in athletic performance.

There are many other common overtraining symptoms beyond fatigue and poor performance. They aren't the same for all athletes, probably due to individual hormonal strengths and weaknesses, and to the unique characteristics of the training that caused the condition. This usually comes down to the interplay of workout duration and intensity over several weeks.

The cure for greed is patience. But that's easier said than done. Given the need to train from time to time with some degree of risk—meaning overreaching—the advanced athlete frequently experiences fatigue. That's normal and to be expected. But if the fatigue is extremely high for a long period, usually several weeks, then the rider experiences exhaustion and overtraining kicks in.

Before arriving at overtraining syndrome, the athlete often becomes sick or injured, forc-

In training, greed is the greatest emotional challenge for advanced athletes.

ing a termination of hard training for some time. While these certainly aren't desirable training outcomes, they are preferable to overtraining syndrome and beneficially interrupt excessive training. They force at least a temporary return to a manageable training load. This is the body's way of protecting itself from your avarice.

All of these setbacks can generally be avoided by following a carefully designed training plan as described in Chapters 7 and 8. For the serious rider, a well-wrought training plan will allow room for deliberate overreaching—training only slightly beyond what the body can handle—while including extended recovery breaks from training every 3 or 4 weeks.

The bottom line is stress. Getting the right amount of stress in your training comes down to experience. There is no one-size-fits-all formula for determining what your training load should be. You must determine what you can handle over time; it's highly individualized. You will know when you've done too much in a workout or a closely spaced series of workouts. The most common sign is that your readiness to go hard again will slow. It may take more than 36 hours to recover. If you are still fatigued 48 hours after a workout, you might reasonably assume the preceding training was too hard. In this situation, "fatigue" means you are unable to repeat the workout or another similarly challenging session. You've achieved stage 2: functional overreaching (see Table 10.2). Of course, over time, as your fitness increases with patient training, what was once an overly hard stage 2 workout becomes a moderate stage 1. That's the result of deliberate and measured overreaching.

There are times when an experienced rider may decide to take a bit of risk by doing a stage 2 workout or even doing several stage 1 sessions in a brief period of time, as with crash training (see Chapter 8 for details). But the risk must be carefully calculated and your fatigue closely watched. Avoiding injury, illness, and overtraining at such times still requires some degree of moderation. Your season could come crashing down if you push your body just a bit too far for even a few days. Patience is always necessary, especially with such risky training.

On the other hand, if you aren't tired after 2 or 3 weeks of training in the base or build periods, you aren't training hard enough. The risk is much too low to produce a reward. As explained in Chapter 3, fitness and fatigue trend the same direction. If fatigue doesn't occasionally happen, neither will fitness. You must frequently become tired if you are to become fitter. So fatigue is a good thing, not something to be totally avoided. The only issue at hand is how long the fatigue lasts. That conundrum is at the heart of overtraining.

Effective training is the balanced blending of stress and recovery. That's it. Nothing else. This chapter looked at only half of this: the stress part. Now let's examine the other half: recovery.

FATIGUE, RECOVERY, AND ADAPTATION

IN CHAPTER 3, I told you that a hard workout creates fatigue that represents the potential for fitness. That new level of fitness is realized as you recover. When you take it easy during recovery, the body's adaptive process kicks in and your body goes through a gradual change. The body restores and rebuilds itself by repairing damaged cells, creating new neural pathways, expanding capillary beds, rebalancing chemistry, developing muscle fibers, and much more.

The physiological reconstruction that follows a hard workout makes all of the body's affected systems slightly better able to handle the stress that produced the fatigue (and therefore the need for recovery). This is called *overcompensation.* Overcompensation is at the heart of adaptation. The ultimate result is that the three determiners of your endurance fitness—aerobic capacity, anaerobic threshold, and economy—improve slightly following recovery after a hard workout. The degree to which your fitness improves

is determined by the type and magnitude of the workout stress applied and the quality and quantity of the recovery.

Recovery and adaptation are, to some extent, the same thing. Both take time and can't be hurried. How much time you need to reduce fatigue and gain fitness depends on how great the preceding workout stress was. If it was only slightly more difficult than what your body was already adapted to, you will probably be ready for another stressful workout again in around 48 hours or less. A workout that was a great deal harder than your current level of adaptation requires a longer period of recovery.

The fatigue you experience following a hard workout is how nature tries to keep you from doing back-to-back hammer sessions that would tear your body down so much it could no longer adapt. An exceptionally high level of fatigue, indicating a very stressful workout, is risky. Combine this with too little recovery time, and you're on the way to overtraining. But the other side of the workout coin isn't much better. Only doing easy rides day after day or frequently taking days off results in a loss of fitness. This is the opposite of overcompensation and takes us back to the discussion of the reversibility principle in Chapter 3.

The key to effective training is to strike a balance between stress and recovery so that fatigue is created by a hard workout and then reduced as adaptation occurs. In this chapter, we look at how adaptation is enhanced by paying close attention to fatigue and recovery.

There is no improvement in fitness without at least some fatigue. How much fatigue is necessary for improvement? Unfortunately, that's hard to nail down because fatigue isn't as easily measured as fitness, at least not yet. While there are a few ways of measuring it, precise tests, such as those used in measuring VO_2max or anaerobic threshold, don't exist for fatigue. That makes recovery more art than science and requires some guesswork in order to come up with the proper recovery dose for the given stress load that produced it. And it means that recovery from fatigue is mostly based on self-perception and sensations.

Sports science, however, is slowly getting better at measuring what the body experiences after a hard workout. These scientific breakthroughs allow us to make better-educated guesses at how much recovery may be needed on a given day. We'll examine some of these tools for measuring fatigue in this chapter. But since we currently know much more about using perceived sensations to gauge recovery from fatigue, I'll place a greater emphasis on that.

What further confounds this search for precision is that recovery is highly specific to the individual. Not all of the recovery methods described in this chapter work equally well for all athletes, even after similar training sessions with similar levels of fatigue. The challenge is to figure out what works for you by trying several things. Even then, the effectiveness of your chosen recovery methods may vary from one workout to the next.

Working your way through all of the recovery suggestions in this chapter won't be easy, not only because there are quite a few but also because some involve using special and somewhat expensive gear. On the other hand, you probably already have a great deal of experience with some of the methods described here. Most advanced athletes soon figure out these things as their racing careers progress.

Here's an example of the individuality of recovery. Most advanced athletes find that an easy ride—called "active recovery"—stimulates recovery and therefore contributes to adaptation. Most novice riders and many intermediates, however, find that a day off the bike—"passive recovery"—is usually the better option (for an example of an active recovery workout, see AE1 in Appendix B).

Connecting the dots leads to the conclusion that fatigue is good because it implies the potential for fitness and decreasing fatigue over time is an indicator of adaptation and therefore represents realized fitness. That's a big deal. So the overarching lesson in this chapter is that recovery is just as critical to success in cycling as hard workouts. If you are good at doing one but not the other, you will fall well short of your potential in the sport. It takes both the stress of training and the adaptive process of recovery to be well adapted and race ready.

The key to effective training is to strike a balance between stress and recovery.

Most advanced athletes find that an easy ride—called "active recovery"—stimulates recovery and therefore contributes to adaptation.

MEASURING FATIGUE

How do you know when you're tired? Dumb question? Perhaps not, as there are many subtle levels of tiredness. In Chapter 4, we used a 0 to 10 scale to rate your perception of workout intensity; we can rate fatigue on a similar scale. The higher the rating, the greater your fatigue. At some point on this scale, you will say you're tired. Actually, you're probably always at least a bit tired—that just comes with being a serious athlete. A level of fatigue that's related to fitness-enhancing adaptation during recovery is higher on the scale, however. So let's say that such a level of fatigue officially occurs when you rate it as 7 or higher. That should happen fairly frequently after hard workouts or a densely spaced series of moderate to hard workouts. It will also happen at the end of several weeks of training. So when you sense your fatigue is 7 or higher, it's time for a recovery day—or several.

Now let's throw a monkey wrench into the works: There are other things in your life besides riding a bike that add to the stress you experience and contribute to your self-perception of fatigue. These other stressors could be related to your career, family, friends, finances, domestic stability, or any number of other important aspects of your life. These have the potential to be Hans Selye's *distressors*, making your fatigue level even higher. When there are so many lifestyle stresses in addition to hard workouts, is there any sure way of knowing that you've reached your limit and need a break from training?

The short answer is no. There is nothing that tells you with certainty that non-training stress in your life has pushed your cumulative fatigue too high. Someday we may have a way of measuring and quantifying emotional stress so that it can be factored into the recovery process, but we're not even close to that now. So we'll stay focused here on training stress as it relates to recovery. Just keep in mind that you cannot discount or ignore your daily lifestyle stressors. They must always be taken into consideration when it comes to the fatigue-recovery process.

Fatigue-Measuring Devices

While we don't have a way to objectively measure fatigue related specifically to training, there are some high-tech gadgets that allow us to measure total fatigue. The three devices presented below have been around for a while, but they are relatively new to sport. We are still learning their nuances. But they do allow you to get a rough idea of how fatigued you are. As with similar devices, you will need to take some time to learn how to interpret what the collected data mean.

Heart rate variability. Tools to determine heart health have long been used on cardiac patients. All measure the interval between heartbeats and then compare those time differentials to draw conclusions about a person's rested or fatigued status. In the early 2000s, sports scientists began studying heart rate variability (HRV) to see what could be learned about an athlete's level of fatigue.

Essentially, what HRV tells us is how the body is reacting to stress. It does this by using the autonomic nervous system (ANS) to reflect one's stress status. The ANS is in control of many of the body's systems, such as breathing, digestion, the need to pee, and heart rate. You usually aren't aware that any of this is going on in the background of your daily life. The ANS's control over heart rate is especially interesting.

> Heart rate variability tells us how the body is reacting to stress.

Within the ANS there are two branches: the sympathetic and parasympathetic nervous systems. They operate in opposite ways to control the body. The sympathetic system contributes to the fight-or-flight response that has helped humans cope for eons with stressful situations such as being attacked by a saber-toothed cat. While such animal attacks are unlikely now, there are other things in our lives that the sympathetic nervous system still considers threats. In its own way, a hard workout or race is one of them. The parasympathetic system, on the other hand, keeps you calm and dampens your physical reaction to excitement. When you go to a race start line, the sympathetic system makes your heart beat faster to get you ready for the "fight" while you try to stay calm by concentrating on breathing slowly and relaxing, activities that are related to the parasympathetic system.

As your workouts become increasingly demanding over time and fatigue accumulates, the sympathetic nervous system becomes dominant. This causes a reduction in heart rate variability. In other words, the timing between beats becomes more consistent. When you're thoroughly rested, the parasympathetic nervous system is in control of your heart rate, and that results in greater variability—in other words, the time between beats varies a lot and is inconsistent.

Measuring HRV at a standard time, such as first thing in the morning, provides feedback on which of the two opposing systems is dominant. If variability is low, meaning the sympathetic system is running things, fatigue is high. If variability is high, fatigue is low. Realize that "low" and "high" are relative terms. It takes a fair amount of collected HRV data to know what all of this means for you. The software instructions that come with HRV devices help you understand what the numbers mean. With such knowledge, you have a more precise way of determining how tired you are as opposed to simply estimating fatigue on a 10-point scale.

There are several tools on the market in this category, and most involve using a chest strap, finger sensor, or wrist sensor. You can do a web search for "heart rate variability" to find what is currently offered.

Muscle glycogen content. There are several physiological indicators that fatigue has occurred following a hard workout. One of the most widely accepted in sports science is the depletion of muscle glycogen levels. Glycogen, a form of carbohydrate, is one of ways the body stores energy. Most of this energy source is stockpiled in the muscles, where it can be quickly accessed during exercise. While riding, your body uses glycogen along with stored fat to produce the energy necessary to turn the pedals.

Compared with stored fat, there is relatively little glycogen in the body, even for the skinniest rider. When glycogen starts to run low, fatigue sets in. As glycogen levels become very low, an athlete is said to have "hit the wall" or to have "bonked." This results in an extreme level of fatigue and makes even soft pedaling an ordeal.

After a hard ride that leaves you with reduced muscle glycogen levels, the food you eat restocks glycogen in the muscles so you can ride hard again. This restocking process takes several hours. Restored muscle glycogen levels are an indicator that recovery, at least in part, has been successful. In the past, the only sure way to measure your glycogen level was to snip out a small sample of muscle, usually from the thigh. Doing this repeat-

The sympathetic system contributes to the fight-or-flight response that has helped humans cope for eons with stressful situations.

The parasympathetic system keeps you calm and dampens your physical reaction to excitement.

edly for several hours would reveal the changes happening during recovery. This procedure is called a "biopsy" and is not the sort of thing anyone would do, except in a scientific study.

Now, however, there is a tool on the market that measures muscle glycogen levels without the need for a biopsy. It's called MuscleSound, and it uses a wand-like device to non-invasively measure muscle glycogen levels. With data gleaned from the device, an athlete can adjust nutrition, rest, workload, and view muscle energy trends over time to optimize training by getting this portion of recovery right. The downside is cost. At several hundred dollars per month for use, there are few riders or even cycling teams that can afford this tool. At the moment, it's used mostly in clinics and by professional and collegiate baseball, football, and basketball teams. While it's currently not practical for personal use, expect to see the price come down as this technology becomes more competitive.

Your smartphone and computer. While MuscleSound is beyond reach for most of us, you probably have a smartphone and a computer. All you need in addition to that is some reliable fatigue-measuring software. There are a few apps and web-based software systems that help you measure fatigue. A couple of examples as of this writing are HRV4Training and Restwise. HRV4Training measures heart rate variability using the camera on your phone—an ingenious idea. Restwise is a website that assesses 11 markers of overtraining-related fatigue such as resting heart rate, body weight, sleep, hydration, appetite, and muscle soreness. It asks you a series of self-perception queries and plugs your answers into an algorithm that gives you feedback on how to train on any given day. It also helps you spot gradual trends over time that may not be obvious to you.

Morning Warnings

Even with sophisticated recovery-measuring devices, apps, and software, determining fatigue still comes down to paying close attention to how you are feeling. So far, there is really no device that tops this. While the abovementioned tools can give you a fairly good idea of how fatigued you are, it's still important that you judge how you are feeling every day based on the 0 to 10 fatigue scale. This can be done by rating various indicators of overreaching, which are nothing more than the early stages of overtraining. Do this at the start of every day. I call these "morning warnings" because they are most obvious when you wake up, first thing in the morning.

Routinely paying attention to these indicators at the start of every day provides feedback on how your stress-recovery balance is doing. Occasionally, you may realize that your fatigue is high. This realization is signaled by several sensations. Some of these sensations are warnings. But they aren't always actionable. You may have one or even two overreaching warnings even when things are going well with training and your life. That just comes with the athlete's lifestyle. It's the cumulative weight of several warnings that tells you how great your fatigue is—and that recovery is needed.

Table 11.1 lists several common morning warnings. I suggest making a copy of this list and placing it by your bed. The first thing in the morning, before getting up, quickly scan the list and reply yes or no to each warning question in the middle column. Don't pause to think about

Even with sophisticated measuring devices, determining fatigue still comes down to paying close attention to how you are feeling.

them. Just give each a quick and dirty evaluation. We aren't talking about subtleties here, only that you're experiencing a fatigue warning sensation (a yes) or not (a no). Note the "yes score" every time you answer yes. Add up the yes scores for the day. If the total is fewer than 7, you have a normal training day ahead. But if the score is 7 or higher, you need recovery. That could be an active (easy ride) or passive (day off) training day.

Again, any one of these warnings by itself is probably not enough to warrant a recovery day, unless it is extreme. For example, consider the "Health" warning. If you awake with a sore throat, it's probably a good idea—regardless of your total score—to significantly lower your stress that day.

The warnings on this list may serve not only as indicators of your recovery but also as a measure of your training load. If you seldom experience any of the warnings in Table 11.1 and your score

is nearly always less than 7, then your training is probably not hard enough. You could do more. Frequently identifying warnings of fatigue with scores of 7 or higher every few days means you are doing something right in training. Frequent fatigue is normal for a serious athlete; as discussed in Chapter 3, fitness and fatigue go hand in hand. They trend in the same direction. When fatigue increases, so does fitness. Conversely, if there is never fatigue, there is never fitness. So paying close attention to how fatigued you are on a daily basis serves a double role in your training.

RECOVERY AND ADAPTATION

Recovery is more than just a marker of your readiness to train hard again or of the difficulty of your workouts. And it's not merely about

Frequent fatigue is normal for a serious athlete.

TABLE 11.1 **Common Morning Warning Indicators**

INDICATORS	WARNINGS (YES OR NO)	YES SCORE
Appetite	Very high or very low?	1
Waking pulse	High?	1
Enthusiasm	Just want to stay in bed?	1
Motivation to train	Low?	1
Overall feeling	Very fatigued; very stressed?	1
Training Stress Balance (TrainingPeaks.com)	Lower than -30?	1
Mood	Unusually grumpy; easily angered?	2
Sleep	Very poor quality and/or inadequate length?	2
Lying-standing heart rate comparison	High differential heart rate?	2
Health	Something not right with health?	2
Muscles, joints	Soreness?	2
Heart rate variability	Low?	2

These indicators suggest that your stress may be too high and that recovery may be needed that day. On awaking, answer yes or no to each item in the "Warnings" column. A combined "Yes Score" of 7 or higher suggests that you need more recovery and less stress that day.

avoiding overtraining. There's another important dimension to recovery. As explained at the start of this chapter, the sensations of diminishing fatigue that tell you recovery is happening are indirect indicators of adaptation and the higher level of fitness that comes with it.

This last aspect of recovery is critical to race performance. If you focus solely on recovering as quickly as possible, as most riders do after a hard session, you risk abbreviating the adaptive process and not reaping all of its benefits. Rushing back into a workout that tests your limits too soon—before recovery is complete—reduces your body's adaptation. That means you'll gain less fitness than if you'd rested a bit longer. So how long should you recover in order to reap all of the adaptive benefits? That question can't be answered without knowing how fatigued you are and how quickly you generally recover. Table 11.1 will help answer the first question: The more warnings you experience, the more tired you are. The second question—how quickly you recover—is highly specific to you. But I can give you some broad generalizations about recovery.

It takes about 48 hours for all of the body's systems to adapt and grow stronger after a very high-stress workout. You've undoubtedly experienced a delayed onset of muscle soreness after a tough training day. Your muscles aren't sore in the first 24 hours or so after, say, a hard weight lifting session. But you may be quite sore after about 24 to 48 hours. That's your body's way of saying it needs more downtime. After about 48 hours, the soreness recedes. Adaptation has occurred in the muscular system. Muscle protein synthesis, when the muscles are repaired and grow stronger, also takes about 48 hours. Other systems affected by stressful exercise have not been studied as closely as the muscular system. But it is probably safe to assume that it takes about the same amount of time for each system to recover and adapt.

So can you safely conclude that your recovery and adaptation will take 48 hours? Maybe. It depends on how quickly you recover and adapt. Athletes who typically recover the fastest are those who are young—typically in their 20s. Recovery slows down as we age. By the time a rider is in his or her 50s, the recovery and adaptation process may take up to twice as long. And adaptation continues to slow after that. We also know that the fitter the athlete, the shorter the time needed to recover and adapt. In this regard, novices need more time to bounce back than do intermediates, who in turn need more downtime than advanced riders.

Given all of this, how much time should *you* devote to recovery? Again, I can't answer that question with a broad-brush answer. If you're a master racer in your second or third year of the sport, you may need 60 hours following a race or an extremely hard ride to make sure you have recovered. You won't be able to bounce back for another hard workout as quickly as a category 1 rider who is 25 years old and needs only 36 hours to be ready to go hard again.

I realize that such a general guideline is not really all that helpful. It merely reflects where sports science currently stands on the topic of recovery. Until we have more precise tools to measure an athlete's recovery and accompanying adaptation, you should err on the conservative side. If there is any doubt about your recovery status—a morning warning score of 6, perhaps—allow a bit more time for rest or reduce the workout stress somewhat for that day. Of course, most

It takes about 48 hours for all of the body's systems to adapt and grow stronger after a very high-stress workout.

Until we have more precise tools to measure an athlete's recovery and accompanying adaptation, you should err on the conservative side.

of the indicators of your recovery and adaptation status are the sensations and feelings suggested in Table 11.1. So you need to become adept at gauging your fatigue symptoms.

Besides the morning warnings, there are likely other things in your daily life that contribute to or detract from recovery and adaptation. Below I will address some that are known to enhance the process. The detractors, unfortunately, aren't nearly as well understood. But sports scientists are slowly learning about things that may negatively affect your fitness gains during recovery. For example, there are a couple of studies showing that vitamin C and E antioxidant supplements, which are commonly used by athletes and seen as insurance against illness, actually reduce the fitness benefits of adaptation during recovery.

There are probably many more such nutritional aids that are detractors, but we don't know about them yet. That's why I always emphasize to athletes that they should eat a healthy diet rich in micronutrients—vitamins, minerals, and phytochemicals—and avoid supplements altogether. There is no evidence that supplements contribute to improved performance or prevent illness, and some may actually be detrimental. In addition, regulation of these supplements is poor, especially in the United States. You cannot be sure that what is inside the bottle fulfills the claim on the label. You're much better off avoiding supplements and eliminating junk food from your diet. I'll come back to this topic below.

Another detractor from recovery appears to be the application of cold to tired or sore muscles. In one study, 15 minutes of icing following a hard strength workout delayed the removal of creatine kinase, a marker of muscle cell break-

down, when compared with a made-up recovery method that was really nothing more than rest. In another icing study, the subjects rode for 90 minutes to deplete glycogen energy stores. Following the workout, one leg was iced and the other was merely rested. Muscle glycogen stores were reduced by 30 percent on average in the iced leg. So icing weary or sore muscles after a workout is probably not in your best interest in terms of recovery. But icing to treat an injury may still be warranted.

In a similar manner, nonsteroidal anti-inflammatory drugs (NSAIDs) such as ibuprofen have been shown to inhibit the positive muscular adaptations of exercise. As a double whammy, they have also been shown to delay the healing of an injury, even though they may reduce soreness. Routinely taking such medications before challenging and highly stressful events, as some athletes do, not only negatively affects adaptation and healing but may also cause other health complications. Their use is not recommended except in the treatment of extreme injury.

As discussed previously, when you are fatigued and decide to take it easy for a day or so, such as with an active or passive recovery day, the accompanying adaptive process accounts for your fitness gains. This takes us back to the concept that only the *potential* for fitness is created during a hard training session; fitness is not realized until you recover. So being recovered means you've reaped all of the potential fitness gains. But is that necessarily the case? Perhaps not; it appears that there is a process the body must go through to fully realize those physiological fitness gains.

So far I have been referring to recovery and adaptation as essentially the same process. This

There is no evidence that nutritional supplements contribute to improved performance or prevent illness, and some may actually be detrimental.

Only the potential for fitness is created during a hard training session; fitness is not realized until you recover.

is likely not so. Just because you feel recovered and have a low morning warning score doesn't necessarily mean that the adaptive process is complete. Adaptation may take more time than recovery does. In other words, full recovery, indicating a perceived readiness to train hard again, may occur before all of the adaptive changes that result in greater fitness take place. If so, then the recovery from fatigue and the adaptation that results in greater fitness are somewhat separate occurrences.

What this means is that it may not be in your best interest to try to artificially shorten the recovery process that follows your hard workouts or races. You probably strive to shorten recovery; I've certainly seen a lot of athletes train that way. But it could be the wrong thing to do when you want to produce the highest possible level of fitness for high performance.

Chances are that some recovery-enhancing methods never interfere with adaptation and others do. We'll look at both categories shortly.

This does not mean, however, that you should never try to shorten the recovery cycle. There are times when doing so is obviously necessary, such as with a stage race. In that case, the purpose is not creating maximal fitness through adaptation, but rather being optimally rested for the next stage. Quick recovery is also necessary when going through a crash period, as described in Chapter 8. This could happen during an early season training camp, when training stress is high every day. After a period of unrelenting high-stress workouts, the crash training method calls for a few days of recovery to regain physiological balance. That is likely all that's needed to elevate your fitness to the highest level possible at the time. Experience tells me that this works quite well, but only if the balance between stress and recovery is achieved in the short term.

For the serious rider, the majority of the training days in a week should be devoted to recovery rather than to the stress of hard workouts. For most riders, stress is easy to get right. Simply do the hard workouts as planned. But riders often undervalue the recovery and adaptation process. Here's what I mean. You may have done a hard two- or three-hour ride. If so, then the remaining hours in your day should be dedicated to recovery. If you aren't currently thinking of recovery in the hours following a hard ride, your training may be out of balance. You can probably perform at a higher level by focusing on recovery after such challenging rides. As strange as it may seem, I've seen athletes improve their performances remarkably by merely training easier more often. This takes us back to the polarized 80/20 training concept discussed in Chapter 4: Train very easy (at or below the aerobic threshold) when the plan calls for it, and train very hard (at or above the anaerobic threshold) at other times, with little training time between the thresholds.

Throughout the remainder of the day following a hard workout—whether at work, with family, with friends, or whatever you may be doing—it's important to stay focused on a natural recovery from fatigue. "Natural," in this case, means something that doesn't artificially shorten the adaptive process. Sleeping, eating, and drinking (which I'll address below) are all part of this. Natural recovery could also include simply resting and avoiding physical stress throughout the day. For the advanced rider, natural recovery is typically the norm, and it's something all athletes, regardless of experience level, should become good at doing. It enhances the recovery process, improves your

As strange as it may seem, I've seen athletes improve their performances remarkably by merely training easier more often.

adaptation and thus fitness, and allows your ensuing hard workouts to become even more challenging. Recovery is perhaps the single most important aspect of the athlete's daily lifestyle. It must be a habit you do without thinking.

So what does it mean for recovery to become a habit? Let me give you a really basic example of how an athlete should act after a hard ride. There's an old saying that's common among serious athletes: Never stand if you can lean, never lean if you can sit, and never sit if you can lie down. Without even thinking about it, an advanced rider follows this simple rule throughout the day. It's a small and almost insignificant concept, yet it lies at the heart of the matter: Recovery and adaptation are critical to success and should be second nature. No thinking is necessary.

Natural Recovery Aids

There are many effective ways to enhance recovery and adaptation. You are certainly already doing some or all of these. They are obvious and natural for everyone, regardless of athleticism. But the issue is the extent to which you are doing them in your daily life, in both quality and quantity. As you read what follows, consider how you can better incorporate these recovery aids into your daily life to enhance the natural adaptive process.

Sleep. You already own the best recovery device for athletes: your bed. Nothing is better. After all, the purpose of sleep is to rejuvenate and rebuild the body, including its aerobic, muscular, skeletal, and immune systems.

Sleep is absolutely critical to athletic success, and yet some athletes intentionally shorten their sleep time in order to fit more stuff into their daily lives. It's quite common for athletes to stay up late watching their favorite shows on television and then set an alarm so they get up early the next morning. If this describes you, then I'll guarantee that you aren't getting enough sleep. You're artificially shortening recovery and thus reducing adaptation. This is one of the greatest mistakes you can make as a serious athlete. The key is going to bed earlier and sleeping until you wake up naturally. More than anything else you do in your off-the-bike life, this one thing will improve your training and performance above all others. More sleep may also improve your life in other ways, including better health and a more positive attitude about life in general. Sleep is the most powerful form of recovery and fitness enhancement there is.

Sleep is so effective for recovery because that's when the body releases anabolic (tissue-building) hormones that repair the damage done to muscles and other soft tissues during hard sessions. Sleep also restores the immune system, restructures bone, heals niggling injuries, restocks energy stores, and much more. When you shorten your sleep, you are potentially giving up some portion of your most important tool for fitness enhancement every day.

And forget about trying to "catch up" on sleep on the weekends. The body doesn't operate that way. You can't save it up for later in the week.

Of course, I fully understand that you have a lot of demands on your time. Getting enough sleep can be difficult. You may have a family and a career that require your time on both ends of the day. So you go to bed later than you'd like due to the family and then get up early in order to be at work on time. Understood. That's a common situation. I'm not suggesting that you abandon

Never stand if you can lean, never lean if you can sit, and never sit if you can lie down.

You already own the best recovery device for athletes: your bed.

your family or quit your job. But I do want you to understand the consequences of your lifestyle, and I encourage you to do something about it, like getting to bed earlier every day, especially after a hard ride. When you do, you'll soon discover that more sleep means more fitness and better race performance. It's the single most important thing you can do besides riding hard.

Nutrition. In terms of recovery, food—especially the "when" and the "what" of putting food in your stomach—is second in importance to sleep. The nutrients in food provide the building blocks the body uses for recovery and adaptation after hard workouts. And when does that happen? While sleeping. So sleeping and eating are closely related.

The quality of what you eat is critical for recovery and adaptation. The old saying "You are what you eat" has a lot of truth to it. If you waste the opportunity for refueling on a low-nutrient diet—junk food—your body will find it difficult to repair damaged muscles, restore the immune system, restructure bone, heal injuries, and everything else that must be accomplished while sleeping. You may have gotten away with eating lots of junk when you were younger, but aging adults experience a gradually increasing loss of health by continuing to eat that way. The body changes with age. Your diet must also.

High-stress training also increases the need for high-quality food. And you can't make up for a poor diet by taking pills—vitamins, minerals, and other supplements—no matter how many scientific claims are attached to them. Nutrition science is still millions of years behind Mother Nature's real food when it comes to the needs of humans, especially athletes.

What you eat has to do not only with the macronutrients your body needs—protein, carbohydrate, and fat—but also the micronutrients. The micronutrients include vitamins, minerals, and phytochemicals. How rich the foods you eat are in all of these critical nutrients determines how quickly and how fully you recover from a hard workout. While junk foods may provide macronutrients, they are nearly devoid of micronutrients. That's because they are highly processed. The more processing a food undergoes, the more micronutrients that are lost. Manufacturers then try to reintroduce micronutrients as part of the processing so the product can be advertised as high in micronutrients. Don't believe the claims. The less processed your food is before you prepare a meal and eat it, the better it is for your health, recovery, adaptation, and, ultimately, race readiness.

Other than getting more sleep, eating nutritionally dense, real foods following your workouts is probably the most effective thing you can do to improve recovery and adaptation. These same concerns should be considered when eating meals throughout the day. Stick with real foods. Don't waste your calories on highly processed foods, even if they are marketed to athletes. It doesn't matter how many pro cyclists say they use their product. I can guarantee you athletes are only doing it for the sponsorship, not the performance benefits.

There are times when junk foods are hard to avoid, of course. On a long ride, it may be necessary to carry food of some sort, and convenience is the name of the game. Sports drinks, bars, and gels—while most certainly junk food—are easy to carry in your back pocket. But they are a lot more expensive than real foods. Carrying real food,

You can't make up for a poor diet by taking pills—vitamins, minerals, and other supplements—no matter how many scientific claims are attached to them.

such as fruit, used to be common among cyclists, but if you find yourself in the convenience camp on a long ride, that's OK. A few calories from imitation food won't do much harm.

How about when a friend has a birthday party? Will you eat some sugary food then? Sure. We all will. The real issue is how often you eat such stuff. I suggest that it should be infrequently. You need to decide what that means. The answer has to do with how serious you are about cycling.

Hydration. Another critical contributor to recovery after a hard workout is fluid replacement. It doesn't fall into the top tier with sleeping and eating, but if you don't replace the water lost mostly to sweat during a workout session, you are likely to come up short of full recovery and adaptation.

Compared with food, replacing fluid is relatively easy. All you have to do is drink enough to satisfy your thirst. There is no need to weigh yourself before and after the session and then drink that exact amount. People have a sensitive thirst mechanism; all you need to do is not ignore yours. Studies of elite athletes who drank only to satisfy their thirst over several days show that they successfully replaced lost fluids and maintained body weight. So just pay attention to your thirst sensations. If you're thirsty, drink. If you're not thirsty, don't drink. There's no need to make it complicated.

There's one possible exception to this easy solution. It has to do with aging riders. There is some research showing that getting older is associated with a decreased thirst sensation compared with younger subjects. But none of the subjects in these studies were athletes. It may be that an older athlete is more sensitive to changes in body fluid levels than a nonathlete. But if

you're over the age of 60, it is probably in your best interest to pay closer attention to hydration after a workout. You may need to drink just a bit beyond thirst. How much I can't say. But I can tell you that excessive hydration beyond thirst has *not* been shown to improve performance.

What should you drink? The best option is water. I suggest that it's better to get your caloric needs satisfied by eating and drinking real stuff rather than sports drinks, which are usually high in sugar. The only exception might be while riding, when convenience is important. But even then, many riders don't need sugary drinks. If you're an advanced athlete riding less than about 90 minutes, even in a high-stress ride or race, water will do fine. Beyond that duration, the need for carbohydrate increases for those who eat a high-carb diet. Chronically low-carb riders will do fine with very little if any carbohydrate during several hours of riding.

And while we're on the subject, it seems that the old belief that coffee and alcoholic beverages cause dehydration is not true. There is considerable research showing that both contribute to positive hydration. This doesn't mean you should necessarily use an espresso or a beer to recover. I'm just saying.

Alternative Recovery Aids

A few research studies have revealed some other things you can do to speed up recovery. These, however, do not fall into the same certain and natural categories as sleep, nutrition, and hydration. So while the following have been shown to shorten recovery time for some, they may also interfere with the adaptive process by producing the sensations of being recovered even though adaptation is incomplete.

If you don't replace the water lost mostly to sweat during a workout session, you are likely to come up short of full recovery and adaptation.

If you're over the age of 60, it is probably in your best interest to pay closer attention to hydration after a workout.

Not all studies of the following alternative methods agree on the recovery benefits. And, in keeping with that caveat, not all athletes respond equally well to each of these methods. The recovery benefits, if there are any for you, are relatively small, but you may find there is something here that works quite well. If so, use it when appropriate.

Compression garments. Tight-fitting elastic apparel, such as stockings, calf sleeves, thigh sleeves, briefs, tights, and full-body suits, have been worn by athletes to assist recovery. Some athletes also propose that wearing such garments during exercise, especially stockings, may improve performance.

Compression garments have been around for a long time as medical devices intended to aid blood flow in people who have conditions such as varicose veins, deep-vein thrombosis, and pulmonary embolism. In the early 2000s, some endurance athletes began using them during and after races to improve performance and to speed recovery. By the late 2000s, they became a common sight at running races and triathlons.

Do they work? There has been a lot of research, but there are no clear-cut answers. Part of the reason for this is that the studies have not focused on any single sport or activity but have instead looked at many, such as soccer, walking, weight lifting, basketball, netball, sprinting, plyometrics, and more. The types of compression garments studied have also varied a lot, not only in terms of the part of the body they are worn on but also in terms of how much pressure they apply to the muscles (there are various compression ratings). All of this has muddied the water in research. The benefits have varied from positive to negative.

In such situations, when the results are so diverse, we can conclude that the benefits are probably quite small if they exist at all. In keeping with this, my sense is that the performance gains of compression garments are minimal and perhaps nonexistent.

When it comes to speedy recovery, however, I believe there really may be some benefit. Most of the research suggests this too.

I've talked with many athletes who have used different types of compression garments both during workouts and in recovery. Their opinions are divided when it comes to performance, but most sense that the garments help to hasten recovery. Could this be a placebo effect? Possibly. It all comes down to what works for you.

Pneumatic compression devices. While similar to compression garments, pneumatic compression devices are more powerful and, like garments, appear to shorten the time needed for recovery. They are made up of chambers that are filled with air by a pump that gradually inflates each of several chambers and then deflates them to help the body's circulatory system remove metabolic waste from the muscles. They provide both compression and a small amount of something similar to massage. Commonly used compression devices as of this writing are NormaTec, Recovery Boots, and RevitaPump. The most common types fit over the legs from toes to hip.

Compression devices are rather pricey. They are most commonly used at "recovery stations" in health clubs, clinics, and bike shops, where customers pay a fee to use them.

Do they work? The consensus seems to be yes. Then again, as with other recovery products, there could be a placebo effect. The research on

Compression garments probably do not aid performance, but they may hasten recovery.

their effectiveness, however, is generally positive. My impression from having used one of these brands for a considerably long time is that they are beneficial in shortening the recovery time. Not everyone agrees.

Massage. Cyclists have used massage since at least the early 1900s to reduce fatigue after a workout or race. Athletes in many other sports also depend on it, and its use seems to have started with Roman gladiators a couple of thousand years ago. So it's certainly been around for a while. But does it work?

It's hard to say. Massage varies considerably, and its effectiveness comes down to the type of massage (there are many) and the masseuse's skill. This makes measuring its benefits quite a challenge. But that hasn't stopped sports scientists from trying.

In one classic study, for example, both legs of the subjects were intensely exercised to produce muscle soreness. Then one leg was massaged for the following four days and peak torque for each leg was repeatedly measured. There was no difference between the legs in either performance or blood flow as measured with Doppler ultrasound. However, the subjects' perceived level of muscle soreness was reduced to a greater extent in the massaged legs than in the non-massaged legs.

This study's results may lead us to believe that the benefits of massage are more psychological than physiological. What athletes report after a massage seems to support this: an increased sense of well-being, a reduction in anxiety, and improved mood. But a few studies have reported measurable benefits such as reduced heart rate and blood pressure, as well as higher heart rate variability.

Is massage something you should do in order to enhance recovery? As with most recovery protocols aside from sleeping, eating, and drinking, the benefits are limited and highly individualized.

Other recovery aids. This discussion of alternative recovery aids could go on to include such high-tech methods as hyperbaric oxygen therapy, low-frequency electromyostimulation, and ultrasound. There are also many low-tech methods, such as alternating hot and cold water immersion, listening to music, meditation, elevating your legs, using a foam roller, stretching, Jacuzzi, water flotation, drinking chocolate milk, and many more. The list is rather long. Each of these has been demonstrated to speed recovery in one or more studies—but not in all such research. Once again, none of these aids works for all athletes.

The challenge is to find the recovery aids that work best for you and then use them at the right times (should you decide to use them at all). The only ones you *must* apply consistently are sleeping, eating, and drinking. Don't ever skip those.

STRATEGIC RECOVERY

When describing training stress in Chapter 10, I suggested that you periodize it as explained in Chapters 7, 8, and 9. Since training and therefore greater fitness through adaptation is made up of both stress and recovery, does that also suggest that recovery should be periodized? Yes. Probably.

I qualify the answer in part because we don't all respond to recovery in the same ways. For example, recovery depends to some extent on the source of the training stress that produced the fatigue. After a high-duration training period,

> The only recovery aids you must apply consistently are sleeping, eating, and drinking.

you may require a different recovery method than you would following a high-intensity block. During periods when high duration is the focus, recovery is largely based on sleep, nutrition, and hydration. But the nervous system needs greater attention when you're recovering from a high-intensity workload. This is when alternative recovery methods may also prove beneficial.

Why else did I say "probably" above? Other than individual responses to unique training loads, there is another reason. Some riders are very good at monitoring their need for recovery. For these few, recovery on demand is often the way to go. This doesn't work for most athletes, however, due to their high levels of motivation. When an A-priority race looms in our not-too-distant future, most of us lose our sensitivity to fatigue or fail to heed its warnings. We're likely to decide that recovery is not needed and press ahead with hard training—to our own detriment.

Scheduling recovery in the seasonal and weekly training plans bypasses the necessity for continually assessing your fatigue status, and it ensures that you recover frequently. There's no second-guessing yourself when the plan calls for reduced training. When the schedule says "recovery," you just do it.

Both planned recovery and recovery on demand have advantages and disadvantages. We'll start by looking at those times when periodized recovery is commonly scheduled and then examine the concept of recovery on demand.

Hard-Easy Days

I'm sure it's obvious that you can't do a killer workout every day. Your body won't allow that to happen. But even if you were so highly motivated that you could overcome the debilitating fatigue,

you'd soon wind up overtrained. You must have a balance between hard and easy workouts throughout your training weeks. Creating a standard weekly schedule, as suggested in Chapter 8, will help you balance your training. A typical way of doing this is to plan on an easy ride, or even a day off, the day after a highly stressful session. That would suggest your weeks would follow a pattern of hard-easy-hard-easy-hard-easy. That would leave a seventh day in the week to be assigned. For some riders, I suggest that be another easy day. Others may be able to handle a moderate day.

Don't feel, however, that you must follow such a weekly pattern. You could also do something such as very hard-easy-easy-hard-easy-hard-easy. That very hard day could be a group ride or C-priority race. The two easy days scheduled after the very hard one ensure that you don't allow your motivation to get the best of you. The harder the hard workouts, the easier—and longer—the recovery break must be.

However you plan your weeks, the bottom line is that there should be a balance between hard and easy days, because bad things happen when they become imbalanced. Too many hard days, and the risk of overtraining appears. Too few hard days, and you make little progress toward your race goal.

You may recall that in Chapter 9 I suggested that slow-recovery riders may benefit from training with 9-day weeks. That provides a nice balance that often solves the problem of getting enough recovery time following hard sessions. The downside, however, is that it often conflicts with standard 7-day weeks built around a work schedule. Your boss may not like it if you show up late for work because you had to fit in a long

> However you plan your weeks, there should be a balance between hard and easy days.

ride. Bosses can be like that. So such a routine generally works best for retired riders or those who have a very flexible weekly schedule.

Base and Build Period Recovery

In Chapters 7 and 8, I suggested planning a few days of recovery every third or fourth week in the base and build periods. The reason, of course, is to get rid of some of the fatigue that has accumulated in the preceding weeks of high-load training. Doing 3 weeks or so of training in these periods, followed by a few days of rest and recovery, is what I suggest for athletes who seem to recover quickly. That usually implies younger riders—those under the age of 50.

For those who recover more slowly—older riders and perhaps novices—about 2 weeks of training followed by a break lasting a few days is generally necessary. But, as I suggested in those previous chapters, I've known 50-something riders who recovered quite quickly and younger athletes who recovered slowly. So this rule isn't carved in stone.

How do you know which category you fit into? It simply comes down to how soon you sense accumulating fatigue when the training load is high for 2 or more consecutive weeks. It may not be the same throughout the season. Some riders can easily manage highly aerobic training, as is typical in the base period in classic linear training. But when these same riders get into the following build period with its great deal of anaerobic endurance work, they find it hard to do 3 weeks without a break. So the training plan may then call for about 2 weeks of focused training before backing off for a few days.

It simply comes down to you making the call. You're the only one who knows how you feel in the second and third weeks of hard training. If you're not very good at sensing the need for rest, as I'm afraid many cyclists are not, pay a lot closer attention to the morning warnings described above. What warning trends are you seeing as the training weeks proceed?

Past experiences with training may also help you determine your usual hard-training limit and therefore your periodization plan. If you're unsure, I'd suggest making your periods 2 weeks or so of hard training followed by a few days of rest and recovery.

How long should the scheduled rest and recovery break last? That, again, depends on how you feel. And it can vary from one training period to the next. I would suggest that 3 days of a greatly reduced training load should be the minimum for an extended break from training. As for a maximum, most riders are fully recovered within 5 days. So those are the two extremes. But then again, there may be a time during the season when 6 or even 7 days of rest and recovery are needed. That's why I keep saying that your hard training should last for 2 or 3 weeks "or so." If you need only 3 days to recover from accumulated fatigue, you will then have a total of either 18 or 25 days of training in the next period, when you start back into your workouts.

The first day after you feel fully recovered is the time to test your fitness and measure your progress. At that point, you might also set new training zones. You can use an FTP test, as described in Appendix B, or you can use a B- or C-priority race. If you are doing a C race on the weekend with only 3 days of recovery earlier in the week, then normally hard training (perhaps including testing) would lead right into the race. So the week of a Saturday race may follow a pattern of rest-rest-rest-test-rest-race-rest. Remember that C races are to be treated as hard workouts. If it's a B race, which calls for a few days of rest prior, then I'd suggest timing your rest and recovery period so that it immediately precedes the race. That may mean starting the recovery break on Wednesday instead of Monday.

During a rest and recovery week, your workouts should consist of short, easy rides. When your legs and attitude start to feel like normal—which may take 2 to 4 days—then it's time to do a cautiously harder workout the next day with a few short intervals appropriate for the training period you're in to see if you're ready to go again. It's probably better to do that than to assume that your body operates on the same recovery schedule every time. This is a little bit like recovery on demand, as you'll see below.

Race Week Recovery

It's important that you come to your A-priority race day recovered and ready to go. The purpose, of course, is to be on form, as discussed in Chapter 3. Form refers to how race ready and fresh you are when it's time to race. Freshness is the absence of fatigue. When fresh, you feel vigorous, alert, and energetic instead of tired, sluggish, and lethargic. You're ready to give it your all. It is so critical to race success that I've devoted Chapter 13 to it. There I will take you through the subtle nuances of peaking and coming into good form for a race from the start of the taper until you place a wheel on the start line.

Transition Period Recovery

After an A-priority race, regardless of when it may occur in the season, it's generally a good idea to take a recovery break from training. This is the transition period described in Chapters 7 and 8. The length of these post-race transition periods varies considerably depending on when they occur in the season, how long your race preparation lasted, how stressful the training load was in those weeks, and how fatiguing the race was.

Chapter 7 suggested that you not have more than three A-priority races in a season, since tapering for each of these races causes a slight loss of basic fitness, especially aerobic endurance. A season schedule of three or fewer highest-priority races usually allows you to regain your basic fitness before the next taper for a race.

Generally, after the first race of the season, you need a very short transition break. After the second A race, you may need a bit more downtime. And there's little doubt that you will be cooked and in need of a lengthy recovery break after the last A race of the year. So these transition periods typically vary from a couple of days to as much as 6 weeks.

Of course, all of that may go out the window if the first A race of the season is a multi-day race with several grueling stages. In that case, a week of recovery may be called for. And if the last race of the year was a short criterium or time trial that placed less demand on you than races early in the season, your post-season transition may be quite short. That could even lead you into a short cyclocross season in the winter months. But be cautious if you do this. Making the winter months into another fatigue-inducing season following on the heels of a long and grueling summer of road racing could easily result in the symptoms of overtraining syndrome. That could significantly shorten your next base period if there is an early spring road

A season schedule of three or fewer highest-priority races usually allows you to regain your basic fitness before the next taper for a race.

During a rest and recovery week, your workouts should consist of short, easy rides.

race on your calendar. At that point, you're setting yourself up for a miserable year of racing.

Such accumulating fatigue is like a snowball rolling downhill—it just keeps getting bigger. You're only capable of handling so much stress. Pushing the limits throughout the year with little or no break from training is dangerous, not only to your racing results but also to your health.

I have always told the athletes I have coached that they should plan on a 2- to 6-week transition period following their road race season. But if they want to also race 'cross, then that should be considered an extension of a shortened road-only season in order to avoid long-term burnout. So they may have one or two A-priority road races followed by one or two A-priority cyclo-cross races. You may be an accomplished cyclist, but I'm pretty sure you don't have the superhero powers required to race at a high level all year. On the other hand, should you decide to make the 'cross races B- and C-priority races only (no A races), then the training load shifts in favor of the road season and it becomes more manageable.

Recovery on Demand

In Chapter 7, when discussing periodization and the need to make your training flexible, I mentioned recovery on demand. It's related to periodization on demand.

Periodization on demand means that when you have achieved your targeted training objectives in a period, you move on to the next period with slightly altered training loads regardless of how long the period lasted. Recovery on demand is much the same. It simply means that when you feel the need for recovery, you back off from training for a few days regardless of what the plan calls for. In fact, the word "plan" takes on a whole

new meaning when training with both periodization on demand and recovery on demand. It now becomes unplanned and perhaps even more *natural*, if I can use that word to imply unstructured in a good way that meets the demands of your body precisely when needed.

That has the potential to be a great way of training—if you are in touch with how your body feels. I'm afraid most riders are not. If left to their own devices, when it comes to making a decision to either train hard or recover, most will usually decide they need to train more and rest less. But for athletes who are in touch with how their bodies are responding to training, periodization on demand and recovery on demand are excellent options. But realize that if you decide to go this route you must pay close attention to your morning warnings.

SUMMARY: FATIGUE, RECOVERY, AND ADAPTATION

The most important message from this chapter is that adaptation takes place during recovery from the fatigue of a hard ride, and after adaptation, performance improves. But recovery and adaptation don't appear to be exactly the same thing. It is possible to feel recovered before adaptation is complete. While it's certainly wise to pay close attention to how you feel in the hours following a high-stress workout—that's the reason for the morning warnings described in Table 11.1—be aware that your primary mission then is to become more fit, not simply to feel less tired.

There is a lot going on during this adaptive time, which sports scientists call "overcompensation." Muscle strength improves. The heart's

---

Pushing the limits throughout the year with little or no break from training is dangerous.

Your primary recovery mission is to become more fit, not simply to feel less tired.

stroke volume (the amount of blood pumped per beat) increases. The tiny blood-delivering capillary networks in the muscles become more dense, allowing for an increased delivery of oxygen and fuel. Blood volume becomes greater, also enhancing oxygen availability. The aerobic enzymes that help produce energy from fuel increases further, contributing to your endurance. Glycogen stores are restocked, allowing for harder workouts in the next few days. These are only a few of the physical changes that result from overcompensation. The full list is quite long. With well-timed and managed fatigue, recovery, and adaptation, the performance gains over a few weeks can be enormous.

Consequently, the biggest mistake you can make is to destroy an easy day or a recovery week by training hard through it. You might want to do it because you feel the need to gain more fitness in the last few weeks before an important race. But even if you manage to avoid a breakdown, the quality of your training will decline as fatigue continues to accumulate. And your subsequent race performance will suffer. You must accept and make time for adaptation in your training plan along with your workouts.

Another common mistake shared by serious riders is to make easy-day workouts slightly too hard. Instead of doing workouts in zone 1, as called for in the training plan, the rides become zone 3. Or what was supposed to be a short active recovery session becomes a long one. On the surface, making such adjustments seems like a good thing, since raising the average workload appears to be a logical way to improve fitness. That is sometimes true, but this isn't one of those times. Making the workout slightly harder should not be done on a recovery day. These days *must* be easy. It's during highly intense sessions when

increases in the workload pay off with increased fitness—not when you're trying to recover. This is merely another way of looking at the polarized 80/20 training methodology described in Chapter 4.

Recall that a rest and recovery "week" that follows 2 or 3 weeks of training should not be literally taken to mean 7 days. Some athletes recover very quickly when focused on sleep, nutrition, and hydration, and they may find they are ready to go again in 3 days. Others need 5 or more days. Older athletes are likely to need more recovery and adaptation than younger athletes. Less fit athletes also need more than those who are highly fit. Experience is the only way to know what works best for you.

Recovery and adaptation are moving targets; they won't always require the same number of days. Three days may be all you need in one training period, while in the next one you still feel tired after 3 days and so need more downtime.

Second in importance only to these frequent multiday recovery breaks are the easy days that are included every few days throughout the season. These can be planned so you routinely follow a hard workout with an active recovery day or even a day off. Or, for the experienced and highly self-aware athlete, they may be included based on demand. In other words, when sensing that recovery is needed, the perceptive rider decides to take an active recovery day regardless of what is called for in the plan. This is when the suggested morning warnings listed in Table 11.1 may prove helpful in making a decision.

The activity level of your active recovery day depends on your capacity for training loads. Recall from Chapter 3 that duration and intensity are the only two training variables you can

Recovery and adaptation are moving targets; they won't always require the same number of days.

manipulate to make a workout easy or hard. When it comes to intensity, defining an easy day is simple. It's a zone 1 workout. Duration is a bit harder to be so precise about. If you're an elite athlete who trains upwards of 20 hours per week, an easy workout duration may be a 2-hour ride. But if you train 6 hours a week, then an easy duration may be something more like 20 minutes.

Two other times in the season when rest and recovery are especially critical are in the week immediately preceding an A-priority race and in the week that follows. If you don't cast off a significant amount of fatigue before an important race, you are likely to have a poor performance. Chapter 13 will thoroughly discuss the matter of coming into form for an A-priority race.

Taking a rest and recovery break in the days following a hard A-priority race, will allow you to rejuvenate, both physically and mentally, before starting the buildup to your next race. Such a post-race break typically lasts only a few days during the season. After the last race of the season, though, this break could be 2 to 6 weeks. And there are times when even that may not be long enough.

Adequate rest and recovery, regardless of when in the season you may do it, is what gets you race ready. Remember that workouts only create the potential for fitness. True fitness is realized when you recover and allow adaptation to occur. Throughout the season, the key to getting the right mix of stress and rest is to be conservative. It's better to do too little training than too much. You're much better off being slightly undertrained and enthusiastic than constantly tired and apathetic.

PART VI

THE COMPETITIVE EDGE

The next three chapters take us back to the topic of periodization, which was last discussed in great detail in Part IV. The first two chapters are about training methods that you should plan to include on either end of your preparation for your first A-priority race of the season. Chapter 12 examines how to organize your muscular force training so that you reach a peak of functional strength early in the season. In Chapter 13, we'll go to the opposite end of your periodization plan, and I'll show you how to peak for a race. The final chapter walks you through using a training diary to plan your season and analyze your progress toward goal accomplishment.

Aside from riding your bike, muscular force workouts are the most effective training you can do to boost performance. And yet this is the most commonly eschewed ability of the six you read about in Chapter 6. I suspect that for most riders, the reason is time. When your life is full to the brim with family, career, and riding your bike, fitting in a gym workout is nearly impossible. But time spent in a gym building functional strength with weight lifting can have a significant positive impact on your on-bike training and race results. If you simply don't have the time, though, I'll show you how to accomplish much the same results by doing muscular endurance workouts on your bike.

That brings us to another topic of great importance: tapering for a race. Riders are often confused about how to do this properly. Most understand the concept of tapering but are confused when it's time to come into race form. This topic was introduced in Chapter 7, where I described the peak and race. There I showed you how to plug these periods into your periodization plan, but I didn't explain what they are actually like. Chapter 13 will fill in the blanks.

In Chapter 14, you'll learn why a training diary is your most important tool (apart from your bike) for racing to your potential. Even if you like to do everything online, a printed paper diary that is always "on" and makes you more thoughtful about your progress is hard to beat for keeping your training on track. I'll show you how to use a diary not only for planning the season but also for measuring progress toward your season's goals. To limit the time you spend poring over seemingly never-ending training numbers, I'll point out the most critical workout and race data to record and then show you how to analyze only what's important.

Your diary will prove most valuable as you follow the race plan you laid out in Part IV.

While often overlooked, the three topics covered in Part VI—muscular training, tapering, and recording data—are all about gaining a competitive edge. They will help you plan and manage your season as you prepare for high-level racing.

MUSCULAR FORCE TRAINING

POWER. It's what separates the best from the rest. The greater your power, the better your results. Power is essential to performance in cycling. So what exactly is power and how do you improve it?

Let's start with physics. From that perspective, power is the product of force and velocity, and it can be expressed with the formula *power equals force times velocity*:

$$P = F \times v$$

From a cycling perspective, *force* is the pressure you apply to the pedal and *velocity* is how fast you turn the pedals—your cadence. You can increase power by turning the cranks faster, or you can keep the cadence steady and increase gear size so that you're applying more force to the pedals. So the key to becoming faster has to do with how much force you can apply to the pedals and how quickly you can turn them. Riding fast is nothing more than turning a high gear with a high cadence. In this chapter, we'll address the force component of the formula.

Delivering greater force to the pedals has a lot to do with becoming muscularly stronger. If you want to increase power, one of the most effective methods is to develop greater strength, especially in the muscles that drive the pedals. You also need strength in your hips and torso to provide stability so that the force you generate is fully transmitted without power leaks.

There are a few ways to develop greater force. The method most commonly used by cyclists is weight lifting. Chapter 8 briefly described how to include a weight lifting program in your annual training plan. In this chapter, we'll examine the details of such training for the high-performance cyclist. I'll also introduce an alternative force-development method—functional force training. We'll get into the details of these options to help you make a decision about which you will use.

THE NERVOUS SYSTEM AND FORCE

The strength-development methods described in this chapter offer a unique way of developing the muscular system. They also have the potential to improve the nervous system's contribution to muscular force production. We seldom think of the nervous system when it comes to building strength or even to pedaling a bike. But the nerves play an important role in both, perhaps in ways you've never considered. We used to think of strength only in relation to muscle size. The bigger the muscle, the stronger and therefore more powerful it is. While that is certainly true, we now understand that the nervous system also plays a key role in strength—or muscular force production—and therefore in power. The muscles don't have to become bulky to create high force.

Ultimately, greater force means improved sprinting, climbing, and time trialing. That power improvement comes from the combined benefits of muscular and nervous system training. Both systems contribute to increased power.

How does the nervous system contribute to greater pedal force and therefore increased power? There are three ways. The first is muscle recruitment. What makes it possible for you to quickly lift a heavy weight or drive a pedal down rapidly with high force is how many muscle fibers you can recruit from those that are available in the active muscle group. Developing the nervous system with high weight loads and fast movements trains the individual muscle fibers to respond in order to produce the necessary high power when it's needed. Without such training, some of those fibers are likely to remain dormant.

A second aspect of neuromuscular training has to do with the coordination of muscle fibers specific to the movement being attempted. This is the complete recruitment of the proper fibers *when they are needed*. That's why throughout this chapter I strongly emphasize simulating the key movement of the sport—driving the bike pedal down—in nearly all of the training methods I describe. By doing that, the nervous system is trained to produce high power by recruiting all of the available and appropriate muscle fibers. Those that aren't needed remain inactive. That's just as important as recruiting the right muscles to do the work. If inappropriate muscle fibers are recruited, they not only detract from the efficiency of the movement, they also add to the metabolic cost of pedaling. Wasting energy is never a good thing.

Neuromuscular training also improves the synchronization of muscle fiber recruitment. This has to do with the sequencing of muscle activation. Fibers must fire at the right times if the pedal stroke is to be effective. That may sound like a rather simple process, but it's actually quite complex; a dozen or so muscle groups must fire in order to make one revolution of the cranks in an efficiently synchronized manner in less than one second. By simulating the pedaling motion, you'll become better at increasing the rate at which muscle fibers are activated. The benefit is that you become more powerful and therefore faster. Neuromuscular training is the most effective form of physical preparation for high-performance racing you can do off the bike.

Let's get started on this topic with the one neuromuscular training method you are likely already familiar with: weight lifting.

Developing the nervous system with high weight loads and fast movements trains the individual muscle fibers to respond.

Neuromuscular training is the most effective form of physical preparation for high-performance racing you can do off the bike.

WEIGHT LIFTING

Should you lift weights? Every winter, when riders often start gym training, you'll find quite a discussion of this topic on Internet cycling forums. Some argue that it's a waste of time. Others point out the research that supports its use. Actually, there's research that goes both ways. I come down on the side of lifting in order to improve force, the strength-based aspect of power. I've seen many riders improve their power after following the weight lifting program I'll describe here.

But should *you* lift? It's probably not for you if you don't like going to a gym or simply don't have the time to fit anything else into your daily routine. In that case, you may want to consider following the functional force program below. I've coached several young men over the years who had too much muscle, especially in the upper body. They didn't need more strength. They needed endurance. On the other hand, I've found that those who benefit most from a weight lifting program are women, novices, skinny ectomorphs, and older riders. If you are in one of these groups, I strongly suggest you lift weights as described below. For other riders, I suggest giving it a try. You may be surprised to find that it's just what you needed to take your racing up a notch.

What are the benefits of weight lifting? The obvious one is an improvement in strength, which delivers greater force when pedaling and therefore more power. Strength improvements occur in the hours following a weight lifting session because of the body's increased production of tissue-building anabolic hormones such as testosterone and growth hormone. Bone density also improves, a benefit for serious cyclists, who have been shown to have rather weak bones. In terms of performance, positive pedaling changes occur in the nervous system as a result of lifting weights, as described above, but only if the exercises are done in such a way as to closely simulate the key movements of riding a bike.

In this regard, lifting weights is a skill, just as pedaling and cornering are skills. To reap the bike-specific benefits, the exercises must be done with proper technique, as you'll soon read. It takes many repetitions over time to refine the skills required of each lift. Until the skills are mastered, the benefits of weight lifting will not be as great.

The first sign of improved weight lifting skills is an increase in the loads you are capable of lifting. After this initial stage of development, improvements in cycling strength will follow. That's why the weight lifting program I'll lay out for you next starts with what is called the anatomical adaptation (AA) phase. That's when the skills are developed. Skipping this in order to get to the heavier loads, as is sometimes done, is counterproductive.

Weight Lifting Guidelines

We need to lay the groundwork for your gym-based training before we get into the various phases and exercises. Stay with me here while I briefly explain several topics that affect your weight lifting program.

Your gym. The most common weight lifting facilities used by riders are membership health clubs, YMCAs, schools, and pay-as-you-go public gyms. The downside of most of these is the time it takes to get to them. As an alternative,

Lifting weights is a skill, just as pedaling and cornering are skills.

you can have your own personal gym in your basement, garage, or a spare room for a couple hundred dollars. A few handheld dumbbells and other simple equipment that you'll see in the accompanying illustrations in this chapter will get you started and save you a lot of time every week. Watch the local newspaper and the Internet for good deals on weights from sporting goods stores and individuals who are selling their weights. In addition to the time you'll save, you're also more likely to use a home-based gym because of its convenience.

Free weights and machines. In the accompanying illustrations, the athlete is using free weights for many of the exercises, such as squats (Figure 12.2) and lunges (Figure 12.5). Free weights are held in your hands and require balancing during the exercise. This balancing strengthens many small muscles and helps develop core strength. But free weights are also risky. You could fall or drop the weight. Some of the other exercises illustrated in this chapter show the athlete using machines, such as for the leg press (Figure 12.6). Balance is obviously not needed when using a machine, making it safer. The downside is that the small muscles that assist with balance are not strengthened. If you are new to weight lifting, you are likely better off starting with machines and gradually shifting to free weights over time.

When to lift weights. For best results, I suggest doing a weight lifting session after riding or on a day off the bike. If you can't lift then and must lift before another workout, you need to be very cautious, as the muscle strain and fatigue can greatly affect the following workout, especially when you are in the muscular strength (MS) phase

with its heavy loads. Pedaling technique is likely to be negatively affected if you do an MS weight workout immediately prior to a long ride. The problem is compounded if you lift weights, especially MS, right before a high-intensity workout such as intervals. Such combinations are best avoided. In fact, in the MS phase, the day after a weight session may even be too soon for some to do long or intense rides. If you must lift weights before another workout, it's probably best if the bike session is a short and easy recovery ride. If you're doing a weight room session prior to a long or intense ride, separate the two sessions by several hours. For example, a weight lifting session early in the morning with a ride late in the day is less likely to have negative consequences than if the ride is immediately after the gym session. As you'll see, it's best to avoid such combinations altogether by following the periodization routine suggested later in Table 12.3. There's more on this matter later in this chapter. But for now, anytime you are in doubt about your readiness to ride after weight lifting, regardless of how much time separates the two sessions, ride short and easy.

Sets and reps. A weight lifting workout consists of several exercises. Each exercise involves several repetitions. One of the strength-building phases, for example, calls for 8 to 12 reps of each exercise. Those reps make up one set. The following guidelines often suggest doing 3 sets with a brief recovery break after each.

Set progression. It's generally best to focus on only one exercise, completing all of its sets before moving on to the next exercise. That maintains muscle warm-up throughout the exercise, and

If you are new to weight lifting, you are likely better off starting with machines and gradually shifting to free weights over time.

If you're doing a weight room session prior to a long or intense ride, separate the two sessions by several hours.

completing the set is often a necessity in a gym, given that there are other people who want to use the same free weight or machine stations. Staying with each exercise to completion of all of the sets prevents you from standing around and waiting for the station to become available again. If your gym is not crowded, however, you may want to use a routine called "supersetting." This simply means alternating the sets of two exercises, especially exercises that aren't focused on the same muscle groups. It maintains the warm-up effect while reducing the workout time.

Recovery between sets. Each of the phases in the following weight lifting program lists how many minutes you should spend recovering after each set. The purpose is to make sure your short-term recovery is adequate before you do the next set. If the recoveries are too short, you will be unable to lift as heavy a load as you are capable of lifting for the prescribed number of reps. Or, if the load remains the same, then the reps per set must be reduced. Reducing the recovery breaks shifts the workout focus to endurance and away from strength. Since you are already doing plenty of endurance training on the bike, there's no need to do more of it in the gym. To build neuromuscular force and therefore power, you need to challenge yourself with each set's load. That means starting each exercise adequately recovered. While fatigue contributes to endurance, it prevents strength development.

Load. The "load" is the amount of weight you are lifting. Throughout most of the weight lifting program described below, the loads are increased at the same time the number of reps for each exercise are decreased. By gradually increasing the

loads over several weeks, the body slowly adapts and grows stronger. The load increases should be made conservatively to reduce the risk of injury.

One-repetition max. To make a weight lifting program effective, it's critical that you use the right amount of load for each exercise. The size of the load for a given exercise in a given phase is based on the greatest weight you can lift one time. This is called one-repetition max, or "1RM." The loads for each neuromuscular training phase are prescribed according to percentages of your current 1RM. For example, the plan may call for a load that is 80 percent of 1RM. The downside of this method is that you must challenge yourself every few weeks to do one maximal effort for each exercise to find your 1RM. That raises the risk of an injury. Highly experienced weight lifters have a lower risk due to their years of experience. But since you are a cyclist and not a serious weight lifter, I suggest a less perilous method.

Loads can be determined based on multiple reps by using Table 12.1. The loads are lighter, making this much less risky than the 1RM test. To use this table, determine a load you think you can only lift 4 to 10 times for a given exercise. Then see how many reps you can do with that load. Find that number of reps in the left-hand column and look to the right-hand column for the associated factor. To determine your predicted 1RM for that exercise, divide the load you lifted by that factor. For example, if you did 9 squats with a load of 80 pounds, Table 12.1 lists the factor as 0.775. Dividing 80 by 0.775 predicts a 1RM of 103 pounds. So for this exercise, you would use a 103 when determining exercise loads. This is a much less risky way of finding your 1RM for each exercise you do.

The size of the load for a given exercise in a given phase is based on the greatest weight you can lift one time. This is called one-repetition max, or "1RM."

TABLE 12.1 **Determining Your 1RM**

REPS	FACTOR
4	0.90
5	0.875
6	0.85
7	0.825
8	0.80
9	0.775
10	0.75

Find how many reps you can do with a given load for an exercise. Divide that load by the corresponding factor to estimate your 1RM for that exercise.

Of course, given improvements in strength over time, your 1RM for each exercise should change periodically, which means revisiting the table from time to time. But there's an easier method that doesn't involve testing.

An even simpler and less risky way to find your load for an exercise is to guess how many reps you can do based on experience. This requires no testing. If you are able to do more reps than are called for, increase the load appropriately and do the next set. You'll soon determine the correct load for the exercise. Adjust the loads up and down from then on based on how many reps you're supposed to do in a certain phase.

Spotter. Some exercises, such as squats, can be risky when using heavy loads. For such exercises, it's a good idea to have a spotter who can assist you with balancing the load throughout the exercise.

Concentric and eccentric contractions. Your muscles contract both concentrically and eccentrically. In a concentric contraction, such as doing a biceps arm curl with a handheld weight, the muscle shortens as you lift the weight up. In an eccentric contraction, the muscle lengthens as you lower the weight. Imagine doing an arm curl starting with the weight near your shoulder, where it was when you finished the concentric curl. From this shoulder-high position, slowly lower the weight to the waist. As you do this, the muscle, which is contracting, gets longer as the elbow joint opens up. The muscle is stretching as it tries to control the weight going down. Every strength exercise has a concentric and an eccentric component. You lift the weight (concentric) and then you set it back down (eccentric).

You are capable of handling a much greater load when making eccentric (lowering the weight) movements. But eccentric movement with a high load can also place a much greater strain on the muscle. Essentially, eccentric movement with a heavy load strains the muscle fibers because they are trying to contract while lengthening. That has the potential to damage the muscle. Setting heavy loads down after each rep should be done cautiously.

Speed of movement. One of the exercises in this chapter calls for ballistic movement. Such a lift is often called "explosive." In ballistic movement, the concentric movement is done very quickly—as fast as you can move given the load. The eccentric movement is done slowly. The loads are considerably lighter than for the more traditional exercises done with heavy loads—usually 50 percent or less of 1RM. This type of exercise is great for producing sprint-like power. Be aware that ballistic exercises can be highly risky, even with light loads. You must start by learning to make the movements with extremely light loads before adding more weight. This can take several sessions.

Later in this chapter I'll describe the movement speeds for the two portions of the various ballistic exercises. Although you move the weight quickly in the concentric portion, you must move it slowly for the eccentric portion. The time ratio for the two portions is something on the order of 1:2, meaning the weight is lowered in about twice the time as it is raised.

Simulating pedaling. There is little reason to do exercises that don't closely replicate the positions and movements of cycling, especially pedaling. Nonspecific exercises are not productive when it comes to improving performance. For example, doing arm curls will obviously not make you a faster cyclist. Seated knee extensions are certainly more similar to pedaling a bike than arm curls, but there are even better exercises for sport specificity. Multi-joint exercises such as squats, leg presses, and step-ups are much more similar to the positions and movements of pedaling a bike.

Multi-joint exercises. Pedaling a bicycle requires moving joints in the hips, knees, and ankles driven by contracting muscles in synchronization. In pedaling a bike, the knee doesn't extend in isolation from the hip and ankle. They all move at the same time. Gym exercises are all about becoming more forceful in making certain movements, not just building random muscular strength. That's why doing squats is preferable to doing knee extensions.

Balancing muscle strength. The exception to the multi-joint exercise guideline has to do with the balancing of muscles that control both basic movements of a joint. Each joint is operated by two or more opposing muscle groups. The primary working muscle for a given movement of a joint is called the "agonist." Returning to our example of the curl exercise, the agonist for the concentric movement is the biceps muscle group. When the agonist is working, the other muscles for that joint are relaxing—or at least they should be. They are the "antagonists." Movement is inefficient and there is a lot of wasted energy if the antagonists are fully recruited at the same time as the agonists. For the arm curl, the triceps is the antagonist. But when doing a push-up, the triceps becomes the agonist and the biceps the antagonist. So the terms are used based on what you intend to do with the joint at the time.

There should be a healthy ratio of strength between the two opposing muscle groups. If the agonist becomes too powerful, there is a risk of damaging the antagonist during a powerful movement such as a ballistic lift. So it can be a good idea to also build strength in the antagonist to protect it from injury. The best example of this is the quadriceps muscle, which is on the front of the thigh; it can become very strong when doing exercises such as squats. That presents some risk to the hamstrings, which are the antagonist when doing a squat.

The antagonist can be strengthened using a muscle-isolated single-joint exercise. So then you'll see leg curls in the following program to strengthen the hamstrings. Also, the loads and reps for the antagonist muscles are not the same in every phase as for the agonists. In other words, there will probably always be a normal difference in their strength. That's OK so long as the difference is not too great.

There is little reason to do exercises that don't closely replicate the positions and movements of cycling.

Workout spacing. Weight lifting sessions should be evenly spaced throughout the week. If you are doing 2 or 3 gym workouts in a week, as is recommended for the early base period, and they are too closely spaced, you will have several back-to-back days with no strength sessions. That's to be expected in the later-season maintenance phase (SM) with only 1 session per week, but it's counterproductive when trying to build strength. Excessive workout spacing makes it difficult to make gains, as recent strength gains are lost during those several consecutive days when there is no weight lifting. Spacing them as evenly as possible throughout the week allows time for the muscles to adapt, which occurs during a couple of days of recovery but doesn't take so much time away from strength work that previous gains are lost. For example, 2 weekly sessions of weight lifting on Monday and Friday are preferable to lifting on Monday and Tuesday. In the same way, if you do weight lifting workouts 3 times per week, Tuesday, Thursday, and Saturday are preferable to Tuesday, Wednesday, and Thursday.

Warm-up and cooldown. Just as with your on-the-bike workouts, you need to warm up before starting a weight lifting session. And a cooldown afterwards is also beneficial. Let's start with the warm-up.

There are two steps in a strength training warm-up routine. The first is to slowly increase blood flow to the muscles that will soon be challenged by lifting heavy loads. Most of the exercises in the following program involve the legs. You can increase blood flow to the legs by riding a stationary bike; it only takes 10 to 15 minutes of gradually increasing the workload to accom-

plish this. Then you are *almost* ready to do the first strength-building exercise.

The second stage of warm-up involves making the movement of the first weight lifting exercise with a few reps done with a light load. For example, as you begin a routine involving squats, you might start by doing a few with body weight only. Emphasize good technique while doing this. Now you're ready to start the exercise. Do this second-stage warm-up before each subsequent exercise.

After a strength session, cool down by spinning on a bike easily at a comfortably high cadence for a few minutes. Five minutes is plenty. You will have most likely done some heavy lifting for your legs, which may negatively alter your pedaling mechanics and cadence. You're likely to be pedaling in squares following such a session. A few minutes spent spinning with good technique at a relatively high cadence will help to restore and reinforce the proper neuromuscular firing sequence.

Exercise order. As you'll see later in this chapter, there is a preferred order for strength exercises. I recommend doing the exercises that involve the heaviest loads first. It's physiologically better to lift heavy loads when you're fresh. It's also better from a safety perspective. For the same reasons, you should alternate muscle groups and movements. Avoid doing two hip-, knee-, ankle-extension exercises (such as squats and step-ups) back to back. Instead, insert another exercise with a different movement and muscle group between them.

Starting a new phase. When starting a new phase of strength training that involves heavier loads than you've recently been using, be conservative in determining loads in the first couple of sessions. While challenging yourself to lift heavier loads is called for at certain times in the phase progression, the first session or two of a new phase is not a good time for that. Save it for the subsequent workouts when you are likely to have a better idea of what you can safely manage.

Unusual exercises. If you're unsure about how to do a new exercise, have someone who is experienced at weight lifting show you. Strength building is certainly a high risk–high reward form of training. The risk of injury from doing the exercise incorrectly or with too much load is quite high. Improper technique for many of the exercises, especially those involving heavy loads or ballistic movements, greatly increases the risk. Ask for help. You might also have someone shoot a video of you doing the lifts and then search the Internet for examples of good technique to see how you compare.

Lifting to failure. Lifting to failure, which is common practice in serious weight lifting, calls for doing reps of a given workout until you are unable to lift the weight one more time and need help setting it down. It is effective for hard-core weight lifting, but I wouldn't recommend it for a cyclist. The injury risk is too great. Instead, pay close attention to how your muscles feel during each exercise and stop 1 or 2 reps short of failure. Stopping just short of failure doesn't produce quite as much strength—although the difference is quite small—but it reduces your risk of injury considerably.

Number of exercises. The weight lifting program described on the following pages assumes you have limited time for training and therefore recommends doing only a few exercises in each phase. The exercises I suggest are the ones most likely to result in performance gains. But feel free to do more than listed here if you have the time, energy, and inclination.

Muscle mass. Some athletes, especially young males, are likely to bulk up when lifting weights. While that's good for lifting heavy objects, it can be counterproductive for bike performance. That's a good reason to limit how much strength training you do and how many exercises you include in your weight lifting program. It's also why I suggest limiting the emphasis on serious weight lifting to only a handful of weeks. After those few weeks are over, weight lifting goes into a maintenance mode with a greatly reduced training load.

Loads also play a role here. The program recommended below increases the loads and decreases the reps over a few weeks' time. While there is research showing that a high number of reps with lighter loads lifted to failure produce much the same muscle strength, the high reps are also more likely to produce excessive muscle mass. Very few cyclists need to weigh more.

Food and strength. What you eat and when you eat it plays a role in strength development. The research suggests that neuromuscular gains are enhanced by eating 10 to 25 grams (0.35 to 0.875 ounces) of leucine-rich protein immediately after a weight lifting session (or within three hours of completion). Body size and the difficulty of the preceding workout determine how much you eat. The leucine amino acid will help your body rebuild the tissues that have broken down due

If you're unsure about how to do a new exercise, have someone who is experienced at weight lifting show you.

to the strain of lifting heavy loads. The protein source doesn't have to be anything expensive, exotic, or designed by a scientist. Real food will do quite nicely. Common protein- and leucine-rich foods that can be stored in your refrigerator for a quick post-workout snack that provides about 10 grams of protein and roughly 1,000 milligrams of leucine are boiled eggs (2 medium), cheddar cheese (1.5 ounces), or milk (10 ounces).

Special groups and weight lifting. Junior cyclists, especially those in their early teens, should be extra cautious when weight lifting. The bone growth plates in young athletes are still developing and are susceptible to damage from heavy loads. This is more likely to be an issue for juniors under age 16, but there is a considerable difference in physical maturity from individual to individual. That doesn't mean juniors shouldn't lift at all. For those who show an interest, I recommend starting a weight training program at about age 12 with very light loads and a focus on developing and refining the techniques of common strength exercises. Teens may also benefit from doing ballistic exercises with very light loads. As with all exercise programs for youth, weight lifting should be driven only by fun. At this stage of development, training schedules and strict routines are not recommended.

Riders over 50 may reap the greatest benefits from weight lifting. Older endurance athletes' race performances are often limited by a loss of muscle mass. They are also likely to experience a decrease in bone density, making them susceptible to fractures. Neuromuscular training is likely to produce significant improvement in muscle power while rebuilding bones. I've seen

Junior cyclists, especially those in their early teens, should be extra cautious when weight lifting.

Adult riders new to the sport are likely to benefit significantly from weight lifting.

many over-50 riders become much better racers by simply lifting weights regularly.

Twenty-something cyclists, both male and female, who have been training and racing for a long time probably don't need as much resistance training as older riders. They are likely to reap a much smaller gain in performance. Their youth yields a lot of natural power. And the mere fact that they are racing at a high level says a lot about their innate physiology. Yet I am aware of many riders at the highest levels of performance in the sport who swear by their weight lifting programs.

Regardless of age, adult riders new to the sport are likely to benefit significantly from weight lifting. The most common issue for novices, however, is finding the time. In their first year in the sport they are typically going through a lifestyle change. Trying to fit bike workouts into their weekly routines is difficult enough. Wedging in yet another sport-related activity in the gym may not seem possible. Although weight lifting would definitely benefit their growth as cyclists, newbies will make rapid performance gains just by frequent riding. If you are new to the sport and decide to lift weights, I'd recommend omitting the muscular strength (MS) phase that is described later in this chapter. You will make great gains without it and keep your risk of injury low. Save that phase for year two.

The Weight Lifting Program

I'm going to suggest several weight lifting exercises for your program. Then I'll lay out the phases and workout procedures. As with all forms of training, there are many ways to improve neuromuscular force through weight lifting. If you have a program that has worked well for you in the past, you should stay with it. If you do not have a program, but your poor power output leads you to believe that a lack of neuromuscular force is limiting your performance, then I strongly suggest incorporating a weight lifting program into your periodization plan as suggested in Chapters 7, 8, and 9.

Don't do all of the lifts described below. This is merely a shopping list of the exercises available to you so you can establish a personal weight lifting program. You should decide which you will do and when in the season you will do them. If you plan to follow a traditional weight lifting program, I strongly recommend including at least one hip-, knee-, and ankle-extension exercise such as a double-leg squat, single-leg squat, dead lift, step-up, lunge, or leg press. Also consider including a leg curl exercise to maintain agonist-antagonist muscle balance. And do one or more of the core strength exercises. You may also decide to use a ballistic lift in place of a traditional hip-, knee-, ankle-extension exercise. All of these exercises are described here, along with illustrations.

Traditional lifts. Heavy-load weight lifting has been shown by many research studies to be quite effective at improving cycling performance. The key to making significant gains is to do exercises that primarily work the extension of the hip, knee, and ankle joints at the same time, eventu-

ally lifting heavy loads with a low number of reps. This extension of the three leg joints is the primary movement that propels you forward when you're riding a bike. The power you produce results, in part, from how much force you apply to the pedal in the downstroke as the three joints extend. The more force you can generate without an increase in perceived effort, the better your race results. You'll climb, sprint, and time trial better. Of course, great muscular force isn't the only determiner of bike power. The other component is cadence. That comes largely from time in the saddle and the refinement of pedaling skills. Here we will look strictly at how to produce more force through developing stronger muscles that extend the hips, knees, and ankles.

There are six common weight lifting exercises that develop the muscles to drive the hip, knee, and ankle joints. While each is unique in some way, they all benefit muscular force for pedaling. The exercises described below are the two-leg squat, single-leg squat, dead lift, step-up, lunge, and leg press. Choose one or two of these exercises that you will do during each weight lifting session. You can also alternate several of them throughout the season for variety. Note that the first five exercises use free weights; only the last one uses a machine. Many health clubs and gyms have machines that may be used for some of the first five should you decide to avoid the risk of free weights.

The more force you can generate without an increase in perceived effort, the better your race results.

Double-Leg Squat

Of these hip-, knee-, ankle-extension exercises, the double-leg squat is probably the most commonly used by experienced riders. Figure 12.1 illustrates how the exercise is done. This figure shows the athlete using a barbell, but double-leg squats can be done just as well with a dumbbell in each hand or even while wearing a weight-loaded heavy-duty backpack. The following instructions will help you learn the movement if you've not done it before.

→ Consider wearing a weight belt to support your back, especially during the muscular strength phase.

→ Stand with a barbell on your shoulders just above the scapulae (or a dumbbell in each hand by your sides) with your feet about pedal's width apart. That's about 7 to 8 inches (18 to 20 cm) between your insteps. Your feet should be pointing straight ahead just like when you're pedaling a bike.

→ Keep your back straight, head up, and eyes looking straight ahead (not at your feet).

→ Squat until your thighs are almost parallel to the floor—about the same knee bend as when your pedal is at the 2 o'clock position. You can use a low stool or bench to gauge squat depth. When your butt touches the seat, stand up.

→ Keep your knees pointed straight ahead and over your feet as you squat.

→ Return to the start position with your back straight and eyes still looking straight ahead so that your head is up. Do *not* look down.

FIGURE 12.1 The double-leg squat

Single-Leg Squat

The advantage of the single-leg squat is that the load can be considerably lighter than for the double-leg, reducing the risk of injury. It also mimics the way you pedal: one leg at a time. The downside is that it requires good balance because you're standing on only one leg with the other supported behind you, as shown in Figure 12.2. It also takes more time to do all of the sets since there are twice as many.

→ With a barbell across your shoulders and just above the scapulae (or with a dumbbell in each hand by your sides), stand about 2 feet (60 cm) from a bench or other knee-high platform, facing away from it.

→ Reach back with one leg and place the top of that foot on the bench.

→ With your back straight and head up, squat on the forward leg until your thigh is almost parallel to the floor. The knee bend for the forward leg should be similar to the 2 o'clock pedaling position. You may need to adjust your distance from the bench to get the proper knee bend. You may need to adjust your stance forward or backward to keep your forward knee over the foot.

→ With your back still straight and eyes looking forward, not down, return to the starting position.

→ Repeat the exercise in the same way with the other leg.

FIGURE 12.2 The single-leg squat

Dead Lift

The dead lift is an excellent exercise for building leg extension strength, but it is riskier than the squat exercises because people new to this exercise nearly always use their back muscles to do most of the lifting instead of their legs. To get it right, I suggest getting some expert assistance. Ask a personal trainer at your gym to provide feedback on your dead lift skills. Another problem is if you are using a fairly light load, as you should be when starting the season: The plates on the ends of the bar are small, thus requiring you to reach quite low, with your knees considerably bent. This also overemphasizes the back. Some gyms have dead lift floor racks or lightweight adaptors resembling large plates that may be put on the ends of the bar so you start in a higher position. You can also do this exercise with dumbbells, which may be better for novices. Figure 12.3 illustrates how to do a dead lift. Note the head-up and straight back positions.

→ Stand facing the barbell with your feet about the width of your bike pedals: approximately 7 to 8 inches (18 to 20 cm) apart.

→ Start in a full squatting position with your knees bent so that your thighs are approximately parallel with the floor.

→ With your back straight, head up, and eyes looking forward (never down), reach down and grasp the bar with both hands, placing them slightly wider than your feet.

→ Stand up using only your legs to do the heavy lifting—not your back. Your back should be straight, not rounded.

→ Return to the starting position using your legs while keeping your back straight, head up, and eyes looking forward.

FIGURE 12.3 The dead lift

Step-Up

The step-up is another great exercise for building combined hip-, knee-, and ankle-extension strength while simulating the pedaling motion. While Figure 12.4 shows the athlete using a barbell, you can do it with dumbbells, which is somewhat safer because your center of gravity will be lower. It's very important that you get the height of the bench or other platform right for this exercise. You're trying to replicate the position your legs have on the bike when one pedal is at 6 o'clock and the other is at 12 o'clock.

→ Stand facing a low bench or other platform such as a very sturdy box that is about 13 to 15 inches (33 to 38 cm) high, with a barbell across your shoulder just above the scapulae (or with a dumbbell in each hand by your sides). Tall athletes need a higher bench than short athletes.

→ Place one foot on the bench. Your raised knee should be slightly below your hip joint with your thigh about parallel to the floor. You may be tempted in the early phases to use a higher platform so that your knee is above your hip. Don't do this; it will eventually prove to be counterproductive and risky when the loads become heavier.

→ With your back straight, head up, and eyes looking straight ahead (not down), step up onto the bench so that both feet are on it.

→ Step back down with the same foot, returning to the start position, and then repeat the movement. After all of the sets are completed for one leg, repeat the exercise using the other leg.

FIGURE 12.4   The step-up

Lunge

The lunge uses a lot of floor space because it involves taking long steps forward. It's a simple exercise but requires that you get the step distance right every time. Too short, and you'll have a hard time getting low enough; too long, and you'll place a great strain on the back leg's hip flexor. Figure 12.5 shows how it's done.

→ Stand tall with your feet together and a dumbbell in each hand (you can also use a barbell across your shoulders).

→ Step forward placing your foot flat on the floor with your toes pointing straight ahead. Your knee should be aligned with your ankle and your weight mostly on that leg. The rear leg helps to maintain balance.

→ Lower your body until the forward thigh is almost parallel to the floor. The rear knee should come close to touching the floor.

→ Stand up and step forward with your back foot so that you return to the starting position.

→ Repeat with the other leg in the same way. Continue alternating steps until you've completed the suggested reps *with each leg*.

→ Keep your back straight and head up throughout the movement.

FIGURE 12.5 The lunge

Leg Press

The leg press is the safest of the leg extension exercises since it's done with a machine and doesn't require balancing heavy loads. Its safety means that the loads can be much heavier than for the other hip-, knee-, ankle-extension exercises—in part because there is no balancing, and also because you're no longer lifting your body weight. Figure 12.6 illustrates the movement.

→ Place your feet on the platform so they are about pedal-width apart, roughly 7 to 8 inches (18 to 20 cm). Your feet should point straight up—not flare out.

→ In the lowered-platform position, your hips, knees, and ankles are at about the same bend as when pedaling with a foot at the 2 o'clock position. This means your knee angle will be slightly greater than 90 degrees. Some machines have a handy locking mechanism that prevents the platform from going too low. Use this to gauge the depth of your movement.

→ Press the platform up until your knees are almost straight and just short of locking out.

→ Lower the platform back to the starting position.

→ Your knees should be in line with your feet throughout the movement—never flared out or angled in.

FIGURE 12.6 The leg press

Leg Curl

The leg curl is not a primary power-enhancing exercise for cycling. Its purpose in this weight lifting program is to balance the strength of the three muscles that make up the hamstrings on the back of the thigh with the quadriceps muscles on the front of the thigh. This does not mean that the strength will be equal, with the capability to lift similar loads. The hamstring muscle group is not as effective as the quads for several reasons, including its relative mechanical limitations and size. So "balance" here doesn't mean a 1:1 strength relationship. The quads will always be stronger, perhaps twice as much.

The purpose of doing leg curls is to help prevent hamstring strains due to an imbalance in favor of the quads. Such an imbalance can lead to many types of injuries. Some research suggests that women may be in greater need of strengthening their hamstrings because their quad-hamstrings imbalance may be greater than men's. Focusing only on leg-extension strength may compound the problem.

Figure 12.7 shows a common hamstring exercise done on a machine. There are other types of machines that also work the hamstrings. If you are strength training in a home gym and don't have access to a machine, you can use an elastic band, as shown in Figure 12.8.

Later in this chapter you will read how many sets and reps you should do during various training periods. Note in Table 12.4 that the leg curl exercise has smaller loads and more reps in the muscular strength phase than do the hip-, knee-, ankle-extension exercises. I suggest using those lighter loads because the hamstrings are a fragile muscle group for many athletes.

FIGURE 12.7 The leg curl

→ Stand on the platform and bring one leg back so your ankle is in contact with the lever.

→ Curl your leg to about a right angle at the knee. Return to the starting position.

FIGURE 12.8 The alternative leg curl

→ Anchor one end of the elastic to a post or sturdy table leg and place the other loop around one ankle.

→ Lying prone, curl your leg to about a right angle at the knee. Return to starting position.

Core Exercises

You're probably familiar with core strength training, but you may not be aware of what your core is. You might also call it torso strength because that's the part of the body it's intended to strengthen.

Your core includes the muscles from your armpits to your groin. These muscles stabilize the spine, support the shoulders and hips, and transfer force between the arms and legs. Having a strong core ensures that any strength gains made in the arms and legs can be used effectively. The core is much like your car's transmission. The engine produces the torque, but it's the transmission that delivers torque to the wheels. If the transmission is weak, power output is compromised. So how does that work on a bike? When you climb a steep hill out of the saddle, your legs are creating the torque to drive the pedals. But to keep the bike stable so that it doesn't fall over, your hands and arms are countering the legs' torque by alternately pulling up on the handlebars with a force equal to that applied to the pedals. When the right leg drives the pedal down, the right arm pulls up on the bars. At that moment, torque is being transmitted from the right leg to the right arm through the torso, or core. If the core is weak, the power isn't balanced, and so it isn't fully transmitted.

Core strength, or lack of it, is also evident when riding at a high effort on flat terrain while seated, especially at a low cadence. The hips of a rider with a weak core will rock from side to side when he or she slowly turns a big gear at near max power. That will also cause the spine and shoulders to sway from side to side. All of this indicates a weak core.

There is also an injury-prevention benefit to strengthening your torso. Good core strength reduces the likelihood of lower back problems, which are all too common among riders.

There is little doubt, even if it's not obvious in the athlete's movements, that poor core strength results in a loss of muscular force. Core strength is necessary for high performance, to develop both the muscles that drive the pedals and the muscles that effectively transmit the power. Having powerful legs but a weak core is like shooting a cannon from a canoe. It's very ineffective.

How do you know if your core strength is sound? One way is to have a physical therapist do a total body assessment at the start of each season, as suggested in Chapter 5. Find one who works with endurance athletes, especially cyclists, and schedule an appointment for a head-to-toe exam to pinpoint weaknesses and imbalances that could reduce performance or lead to injury. The PT should recommend ways to correct any shortcomings. These fixes may include exercises to improve strength, joint range of movement, or postural improvement.

He or she may also suggest a bike fit, orthotics for your cycling shoes to correct pedaling imbalances, or even wedges that go under your cleats. However, I've found that for the athletes I've coached, improving core strength is one of the most commonly suggested solutions physical therapists make. An exam with a PT is the best way of finding out if you need to improve your core strength, but there is an out-of-pocket cost. It's cheaper to assume that your core needs strengthening and to work on it. It takes little time and has shown to be quite effective.

Let's take a look at a few common core strength–building exercises. There are many similar exercises in addition to those illustrated here. I'll show you only a few of the possibilities. You

Core strength is necessary for high performance.

can easily fit these exercises into your training, no matter how you develop strength: with traditional weight lifting sessions at home or at the gym, or on-the-bike functional exercises. They can also be done as a stand-alone workout whenever time is available, since they only take a few minutes to do. Or they can be included before or after a ride. A benefit of using free weights for the front plank with rows is that they will also help to develop a stronger core.

There are three core strengthening exercises suggested here. The most basic of these is the front plank. The side plank engages and develops a different group of core muscles, and the front plank with rows is an advanced exercise that places a greater strain on the core muscles.

Front Plank

The key to this exercise is maintaining a straight line from your head to your toes without sagging or raising your hips. It helps to have someone monitor and correct your posture the first few times you try it.

→ Assume the position shown in Figure 12.9 to form a rigid plank-like pose.

→ Your elbows should be shoulder-width apart and directly below your shoulders.

→ Your arms should point straight forward from your elbows or be pointed in slightly.

→ Hold the pose for about 30 seconds. That's 1 rep.

→ Rest for a minute or so after each rep and then repeat. Do 3 of these 30-second reps in a session.

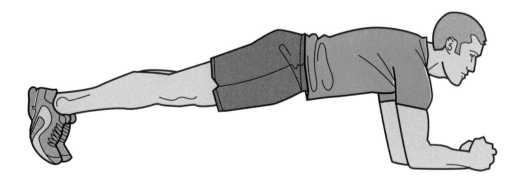

FIGURE 12.9   The front plank

Side Plank

The side plank engages and develops a different group of core muscles from those of the front plank.

→ Start with one hip on the floor while lying on your side with your feet stacked and your upper body resting on a bent elbow.

→ Raise your hips up off the floor. Balance on the side of your lower foot and elbow as shown in Figure 12.10.

→ Your legs, hips, shoulders, and head should form a straight line. It's beneficial to have an assistant help you get into this posture the first time, as it's difficult to sense when you have it right. A mirror may also prove helpful.

→ The free hand may either be raised high, as shown in the figure, or placed on your hip.

→ Hold this position for 30 seconds. Rest for about a minute and repeat 2 more times.

→ Switch to the other side and repeat.

FIGURE 12.10 The side plank

Front Plank with Rows

This is an advanced exercise that places a greater strain on the core muscles. Master the front plank position before attempting this one.

→ Assume the same basic starting position as the front plank, but instead of resting on your elbows, keep your arms straight, as in a push-up position, with your weight on your hands while holding lightweight dumbbells.

→ Wearing bike gloves may help take the stress off of your palms.

→ Space your feet shoulder-width apart.

→ While maintaining a straight-line posture from your head to your toes, slowly lift one of the weights to your shoulder as shown in Figure 12.11. Set it slowly back down to the floor and then do the same with the other arm. That constitutes 1 rep.

→ Do 5 reps in a set and then rest for a minute or so before repeating. Complete 3 sets in a session.

→ For a more advanced version, widen your foot position and alternately lift the weights to the sides until your arm is parallel with the floor.

FIGURE 12.11   The front plank with rows

Ballistic Lifting

Recall from the "Weight Lifting Guidelines" section earlier that ballistic exercises are done very rapidly during the lifting portion. Ballistic lifting not only builds neuromuscular force, it also develops power. Remember that in cycling, power is the result of force applied rapidly. Ballistic lifting trains this muscular action.

I've said this a few times now, but here it is once more to be certain that you understand: Ballistic lifting is risky. To minimize the risk, whenever you lift weights this way the loads must be considerably lighter than when you make the same movement more slowly. Consequently, for such exercises use loads of 50 percent of 1RM or less.

The number of reps should also be relatively low, on the order of 3 to 6 within each of the sets, because fatigue is likely to cause poor technique and increase the risk of injury. Be careful. Warm up with a very a light load, perhaps only body weight or an empty bar, before progressing to somewhat heavier loads in the ensuing sets.

There are many ballistic power-building exercises you could choose from when design-ing a neuromuscular program. In fact, any of the traditional weight lifting exercises described above could also be done explosively. You would simply lift the load rapidly and then set it back down slowly. But there is one ballistic exercise I highly recommend for building explosive cycling power: the power clean.

The power clean, shown in Figure 12.12, is an advanced power-building exercise that requires mastering a somewhat complex movement. Combining a load with an explosive movement makes for a risky exercise. To reduce the risk, you must master the movement. It's a skill that you learn through measured repetition.

Start by moving slowly with a very light load. At first that load may be something as light as a broomstick. Eventually, as your technique improves, you will progress to a bar only, and then, perhaps, to a bar with plates loaded on it. Again, always keep the load less than 50 percent of 1RM. If you're unsure what that load should be, err on the low side. Keep it light until you master the exercise. The explosive nature of this exercise is more important than the weight of the load, especially initially.

Ballistic lifting is risky.

Power Clean

Do not attempt this exercise if you are new to weight lifting. Save it until you've mastered the other hip-, knee-, ankle-extension exercises shown previously, especially the dead lift. Figure 12.12 shows how the power clean is done.

→ Start with a barbell near the floor with the bar held about halfway up your shins. Your knees should be bent, your head up, and your eyes looking forward (not down). Your butt is about the same height as your knees. This is a position similar to that described for the dead lift in Figure 12.3.

→ Grasp the bar with your hands slightly wider than your thighs and your palms facing down, with the knuckles forward of the bar.

→ In one continuous and explosive movement of the legs, torso, and arms, bring the bar to thigh height (your heels should come off of the floor if it's truly explosive) and then continue moving the bar upward to shoulder height with your elbows flaring out. Without pausing, rotate your arms so that the bar is resting on your hands with your elbows below the bar. This must be a nonstop explosive movement as you raise the bar from the shins to the shoulders. Use primarily the legs for lifting—not the back.

→ Set the weight down slowly using your legs, not your back. Rest for a few seconds, and then repeat. A full recovery between sets is necessary for building power.

FIGURE 12.12 The power clean

Weight Lifting Program Details

So far I've suggested several weight lifting exercises for you to consider in order to improve your neuromuscular force. You certainly don't need to do all of them. In fact, I think it's best to do the fewest number of exercises you can to produce the desired results, as I'm sure the time you have available for training, whether on the bike or in the gym, is limited.

Your goal for your weight lifting program is not to become a muscular hulk, but rather to improve your power. Pedal force and cadence are the keys to doing that. The purpose of most of the weight lifting exercises described here is to increase your force, or torque, without increasing the sensation of effort when you're pedaling at a high power. For example, your current functional threshold power (FTP) requires a maximal effort if you maintain it for a long time, such as 40 to 60 minutes. What weight lifting can do for you is to increase your power output for a long duration without it feeling any harder. This is how you know you're more aerobically fit: greater power with the same effort as before.

The exception is the ballistic power clean lift described above. Its purpose goes beyond increasing torque. With that exercise, you are combining speed of movement with force. That's power. But, as I keep saying, you must treat ballistic exercises with great respect, even if you are

an experienced lifter. This is not to discourage you: Recall from Chapter 10 that high-risk training also means high-reward results. Just respect the process.

In Chapters 7, 8, and 9, I presented an overview for how to periodize your weight lifting program. Let's review that. Table 12.2 lists the four phases of the weight lifting program in the order they should be followed, along with the purpose of each phase.

Table 12.3 shows a more detailed look at how the weight lifting phases advance from the first period of the season—the prep period—to the last—the peak period. (Note that there is no weight lifting in the 1-week race period.)

I suggest following this relationship between on-bike training periods and the weight lifting phases as closely as possible. The key message is that there is a shift in emphasis from weight lifting to riding as the season progresses. When you're doing a lot of weight lifting, training on the bike is minimal. That's why the most stressful weight lifting phase—muscular strength (MS)—is best scheduled in the base 1 period, when on-bike training is not very stressful at all. And when bike training is the primary focus, you cut back to minimal weight lifting. Trying to do a stressful weight lifting program at the same time you are doing very high-intensity bike training will cause both to suffer. Build neuromuscular force

Your goal for weight lifting is not to become a muscular hulk, but rather to improve your power.

TABLE 12.2 The Weight Lifting Phases and Their Purposes

WEIGHT LIFTING PHASE	PURPOSE
Anatomical Adaptation (AA)	Become accustomed to the various exercises
Muscular Transition (MT)	Gradually adapt to heavier loads
Muscular Strength (MS)	Build neuromuscular force
Strength Maintenance (SM)	Maintain the strength gains made in MS

TABLE 12.3 Details of the Weight Lifting Phases

WEIGHT LIFTING PHASE	PERIOD	TOTAL SESSIONS	SESSIONS PER WEEK	LOAD (% 1RM)	SETS PER SESSION	REPS PER SET	RECOVERY BETWEEN SETS (IN MINUTES)
Anatomical Adaptation (AA)	Prep	4–6	2–3	40–60	3–5	15–20	1–1.5
Muscular Transition (MT)	Prep	2–3	2–3	70–80	3–5	8–12	2–3
Muscular Strength (MS)	Base 1	8–12	2–3	85–95	3–4	3–6	3–4
Strength Maintenance (SM)	Base 2 Base 3 Build 1 Build 2 Peak	Indefinite	1	60–85	2	6–12	1–2

TABLE 12.4 Typical MS Session

EXERCISE	LOAD (% 1RM)	SETS	WEIGHT REPS OR CORE DURATIONS IN SECONDS	DURATION IN MINUTES
Warm-Up (Stationary Bike)	—	—	—	10
Double-Leg Squat	85–95	3	3–6	15
Front Plank	Body Weight	3	30	5
Step-Up, Ballistic	40–50	3	3–6	15
Side Plank	Body Weight	3	30	5
Leg Curl	70–80	3	8–12	10
Cooldown (Stationary Bike)	—	—	—	5
Total Workout	—	—	—	65

This table provides an example of how a weight lifting session in the muscular strength (MS) phase might look. In the AA and MT phases preceding MS, the exercises may be the same, but the loads and reps are different, as shown in Table 12.3. Note that this is only an example; you may choose other exercises.

first (AA, MT, and MS phases) in the prep and base 1 periods and then maintain it (SM) while developing a high level of bike fitness in all of the remaining periods.

Now let's examine what a weight lifting workout might look like in the key muscular strength (MS) phase. These are suggestions; you may do different exercises from the discussion in "Weight Lifting Guidelines" section earlier.

FUNCTIONAL FORCE TRAINING

I've coached many athletes over the years who didn't enjoy going to the gym to lift weights. I understand. That's a common feeling among cyclists. There have also been some who didn't have easy access to a gym or simply didn't have the time to devote to lifting.

How about you? Can you fit a gym workout into your busy day? What if you have the time and would like to do some weight lifting but don't have a gym handy? A home-based gym is one possible solution, though not always practical. Or what if you simply don't enjoy weight lifting and you'd much rather be riding? Should you lift anyway? The answer comes down to why you race bikes. If it's for fun, a reason I expect plays a major role, then don't do things that aren't fun. That may mean not lifting. If you don't enjoy it, don't do it.

Of course, not lifting weights means you are less likely to reach your potential for high-performance cycling. As you've read in this chapter, neuromuscular training has many benefits. If you've decided not to lift weights, wouldn't it be nice if you could reap similar benefits in another way? Well, you can. There are bike workouts you can do that develop neuromuscular fitness without requiring you to ever lift a barbell. Such on-bike workouts can increase your pedaling force and make you a more powerful rider. They're a great alternative if you don't have the time, the facilities, or the interest for weight lifting. Let's take a look at how to do this.

As with weight lifting, these alternative neuromuscular workouts require putting great loads on your muscles, tendons, and joints. There is simply no way to get around this if you want to build force. In the gym, when lifting heavy weights, the risk of injury is generally obvious. It may not be quite so obvious when you're doing force-development training on the bike. But the risk is still there. Doing these workouts to excess certainly could cause an injury and interrupt your training, perhaps for several weeks.

You will be putting a great deal of stress on your knees. If you are prone to knee injuries, it's

On-bike workouts can increase your pedaling force and make you a more powerful rider.

best to avoid the bike workouts I describe below. In any case, moderation is key. The first time you try either of the two workouts that follow, do only 1 set of 3 or 4 reps and hold back a bit on how much effort you put into each. You can slowly increase the reps and the effort in subsequent sessions as your body adapts to the loads. And, of course, be sure to warm up well before doing these workouts.

I call these two workouts "force reps." One is done on flat terrain and the other on a short hill. They're basic on-the-bike workouts for building strength. Each involves pedaling in a very high gear with a low cadence and maximal effort while seated.

Does this description sound familiar? It should. This is very much like doing double- or single-leg squats, step-ups, or lunges with heavy loads. The hip, knee, and ankle extend in the same way. In doing these workouts, you are working specifically on building your capacity to deliver force to the pedal.

A power meter is very beneficial for these workouts because it gives immediate feedback on how great the load is for each rep. If you don't have a power meter, you'll have to go by feel, which is not very precise when it comes to determining if you are, for example, making progress over time. A heart rate monitor is of no use in these workouts.

Flat Force Reps

As the name implies, this workout is done on flat terrain. It calls for using a high gear such as 53 × 14. It should be such a hard gear to turn that even when using full force, you can only initially manage a cadence of about 50 rpm. You'll probably need to do some experimenting with gears the first time you do this workout to find the right gear for keeping your cadence that slow. While staying in the saddle, otherwise pedal as usual, but with a very high effort. It's important that you stay seated. Do not stand. This workout is also described in Appendix B in the Muscular Force Workouts category as workout MF1. Here's how this workout is done following the warm-up.

On flat terrain, shift to a high gear, such as 53 × 14, and slow down so that you nearly come to a stop.

Now accelerate by turning the cranks only 6 or 8 strokes so that you do a total of 3 or 4 pedal strokes for each leg. (Of course, you are alternating legs pedaling as you normally do—it's not just pedaling with one leg.) The effort should be extremely high for each pedal stroke.

While the first couple of pedal strokes will be quite slow—around 50 rpm or lower—by the last couple of strokes the cadence will increase.

If there is reason for concern about your knees, do only one set of 6 to 8 total pedal strokes and be a bit conservative with effort.

If you do a second set, recover by riding slowly in a low gear for 3 to 4 minutes. Do no more than 2 sets the first time you do this workout. Table 12.5 provides the details.

Hill Force Reps

This workout is the same as flat force reps, but it's done on a hill to increase the neuromuscular stress. Before doing this workout, you should have previously done at least 4 of the flat force reps and know that your knees do not complain about the high load required.

- After warming up well, go to a short, steep hill (about an 8 percent grade is perfect) with little or no traffic. You need to be able to safely make a U-turn at the top and at the bottom.
- Shift to a high gear. It won't be as high as for the flat force reps; for example, it may be 53 × 15.
- Come nearly to a stop at the bottom of the hill.
- While staying seated, alternate driving the pedals down 3 to 6 times with each leg while otherwise pedaling in a normal manner. That's 6 to 12 total pedal strokes.
- Do up to 3 sets in a workout with 3 to 4 minutes of easy pedaling in a low gear for recovery between them. See Table 12.5 for all of the details.

Since the force reps portions of these two workouts only take, at most, 15 minutes per set (not including the warm-up), doing 3 sets takes about 45 minutes. Your planned ride for that day may be considerably longer and could include another workout portion, such as the aerobic endurance ability. It's quite common to combine two workouts from Appendix B to create sessions specific to your training goals. If you do combine another workout with force reps, do them first, followed by whatever else you may include. It's best not to do muscular force workouts near the end of the ride when you are fatigued; you cannot make a tired muscle stronger. Another option if you are doing only a force reps session is to include a lengthy cooldown following the force reps.

I advise you to do a recovery ride the day following a session that includes 2 or 3 sets of hill force reps. This is most likely in the base 1 period, as suggested by Table 12.5. While this workout may not seem all that challenging when you're doing it, it often makes itself known the next day.

Do a recovery ride the day following a session that includes 2 or 3 sets of hill force reps.

TABLE 12.5 Periodization of Force Reps Done as an Alternative to Traditional Weight Lifting

PERIOD	TYPE OF WORKOUT	TOTAL SESSIONS	SESSIONS PER WEEK	SETS PER SESSION	REPS PER SET (EACH LEG)	RECOVERY BETWEEN SETS (IN MINUTES)
Prep	Flat Force Reps	4–6	2–3	1–2	3–4	3–4
Base 1 (may continue into early base 2)	Hill Force Reps	8–12	2	3	3–6	3–4
Base 2	Hill Force Reps	Indefinite	1	1	3–4	—
Base 3						
Build 1						
Build 2						
Peak	Hill Force Reps	1 or 2	1	1	2–3	—
Race	None	None	—	—	—	—

TSS AND WEIGHT LIFTING

I'm often asked how to apply the Training Stress Score (TSS) system to weight lifting. I introduced the concept of TSS in Chapter 4 as a more meaningful way of expressing training load than using hours, miles, or kilometers. You may recall that TSS is the combination of both duration (time) and intensity (power or heart rate). Of course, there is no need to be concerned with this if you are doing functional force training on the bike instead of weight lifting, as your power meter or heart rate monitor will record the TSS for all portions of your rides, including force reps (note that heart rate is much less indicative of the stress of such a workout because the reps are quite brief and your heart rate will lag behind your actual effort). So how can you apply TSS to weight lifting?

Let's start this discussion with the observation that duration has no bearing on strength building. Time is only important when developing endurance. It doesn't matter how long you were in the gym for a weight lifting session. The

only thing that matters in weight lifting is how great the weight load was for the workout.

But if you are using TSS to measure your bike training load, how can you come up with a TSS score for a weight lifting workout in order to express the total workload you're doing? (As an aside, let me note that it's probably not necessary to do this—most cyclists do not—but as a numbers person myself I do understand the interest.)

To have thorough training load data that includes weight lifting, you need to have a TSS number for each gym workout. So how can you do that? We don't have a perfect method yet, although technology may give us one. I expect to see a type of weight lifting device soon that can do this. It would consist of a magnetic accelerometer attached to a barbell. After indicating the total load on the bar on a smartphone app, it would then calculate the training load including the number of reps, the range of movement, and the speed of each lift. From that data, TSS could be determined just as with a power meter. This would have the potential to revolutionize weight lifting and make it a much more effective train-

Recall that TSS is the combination of duration and intensity.

ing method for endurance athletes. But we're not there yet. Right now, we're stuck with some low-tech approaches.

The first is to simply use a Rating of Perceived Exertion (RPE), as shown in Table 4.1. That's subjective, but it works. For example, if you do a hard weight lifting session in the MS phase, you may rate the total workout RPE as 9 (on a 10-high scale). Multiply that by 10, and you have an estimated TSS of 90. Before you send me a letter of complaint, let me acknowledge that there are lots of weaknesses with this system. Nevertheless, it can give you a fair estimate.

A more definitive method used by serious weight lifters involves measuring "tonnage": how much total weight was lifted in a workout. Tonnage is based on the load lifted for a given exercise multiplied by the number of reps of that exercise. That's the training load for a single set. At the end of the session, you add up all of the set tonnages for each of the exercises you did, divide by 2,000, and you have the session tonnage. Multiply that by 10, and you now have a reasonable estimate for the weight lifting session TSS. Of course, there are still problems. For example, this doesn't include the core exercises that are more difficult to quantify, because they *do* include time (for example, a 30-second hold of the plank position). And the reps are stationary since it's an isometric exercise.

I realize that this is kludgy. There aren't too many options, however, since we are lacking the technology that would drive this system—at least as of this writing. Then again, I'm not completely convinced that such measurement is necessary in the first place. As much as I would like to put a number on it, you may simply decide to accept that weight lifting is beneficial to performance and that your workouts are sufficiently challenging to reap such a reward, and therefore not mess with quantifying it.

SUMMARY: MUSCULAR FORCE TRAINING

The muscular force you apply to the pedals is one of two critical components that account for your power on the bike. The other is the speed at which you turn the cranks: cadence. You become a more powerful rider by developing both. That means faster racing, whatever your focus: time trialing, climbing, sprinting, or all-around performance. The time to develop both of these power-producing elements of cycling is early in the season, in the prep and base 1 periods.

Muscular force training has to do with building stronger muscles. Strength is not necessarily big muscles. In fact, we want to avoid bulk if at all possible. Strength is the result of training both the muscular and the nervous systems to deliver force to the pedal whenever needed. One without the other is inadequate for high-performance racing. The nervous system's contribution to pedal force has to do with the recruitment of muscle fibers. When it's time for a force-producing muscle, such as the quadriceps, to fire, the nervous system ensures not only that the timing of the force application is right but also that the proper number of fibers is called upon to contract. A well-trained nervous system also means that the muscles are properly synchronized when pedaling.

To achieve these muscular force goals, your training must apply stress to both systems. You can accomplish this with traditional weight lifting and with functional, or on-bike, force training.

That brings us to the two types of neuromuscular strength training suggested in this chapter. The first is traditional weight lifting. When doing such a gym-based workout, the emphasis must be on mastering the movements of pedaling a bike under a heavy load, not merely lifting weights to have a strong-looking body.

With the exception of the core exercises and hamstring curl, all of the weight lifting exercises described in this chapter—the double-leg squat, single-leg squat, dead lift, step-up, lunge, and leg press—involve concurrent extensions of the hip, knee, and ankle. I recommend that you also build your core strength with the front plank, side plank, and front plank with rows.

The leg curl exercise will help reduce the possibility of a muscle injury by maintaining a safe level of strength balance between the hamstrings and the quadriceps.

An alternative to the hip-, knee-, ankle-extension exercises is called the power clean. This is a ballistic Olympic lift—one that is done very rapidly. It's often called an "explosive" exercise. The hip-, knee-, ankle-extension lifts may also be done explosively. Whenever you do lifts like this, use loads that are 50 percent of 1RM or less in order to reduce your risk of injury.

The key to successful weight lifting lies in mastering the movements of each exercise during the anatomical adaptation (AA) phase of training in the prep period. After a few such sessions in which you use light loads while learning the movements, you progress to the muscular transition (MT) phase. During this phase, usually in the late prep or early base 1 periods, you gradually increase the loads for each lift while reducing the number of reps in a set.

The most critical phase of weight lifting for the advanced rider is the muscular strength (MS) phase in the base 1 period, possibly spilling over into early base 2. Following MS is the strength maintenance (SM) phase, which lasts until the week of your first A-priority race of the season.

Athletes are tempted to skip AA early in the season and jump right into using heavy loads with few reps. This is usually a mistake. In order to avoid injury and get the greatest possible benefits from the exercises, you must learn effective movement patterns before going to heavy loads. This involves lifting positions and posture. Each of the above exercise descriptions emphasizes positions, such as simulating foot positions on the pedals and depth of each lift. Body posture mostly has to do with back and head positions. Many of the exercises call for keeping the eyes looking forward, not down. That keeps the load primarily on the legs and not on the low back.

Functional force training simulates weight lifting, but it's done on the bike. Since most of the weight lifting exercises described in this chapter simulate pedaling movements while lifting a heavy load, it's possible to reverse that and do on-bike exercises to build force, simulating weight lifting. This is an effective way of accomplishing much the same thing as weight lifting without trying to fit gym workouts into an already busy schedule. It also works well for the athlete who doesn't enjoy lifting weights and would be much happier riding a bike instead.

The functional exercises on the bike involve using very high gears and low cadences while staying seated on the saddle. These workouts start with flat force rep sessions before progressing to hill force reps that increase the load.

> In order to avoid injury and get the greatest possible benefits from the exercises, you must learn effective movement patterns before going to heavy loads.

These workouts are best avoided by riders with tender knees.

The periodization of on-bike muscular force training is similar to that of weight lifting. Start with flat force reps and gradually transition to hill force reps. Do them early in the season in the prep and base 1 periods. Following that, do a greatly reduced version of the hill force reps workout for the remainder of the season.

Riders who like to carefully quantify their training using TSS may use a system suggested in this chapter for assigning a Training Stress Score to a weight lifting session. Bear in mind that should you decide to do this and you've not done it in previous seasons, you will likely want to increase your weekly TSS by the anticipated weight lifting TSS for the week. If you don't do this and keep your weekly TSS the same as in previous seasons, your on-bike TSS will be reduced.

This chapter was perhaps a heavy load in many ways. It may have challenged your thinking about developing your muscular force. Increasing it is imperative if you want to be a more powerful rider. This is mostly accomplished very early in the season. In the next chapter, we will look at what you can do late in your seasonal buildup to also improve performance.

TAPERING TO RACE

IF YOU'VE NEVER TAPERED for a race before, this chapter is likely to seem strange—and perhaps even scary. I'm going to suggest in the coming pages that you reduce your training load—hours, distance, or TSS—in order to race better than you may have otherwise thought possible.

The training load reduction will occur in the last 2 or 3 weeks prior to your A-priority race. That is certainly the scariest time there is to cut back on training. Most athletes' guts tell them to do more, not less. Deep down, they sense that physical fitness is the only concern when it comes to race success. That seems to make sense. But it's wrong.

I can tell you from years of training athletes for races of all types that the best predictor of race success is not *fitness*, but *form*. Of course, your fitness must be high, but trying to get it even higher in the last 2 weeks before the race is not going to do it. For example, given two riders who are the same in many ways—including having the exact same level of fitness 2 weeks prior to a race—the one who focuses mostly on form in the coming few days will beat the rider who is intent on increasing fitness. I'd put my money on form over more fitness every time.

So what are fitness and form? We covered them in Chapter 3, but since they are so important to your race taper, it's a good idea to review them briefly here.

FITNESS

High-level fitness results from many small physical performance gains made over the course of consecutive workouts. With consistent training, fitness grows over weeks, months, and years. Cycling fitness is usually defined in sports science as an individual's mix of aerobic capacity, anaerobic threshold, and economy (see Chapter 6 for details). These three physical markers are the most basic components of race readiness.

Fitness may also be thought of as the product of an increasing training load. Some combination of your saddle time, distances traveled, training intensities, and TSS have gradually made you more physically fit than you were earlier in the season. As you read in Chapter 3, it's your increasing training load over time that produces fitness. This is the starting place for race readiness. To be race ready, you must first of all be physically fit.

But since greater fitness is a product of an increased training load, it then must also hold true that a decreased training load causes a loss of fitness. You can't become more fit by training less. Experienced athletes almost always accept this explanation that an increase in fitness results from an increase in training load—until we come to the topic of tapering. Those who have done a pre-race taper will now argue that training *less* at this time in the season makes them more fit. After all, they race better when they taper than when they don't. They even feel more fit. Well, they can't have it both ways. It's either one or the other. Which is it? In fact, it is not an increase in fitness that causes this phenomenon. It's form.

FORM

What we've been talking about so far could be called "race readiness." That means being physically ready and mentally prepared for the demands of the A-priority race. This is the fitness component of race-day readiness. But in the context of form, race readiness goes beyond what we've been calling "fitness." Race readiness embraces topics beyond physical fitness, including, for example, a well-planned strategy and a wide array of tactics that have been rehearsed for potential use in support of the strategy. Also included as subsets of race readiness are prepara-

tion for the expected environmental conditions of the race, such as heat, humidity, cold, wind, rain, and snow, and course conditions like hills. Another consideration that could impact race readiness is nutrition, both before and during the race. We might also add hydration and equipment selection; both play a role in your readiness to race. All of this is just a part of what I'm calling "form."

The other key portion of form is "freshness." By that, I mean the absence of fatigue. Eliminating fatigue gets you ready to race. And the only effective way to remove fatigue is to reduce your training load. In other words, less training means more form.

The athlete who has tapered properly sees form play out as faster racing. Fitness does not increase when you're tapering. In fact, as explained in Chapter 3, a small amount of fitness is lost prior to the race.

The portion of your training load that you *must* decrease is duration—not intensity. During this time, intensity, as you'll see shortly, must remain high.

So what tapering means, in a nutshell, is a reduction in workout duration resulting in an increase, percentage-wise, of your training load intensity. That's the bottom line for tapering.

There are a lot of moving parts to a successful taper. Let's dig into the details.

THE COMPONENTS OF TAPERING

The pre-race taper stretches across the peak and race periods that you scheduled for the last 2 to 3 weeks prior to your A-priority race. This training is called "tapering" because you reduce, or taper,

To be race ready, you must first of all be physically fit.

Eliminating fatigue gets you ready to race. And the only effective way to remove fatigue is to reduce your training load.

your training load by cutting workout duration before the race in order to gain freshness and come into form.

If done right, reduced weekly training volume during the taper results in greater form on race day and faster racing. The most common mistake in these last few weeks is not becoming fresh enough, and that is usually due to including too much volume in an attempt to maintain or even increase physical fitness. You may recall from Chapter 4 that the key to racing success for the advanced rider is intensity—not how many hours he or she rides in a week. For the highly experienced rider, the last few weeks prior to a race are the worst possible time to try to increase fitness with more saddle time. If you don't have good aerobic fitness by now, you will never have it by race day. Instead, the key to a successful taper is race-like intensity. These are the hard workouts that are done only a few times in these last couple of weeks, as I will explain shortly.

The high-intensity workouts you do during the taper period are often interval workouts, no matter what type of race you're doing or its duration. These intervals must, first of all, simulate the strategic intensities you anticipate during your race. If there is a hill that is likely to have a significant impact on your race outcome, then you need to be prepared for the intensity of that climb. That usually means doing hill intervals with a duration and volume closely related to, or greater than, what you expect on race day. (You can also simulate the race with a fast group ride that includes a similar hill.) If sprinting will likely determine your outcome, then you need to include sprints in your key taper workouts. If it's a time trial, then you need to rehearse the greatest intensity you expect, or can sustain, in

the race. Essentially, you must use workouts that mimic those moments in the race that will have the greatest impact on your performance. And the unifying piece here is high intensity.

The next important component of tapering is frequent recovery. You need to come into your race-simulation workouts rested and ready to ride at a high level. That means maintaining low intensity and low duration through the two days prior to your key workouts so that every third day you are champing at the bit to go fast. The best workouts during this period may be races, especially ones that are shorter than your goal event but which are likely to have a similar or greater intensity. You can also use fast group rides if you are tapering for a road race or criterium. The third option is interval workouts done with another rider. The final option is doing interval workouts by yourself.

Any races you do during this period should be C priority and kept shorter than the goal race to make sure that you can recover and be ready to go hard and fast again following two days of easy riding. Avoid any race that is likely to prevent such recovery, or intentionally abandon the race at some preplanned point. I know that dropping out may not be in your nature, especially if you're turning a big gear and feeling good, but taking an extremely stressful race all the way to the finish line could easily mean that in three days you won't be ready to go hard again, thus screwing up the taper and threatening your A-priority race results. If you're unsure about the C race, don't do it. Stick to your plan.

Whatever races or workouts you do on these hard days should prepare you in some way for what is critical to the outcome of your goal race. That likely includes climbing, sprint-

Reduced weekly training volume during the taper results in greater form on race day.

ing, or time trialing. Races that challenge the key determiner of your A-race outcome should be your first choice when considering race options at this time. But if you normally don't race very often, then doing a race of any type, regardless of your A-race demands, can be beneficial because it will help prepare you in many subtle ways for race day. Those preparations may include mental, nutritional, logistical, environmental, or other factors that help you become race ready.

Having successful high-intensity workouts or C-priority races throughout this period also builds confidence. We all know how much that counts when it comes to putting your wheel on a start line. Being rested prior to high-intensity sessions not only ensures freshness but also increases your chances of having good race-simulations. You should come to race day feeling convinced of your race preparation and readiness.

An important point is that you must trust your training plan and its reduced volume throughout the taper. The scariest part is the reduction in workout duration, especially on the easy days between the high-intensity sessions. If you have never followed such a tapering plan before, you'll be skeptical, if not intimidated, by the low workout durations on these days. You're likely to be afraid of losing too much fitness. That's a common concern. But be resolute in your conviction that this reduction is necessary for gaining form. If you make the durations longer in an attempt to maintain fitness, you'll be giving up form. Big mistake.

The two back-to-back recovery days after each hard ride should be about half your normal workout duration. Even the high-intensity sessions must be shorter. But they can be about 80 percent of what you normally do when in the build period for a high-intensity workout.

Throughout the entire taper, do all of your hard rides on the bike you will use on race day. If you're training for a stage race with road and time trial stages, use both bikes at appropriate times with workouts that match the bike and stage type. Get dialed in.

PEAK AND RACE PERIOD ROUTINES

Tapering consists of everything I've described above, and it's a lot to think about when you're preparing for a race. To make tapering a little easier to understand and apply, let's dig a little deeper into the peak and race periods by looking at training routine examples.

The Peak Period

The peak period typically lasts 1 to 2 weeks and ends several days prior to the race. That's when the race period begins. A 2-week peak period is typically included before late-season races following a long and stressful build period. It's also common before very long races, including stage races.

A short peak period may only last 3 to 5 days. This is common for highly fit and experienced riders who recover quickly. It's also more common for an early season race or for a very short A-priority race such as a criterium of 1 hour or less.

As explained earlier, there are two purposes to the peak period. The first is shedding accumulated fatigue by increasing the easy recovery days. The second is keeping fitness at a high level with high-intensity training. This combination produces both race readiness and freshness.

The key to a strong peak is a race-like workout that simulates a portion of the race. Workouts on the following two days are short rides at low

You should come to race day feeling convinced of your race preparation and readiness.

The key to a strong peak is a race-like workout that simulates a portion of the race.

TABLE 13.1 Two-Week Peak Period Routine for an Advanced Cyclist

Monday	Muscular Force (see Tables 12.3 and 12.5 for details), or day off if you haven't been doing Muscular Force workouts
Tuesday	HIT
Wednesday	Easy
Thursday	Easy
Friday	HIT
Saturday	Easy
Sunday	Easy
Monday	Muscular Force and/or HIT
Tuesday	Easy
Wednesday	Easy
Thursday	HIT
Friday	Easy

This is an example of a 2-week peak period routine for an advanced cyclist. The high-intensity workout abilities (muscular endurance, anaerobic endurance, and sprint power) are indicated as "HIT." The "easy" workouts are active recovery sessions done mostly in zones 1 and 2. The workouts may be rearranged to better fit your particular situation, such as when you schedule a C-priority race.

intensity. Of course, "short" is a relative term. If you ride 20 hours per week, your ride may be 90 minutes to 2 hours long. But if you train 10 hours per week, it could be 45 to 60 minutes. These recovery rides will stay appropriately short throughout the peak period while the durations of the high-intensity race-like workouts gradually get shorter. As these rides become shorter, your weekly volume—hours or TSS—drops rather rapidly. By the end of the peak period, it should decrease 30 to 50 percent from what it was in the build 2 period.

With all of this in mind, Table 13.1 offers an example of how a 2-week peak period may look. In this example, the high-intensity workouts emphasize muscular endurance ability for an A race that is a time trial, anaerobic endurance if it's a road race or criterium, and sprint power for sprint preparation. These workouts should also simulate the expected conditions of the race, including the key portions that are most important to your race-goal success. The easy workouts are done in zones 1 and 2. The example in Table 13.1 may not exactly work for you, but it will help you get started in designing your own routine. Regardless of how long the peak period lasts, the pattern is always race-like intensity followed by recovery.

The Race Period

There are several ways to taper in order to achieve the twin goals of race readiness and freshness on the day of your A-priority race. Regardless of exactly how you do it, the underlying principles remain the same: Reduce the volume of training while emphasizing race-like intensity. That combination will bring you to a peak. The trick is doing this without losing too much fitness. In the peak period, I described how to taper with a high-intensity ride every third day and recovery workouts in between. Now as you come to the last few days before your race, I suggest making some changes.

Training in the week of the race is unlike the way you've been training throughout the season, or even in the immediately preceding peak period. Both rest and intensity are emphasized even more than they were in the peak period, but in a unique way. The rides are all very short and highly focused on race intensity. Let's take a look at the details of this last critical week of training using a somewhat unusual routine.

In the race period, the athletes I train do three or four interval workouts, depending on whether their race is on Saturday or Sunday (see Table 13.2). Following a warm-up, they do several 90-second intervals with 3-minute recoveries. That's followed by a short cooldown,

making for a rather brief session. This ensures both race readiness and freshness by the end of the week.

The intervals are done at the highest intensity expected in the race. While 90-second intervals are appropriate for muscular endurance and anaerobic endurance intervals, they are a bit long for a sprint. Sprinters should still do 90-second hard efforts, but with two parts: a sustained high effort, as when following a leadout man or coming out of a corner in a criterium, and then an all-out sprint at the end of the interval. The number of intervals decreases during the week, which means the individual workout times also gradually decrease. The rides should be quite short. Table 13.2 suggests how many intervals to do each day of the week depending on whether your race day is Saturday or Sunday.

TABLE 13.2   Example of a Traditional Race Period Routine

	SATURDAY RACE	SUNDAY RACE
Monday	Easy or day off	Easy or day off
Tuesday	HIT (4–6 intervals)	HIT (4–6 intervals)
Wednesday	HIT (3–5 intervals)	HIT (3–5 intervals)
Thursday	Day off from training or very easy and short ride; possible travel day	HIT (2–4 intervals)
Friday	HIT (1–3 intervals)	Day off from training or very easy and short ride; possible travel day
Saturday	Race	HIT (1–3 intervals)
Sunday	Day off from training or easy ride	Race

This table provides an example of a traditional race period routine for a Saturday or Sunday race for an advanced rider who finished the peak period with a HIT ride or C-priority race on Sunday, as suggested in Table 13.1. The HIT workouts in the race period continue the emphasis on the key ability relative to your race (muscular endurance, anaerobic endurance, or sprint power). The HIT rides start with your standard warm-up followed by 90-second intervals done at the appropriate ability with 3-minute recoveries. Finish with a short cooldown. The HIT workouts each day have a gradually decreasing number of 90-second intervals as the week progresses, as suggested by the number in parentheses.

Note that heart rate cannot be used to gauge intensity for these intervals; they are too brief. Your heart would not have enough time to respond and achieve the targeted zone in 90 seconds. Once again, power is the preferred measure of intensity throughout this week.

For most athletes, I've found that the easiest day of race week is best scheduled two days before the race, as shown in Table 13.2. This is usually a day off or, at most, a short and low-intensity ride. It may also be a day of travel to the race venue. The greater the venue's heat or altitude relative to where you've recently been training, the earlier in the week you should arrive. Even a little adaptation is better than none. Note that the day before the race also includes some race-like intensity with a very brief session. Stay off your legs as much as possible the remainder of the day.

Regardless of how well you manage the many details of tapering, the racing truth is that sometimes it works and sometimes it doesn't. You're a human, not a robot. That's just the way the world is. But that doesn't mean you have no other levers to pull. To improve your chances of racing well, in the final few days before every A race keep a record in your training diary (see Chapter 14) of what you do. This could include travel details, sleep patterns, when and what you eat, mental and physical stressors, race equipment selections such as wheels, pre-race warm-up, and anything else that may affect race preparation. If the race goes well, try to repeat these details for subsequent races. If things don't go well, study what you did and make appropriate adjustments before the next race. Remember, even Eddy Merckx didn't win the road world championship on his first try. But he did win it the next time.

SUMMARY: TAPERING TO RACE

The closer you get to race day, the more critical your training becomes. What you do in the final two or three weeks can have a bigger impact on performance than what you did in the preceding two or three months.

No matter what taper methodology you decide to follow, there are two critical components that all good coaches take into consideration: volume and intensity. To be fresh on race day, you must reduce training volume. There are two ways to do this. You can do fewer workouts each week, or you can make your workouts shorter. Other than possibly taking a day off once per week during the taper, I'd recommend doing shorter rides at this time.

The other critical component of the taper is workout intensity. It must frequently be high if you are to come to the start line race ready. Doing the opposite—increasing volume and decreasing intensity—is highly likely to produce a poor race. You'll simply lose race-like fitness and race with tired legs.

What I've proposed in this chapter is that you manage your taper by doing a high-intensity ride every third day with two easy recovery days in between. That is the routine until the race period starts. The race period is generally the last six or seven days before the race. In these few remaining workouts, I have riders do short intervals at race intensity several times on most days of that week. This is the time to closely simulate the race conditions that will determine its outcome. So, depending on what type of race it is, these intervals may be done on a race-like hill that is likely

To be fresh on race day, you must reduce training volume.

to cause a break; or on a time trial bike, rehearsing pacing; or as long lead outs, finishing with sprints. In other words, rehearse what you expect the race situations and intensity to be, as closely as you can. If possible, include environmental conditions that you may experience such as heat, wind, and altitude. All of this also prepares you mentally. You'll go to the start line with confidence. That counts for a lot on race day.

While I've seen this tapering method produce great results for many riders over the years, it isn't foolproof. You could have a poor race performance even if you follow it exactly. It's rare to find a rider who has never had a race setback. Despite the best possible taper plan, things often go wrong in the last few days before your race. For example, you may have had to work overtime and so you missed a key workout. Or you might have caught a cold and so your training suffered for a few days. Or the weather turned nasty and you couldn't get out on your bike. There are any

number of training interrupters. Things happen. There are no guarantees. I can only tell you that what I've described here is the best possible plan you can use to prepare yourself in the weeks and days just before your A-priority race.

Regardless of the outcome, you are best advised to tweak your taper as necessary before the next A race. If, for example, you felt flat on race day, you may need a shorter taper next time, or perhaps harder workouts in the last three days before the race. If you feel tired on race day, you need a lower level of total training load in the last days.

If you fully believe that you are capable of racing at a much higher level of performance, then experiment with the types of workouts, especially their intensity, on the hard days of your taper. The bottom line is that training, especially tapering, is a scientific study with only one subject: you. As with anything else in training, if it didn't work, fix it next time.

THE TRAINING DIARY

ASIDE FROM your bike, the best race-preparation tool is a training diary. Used properly, it can steer your performance in the right direction for your entire cycling career.

A diary makes your training more purposeful by maintaining focus on your goals and objectives. Without frequent reminders of why you ride, it's easy for your underlying purpose to become a vague memory. Without clear goals, you are just riding a bike and accumulating pointless hours, miles, kilometers, or TSS. The hubbub of daily training and the pressing demands of your off-the-bike life can easily cloud your reason for riding so much. A training diary reminds you every day why you train. As one of my clients used to frequently tell me, it's a mission.

A training diary can also help you measure the most important factors to improve your limiters. These essential metrics help you pinpoint unwanted trends early on and make training corrections. A diary answers critical questions about those metrics: Is my FTP increasing? Is my power-to-weight ratio where it should be? How is my training load progressing, and how does it compare with my best race season? What are my workouts predicting for my race performance? How did I taper for this same race last season? What happened in this race last year?

As you will soon see, a training diary is also a great planning tool. Use it to record your seasonal plan to keep you on track. There's no need to search through scattered notes; it's all right there at your fingertips. At the end of the season, as you start thinking about the new one ahead, your training diary provides answers that will guide you to race better in the new season.

Without a written record of your day-to-day training and racing experiences, you're left to memory and speculation. That won't hack it. If you're truly serious about racing, you have to have a training diary.

Aside from that necessity, it's also pretty cool to have a daily record of what you've done over the years. I've known master riders who have diaries going back decades. Their progression from young novice to national champ is described in those pages. That makes a great memorial of an athletic career. And more: An entire training history is recorded there. That's valuable data. Whenever I've taken on a new client, the most helpful information they can give me is in their training diaries. Without that information, I am guessing where to start, and it will be some time before I know exactly what we should be doing. But with a diary I can discover what works and what doesn't. We hit the ground running.

DIARY OR LOG?

For this chapter to be meaningful, it's important that you understand the difference between a training diary and a training log. A diary includes your daily reactions to workouts and to the big picture of training. If all you do is record workout data from your power meter and heart rate monitor but never include comments or critically review the records to consider how your training is going, it's only a log, not a diary. A diary is also built around data, of course, but it's fleshed out by your thoughts, feelings, and training assessments. A diary is a record of not only metrics but also of your reactions to them.

A log is a bunch of numbers. A diary takes you down the path to high-performance racing.

A log is a statistical record of what you did. A well-kept diary helps you to plan your training, recall the details of your past workouts and races, build self-confidence, and stay accountable.

The guidance found in a diary sounds surprisingly similar to what a good coach does. In fact, for the well-informed rider, it's much like having a coach.

The training diary can come in many formats. The most basic format is paper. A plain and simple notebook will do. Or you can use an electronic calendar-based diary that resides on your computer. The third option is to use a web-based diary such as TrainingPeaks.com. There are several other electronic options for which you pay a one-time purchase price or a small monthly user fee.

The advantage of most of the computer- and Internet-based apps is that they can display information in graphs, pull up related data from past workouts, pinpoint how the most important markers of your training are going, and let you rearrange data to examine it in different ways. This will save you a lot of time and help you understand what all of the data are telling you. That's a key consideration, especially if you typically record a lot of power, heart rate, speed, cadence, gradient, and other such data for every workout.

Some electronic training diaries even provide advanced planning and analysis tools that serve as a virtual coach to help you make training decisions. If you are truly serious about race performance, then the electronic versions are probably the way to go.

A diary, however, doesn't have to be complex to be effective. In fact, the simpler it is for you to understand, the more you are likely to get from it. It's possible to get bogged down in too much daily data and forget your long-term training purpose. Simple is OK. In its simplest form, your diary is a frequently viewed list of your season's goals and training objectives (Chapter 5), followed by a seasonal plan (Chapter 7), weekly planned workouts (Chapter 8), historical workout data, race results, and your thoughts on all of this. The diary can also serve as an early warning

Whenever I've taken on a new client, the most helpful information they can give me is in their training diaries.

A diary doesn't have to be complex to be effective.

system to prevent injuries and overtraining. All of this is why I believe keeping a training diary is the single most important thing you can do aside from actually riding your bike.

PLANNING WITH A DIARY

Chapter 7 described how to create an annual training plan (ATP) based on your A-priority race goals. There I introduced a few common periodization routines, along with the pros and cons of each, to help you start planning. We also looked at training volume based on either annual hours or TSS, and I showed you how to distribute that volume by period. That brought us to Chapter 8, where we got into the details of laying out an effective training week.

Those two chapters introduced a lot of scheduling details that need frequent review to be effective. If you never look at it again, all of that work was largely a waste of time. Since an ATP is something that should be reviewed frequently, the best place for it is in your diary. If you are using a paper diary, you can insert your paper plan into the notebook. If you are using an electronic diary, it will probably provide a plan format for this purpose. The best e-diaries can even manage some of the tedious planning tasks for you. Regardless of the format or where you store your ATP, you need to review it and update it regularly—at least weekly and sometimes more often throughout the season.

Your diary is where all of the planning for next season should take place. At the start of the new season, set aside some time to make notes in your diary about what your goals and training objectives are (see Chapter 5 for details). Then lay out your ATP (there's an example in Appendix A) if using a paper diary. Make note of the periodization method you're using (see Chapters 7 and 9), plug your A-priority races into the appropriate calendar weeks (Chapter 7), schedule the periods for your first race (Tables 7.1 and 7.4), note the volume to be completed for every week leading up to your first race (Tables 7.2, 7.5, and 7.6), and design a weekly training routine that fits your schedule (Chapter 8).

This will take a lot of deep thinking the first time you do it, but it will pay off throughout the season as you start each training week. Once you've written everything down, your decisions about weekly workouts are nearly complete. All you have to do is follow the guidelines you've already laid out in your diary as you decide which specific workouts to do (Appendix B). This will prove to be a great time-saver throughout the year while also sharpening the focus of your training.

Using your diary to plan workouts for the coming week is easy. At the end of the current week, most likely on Sunday, open your diary to the next week and write in the workouts you will do each day. To keep it quick and simple, use the workout codes found in Appendix B. If you're also weight lifting, indicate the day or days for your workouts and the type (AA, MT, MS, or SM), as described in Chapter 12. Then indicate the planned workout durations or TSS for each session.

All of this is illustrated in Figure 14.1 using a paper version from my *Cyclist's Training Diary*, available through VeloPress.com. Because of the long-range planning you did at the start of the season, scheduling workouts for next week will only take a few minutes. Knowing exactly what you're going to do each day gives you a head start on the week, more productive workouts, and increased confidence in your race preparation.

Your diary is where all of the planning for next season should take place.

week beginning: _June 3, 2019_

period: _Build 2, Week 3_   planned hours/TSS: _10 / TSS: 880_

MONDAY   _6_ / _3_ / _19_

☐ sleep ☐ fatigue ☐ stress ☐ soreness

resting heart rate _____ weight _____

planned workout _SM & AE1 + SS1_
TSS 50 (WTS 30 min., bike 1.5 h)

_____

weather _____

route _____

_____

_____

_____

dist._____ time _____ TSS _____

zone 1_____ 2_____ 3_____ 4_____ 5_____

avg. HR _____ norm. power _____

workout rating _____

notes _____

_____

_____

_____

_____

_____

_____

_____

nutrition _____

_____

_____

_____

_____

TUESDAY   _6_ / _4_ / _19_

☐ sleep ☐ fatigue ☐ stress ☐ soreness

resting heart rate _____ weight _____

planned workout _M71 + ME4_
TSS 180 (2.5 h)

_____

weather _____

route _____

_____

_____

_____

dist._____ time _____ TSS _____

zone 1_____ 2_____ 3_____ 4_____ 5_____

avg. HR _____ norm. power _____

workout rating _____

notes _____

_____

_____

_____

_____

_____

_____

_____

nutrition _____

_____

_____

_____

_____

FIGURE 14.1 Example of the training diary used for weekly planning

week goals: ▪ *Ride 40 minutes in Sweetspot Tuesday.*
▪ *Do 20 minutes of 25 hill intervals on Thursday.*
▪ *Finish with first group on Saturday.*

WEDNESDAY 6 / 5 / 19

▪ sleep ▪ fatigue ▪ stress ▪ soreness

resting heart rate _____ weight _____

planned workout *AE1*
  TSS 60 (2 h)

weather _____

route _____

_____

_____

_____

dist. _____ time _____ TSS _____

zone 1 _____ 2 _____ 3 _____ 4 _____ 5 _____

avg. HR _____ norm. power _____

workout rating _____

notes _____

_____

_____

_____

_____

_____

_____

_____

nutrition _____

_____

_____

_____

_____

THURSDAY 6 / 6 / 19

▪ sleep ▪ fatigue ▪ stress ▪ soreness

resting heart rate _____ weight _____

planned workout *AE2 + AnE4*
  TSS 180 (2.5 h)

weather _____

route _____

_____

_____

_____

dist. _____ time _____ TSS _____

zone 1 _____ 2 _____ 3 _____ 4 _____ 5 _____

avg. HR _____ norm. power _____

workout rating _____

notes _____

_____

_____

_____

_____

_____

_____

_____

nutrition _____

_____

_____

_____

_____

→

FRIDAY _____ 6 / 7 / 19 _____

□ sleep □ fatigue □ stress □ soreness

resting heart rate _____ weight _____

planned workout _AE1_____

___TSS 60 (2 h)____

_____

weather _____

route _____

_____
_____
_____
_____
_____

dist._____ time _____ TSS _____

zone 1_____ 2_____ 3_____ 4_____ 5_____

avg. HR _____ norm. power _____

workout rating_____

notes _____
_____
_____
_____
_____
_____
_____
_____
_____

nutrition _____
_____
_____
_____
_____

SATURDAY ____ 6 / 8 / 19 _____

□ sleep □ fatigue □ stress □ soreness

resting heart rate _____ weight _____

planned workout _AnE1 (group ride)_

___TSS 290 (4 h)____

_____

weather _____

route _____

_____
_____
_____
_____
_____

dist._____ time _____ TSS _____

zone 1_____ 2_____ 3_____ 4_____ 5_____

avg. HR _____ norm. power _____

workout rating_____

notes _____
_____
_____
_____
_____
_____
_____
_____
_____

nutrition _____
_____
_____
_____
_____

FIGURE 14.1 (continued)

SUNDAY   6 / 9 / 19

- sleep - fatigue - stress - soreness

resting heart rate _____ weight _____

planned workout *AE1*

_____ *TSS 60 (2 h)*

_____

weather _____

route _____

_____

_____

_____

_____

_____

dist._____ time_____ TSS _____

zone 1_____ 2_____ 3_____ 4_____ 5_____

avg. HR _____ norm. power _____

workout rating_____

notes _____

_____

_____

_____

_____

_____

_____

_____

_____

_____

nutrition _____

_____

_____

_____

_____

_____

RACING

race 1

_____

category_____

dist. _____ time_____ TSS _____

result _____ upgrade pts. _____

notes

_____

_____

_____

race 2

_____

category _____

dist._____ time_____ TSS _____

result _____ upgrade pts. _____

notes

_____

_____

_____

_____

WEEKLY SUMMARY

	weekly total	YTD
bike time		
bike TSS		
strength time		
strength TSS		
TOTAL		

soreness _____

notes

_____

_____

_____

_____

_____

_____

Confidence? Most certainly. With a written and detailed plan, you're training with a purpose, not by the seat of your pants. And that's true even though the plan may change. In fact, modifying your plan along the way is to be expected. It would be unusual if you made it through the entire racing season with no changes at all to the plan you created at the start. Something always comes up to force a change.

And, to be quite honest, it's not the plan that builds confidence, but rather the act of planning. When it comes to success at anything in life, planning how to get there, even if the plan changes, is the most important thing you can do.

WHAT TO RECORD

With a workout completed and your diary in front of you, what should you write down about it? First of all, keep it simple. I've known athletes who record everything. That's overkill and is likely to lead to way too much data to analyze. It's easy to get carried away if you are using a power meter and heart rate monitor. What you record and analyze (we'll come to this soon) should be only the info related to your training objectives. Recall from Chapter 5 that these are subgoals that, when accomplished, indicate you are ready to achieve a seasonal goal.

The following six data categories will help you make decisions about training. These data suggestions are minimal, but even so, don't feel you have to record all of them. Customize your diary to fit your specific training needs. Keep a record only of those things you are likely to consider later when you analyze recent training.

Morning Warnings

Chapter 11 introduced the idea of assessing your workout readiness as you awake each day. Table 11.1 lists several "morning warnings" to help you do so. After using this table for a few days, you should be able to decide which of these are the best indicators of unusual stress for you: These are the warnings you will regularly measure. Record your warnings score each day in your diary. Pay close attention to how it's trending over several days. This may prove valuable later on, when you're trying to understand your current level of fatigue or, conversely, what's led to your training high. It may help to reread that section of Chapter 11 and decide how you will keep tabs on your daily training status and how to record it.

Basic Workout Data

The what, where, and when of your daily workouts creates your basic workout data: date, time of day, planned workout, workout as completed, course route or venue, duration of the ride, TSS, and equipment used.

When you look back at the ride data several days, weeks, or months later, you will also want to know about anything that set that ride apart from the norm. Did weather affect your ride? Was it cold, hot, windy, or rainy? Did you have a training partner who caused you to work a little harder or easier than usual? Who was it? Was there anything that happened out of the ordinary, such as a knee that didn't feel quite right or tires that were underinflated? Make note of it. If you've never kept track before, your training will begin to improve as soon as you do this.

Performance-Specific Data

Now we start moving into an area that will have a lot to do with the analysis you'll read about later. To get started, use Table 14.1 to look at examples of the numerical data you *might* record. This table contains suggestions, but it's not intended to precisely match the needs of every rider in each phenotype grouping. There may well be data important for your personal race requirements that are not listed here, and other data that are included won't necessarily match your needs.

Three types of workout data are included in this table. The first is general data for *all* workouts including, for example, recovery rides. The second category is objective-specific workouts intended to simulate portions of your A-priority race. And the third is data from test sessions.

To fully understand Table 14.1, you may want to return to Chapter 2 and Figure 2.1 to review the details regarding common cycling phenotypes. Realize that the phenotypes in Table 14.1 are based on "pure" characteristics. For example, a rider who is both a good time trialist and also has many of the characteristics of a climber (such as a high power-to-weight ratio) will not fit nicely into the "climber" phenotype as suggested in this table and may be thought of as an all-rounder. Such a rider probably would

TABLE 14.1 Commonly Recorded Workout Data Based on Pure Cycling Phenotypes

SUGGESTED WORKOUT DATA TO RECORD	CLIMBER	SPRINTER	TIME TRIALIST
General data for all workouts	Duration TSS Time by zone	Duration TSS Time by zone	Duration TSS Time by zone
Objective-specific data for race-like workouts	HKAE* loads (or force reps peak power) Watts/kilogram (W/kg) Surge power on climbs 5-minute peak power & HR** on climb 20-minute peak power & HR** on climb	HKAE* loads (or force reps peak power) 3–12 second peak power	HKAE* loads (or force reps peak power) 20–60 minute normalized power & HR** 20–60 minute efficiency factor 20–60 minute decoupling Variability index
Test data (see Appendix B)	Aerobic threshold (T1) Functional threshold power (T2) Functional aerobic capacity (T3)	Aerobic threshold (T1) Functional threshold power (T2) Functional aerobic capacity (T3) Sprint power (T5)	Aerobic threshold (T1) Functional threshold power (T2) Functional aerobic capacity (T3) Time trial (T4)

The all-rounder is not included, as it requires a rider-dependent combination of the climber, sprinter, and time trialist phenotype data.

* HKAE = hip-, knee-, ankle-extension weight lifting exercises. ** HR = heart rate.

not be concerned with surge power on hills in order to match a pure climber's brief high-power attempts to create a gap. Instead, the all-rounder will simply maintain a high but steady and sustained power output to bring the pure climber back. But this all-round rider's race goal still requires climbing well, since that is the terrain of the goal race. Consequently, all-rounders are not included in this table. If your training objectives fall into this phenotype, pick and choose the data from the three pure phenotypes that best match your needs. (Some of the power-related data suggested here requires a deeper understanding of power-based training. That is beyond the scope of this book. My *Power Meter Handbook* or *Training and Racing with a Power Meter* by Allen and Coggan offer more details on power measurement and how to use it in your daily training.)

The underlying theme in Table 14.1 is to record the data most applicable to your goals and objectives, and little else. The more superfluous data you record, the less likely you are to find what is really important, spot trends, and make course corrections. You'll simply be overwhelmed with information. That's what paralysis by analysis is all about—too many details to consider, so decisions can't be made. Other metrics may be interesting, but if they're not data that are closely related to your objective, leave them out. The key is to make your diary simple, succinct, and meaningful.

If you have set high goals for the season but hate recording and analyzing data, then I'd strongly suggest you hire a coach. He or she will do all of the data analysis and seasonal training adjustments for you.

The more superfluous data you record, the less likely you are to find what is really important.

Physical Notes

How did the workout go? Did you accomplish what was intended? To keep it simple, you may use an A to F grading system. How did you feel during the ride? Did it seem too hard or too easy? Were you adequately recovered before this ride? Is there anything you'd change about the workout for the future?

Mental Notes

Some athletes view their mental reactions as unimportant, especially when compared with the hard data that was recorded as performance-specific. That's a big mistake. The best indicator of how you are progressing on a daily basis is likely to be your emotions and gut feelings. Record these after the workout. Are you satisfied with how it went? Do you feel as if you are making good progress? How was your motivation? Do you have training concerns? Make note of such thoughts and feelings after every workout. This often provides a treasure trove of valuable information as you look back.

Miscellaneous Notes

Other details you may include in your diary are the unusual items that may affect your training such as travel, career-related stress such as working long hours, injuries and illnesses, and family activities that interrupt workouts. You may also note equipment changes, such as a recent bike fit, different wheels, a repositioned saddle, or a change in gears. Record changes made to your usual diet, especially what and when you ate before or during a race. And, of course, record the details of any races you do (more on this later).

TRAINING ANALYSIS

Am I making progress toward achieving my race goals? Are my goals reasonable? Is this periodization model working for me? Should I make any tweaks to my workouts this week? Do I need more recovery between hard workouts? Is my power-duration curve improving? Is my diet meeting my fueling needs? These are questions you surely ponder often. The answers to these and more are found in your training diary.

The diary should be thought of as much more than a historical record of training. Its most important role is as a tool for spotting trends relative to how your training is going so that you can make adjustments in order to achieve your goal. That determination must be made frequently by analyzing the data based on the what-to-record guidelines above. Analysis is where the rubber meets the road. This is the real value of a training diary.

How do you analyze your training? Think of each bit of recorded data as fitting into one of three broad categories: fitness, fatigue, and form. You may recall that these were described in detail in Chapter 3. They are somewhat vague when discussed in general terms. "Fitness" is especially vague. But in the context of your next A-priority race, all three have a definite meaning. Fitness, for example, is what your particular mix of the three phenotypes—climbing, sprinting, and time trialing—must be for the race. The analysis of your fitness includes your workout performance-specific data along with physical and mental notes. Look for trends in your workout data that suggest how your fitness is progressing. They should be rather evident if

you've only recorded info that is appropriate to your goal.

"Fatigue" has to do with how well recovered you are coming into each of the hard workouts. You'll seldom be completely recovered, so the issue becomes the level of fatigue you experience when starting a key training session. If you are overly fatigued, the session performance data will be rather uninspiring. But if you are frequently overly rested, you may be wasting valuable time that could be devoted to hard workouts. You can determine all of this by looking back at your recent morning warnings along with your physical and mental notes related to how well-rested you felt during hard rides. Morning warnings should seldom be 0 before hard rides. Higher warning scores, even an occasional 7, indicate that you are working at about your limit.

"Form" refers to the combination of your race readiness and freshness on race day. Race readiness, you may recall, goes well beyond fitness; it also includes adaptation to anticipated race-day conditions such as hot or cold temperatures, wind, rain, or snow, and more. Also a part of race readiness is having a race plan that includes strategies and tactics. Getting the blend of race readiness and freshness right is what ultimately produces an exceptional performance. The physical and mental notes in your training diary, especially during the last two or three weeks before the race, will help you determine if you are achieving the appropriate balance of race readiness and freshness.

One of the best gauges of fitness, fatigue, and form I've ever seen is the Performance Management Chart found at TrainingPeaks.com.

> The diary should be thought of as much more than a historical record of training.

This chart is the brainchild of Dr. Andrew Coggan, who was mentioned in previous chapters, and I've relied on it extensively for the athletes I've coached. It indicates how training is progressing throughout the season. When using this chart, you soon find that you can manage fitness and fatigue to increase seasonal progress by making daily adjustments to your workout TSS. It's even possible to achieve a planned level of form on race day that is likely to produce your best possible race. Of course, achieving good form also requires managing other aspects of your daily life to ensure that you get the most possible benefits from training. This is why I suggested above that you record physical, mental, and miscellaneous notes along with basic workout and performance data in your training diary.

Based on how your training and B and C races have gone for the past several weeks, you should be able to predict how your A race will go. This assessment of how you think you'll perform on race day usually becomes clear during the pre-race taper.

RACE ANALYSIS

Your race plan is the starting place for post-race analysis after an A-priority event. As with all preparation for a high-performance race, this plan is based on your goals. It doesn't have to be complicated, but your plan should address, at the very least, the anticipated key episodes and demands of the race and how you plan to deal with them. For example, if the race is a criterium, your plan could include your readiness for frequent, early attacks as teams and individual riders vie for control of the race. The attacks

generally become less frequent as the race progresses, but they become more strategic. You must be prepared to respond to or initiate these. How well you do that determines your success. Were you physically and mentally ready for these episodes?

If your A race is a time trial, the usual determiner of race-day success is pacing. In your planning, I suggest breaking the course into segments based on terrain or distance, with each having a specific plan. You should rehearse your plan for each of these segments repeatedly in training during the build period and the taper. The first such segment almost always calls for controlled effort, since the most common error is to go out too fast, build a lot of fatigue, and then fade later in the race. You can't win a time trial in the first few minutes, but you can lose it. The plan then usually comes down to power management. The key question to ask after the race is, did you pace it as planned?

Road race plans often come down to tactical moves relative to hills, corners, wind, and other race variables that provide opportunities for strategic attacks. The plan should include how you will respond to and initiate these attacks. The goal is to have nothing occur in the race that was unexpected unless it was initiated by you or your team. In the post-race analysis, you should be able to answer two key questions: Were you prepared for the other teams' and individual riders' attacks? And did you take advantage of your strengths to achieve your race goal?

The race plan should be refined in the last few weeks prior to the race and rehearsed many times in workouts and lower-priority races in the build and peak periods. Give a great deal of thought to how your personal plan dove-

Your plan should address the anticipated key episodes and demands of the race and how you plan to deal with them.

tails with the team's. Long before race day, you should know exactly what your role is and how you will carry it out.

Following the race, your in-depth analysis of how you performed goes back to the race plan. This is the time for individual and team introspection. Be aware that analysis immediately following the race may be influenced by emotions that lead to impulsive conclusions. It's often better to wait a day before digging into the questions that must be answered. Those key questions are usually:

- Did you achieve your race goal? If not, why not?
- Criterium and road race: What were the key episodes in the race and how did you manage, initiate, or respond to them?
- Time trial: How was your pacing throughout the race?
- Were there unanticipated factors that played a role in the outcome such as poor equipment selection, weather, mechanicals, crashes, road conditions, nutrition, or something else? Were these preventable? Did you react to them appropriately?
- What would you do differently in preparing for and racing this and similar races in the future?

Good or bad, after every race, but especially A races, you and your teammates must assess how you did. If the race didn't go as planned, it's critical that you search for why that happened and what you can do about it in future races. It may be painfully obvious or require a lot of deep thought. And it all belongs in your diary for future planning and reference.

SUMMARY: THE TRAINING DIARY

The training diary is a valuable tool in preparing to race. Here, your season's goals should be recorded so you see them every time you open your diary. That keeps them uppermost in your mind throughout the season. If you are using a paper diary, you can write your goals on the cover, the first page, or on a card that serves as a page marker. With an electronic diary, you may also record your goals and review them frequently.

Next, your diary should be used to create seasonal and weekly plans for how you will achieve your goals while also measuring your progress toward them. The annual training plan may take an hour or so each year to construct, but once done, it will prove invaluable to your goal achievement. At the end of each week, you need to record the plan for the coming week in your diary. This will take only a few minutes, but writing it down keeps you focused on what's important. All of this pays off with improved training.

There are many approaches to using a diary on a daily basis. My recommendation is to record only what is relevant to your race goal and accomplishing your training objectives. Don't record more data than you are likely to scrutinize later on. For riders who are detail oriented and enjoy analysis, the diary may contain quite a bit of information. If you're not into charts, graphs, and data analysis, though, keep the data rather bare bones by recording only the most critical goal-related data. Bear in mind that recording too little data is as bad as recording too much. Either way, be sure to always include your perceptions of how the workout went. The diary should not be solely a compilation of numbers.

Don't record more data than you are likely to scrutinize later on.

Regardless of your penchant for data analysis, the basic details to include throughout the season are your periodic test results and race performance info. These should consist of both numerical outcomes and subjective assessments. Such data are valuable and probably the best indicators of your progress toward goal and objective achievement. These are also the endeavors that are most likely to help you achieve your objectives. Whenever you go into a test or low-priority race with some degree of freshness, you are likely to attain an objective that serves as a predictor of race goal achievement. Anticipate and watch closely for these to happen. That's what focused training is all about.

Periodically do an in-depth review of your training diary, looking for trends. It's essential to do this following a rest and recovery week because that is when you are fresh and ready to perform at a high level. Compare that week with where your performance was during previous R&R weeks. Are you seeing progress toward your goals? If not, why not? If you are, what's working well? Progress may be marked by better performance numbers, such as improved phenotype metrics (see Table 14.1), and also by subjective markers of progress, such as feelings of greater ease in doing what previously were hard workouts. All of this requires comparing current data with what you achieved in past tests and low-priority races.

So the primary purpose for collecting workout, test, and race data is to spot trends and consequently make training adjustments as the season progresses. By "spotting trends," I mean that you are determining how a specific metric, such as hip-, knee-, ankle-extension loads or FTP, is progressing. If these numbers are not

increasing, you need to give some thought as to why. The most common reason is missed workouts. If that's the case, you need to become more consistent in training. Whatever the cause, you must seek to correct the direction you are heading immediately.

Another training indicator of fitness progress is your power output for given durations that are key to your phenotype success (see Figure 2.1), as shown in Table 14.1. Is your power increasing for the durations listed there? As the season progresses, power should rise after occasional plateaus. If not—or if it's decreasing—then there's a problem that needs to be addressed. Once again, the most common reason for negative changes or extended power plateaus is inconsistent training. That's pretty easy to determine simply by looking at how consistently you've been doing the workouts associated with a race-specific training objective (see Appendix B). But it could be something else. Perhaps you are training too densely, with hard workouts too closely spaced, and so fatigue is limiting your power performance. In that case, you need more recovery and adaptation time. That's the second most common reason for a negative fitness trend and is common even among highly motivated riders. There could be many other factors, such as nutrition, sleep, stress, and more. That's why you record more than just numbers in your diary. The nonnumerical data you've also recorded can help you resolve this conundrum.

Use your training diary to prepare for a race by developing a plan to achieve a specific goal. The more important the race, the more thought you need to give to your plan. The race plan should always be based on what you are capable of accomplishing based on all of the trends you've spotted up to that point in the season. As the season progresses, you should be capable of achieving higher levels of performance, and your race plans should reflect this.

The day after the race—good or bad—evaluate how you did. Poor race performances aren't fun to relive, but it's necessary. At the very least simply consider what you would do differently in preparation for the race, and in the race itself, if you could do it all over again. That may help you with the direction of your training before the next race. If the race went well, review what you did to prepare: specific workouts, especially during the taper; the race plan; pre-race nutrition; equip-ment selection. Your performance is directly related to workout and race management. Is your training effective and are you preparing for and conducting races in the best possible way? Your diary provides the answers.

Later in this or subsequent seasons, your collected and analyzed volumes of training and race data will help you understand your race performances. The best use of all of this data is making training adjustments on the fly—a little more of this or less of that. The key is to ask the question, what's important? after each workout, as suggested in Table 14.1, and then record and decide what all of the data are saying to you.

EPILOGUE

You've now read my take on how to train for the endurance sport of cycling. This method is the best one I know, but it's not the only way; I've simply described the method I use. And though I use it now, that doesn't mean I won't make changes to it in the future. Training, and my opinion of how to do it, evolve and will continue to do so. The ever-growing body of knowledge on this topic shows no sign of plateauing. As long as athletes, coaches, and sports scientists persist in seeking better methods, training for high performance in the sport will continue to develop. Your ongoing mission as an athlete, and mine as a coach, is to keep up with the inevitable evolution of training methodology. That's not a simple task.

Sometimes the future of training may even be found in the past. In the early days of the sport, before all of our current technology and interest in sports science, riders trained in a simple way: They put in a lot of saddle time with other fast athletes. That was about it, and some of the best athletes the sport has ever known developed that way. I encourage you to read the biographies of past champions such as Anquetil, Merckx, Hinault, and LeMond to see how they trained and what got them to the top of the sport. There is much to be gleaned from the past.

What you will undoubtedly learn from reading of such riders goes well beyond their training methods. The underlying keys to their success were mostly mental: dedication and discipline. They were driven to succeed. Drive is still the ultimate determiner of high performance. In the final analysis, it comes down to how badly you want it.

Of course, these champions were blessed with the two other components of success: genetics and opportunity. These are often referred to as nature and nurture. There are many people who were born to be world-class cyclists. Nature gave them the genes of champions. But they never had the opportunity. Life got in the way. They didn't take up cycling. Their genes weren't nurtured. They became decent accountants and piano players. Well, the world does need accountants and piano players, but at the same time, it's somewhat sad they never realized their true calling. That's why there are youth programs—to provide an opportunity to those whom nature blessed with a rare combination of genes.

Then there are others who did not win the cycling-gene lottery. Nature gave them a different potential. But they love the sport and have been riding and racing enthusiastically for a long time, even though they may finish well back in the pack. It's unlikely they will ever be on the podium. Most of them know that, and they really don't care. They're "completers" not "competers." That's also OK. They just want to be there for their own enjoyment and self-satisfaction, although racing faster and achieving high goals still motivates them.

Which nature-nurture category are you in? You obviously have the opportunity to race, or you wouldn't be reading this book. But do you have the genetics to excel as a cyclist? If you've been in the sport for several years, you undoubtedly know the answer to that question. If you are a novice or even an intermediate rider, you may be unsure. In either case, it's likely you want to perform at a higher level. We all do. That's what initially drove me to learn more about training and to eventually write books on the subject. I had a fair amount of nurture but was lacking nature.

In the final analysis, why you train will predict your success as a rider. If you are dedicated and disciplined, regardless of genetics, you will find a way and grow as a cyclist. If you have both of these mental determiners of success, your battle is 80 percent won. The remainder lies in how you train. That's where this book comes in.

My hope is that what you get from reading this latest edition of *The Cyclist's Training Bible* is a better understanding of how to be your own high-performance coach. It should be obvious by now that high-level self-coaching is not easy. It's a complex undertaking with many parts requiring a great deal of study and thought. While the details of planning a successful season, laying out an effective weekly routine, and determining daily workouts are thoroughly described in the preceding pages, the challenge is to make all of it work for you. This requires an understanding of the art and science behind what to do both on and off the bike.

It's not easy. Professional coaches typically devote many years to learning the science of training and developing a unique training philosophy and methodology. Experience helps them understand how to apply all of this to the athletes they coach in the real world.

Having read this book, I'm sure you realize that training is a complex topic that requires a great deal of study. And you must realize that despite this book's length, I've only skimmed the surface. If you want to grow as a self-coached athlete, your journey is just beginning.

If I can recommend one additional training tip, it's this: As you continue to advance as a racing cyclist, you will need to become proficient in the rapidly developing technology of the sport. Currently, that has to do with understanding power-based training.

Power is now the high-water mark in endurance sport technology. (That's true not just in cycling but also in sports such as running and rowing.) Your challenge is to understand the many intricacies of power-based training on the bike in order to become an effective self-coached rider. I'm afraid I haven't helped you much in this task. In this edition, I frequently mentioned some complex power metrics and gave brief explanations of them, but if you want to fully develop the know-how to successfully train with power, I strongly suggest reading my introductory book on the topic, *The Power Meter Handbook*. Once you understand the basics, read *Training and Racing with a Power Meter*, a more advanced book by Hunter Allen and Andrew Coggan, PhD. Then apply the analysis of power to your training and racing.

All of this, of course, takes time, but it's time well spent if you want to be a knowledgeable and effective self-coach and a high-performance athlete.

While I've tried to write a book that will thoroughly guide you through the ins an outs of becoming a successful self-coach, I've still only scratched the surface. From personal experience, I can tell you that it takes a long time and that the learning is never complete. What I've described in this book works well for most riders. But success requires that you be both flexible and meticulous when it comes to self-coaching.

Flexibility as a self-coached rider means that you are willing to make changes regardless of how much time and thought you have invested in your training plan. There are many ways to become a good cyclist, and the key to your success—whether you use this book's training philosophy and methodology or something different—is to accept and apply all the essential parts of it. But despite the need to be flexible within a training plan, mixing what I propose here with another method is risky and may ultimately prove to be unsuccessful.

For example, it's not wise to use my workouts in Appendix B along with someone else's training intensity zones. That won't work. You may be able to successfully make slight tweaks here and there, for example when trying to fit what I propose into your daily schedule. That's to be expected. Be careful, however, with merging widely different methodologies. That's the meticulous part.

Flexibility is especially important at the big-picture level. For example, you must be willing to make changes based on what you are experiencing on a daily basis. If you're tired, you must change your scheduled high-stress workout to something you can more easily accomplish that will allow for recovery. Pressing ahead without change in this case will only dig a deeper hole and may even ruin your season. Rest is often viewed by the ambitious racer as an inconvenient necessity, but it is a critical component of training. Self-coached riders often neglect it, and their results suffer. You must insert recovery into your training when you need it, regardless of whether your plan calls for it that day or not. Being flexible in this regard is critical.

Being meticulous is especially critical when it comes to the details of a workout. Once you've decided to do a certain training session, you must closely follow the guidelines described in Appendix B in order to produce results. That's especially important for high-intensity workouts. For example, an interval workout is composed of two parts: "work intervals" and "recovery intervals." The intensities and durations of both of these components are spelled out in the workouts. Maintaining those intensities and durations is critical to reaping the intended rewards of the workout. Making significant changes to either is likely to reduce or even eliminate the benefit.

While I've tried in this book to simplify a rather complex topic, I hope it's clear that successful training requires study and thought so you can design an individual plan that matches your specific strengths and needs. Nearly every day I get emails from athletes who seem to think that one particular workout will make them race faster. I wish it were so simple. As you surely realize by now, there is no one-size-fits-all method. You are essentially carrying out a research study that has only one subject: you. It takes thoughtful experimentation to figure out what works best. It takes trial and error, and this book should have helped you learn how to do that.

Your performance as a cyclist is determined by mental and physical components. The bottom line is that your success in achieving a goal depends on your desire and knowledge. The desire is created within. Becoming a student of the sport, however, is the road to greater knowledge. That's why I wrote this book.

APPENDIX A: ANNUAL TRAINING PLAN TEMPLATE

Athlete _____

Hours/TSS _____

Year _____

WEEK	MON.	RACE	PRI.	PERIOD	HOURS / TSS	DETAILS	WEIGHT LIFTING	AEROBIC ENDURANCE	MUSCULAR FORCE	SPEED SKILLS	MUSCULAR ENDURANCE	ANAEROBIC ENDURANCE	SPRINT POWER	TESTING
						MOST IMPORTANT WORKOUTS								
01														
02														
03														
04														
05														
06														
07														
08														
09														
10														
11														
12														
13														
14														
15														
16														
17														
18														
19														
20														
21														
22														
23														
24														
25														
26														

Season Goals

1. _____
2. _____
3. _____

Training Objectives

1. _____
2. _____
3. _____
4. _____

WEEK	MON.	RACE	PRI.	PERIOD	HOURS / TSS	DETAILS	WEIGHT LIFTING	AEROBIC ENDURANCE	MUSCULAR FORCE	SPEED SKILLS	MUSCULAR ENDURANCE	ANAEROBIC ENDURANCE	SPRINT POWER	TESTING
								MOST IMPORTANT WORKOUTS						
27														
28														
29														
30														
31														
32														
33														
34														
35														
36														
37														
38														
39														
40														
41														
42														
43														
44														
45														
46														
47														
48														
49														
50														
51														
52														

APPENDIX B: WORKOUTS

This appendix contains the basic cycling workouts categorized into the six abilities as described in Chapter 6. Field tests are included here as well.

Generally, a workout should be preceded by a warm-up and followed by a cooldown. Between the warm-up and cooldown is the workout's main set—the primary focus of the session. Note that the more intense the main set of the workout, the longer the warm-up.

Workout intensities are described using power and heart rate. See Table 4.2 to set your heart rate zones and Table 4.3 for power zones. The power instructions below are based on functional threshold power (FTP). For an explanation of FTP, return to Chapter 4 and read the section "Functional Threshold." Note that heart rate and power zones don't always agree. For a review of their relationship, reread the "Zone Agreement" section in Chapter 4. If you have both devices, the power meter is used to measure performance and the heart rate monitor indicates your effort. The power meter is the preferred intensity gauge for most workouts. There are exceptions as described below.

This is not an all-inclusive listing of workouts. There are many variations on these, including multi-ability workouts. By combining portions of the following, you can create new workouts that more closely match the particular demands of your A-priority race. Merging multiple abilities into one workout is most commonly done in the build period of the season (see Chapter 8 for more on the periodization of weekly and daily training).

AEROBIC ENDURANCE WORKOUTS

AE1: Recovery

Recovery workouts are not included on the annual training plan, but they are an integral part of training throughout the season. Do this workout in heart rate zone 1 or at an intensity of or below 55 percent of FTP. The ride should be of a shorter duration than your average ride. Do it on a flat course. Ride primarily in the small chainring. Pedal with a comfortably high cadence.

You can use an indoor trainer or rollers for this session any time of the year, especially if flat road courses are not available. Crosstraining workouts, such as cross-country skiing on a relatively flat course and various health club machines, are additional options for recovery in the prep and early base periods. Such sessions should be done at a perceived exertion of 2 or 3 on a 10-high scale (see Table 4.1). Note that your heart rate zones for alternative activities such as skiing are unlikely to be the same as your bike zones.

While light exercise on a bike is quite beneficial for advanced athletes who want to speed recovery, novices and intermediates may benefit more by taking the day off from exercise. You can combine this workout with a speed skills workout from below.

AE2: Aerobic Threshold (AeT)

The aerobic threshold was briefly introduced in Chapter 4, where you read about intensity reference points. The purpose of this workout is to boost aerobic fitness by improving your body's capability for delivering and using oxygen to produce energy in the muscles. Early in the base period, use a heart rate monitor to gauge the intensity of this ride. If you haven't been tested for aerobic threshold in a lab recently, assume your AeT heart rate is approximately 30 bpm below your anaerobic threshold heart rate (see Chapter 4, "Setting Training Zones," for details).

After warming up, ride 1 to 4 hours at your aerobic threshold heart rate plus or minus 2 bpm on a flat to gently rolling course or indoor trainer. The longer your A-priority race, the longer the AeT portion of the workout should be. If you race primarily in criteriums or time trials, ride for 1 hour to 90 minutes at the AeT heart rate zone.

If you are also using a power meter, when the workout is finished divide the normalized power for the AeT segment by your average heart rate for the same segment to find your efficiency factor (EF) for this session. An increasing EF over time indicates that your aerobic threshold is improving. Note that it seldom rises linearly but instead ratchets up over several weeks as aerobic fitness improves. When EF plateaus for several consecutive sessions, it's time to change from heart rate to power for gauging the intensity of this workout in order to maintain aerobic fitness gains. For this session, ride steadily at your NP plateau power plus or minus 5 watts.

You can also use the AeT workout as a test of aerobic endurance (see "T1: Aerobic Threshold (AeT) Test" below). This workout should be done year-round to initially build and, later on, to maintain aerobic endurance. Once your EF plateaus, maintain aerobic endurance by doing this workout about half as frequently as when you were initially building aerobic fitness.

AE3: Intensive Endurance

This workout develops aerobic endurance while also boosting muscular endurance. After a warm-up, ride for an hour or more on a flat to gently rolling course while staying mostly in heart rate zone 2 or power zone 3. Remain seated on hills. Most of this ride should be at an intensive endurance RPE of about 4 to 6. The purpose of this workout is to boost your body's capacity for processing oxygen to produce energy. You can also do this workout on an indoor trainer by frequently shifting gears to increase the load to simulate hills.

MUSCULAR FORCE WORKOUTS

MF1: Flat Force Reps

This workout is most commonly done in the prep period to prepare for the more advanced M2 workout. But it may also be done at any time in the season.

Following a warm-up, shift to a high gear, such as 53 × 14, and slow down so that you nearly come to a stop. Then accelerate by turning the cranks for only 6 or 8 strokes so that you do a total of 3 or 4 pedal strokes for each leg (of course, you are alternating legs and pedaling as you normally do—it's not just pedaling with one leg). The effort should be extremely high for each downward pedal stroke. Stay seated. Do not stand. While the first couple of pedal strokes will be quite slow—around 50 rpm or lower—the cadence will gradually rise with increasing speed.

If there is reason for concern about your knees, do only 1 set of 6 to 8 total pedal strokes and be conservative with gear selection and effort.

If you do a second set, recover by riding slowly in a low gear for 3 to 4 minutes before starting it. Do no more than 2 sets the first time you do this workout. Experiment with gearing the first couple of times. If you err, make it on the low-gear (easy) side at first. Table 12.5 provides the details for the workout.

MF2: Hill Force Reps

This workout is the same as MF1: Flat Force Reps, but it's done on a hill in order to develop greater neuromuscular fitness. Before doing this workout, you should have previously done at least 4 of the flat force reps sessions and know that your knees do not complain about the high load required.

After warming up well, go to a hill that is short (30 to 50 yards or meters) and steep (an 8 percent grade is perfect). For safety, there must be little or no traffic. You must be able to safely make a U-turn at the top and bottom of the hill.

As you coast to the base of the hill to start a rep, shift to a high gear and come to a very brief, balanced stop without unclipping from a pedal. The gear you select won't be quite as high as for the flat force reps. For example, it may be 53 × 16 instead of 53 × 14. Then, while staying seated, alternately drive the pedals down 3 to 6 times with each leg while otherwise pedaling in a normal manner. That's 6 to 12 total pedal strokes. Do not stand at any time on each set.

Complete up to 3 sets in a workout. After each set, shift to a low (easy) gear and pedal gently for 3 to 5 minutes for recovery. Do not shorten the recovery time between sets, as this will reduce the workout benefit of neuromuscular development. Be sure your legs are recovered before doing the next set.

This is a high-risk, high-reward workout. At the first sign of any tenderness, stop the workout. Do not continue, even if the tenderness is only slight. Power, not heart rate, is the only gauge of intensity for this session. Strive to pro-

duce very high wattage on each pedal stroke. See Table 12.5 for details. Do this workout no more than twice per week, with at least 48 hours separating workouts.

MF3: Hill Repeats

On a steep hill of about 6 to 8 percent grade that takes 20 to 30 seconds to climb, do 3 to 8 repeats with 2 to 4 minutes of recovery in between each one. Maintain power zone 5 for each uphill climb. Heart rate is not a good indicator of intensity for this workout, as the repeats are quite short.

Climb in the saddle with minimal upper body movement. Do not stand. Select a gear that allows only a cadence of 70 rpm or lower for each rep.

To recover, coast while descending before starting the next rep.

Stop the workout if you find your knees becoming sensitive. Do this workout no more than twice per week, with at least 48 hours between workouts. Do not do this workout if you are prone to knee injury.

SPEED SKILL WORKOUTS

SS1: Spin-Ups

The purpose of this workout is to improve pedaling efficiency as indicated by an increasingly higher maximum cadence without bouncing on the saddle.

On a flat or slightly downhill section of road, or on an indoor trainer set to light resistance, and in a low (easy) gear, gradually increase cadence for about 1 minute to your maximum spin rate. This is a cadence you can maintain without bouncing on the saddle. As the cadence increases, allow your lower legs and feet to relax, especially the toes. Hold your maximum cadence for as long as possible, which will probably be only a few seconds. Recover for at least a minute. Repeat several times.

This drill is best done with a handlebar device that displays cadence. Heart rate and power measurements are not meaningful for this workout.

SS2: Isolated Leg

On a flat or slightly downhill section of road, do 90 percent of the work with one leg while the other rests. Alternatively, on an indoor trainer using a light resistance, the resting leg may be supported by placing the foot on a chair or stool. Spin with the highest cadence you can. Change legs when fatigue begins to set in. Focus on eliminating the dead spots at the top and bottom of the stroke. Heart rate and power ratings have no significance for this workout.

SS3: 9-to-3

As you pedal, imagine that you can drive the pedal forward from the 9 o'clock position on the back side of the stroke to 3 o'clock position on the front side without going through 12 o'clock. Use a low (easy) gear so that you can pedal with a low force at a comfortably high cadence. This will help you to master the most challenging part of the pedal stroke, at the top.

SS4: Fixed-Gear

This workout requires a fixed-gear bike. Your local shop can help you set one up with only one chainring, one cog, no derailleurs, and no freewheel. You are always pedaling and can't coast. When riding a fixed-gear bike, you must learn to relax and let the bike do the work. The first few times you ride your fixie, find a flat area with no traffic or stop signs, such as a large, empty parking lot. Keep the workouts short at first. This can be a dangerous workout until you master the new bike, so avoid busy streets.

SS5: Cornering

On a curbed street with a clean surface and 90-degree turns, practice cornering techniques: Lean both the bike and your body into the turn, lean your body while keeping the bike upright, and keep your body upright while leaning the bike. Avoid streets with heavy traffic. Practice several speeds with different angles of approach. Include a few with sprint efforts both into and out of the corners. Heart rate and power ratings are not important for this workout.

SS6: Bumping

On a firm, grassy field, practice making body contact with a training partner while riding slowly. Increase speed as skill improves. Also include leaning on each other and slightly touching overlapped wheels.

MUSCULAR ENDURANCE WORKOUTS

ME1: Tempo Intervals

Do this workout on a mostly flat road course, slight uphill (1 to 3 percent grade), or an indoor trainer.

After a warm-up, do 3 to 5 work intervals in heart rate zone 3 or power zone 4 with brief recoveries. The work intervals may be 12 to 20 minutes long with recoveries that are about one-fourth as long: 3 to 5 minutes. For example, following a 16-minute interval, recover for 4 minutes.

Power is the preferred measure of intensity for this workout, but heart rate may be used instead. If training only with a heart rate monitor, the work interval starts as soon as you begin pedaling hard—not when zone 3 is achieved. There will be a time lag during the interval as your heart rate is catching up. During these times, use a perceived exertion of 5 to 6 on a 10-high scale (see Table 4.1 for details on RPE).

Avoid roads with heavy traffic and frequent stop signs. Stay seated for each interval. Recover by pedaling easily in zone 1.

ME2: Cruise Intervals

On a relatively flat course, slight uphill (1 to 3 percent grade), or indoor trainer, do 3 to 5 work intervals of 6 to 12 minutes duration. Do each work interval at about the anaerobic threshold: RPE 7 or 8.

Power is the preferred gauge of intensity for this workout, but heart rate may be used too. For power, ride at or slightly below your FTP. If using heart rate, gradually raise your pulse to near FTHR (see Table 4.2) on each. With heart rate, the timed work interval portion begins as soon as the hard effort begins, not when heart rate reaches the goal intensity. As you increase your heart rate, intensity is estimated based on a perceived exertion of 7 or 8 on a 10-high scale (see Table 4.1 for details on RPE).

After each work interval, recover in zone 1 with easy pedaling for one-fourth of the preceding interval duration. For example, after a 6-minute work interval, recover for 90 seconds with easy pedaling.

The first such workout of the new season should total about 12 minutes or less of work intervals (for example, 2 × 6 minutes). Gradually, over a few such sessions, increase the total combined work interval duration to about 30 to 50

minutes (for example, 5 × 6 minutes or 5 × 10 minutes). Stay relaxed. The work interval intensity is very similar to that of a 40 km time trial, making this an especially key workout for time trialists. Pedal with a cadence similar to what you would use at such a race distance.

An optional variation that challenges you to work harder is to shift every 20 to 60 seconds between your normal gear for this intensity and a higher (harder) gear.

ME3: Hill Cruise Intervals

This session is the same as ME2 cruise intervals, except it is done on a long low-gradient hill, such as 2 to 4 percent grade, or into a strong headwind. If you're using a hill, select one that has light traffic and no stop signs. Stay seated for each climb, and work on a smooth pedal stroke with minimal upper body motion.

As with ME2, a power meter is the preferred intensity-measuring tool while riding at near your FTP, but a heart rate monitor may be used to gauge FTHR (see Tables 4.2 and 4.3). If training only with a heart rate monitor, the work interval starts as soon as you begin pedaling hard—not when FTHR is ultimately achieved. Note that you may not reach FTHR during the first or even the second work interval. That's common due to heart rate lag and the warm-up effect. As your heart rate slowly increases, maintain a perceived exertion of 7 or 8 on a 10-high scale to gauge intensity.

Recover after each climb by turning around and returning to the bottom of the hill in zone 1. The coasting descent time makes the recovery intervals longer than when doing ME2 intervals, but it also translates to a somewhat increased intensity for each work interval and a slightly greater benefit for muscular force.

A variation on this workout is to shift between your normal gear for such a climb and a higher (harder) gear every 30 seconds or so.

ME4: Sweet Spot Intervals

After a warm-up, do 2 work intervals on a flat or slightly uphill (2 to 3 percent grade) course. Ride steadily, staying in the saddle for each work interval.

Each work interval should be done at 0.88 to 0.93 percent of FTP. The work intervals are 12 to 20 minutes in duration, interspersed with a recovery of about one-fourth the work interval duration (for example, a 4-minute recovery between 16-minute work intervals).

At the start of the base period, do work intervals that are about 12 minutes long. As you sense adaptation occurring, gradually increase the lengths of the work intervals.

ANAEROBIC ENDURANCE WORKOUTS

AnE1: Group Ride

This is an unstructured ride with a group and should simulate racing. It could also be a B- or C-priority race. This ride should include frequent maximal efforts. The goal is to achieve zone 5 (power) or zone 5b (heart rate) and higher for several seconds to a few minutes several times during the ride. These high-intensity surges are "matches" that should closely simulate the efforts of a race.

In your analysis following the ride, note how much total time you spent in the goal zone during the ride. Be cautious with this workout, not only in terms of how intense it may become but also with regard to road safety. Pay attention to traffic and other riders who may not be skilled at riding in a group.

Power is the preferred metric for this workout, as heart rate is not indicative of performance.

AnE2: VO$_2$max Intervals

The course should be flat to rolling (frequent small hills) with no stop signs and light traffic.

After a long warm-up, do several work intervals of 30 seconds to 4 minutes each. Recover with easy pedaling in zone 1 for as long as the preceding work interval lasted. As fitness improves, gradually reduce the recovery time to half the previous interval's duration. Cadence for these intervals is at the high end of your comfort range.

Start with about 5 minutes of total work interval time within a workout (for example, 10 × 30 seconds), and gradually, over several sessions, build to 15 to 20 minutes in a session (for example, 5 × 3 minutes and 5 × 4 minutes).

A power meter is the preferred tool for measuring intensity for this session. The goal intensity is power zone 5. Heart rate lag makes heart rate monitors ineffective for gauging intensity. If you don't have a power meter, use a Rating of Perceived Exertion of 9 on a 10-high scale for each interval (see Table 4.1 for details on RPE).

AnE3: Pyramid Intervals

This workout is the same as the AnE2 session, except the work interval progression is 1-2-3-4-4-3-2-1 minutes in power zone 5. The recovery after each work interval is equal to the preceding work interval duration. Cadence for these intervals is at the high end of your comfort range.

Heart rate is an ineffective gauge of intensity due to heart rate lag and the short duration of these intervals. If you don't have a power meter, use a Rating of Perceived Exertion of 9 on a 10-high scale for each interval.

After doing a few of these or the AnE2 workouts, reduce the recovery durations by as much as half. For example, following a 2-minute work interval, recover for 1 minute in zone 1.

AnE4: Hill Intervals

Find a relatively steep hill with a 6 to 8 percent gradient that takes 2 to 4 minutes to climb, with light traffic and no stop signs.

Following a thorough warm-up, do 5 to 7 climbs in power zone 5 for a total of 10 to 20 minutes of workout climbing time (for example, 5 × 2 minutes or 5 × 4 minutes). Maintain a steady intensity in power zone 5 for each climb, and pedal at a comfortably high cadence. If you don't have a power meter, ride at RPE 9 on a 10-high scale (see Table 4.1 for details on RPE).

Recover by coasting down the hill and starting a new work interval every 2 to 4 minutes (for example, following a 2-minute climb recover for 2 minutes).

As an alternative, include several surges to zone 6 within each work interval.

This is a very hard workout that is usually best done only once in a week and followed by at least 48 hours of recovery.

SPRINT POWER WORKOUTS

SP1: Form Sprints

Early in a ride, following the warm-up, do 6 to 10 sprints on varying terrain: flat, uphill, and downhill. Each sprint should last 5 to 10 seconds, followed by a 3- to 5-minute recovery. Alternate standing and sitting throughout this main set while focused on posture and technique. This session is done primarily for form, so hold back slightly on intensity.

Power should be in zone 6 and RPE at about 9 on a 10-high scale (see Table 4.1 for details on RPE). This workout is best done alone to avoid competing while refining sprint technique.

SP2: Jumps

Warm up well. Then, early in the workout, on an indoor trainer or the road, do 10 to 20 very brief surges to improve explosive power. Complete 2 to 4 sets of 5 jumps each for a total of 10 to 20 jumps in the session. Each jump is 8 to 12 revolutions of the cranks (each leg) at a high cadence. Recover for 1 minute following each jump and 5 minutes between sets. Power and effort should be maximal for each jump. If on a road, vary the terrain from flat to uphill to downhill. Also include cornering.

SP3: Group Sprints

Within a ride, include several 5- to 15-second race-like sprints. These can be done with another rider or with a group to simulate racing intensity and tactical maneuvering. Designate sprint zones such as segments marked by road signs. Employ all of the techniques of good form sprints, but at a much higher intensity. Power and effort should be maximal. Recover for several minutes between sprints.

FIELD TESTS

T1: Aerobic Threshold (AeT) Test

It is best to do this test of your aerobic fitness after 3 to 5 days of greatly reduced training to allow for rest and recovery. You need both a heart rate monitor and a power meter for this test.

Follow the instructions for workout AE2 above. After the workout, divide your normalized power for the AeT portion by your average heart rate for the same portion to determine your current efficiency factor (EF). Your EF will rise as your aerobic fitness improves over time. During a period of greatly reduced training, for example at the end of the season, your EF will decrease, indicating a loss of aerobic fitness. That is normal and to be expected, as fitness must decline at certain times of the year.

While you may also be doing the AE2 workout during a normal training week, your results after a short R&R break from hard training are a better indicator of your progress, because fatigue is unlikely to be a limiting factor. You should do this test throughout the season, at least every 6 to 8 weeks. If possible, use the same course every time.

T2: Functional Threshold Power (FTP) and Heart Rate (FTHR) Test

The purpose of this test is to determine your functional threshold power and functional threshold heart rate as described in Chapter 4. You must use a power meter to determine FTP, and you need a heart rate monitor for FTHR. Do this test following 3 to 5 days of rest and recovery.

You need a stretch of road that is flat to slightly uphill (3 percent grade or less) with a wide bike lane, light traffic, no stop signs, and few intersections and corners. You will probably need 5 to 10 miles (8 to 16 km), depending on how fast you are and the hill you use. A safe course is critical. The bike for this test should be the same one you will use for your A-priority race. Throughout the test, keep your head up so you can see ahead. You may also do this test on an indoor trainer.

Warm up well before starting the test. Ride as if you are doing a time trial that lasts 20 minutes. Hold back slightly in the first 5 minutes (most riders start much too fast). At the end of every 5-minute portion, decide whether to go slightly harder or easier for the next 5 minutes.

After the workout, note your average heart rate from the 20-minute test portion. Subtract 5 percent, and you have an estimate of your FTHR. Then use Table 4.2 to compute your heart rate training zones. To determine FTP from the same test, subtract 5 percent from your average power (not normalized power), and you have an estimate of FTP. You can then use Table 4.3 to set your power training zones.

As described in Chapter 4, you may also estimate FTP by using 5-, 8-, or 30-minute tests, although the 20-minute test described above is preferred. See Chapter 4 for these alternative tests.

T3: Functional Aerobic Capacity Test

This test measures your functional aerobic capacity power. Aerobic capacity, as determined by a clinic or lab test, is called "VO_2max." This test estimates your power at that high level of intensity. This field test requires a power meter. It is best done following 3 to 5 days of rest and recovery.

The course you use for the test should be safe, with light traffic, no stop signs, few intersections, no turns, and a wide bike lane. For safety, you should look ahead throughout the test. Do not ride with your head down. The selected test course should also be a flat to slightly uphill (3 percent grade or less) section of road that you can use every time you do this test. You may also do this on an indoor trainer, but only if it is very stable, as the test typically involves a lot of forceful side-to-side rocking.

Following the warm-up, ride a steady top-end effort that you can sustain for 5 minutes. Your average power for the 5-minute test portion is a good predictor of your power at aerobic capacity.

T4: Time Trial

Do this field test following 3 to 5 days of rest and recovery. The section of road you use should be safe, meaning light traffic, few intersections, no stop signs, and a wide bike lane. Keep your head up throughout the test so you can see traffic and possible road obstacles such as potholes. Do not ride with your head down. The course should be flat to slightly uphill (1 or 2 percent grade). This test is best done on your time trial bike when preparing for a time trial. Any gear combination may be used, and you may shift during the test. Treat this test as a race.

Note your start and finish points so you can test on the same course every time. You may also do this on an indoor trainer.

After a thorough 15- to 30-minute warm-up, complete a 10 km time trial on a mostly flat course. You should expect faster times (assuming simi-

lar conditions) as your anaerobic endurance and muscular endurance abilities improve. Besides your time, note your average heart rate and power for the test portion in your training diary.

T5: Sprint Power Test

This test will gauge the progress of your sprint. A power meter is required. Do this test following 3 to 5 days of reduced training load.

Following a thorough warm-up, ride a flat to slightly uphill (less than 4 percent) section of road that is roughly 50 to 100 yards or meters long, depending on how fast your sprint is and the gradient. The road section used for the test should have light traffic, a wide bike lane, no intersections, and no stop signs.

From a rolling start, pedal as forcefully and quickly as you can, counting 8 right- or left-side pedal strokes (16 total strokes) in your preferred sprint posture: standing or sitting with your hands on the hoods or in the drops. Experiment to find what works best for you. Your peak power output for the 8 strokes is a measure of your sprint power.

GLOSSARY

Ability. In the context of this book, ability is a category of workouts focused on an intended physical adaptation in preparation for racing. See *adaptation, anaerobic endurance, muscular endurance, muscular force, speed skill,* and *sprint power.*

Active recovery. Low-intensity exercise intended to allow for recovery. See *passive recovery.*

Adaptation. The body's physiological adjustment to a training stress repeatedly placed on it over a period of time. The purpose of adaptation is to improve an aspect of fitness. See *ability* and *fitness.*

Aerobic. In the presence of oxygen; aerobic metabolism primarily uses oxygen to produce energy. Also refers to any exercise intensity below the anaerobic threshold.

Aerobic capacity. The maximal volume of oxygen an athlete can process to produce energy during a maximal and prolonged exertion. Also known as VO_2max. It is determined in a graded exercise test by measuring the oxygen uptake in milliliters divided by the athlete's body weight (in kilograms) and finally divided by the number of minutes at that maximal intensity level ($VO_2max = mL/kg/min$). See *VO_2max.*

Aerobic endurance. In the context of this book, a category of workouts done at or near the aerobic threshold and intended to improve the athlete's aerobic ability.

Aerobic threshold. The exercise intensity at which blood lactate rises above the resting level. Exercise is fully aerobic at this intensity, with fuel being supplied primarily by stored body fat. In terms of heart rate, the aerobic threshold is typically 20 to 40 bpm below the anaerobic, or lactate, threshold.

Agonist muscles. The primary movement muscles that contract with the purpose of propelling the body for activities such as cycling. See *antagonist muscles.*

All-rounder. A cyclist who is able to perform at a high level in at least two of the three cycling phenotypes: climbing, sprinting, and time trialing. See *phenotype.*

Anaerobic. Literally, "without oxygen." Very high-intensity exercise during which the demand for oxygen is greater than can be met. The primary fuel when anaerobic is carbohydrate. Also used to describe the intensity of exercise performed above the anaerobic, or lactate, threshold.

Anaerobic endurance. In the context of this book, a category of workouts done to improve the athlete's ability to maintain a high level of intensity above the anaerobic threshold for an extended period of time.

Anaerobic threshold (AnT). A high intensity level that occurs immediately before becoming anaerobic. Above this intensity, energy production becomes anaerobic, with energy being supplied by stored carbohydrate. High efforts above the AnT can be continuously maintained for a period lasting from a few minutes to about an hour, depending on how great the intensity is.

Antagonist muscles. Muscles that have an opposing effect on the agonist muscles by opposing their contraction. For example, the triceps is an antagonist muscle for the biceps. Whereas the biceps flexes the elbow, the triceps extends it. When doing arm curls with a heavy weight, the triceps are the antagonist muscles. See *agonist muscles*.

Base period. In seasonal periodization, the training period during which the workouts are general, meaning not exactly like the demands of the targeted event. The purpose of training in this period is to prepare the body for the training stresses of the build period. See *build period, peak period, prep period, race period, and transition period*.

Bonk. A state of extreme exhaustion during a very long endurance session; related to the depletion of glycogen. See *glycogen*.

Breakthrough (BT). A challenging workout intended to cause a significant, positive, adaptive response. These workouts generally require 36 or more hours for adequate recovery.

Build period. In seasonal periodization, the training period during which the workouts are specific, meaning very much like the demands of the targeted event. The purpose of training in this period is to prepare the body for the training stresses of racing. See *base period, peak period, prep period, race period, and transition period*.

Cadence. Revolutions per minute of pedal stroke.

Capillary. A small blood vessel located between arteries and veins in which oxygen and fuel exchanges between tissue (such as muscle) and blood occur. Generally, several capillaries at a given site form a capillary bed. As aerobic fitness improves in a given muscle, the capillary beds for that muscle are enlarged.

Carbohydrate loading. A dietary procedure intended to elevate muscle and liver glycogen stores by emphasizing carbohydrate consumption for a few days prior to a race.

Cardiorespiratory system. The combined interactions of the heart, blood vessels, and lungs to supply fuel and oxygen to the working muscles during exercise.

Central nervous system. The brain and spinal cord.

Circuit training. Selected gym exercises or activities performed rapidly in a sequential order. A term often used in weight training.

Climber. A cyclist who has a unique capacity for riding uphill. This talent is usually marked by a high power-to-weight ratio. See *phenotype*.

Compound exercise. In weight lifting, an exercise that uses multiple joints, usually in the same manner in which they are recruited while cycling. For example, the squat is a compound exercise involving the hips, knees, and ankles and is somewhat similar to the lower body's movement when pedaling a bicycle.

Concentric contraction. The shortening of a muscle during its contraction, as when the biceps muscle is used in an arm-curling exercise. When pedaling a bicycle, the quadriceps muscle is used concentrically. See *eccentric contraction*.

Cooldown. Low-intensity exercise at the end of a training session intended to gradually return the body to a resting state.

Cranks. On a bicycle, the levers on which the pedals are attached.

Crosstraining. Workouts that involve activities not common to the athlete's primary sport. For example, weight lifting and cross-country skiing are crosstraining activities for a cyclist.

Drafting. Riding closely behind another cyclist in order to reduce effort.

Drops. The lower portion of turned-down handlebars commonly seen on road bicycles.

Duration. The length of time of a given workout.

Eccentric contraction. The lengthening of a muscle during its contraction as, for example, when the biceps muscle is used to slowly lower a weight that was lifted during an arm curl. See *concentric contraction*.

Economy. The physiological cost of riding a bike, commonly expressed as liters of oxygen consumed for a given duration or distance. The more economical the athlete, the less oxygen consumed at any given pace or power. See *fitness*.

Efficiency factor (EF). In the context of this book, normalized power is divided by average heart rate to calculate efficiency factor for a steady, aerobic workout or segment, such as an aerobic interval. An increasing EF over time suggests improving aerobic fitness. See *normalized power*.

Endurance. The ability to persist, or resist fatigue, for a relatively long duration.

Ergogenic aid. A substance, device, or phenomenon that can improve athletic performance. For example, caffeine is often considered an ergogenic aid for endurance athletes. Some ergogenic aids are banned from endurance sports.

Fartlek. A Swedish term for "speed play." An unstructured interval-type workout in which the intensity and duration of the intervals and recovery times between them are completely subjective, spur-of-the-moment decisions.

Fast-twitch muscle fiber (FT). A muscle fiber characterized by a brief contraction time, high anaerobic capacity, and low aerobic capacity, all making the fiber suited for high-power activities such as sprints. See *slow-twitch muscle fiber*.

Fatigue. In endurance sport, the long-term accumulation of tiredness resulting from training.

Field test. A test that is conducted on the road or on an indoor trainer (as opposed to in a clinic or lab) that is intended to determine a specific aspect of fitness.

Fitness. In endurance sport, the combined product of the athlete's aerobic capacity, anaerobic threshold (as a percentage of aerobic capacity), and economy. See *aerobic capacity*, *anaerobic threshold*, and *economy*.

Force. The muscular work done to overcome a resistance. For example, pushing down on a bicycle pedal exerts force. See *torque*.

Form. The athlete's readiness to race. Specifically, on race day the athlete should have a relatively high level of race readiness and be fresh, meaning without fatigue.

Free weights. Weights such as barbells and dumbbells that are not part of an exercise machine.

Frequency. The number of times per week that an athlete trains.

Functional threshold power (FTP). In cycling, this refers to an intensity level that is similar to the anaerobic threshold or lactate threshold. But instead of being determined in a clinic by measuring oxygen expenditure or lactate accumulation, it is based on a field test. The most common test lasts 20 minutes. FTP is determined by subtracting 5 percent of the average power. See *anaerobic threshold*, *field test*, and *lactate threshold*.

Gear, high and low. On a bicycle, one crank revolution of a high gear results in the bike covering a greater distance than one revolution in a low gear. When riding a bicycle, a high gear generally requires greater force to turn the cranks than a low gear does.

Glycogen. A source of fuel for exercise primarily derived from dietary carbohydrate. It is the body's storage form of sugar.

GPS device. An electronic mechanism, often worn on the wrist or attached to the bike's handlebars, that determines geographical position and is used to measure distance and speed using the U.S. navigational Global Positioning System. Its data may usually be downloaded to a computer following the session for analysis.

Growth hormone. A hormone secreted by the anterior lobe of the pituitary gland that stimulates physical growth and development.

Hammer. A slang term used to describe a fast, sustained, near-maximal effort.

Hamstring. Muscle on the back of the thigh that flexes the knee and extends the hip.

Heart rate monitor. An electronic device that measures and displays an athlete's pulse. Its data may usually be downloaded to a computer following a session for analysis.

Hoods. On drop handlebars, the covers over the brake lever mechanisms.

Individuality, principle of. The concept that a training program must consider the specific needs and abilities of the person for whom it is intended, as athletes are unique in many ways and often vary considerably in their responses to training.

Intensity. The qualitative element of training referring to effort, speed, velocity, pace, force, and power.

Intensity factor (IF). A power metric that quantifies workout intensity. IF is determined by dividing the workout's normalized power by the rider's functional threshold power (IF = NP ÷ FTP). See *functional threshold power, intensity,* and *normalized power.*

Intervals. A system of generally high-intensity work marked by short but regularly repeated periods of hard exercise interspersed with low-intensity periods of recovery. See *recovery interval* and *work interval.*

Isolated leg training (ILT). Pedaling the bicycle with one leg in order to focus on improving technique. Generally done on an indoor trainer.

Kilojoule (kJ). In training with a power meter, an expression of how much energy is expended throughout a workout or portion of a workout. It is the product of average power (in watts) multiplied by the number of seconds within the workout or selected portion and then divided by 1,000. It may also be used in measuring the cumulative training load for a given period of time such as a week. See *workload.*

Lactate. A chemical formed in the body that enters the bloodstream following the production of lactic acid within the working muscle. See *lactic acid.*

Lactate threshold (LT). The intensity during exercise at which blood lactate begins to accumulate due to the body's inability to process it, resulting in labored breathing. This is similar to the anaerobic threshold (AnT). LT is determined by sampling blood lactate, while AnT is measured by sampling inhaled and expired oxygen. See *anaerobic threshold.*

Lactic acid. A by-product of exercise resulting from the incomplete breakdown of glucose (sugar) in the production of energy in the muscles. Lactic acid is produced during both rest and exercise. See *lactate.*

Long, slow distance (LSD). A form of continuous training in which the athlete performs at a relatively low intensity, usually below the aerobic threshold, for a long duration.

Macrocycle. A term used in training periodization. A period of training that includes several mesocycles. Usually refers to an entire season but may also refer to the preparation period for a single race. See *mesocycle* and *microcycle*.

Main set. The primary portion of a workout session that is focused on a specific training ability. Typically follows the warm-up and precedes the cooldown.

Mash. To push a bicycle in high gear at a slow cadence.

Mesocycle. A term used in training periodization. A period of training generally 2 to 6 weeks long. See *macrocycle* and *microcycle*.

Microcycle. A term used in training periodization. A period of training approximately 1 week long. See *macrocycle* and *mesocycle*.

Muscular endurance. In the context of this book, a category of workouts done to improve the ability of a muscle or muscle group to perform repeated contractions for a long period of time while overcoming resistance.

Muscular force. In the context of this book, a category of workouts done as brief repeats at a maximal intensity with long recoveries in between. The purpose is to increase the athlete's ability for pedaling-specific strength.

Normalized power (NP). In bicycle training using a power meter, normalized power is derived from an algorithm that computes the athlete's average power, with a greater numeric weight given to surges. The NP for a workout is typically somewhat higher than the workout's average power. A power meter and software are necessary to measure NP. See *power meter* and *surging*.

One-repetition max (1RM). In weight lifting, the maximum load that an athlete can lift in one attempt.

Overload, principle of. A training load that challenges the body's current level of fitness and causes adaptation. See *adaptation* and *fitness*.

Overreaching. Training above a workload that would produce overtraining if such a training load were continued long enough. See *overtraining*.

Overtraining. A physical and mental condition marked by extreme fatigue caused by training for an excessive period of time at a workload higher than the body can readily adapt to. It's the result of an imbalance between training stress and rest.

Pacing. The act of producing steady speed or power in order to carefully manage the expenditure of energy during a workout, race, or interval while producing the best possible performance. Unsteady pacing wastes energy. See *surging*.

Passive recovery. A day or group of days with no workouts with the purpose of complete rest. See *active recovery*.

Peak period. In seasonal periodization, the training period during which the workouts are specific, meaning very much like the demands of the targeted event, and workout durations are decreased while intensity remains high. The peak period typically follows the build period and precedes the race period. The purpose of this period is to gradually produce form by allowing the body to recover from the previous period of hard training while steadily becoming race ready. See *base period, build period, form, prep period, race period*, and *transition period*.

Periodization. A seasonal planning method of structuring training into periods based on training volume and intensity, with each period focused on a specific training objective. See *intensity, macrocycle, mesocycle, microcycle*, and *volume*.

Phenotype. In the context of this book, the individual cyclist's unique and specific aptitude for performance during a bike race when certain race talents are required. See *all-rounder, climber, sprinter*, and *time trialist*.

Power meter. An electronic device that measures torque and cadence, thus providing a wattage reading that indicates intensity. Its data typically can be uploaded to a computer for analysis following the training session. See *cadence* and *torque*.

Preparation (prep) period. In seasonal periodization, the training period during which the workouts are very general, meaning not exactly the same as the demands of the targeted event. The purpose of training in this period is to gradually return to a structured training program following a break from focused training during the preceding transition period. See *base period, build period, peak period, race period*, and *transition period*.

Progressive overload, principle of. The concept that the athlete's training workload must be gradually increased over time while accompanied by intermittent periods of recovery. **Quadriceps.** The large muscle in front of the thigh that extends the lower leg and flexes the hip.

Race period. In seasonal periodization, the training period during which the workouts are specific, meaning very much like the demands of the targeted event, and workout durations are very brief while intensity remains high. This period typically follows the peak period and culminates with the targeted race. The purpose of this period is to completely recover from the previous periods of hard training and become race ready. See *base period, build period, peak period, prep period*, and *transition period*.

Rating of Perceived Exertion (RPE). A subjective assessment of how hard one is working during exercise, usually using a 0 (low) to 10 (high) scale to express exertion levels.

Recovery interval. The relief period between work intervals in an interval workout. The recovery interval is usually quite low in duration and intensity. See *work interval*.

Repetition (rep). The number of times a task, such as a work interval or lifting a weight, is repeated. See *set*.

Rest and recovery (R&R) period. In periodization, a period of reduced training following a block of hard training. Passive and active recovery are emphasized during R&R. R&R is typically included in training after about 2 or 3 weeks of focused training in the base and build periods. See *active recovery*, *base period*, *build period*, and *passive recovery*.

Session. A single workout or race.

Set. A group of repetitions. See *repetition*.

Slow-twitch muscle fiber (ST). A muscle fiber characterized by a slow contraction time, low anaerobic capacity, and high aerobic capacity, all making the fiber suited for low power, long-duration activities. See *fast-twitch muscle fiber*.

Specificity, principle of. The concept that training must stress the specialized systems critical for optimal performance in a given type of race in order to achieve the desired training adaptations.

Speed skill. Within the context of this book, a category of workouts focused on improving the ability to efficiently move the body in order to produce optimal performance. See *economy*.

Sprinter. A cyclist who has the capacity to produce a very high power output for a brief period of time, usually measured in seconds. This talent is commonly related to a high fast-twitch muscle composition. See *fast-twitch muscle fiber* and *phenotype*.

Sprint power. In the context of this book, a category of workouts done at a maximal effort for a very brief time and typically at a very high cadence with long recovery periods in between. A sprint power workout is intended to improve the athlete's sprinting ability.

Surging. Riding a bike unsteadily with a great deal of energy expenditure during brief accelerations. See *pacing* and *sprinter*.

Tapering. A training method initiated a few days or weeks prior to an important race involving a gradual reduction in training volume in order to come into form on race day. See *form*.

Tempo. Commonly refers to a moderately hard intensity between the aerobic and anaerobic thresholds. See *aerobic threshold* and *anaerobic threshold*.

Time trialist. A cyclist with the capacity for steadily producing a relatively high power output for a long period of time, especially during an individual time trial. This talent is common for a rider with a high slow-twitch muscle composition. See *phenotype* and *slow-twitch muscle fiber.*

Torque. In pedaling a bicycle, the rotational force applied to the pedals. See *force.*

Training. A comprehensive program or portions thereof intended to prepare an athlete for competition.

Training Stress Score (TSS). A method of assigning a numerical value to a session using an algorithm based on session duration and intensity. It requires the use of a power meter, heart rate monitor, or other device for accurately measuring intensity. Since it involves both duration and intensity, cumulative TSS may be used to create a training seasonal plan. See *duration, heart rate monitor, intensity, periodization, power meter,* and *workload.*

Training zones. Consecutive categories of intensity based on heart rate or power that are specific to a cyclist's physical capacity. Training zones are typically based on percentages of an athlete's unique physiological marker such as anaerobic threshold, lactate threshold, or functional threshold. Typically used to predetermine the intensity of a workout or portion of it. See *anaerobic threshold, functional threshold power,* and *lactate threshold.*

Transition period. In seasonal periodization, the training period during which workouts are relatively short and low intensity, allowing for full recovery in the days or weeks immediately following a targeted race. The purpose of this period is to completely recover from the stresses of recent training and racing. See *base period, build period, peak period, prep period,* and *race period.*

Variability index (VI). An indicator of how steadily (or non-steadily) paced a workout, race, or interval is when using a bicycle power meter. It is determined by dividing normalized power by average power. A resulting quotient of 1.05 or less is an indicator of steady pacing. A VI rising above 1.05 indicates progressively non-steady riding marked by surging. See *pacing* and *surging.*

Ventilatory threshold (VT). The moment during steadily increasing exertion at which breathing first becomes labored. VT closely corresponds with the lactate and anaerobic thresholds. See *anaerobic threshold* and *lactate threshold.*

VO₂max. The athlete's physical capacity for oxygen consumption during a maximal endurance exertion. Also known as aerobic capacity and maximal oxygen consumption. It is numerically expressed as milliliters of oxygen consumed per kilogram of body weight per minute (mL/kg/min). VO₂max is closely related to endurance fitness. See *aerobic capacity* and *fitness.*

Volume. A quantitative measure of training that expresses how much training is done in a given time frame such as a week. Volume is commonly based on cumulative Training Stress Score (TSS), total miles or kilometers, or collective hours of training. Volume results from the combination of individual workout durations and the frequency of those workouts in the chosen time frame. See *duration, frequency* and *Training Stress Score.*

Warm-up. The period of gradually increasing the intensity of exercise at the start of a training session with the intent of readying the body for the physical stress of the main set. See *main set.*

Work interval. High-intensity efforts in an interval workout separated by recovery intervals. Work intervals are commonly defined by their durations and intensities. See *intervals* and *recovery interval.*

Workload. The total stress applied in training through the combination of frequency, intensity, and duration for a given period of time, such as a week. Workload expresses both the quantitative and qualitative aspects of training in a single number. Common measurements are cumulative Training Stress Score (TSS) and kilojoules (kJ) for the designated time frame. See *kilojoules* and *Training Stress Score.*

Workout. A complete training session that is focused on a specific outcome and is typically made up of warm-up, main set, and cooldown. See *cooldown, main set,* and *warm-up.*

BIBLIOGRAPHY

Chapter 1

Blanchfield, A. W., J. Hardy, H. M. De Morree, W. Staiano, and S. M. Marcora. "Talking Yourself Out of Exhaustion: The Effects of Self-Talk on Endurance Performance." *Medicine and Science in Sports and Exercise* 46, no. 5 (2014): 998–1007.

Casey, B. J., L. H. Somerville, I. H. Gotlib, O. Ayduk, N. T. Franklin, M. K. Askren, J. Jonides, et al. "Behavioral and Neural Correlates of Delay of Gratification 40 Years Later." *Proceedings of the National Academy of Sciences* 108, no. 36 (2011): 14998–15003.

Hamilton, R. A., D. Scott, and M. P. MacDougall. "Assessing the Effectiveness of Self-Talk Interventions on Endurance Performance." *Journal of Applied Sport Psychology* 19 (2007): 226–239.

Jones, G. "How the Best of the Best Get Better and Better." *Harvard Business Review* 86, no. 6 (2008): 123–127, 142.

Kyllo, L., and D. Landers. "Goal Setting in Sport and Exercise: A Research Synthesis to Resolve the Controversy." *Journal of Sport and Exercise Psychology* 17 (1995): 117–137.

Noakes, T. D., J. E. Peltonen, and H. K. Rusko. "Evidence That a Central Governor Regulates Exercise Performance During Acute Hypoxia and Hyperoxia." *Journal of Experimental Biology* 204, no. 18 (2001): 3225–3234.

Weinberg, R. "Does Imagery Work?: Effects on Performance and Mental Skills." *Journal of Imagery Research in Sport and Physical Activity* 3, no. 1 (2008): 1–21.

Zadow, E. K., N. Gordon, C. R. Abbiss, and J. J. Peiffer. "Pacing: The Missing Piece of the Puzzle to High-Intensity Interval Training." *International Journal of Sports Medicine* 36, no. 3 (2015): 215–219.

Chapter 2

Bentley, D. J., L. R. McNaughton, D. Thompson, V. E. Vleck, and A. M. Batterham. "Peak Power Output, the Lactate Threshold, and Time Trial Performance in Cyclists." *Medicine and Science in Sports and Exercise* 33, no. 12 (2001): 2077–2081.

Bouchard, C. "Genomic Predictors of Trainability." *Experimental Physiology* 97, no. 3 (2012): 347–352.

Bouchard, C., M. A. Sarzynski, T. K. Rice, W. E. Kraus, T. S. Church, Y. J. Sung, D. C. Rao, and T. Rankinen. "Genomic Predictors of the Maximal O_2 Uptake Response to Standardized Exercise Training Programs." *Journal of Applied Physiology* 110, no. 5 (2011): 1160–1170.

Coyle, E. F., M. E. Feltner, S. A. Kautz, M. T. Hamilton, S. J. Montain, A. M. Baylor, L. D. Abraham, and G. W. Petrek. "Physiological and Biomechanical Factors Associated with Elite Endurance Cycling Performance." *Medicine and Science in Sports and Exercise* 23, no. 1 (1991): 93–107.

Ebert, T. R., D. T. Martin, W. McDonald, J. Victor, J. Plummer, and R. T. Withers. "Power Output During Women's World Cup Road Cycle Racing." *European Journal of Applied Physiology* 95, no. 5–6 (2005): 529–536.

Faria, E. W., D. L. Parker, and I. E. Faria. "The Science of Cycling: Physiology and Training—Part 1." *Sports Medicine* 35, no. 4 (2005): 285–312.

——. "The Science of Cycling: Physiology and Training—Part 2." *Sports Medicine* 35, no. 4 (2005): 313–337.

Joyner, M. J., and E. F. Coyle. "Endurance Exercise Performance: The Physiology of Champions." *Journal of Physiology* 586, no. 1 (2008): 35–44.

Lucía, A., J. Hoyos, M. Pérez, A. Santalla, and J. L. Chicharro. "Inverse Relationship Between VO₂max and Economy/Efficiency in World-Class Cyclists." *Medicine and Science in Sports and Exercise* 34, no. 12 (2002): 2079–2084.

Lucía, A., H. Joyos, and J. L. Chicharro. "Physiological Response to Professional Road Cycling: Climbers vs. Time Trialists." *International Journal of Sports Medicine* 21, no. 7 (2000): 505–512.

Lucía, A., J. Pardo, A. Durántez, J. Hoyos, and J. L. Chicharro. "Physiological Differences Between Professional and Elite Road Cyclists." *International Journal of Sports Medicine* 19, no. 5 (1998): 342–348.

Sallet, P., R. Mathieu, G. Fenech, and G. Baverel. "Physiological Differences of Elite and Professional Road Cyclists Related to Competition Level and Rider Specialization." *Journal of Sports Medicine and Physical Fitness* 46, no. 3 (2006): 361–365.

Skinner, J. S., A. Jaskólski, A. Jaskólska, J. Krasnoff, J. Gagnon, A. S. Leon, D. C. Rao, et al. "Age, Sex, Race, Initial Fitness, and Response to Training: The HERITAGE Family Study." *Journal of Applied Physiology* 9, no. 5 (2001): 1770–1776.

Swain, D. P. "The Influence of Body Mass in Endurance Bicycling." *Medicine and Science in Sports and Exercise* 26, no. 1 (1994): 58–63.

Swain, D. P., J. R. Coast, P. S. Clifford, M. C. Milliken, and J. Stray-Gundersen. "Influence of Body Size on Oxygen Consumption During Bicycling." *Journal of Applied Physiology* 62, no. 2 (1987): 668–672.

Chapter 3

Bangsbo, J., T. P. Gunnarsson, J. Wendell, L. Nybo, and M. Thomassen. "Reduced Volume and Increased Training Intensity Elevate Muscle Na+/K+ {alpha} 2-Subunit Expression as Well as Short- and Long-Term Work Capacity in Humans." *Journal of Applied Physiology* 107, no. 6 (2009): 1771–1780.

Banister, E. W., R. H. Morton, and J. Fitz-Clarke. "Dose/Response Effects of Exercises Modeled from Training: Physical and Biochemical Measures." *Annals of Physiology and Anthropology* 11, no. 3 (1992): 345–356.

Borg, G. "Perceived Exertion as an Indicator of Somatic Stress." *Scandinavian Journal of Rehabilitation Medicine* 2, no. 2 (1970): 92–98.

Brisswalter, J., P. Legros, and M. Durand. "Running Economy, Preferred Step Length Correlated to Body Dimensions in Elite Middle Distance Runners." *Journal of Sports Medicine and Physical Fitness* 36 (1996): 7–15.

Burgomaster, K. A., K. R. Howarth, S. M. Phillips, M. Rakobowchuk, M. J. Macdonald, S. L. McGee, and M. J. Gibala. "Similar Metabolic Adaptations During Exercise After Low Volume Sprint Interval and Traditional Endurance Training in Humans." *Journal of Physiology* 586, no. 1 (2008): 151–160.

Busso, T., R. Candan, and J. R. Lacour. "Fatigue and Fitness Modelled from the Effects of Training on Performance." *European Journal of Applied Physiology and Occupational Physiology* 69, no. 1 (1994): 50–54.

Costill, D. L., R. Thomas, R. A. Roberts, D. D. Pascoe, C. P. Lambert, S. I. Barr, and W. J. Fink. "Adaptations to Swimming Training: Influence of Training Volume." *Medicine and Science in Sports and Exercise* 23 (1991): 371–377.

Ekblom, B., and A. N. Golobarg. "The Influence of Physical Training and Other Factors on the Subjective Rating of Perceived Exertion." *Acta Physiologica Scandinavica* 83, no. 3 (1971): 399–406.

Fitz-Clarke, J. R., R. H. Morton, and E. W. Banister. "Optimizing Athletic Performance by Influence Curves." *Journal of Applied Physiology* 71, no. 3 (1991): 1151–1158.

Godfrey, R. J., S. A. Ingham, C. R. Pedlar, and G. P. Whyte. "The Detraining and Retraining of an Elite Rower: A Case Study." *Journal of Science and Medicine in Sport* 8, no. 3 (2005): 314–320.

Hawley, J. A. "Specificity of Training Adaptation: Time for a Rethink?" *Journal of Physiology* 586, no. 1 (2008): 1–2.

Helgerud, J., K. Hoydal, E. Wang, T. Karlsen, P. Berg, M. Bjerkaas, T. Simonsen, et al. "Aerobic High-Intensity Intervals Improve VO$_2$max More Than Moderate Training." *Medicine and Science in Sports and Exercise* 39, no. 4 (2007): 665–671.

Jones, A. M., and H. Carter. "The Effect of Endurance Training on Parameters of Aerobic Fitness." *Sports Medicine* 29, no. 6 (2000): 373–386.

Kubukeli, Z. N., T. D. Noakes, and S. C. Dennis. "Training Techniques to Improve Endurance Exercise Performances." *Sports Medicine* 32, no. 8 (2002): 489–509.

Laursen, P. B., and D. G. Jenkins. "The Scientific Basis for High-Intensity Interval Training: Optimizing Training Programmes and Maximising Performance in Highly Trained Endurance Athletes." *Sports Medicine* 32, no. 1 (2002): 5373.

Lehmann, M., H. Mann, V. Gastmann, J. Keul, D. Vetter, J. M. Steinacker, and D. Haussinger. "Unaccustomed High-Mileage vs. Intensity Training-Related Changes in Performance and Serum Amino Acid Levels." *International Journal of Sports Medicine* 17, no. 3 (1996): 187–192.

Lindsay, F. H., J. A. Hawley, K. H. Myburgh, H. H. Schomer, T. D. Noakes, and S. C. Dennis. "Improved Athletic Performance in Highly Trained Cyclists After Interval Training." *Medicine and Science in Sports and Exercise* 28 (1996): 1427–1434.

McNicol, A. J., B. J. O'Brien, C. D. Paton, and W. L. Knez. "The Effects of Increased Absolute Training Intensity on Adaptations to Endurance Exercise Training." *Journal of Science and Medicine in Sport* 12, no. 4 (2009): 485–489.

Midgley, A. W., L. R. McNaughton, and N. M. Wilkinson. "Is There an Optimal Training Intensity for Enhancing the Maximal Oxygen Uptake of Distance Runners?: Empirical Research Findings, Current Opinions, Physiological Rationale, and Practical Recommendations." *Sports Medicine* 36, no. 2 (2006): 117–132.

Millet, G. P., A. Lambert, B. Barbier, J. D. Rouillon, and R. B. Candan. "Modelling the Relationships Between Training, Anxiety, and Fatigue in Elite Athletes." *International Journal of Sports Medicine* 26, no. 6 (2005): 492–498.

Morton, R. H. "Modeling Training and Overtraining." *Journal of Sports Science* 15, no. 3 (1997): 335–340.

Morton, R. H., J. R. Fitz-Clarke, and E. W. Banister. "Modeling Human Performance in Running." *Journal of Applied Physiology* 69, no. 3 (1990): 1171–1177.

Neal, C. M., A. M. Hunter, L. Brennan, A. O'Sullivan, D. L. Hamilton, G. DeVito, and S. D. Galloway. "Six Weeks of a Polarized Training Intensity Distribution Leads to Greater Physiological and Performance Adaptations Than a Threshold Model in Trained Cyclists." *Journal of Applied Physiology* 114, no. 4 (2013): 461–471.

Taha, T., and S. G. Thomas. "Systems Modelling of the Relationship Between Training and Performance." *Sports Medicine* 33, no. 14 (2003): 1061–1073.

Tanaka, H. "Effects of Cross-Training: Transfer of Training Effects on VO_2max Between Cycling, Running, and Swimming." *Sports Medicine* 18, no. 5 (1994): 330–339.

Westgarth-Taylor, C., J. A. Hawley, S. Rickard, K. H. Myburgh, T. D. Noakes, and S. C. Dennis. "Metabolic and Performance Adaptations to Interval Training in Endurance-Trained Cyclists." *European Journal of Applied Physiology and Occupational Physiology* 75, no. 4 (1997): 298–304.

Chapter 4

Bendke, R., R. M. Leithauser, and Q. Ochentel. "Blood Lactate Diagnostics in Exercise Testing and Training." *International Journal of Sports Physiology and Performance* 6, no. 1 (2011): 8–24.

Estave-Lanao, J., C. Foster, S. Seiler, and A. Lucía. "Impact of Training Intensity Distribution on Performance in Endurance Athletes." *Journal of Strength and Conditioning Research* 21, no. 3 (2007): 943–949.

Estave-Lanao, J., A. F. San Juan, C. P. Earnest, C. Foster, and A. Lucía. "How Do Endurance Runners Actually Train?: Relationship with Competition Performance." *Medicine and Science in Sports and Exercise* 37, no. 3 (2005): 496–504.

Fisketstrand, A., and S. Seiler. "Training and Performance Characteristics Among Norwegian International Rowers, 1970–2001." *Medicine and Science in Sports and Exercise* 14 (2004): 303–310.

Gaskill, S. E., R. C. Serfass, D. W. Bacharach, and J. M. Kelly. "Responses to Training in Cross-Country Skiers." *Medicine and Science in Sports and Exercise* 31 (1999): 1211–1217.

Helgerud, J., K. Hoydal, E. Wang, T. Karlsen, P. Berg, M. Bjerkaas, T. Simonsen, et al. "Aerobic High-Intensity Intervals Improve VO_2max More Than Moderate Training." *Medicine and Science in Sports and Exercise* 39, no. 4 (2007): 665–671.

Impellizzeri, F., A. Sassi, M. Rodriguez-Alonso, P. Mognoni, and S. Marcora. "Exercise Intensity During Off-Road Cycling Competitions." *Medicine and Science in Sports and Exercise* 34, no. 11 (2002): 1808–1813.

Ingham, S. A., H. Carter, G. P. Whyte, and J. H. Doust. "Physiological and Performance Effects of Low- Versus Mixed-Intensity Rowing Training." *Medicine and Science in Sports and Exercise* 40, no. 3 (2008): 579–584.

Ingham, S. A., B. W. Fudge, and J. S. Pringle. "Training Distribution, Physiological Profile, and Performance for a Male International 1500-m Runner." *International Journal of Sports Physiology and Performance* 7, no. 2 (2012): 193–195.

Jacobs, I. "Blood Lactate: Implications for Training and Sports Performance." *Sports Medicine* 3 (1986): 10–25.

Laursen, P. B. "Training for Intense Exercise Performance: High-Intensity or High-Volume Training?" *Supplement, Scandinavian Journal of Medicine and Science in Sports* 20, no. S2 (2010): 1–10.

Laursen, P. B., and D. G. Jenkins. "The Scientific Basis for High-Intensity Interval Training: Optimizing Training Programmes and Maximising Performance in Highly Trained Endurance Athletes." *Sports Medicine* 32, no. 1 (2002): 53–73.

Lehmann, M., H. Mann, V. Gastmann, J. Keul, D. Vetter, J. M. Stewacker, and D. Haussinger. "Unaccustomed High-Mileage vs. Intensity Training-Related Changes in Performance and Serum Amino Acid Levels." *International Journal of Sports Medicine* 17, no. 3 (1996): 187–192.

Loftin, M., and B. Warren. "Comparison of a Simulated 16.1-km Time Trial, VO_2max, and Related Factors in Cyclists with Different Ventilatory Thresholds." *International Journal of Sports Medicine* 15, no. 8 (1994): 498–503.

Midgley, A. W., L. R. McNaughton, and N. M. Wilkinson. "Is There an Optimal Training Intensity for Enhancing the Maximal Oxygen Uptake of Distance Runners?: Empirical Research Findings, Current Opinions, Physiological Rationale, and Practical Recommendations." *Sports Medicine* 36, no. 2 (2006): 117–132.

Mujika, I., J. C. Chatard, T. Busso, A. Geyssant, F. Barale, and L. Lacoste. "Effects of Training on Performance in Competitive Swimming." *Canadian Journal of Applied Physiology* 20 (1995): 395–406.

Munoz, I., S. Seiler, J. Bautista, J. Espana, E. Larumbe, and J. Esteve-Lanao. "Does Polarized Training Improve Performance in Recreational Runners?" *International Journal of Sports, Physiology and Performance* 9, no. 2 (2013): 265–272.

Neal, C. M., A. M. Hunter, L. Brennan, A. O'Sullivan, D. L. Hamilton, G. DeVito, and S. D. Galloway. "Six Weeks of a Polarized Training Intensity Distribution Leads to Greater Physiological and Performance Adaptations Than a Threshold Model in Trained Cyclists." *Journal of Applied Physiology* 114, no. 4 (2013): 461–471.

Ready, E. A., and H. A. Quinney. "Alterations in Anaerobic Threshold as the Result of Endurance Training and Detraining." *Medicine and Science in Sports and Exercise* 14 (1982): 292–296.

Seiler, S. "What Is Best Practice for Training Intensity and Duration Distribution in Endurance Athletes?" *International Journal of Sports, Physiology and Performance* 5 (2010): 276–291.

Seiler, S., and G. Kjerland. "Quantifying Training Intensity Distribution in Elite Endurance Athletes: Is There Evidence for an 'Optimal' Distribution?" *Scandinavian Journal of Medicine and Science in Sports* 16, no. 1 (2006): 49–56.

Seiler, S., and E. Tonnessen. "Intervals, Thresholds, and Long Slow Distance: The Role of Intensity and Duration in Endurance Training." *Sport Science* 13 (2009): 32–53.

Skinner, J., and T. McLellan. "The Transition from Aerobic to Anaerobic Metabolism." *Research Quarterly for Exercise and Sport* 51 (1980): 234–248.

Stöggl, T., and B. Sperlich. "Polarized Training Has Greater Impact on Key Endurance Variables Than Threshold, High Intensity, or High Volume Training." *Frontiers in Physiology* 4, no. 5 (2014): 33.

Swensen, T. C., C. R. Harnish, L. Beltman, and B. A. Keller. "Noninvasive Estimation of the Maximal Lactate Steady State in Trained Cyclists." *Medicine and Science in Sports and Exercise* 31, no. 5 (1999): 742–746.

Chapter 5

Allen, H., and A. Coggan. *Training and Racing with a Power Meter.* 2nd ed. Boulder, CO: VeloPress, 2010.

Jobson, S. A., A. M. Nevill, G. S. Palmer, A. E. Jeukendrup, M. Doherty, and G. Atkinson. "The Ecological Validity of Laboratory Cycling: Does Body Size Explain the Difference Between Laboratory- and Field-Based Cycling Performance? *Journal of Sports Science* 25, no. 1 (2007): 3–9.

Jones, G. "How the Best of the Best Get Better and Better." *Harvard Business Review* 86, no. 6 (2008): 123–127, 142.

McCormick, A., C. Meijen, and S. Marcora. "Psychological Determinants of Whole-Body Endurance Performance." *Sports Medicine* 45, no. 7 (2015): 997–1015.

McGehee, J. C., C. J. Tanner, and J. A. Houmard. "A Comparison of Methods for Estimating the Lactate Threshold." *Journal of Strength and Conditioning Research* 19, no. 3 (2005): 553–558.

Chapter 6

Bendke, R., R. M. Leithauser, and Q. Ochentel. "Blood Lactate Diagnostics in Exercise Testing and Training." *International Journal of Sports Physiology and Performance* 6, no. 1 (2011): 8–24.

Cairns, S. P. "Lactic Acid and Exercise Performance: Culprit or Friend?" *Sports Medicine* 36, no. 4 (2006): 279–291.

Coyle, E. F. "Integration of the Physiological Factors Determining Endurance Performance Ability." *Exercise, Sport, and Science Review* 23 (1995): 25–63.

Coyle, E. F., M. E. Feltner, S. A. Kantz, M. T. Hamilton, S. J. Montain, A. M. Baylor, L. D. Abraham, et al. "Physiological and Biomechanical Factors Associated with Elite Endurance Cycling Performance." *Medicine and Science in Sports and Exercise* 23, no. 1 (1991): 93–107.

Faria, E. W., D. L. Parker, and I. E. Faria. "The Science of Cycling: Physiology and Training—Part 1." *Sports Medicine* 35, no. 4 (2005): 255–312.

Grossl, T., R. Dantas de Lucas, K. Mendes de Souza, and G. A. Guglielmol. "Maximal Lactate Steady-State and Anaerobic Thresholds from Different Methods in Cyclists." *European Journal of Sports Science* 12, no. 2 (2012): 161–167.

Lucía, A., J. Hoyos, M. Perez, A. Santalla, and J. L. Chicharro. "Inverse Relationship Between VO2max and Economy/Efficiency in World-Class Cyclists." *Medicine and Science in Sports and Exercise* 34, no. 12 (2002): 2079–2084.

Lucía, A., H. Joyos, and J. L. Chicharro. "Physiological Response to Professional Road Cycling: Climbers vs. Time Trialists." *International Journal of Sports Medicine* 21, no. 7 (2000): 505–512.

McGehee, J., C. Tanner, and J. Houmard. "A Comparison of Methods for Estimating the Lactate Threshold." *Journal of Strength and Conditioning Research* 19, no. 3 (2005): 553–558.

Myers, J., and E. Ashley. "Dangerous Curves: A Perspective on Exercise, Lactate, and the Anaerobic Threshold." *Chest* 111, no. 3 (1997): 787–795.

Nicholls, J. F., S. L. Phares, and M. J. Buono. "Relationship Between Blood Lactate Response to Exercise and Endurance Performance in Competitive Female Master Cyclists." *International Journal of Sports Medicine* 18 (1997): 458–463.

Pate, R. R., and J. D. Branch. "Training for Endurance Sport." *Medicine and Science in Sports and Exercise* 24, no. 9 (1992): S340–343.

Sallet, P., R. Mathieu, G. French, and G. Baverel. "Physiological Differences of Elite and Professional Road Cyclists Related to Competition Level and Rider Specialization." *Journal of Sports Medicine and Physical Fitness* 46, no. 3 (2006): 361–365.

Swensen, T. C., C. R. Harnish, L. Beltman, and B. A. Keller. "Noninvasive Estimation of the Maximal Lactate Steady State in Trained Cyclists." *Medicine and Science in Sports and Exercise* 31, no. 5 (1999): 742–746.

Chapter 7

Boullosa, D. A., L. Abreu, A. Varela-Sanz, and I. Mujika. "Do Olympic Athletes Train as in the Paleolithic Era?" *Sports Medicine* 43, no. 10 (2013): 909–917.

Fry, R. W., A. R. Morton, and D. Keast. "Periodization of Training Stress: A Review." *Canadian Journal of Sport Science* 17 (1992): 234–240.

Gaskill, S. E., R. C. Serfass, D. W. Bacharach, and J. M. Kelly. "Responses to Training in Cross-Country Skiers." *Medicine and Science in Sports and Exercise* 31, no. 8 (1999): 1211–1217.

Hagberg, J. M., R. C. Hickson, A. A. Ehsani, and J. O. Holloszy. "Faster Adjustment to and Recovery from Submaximal Exercise in the Trained State." *Journal of Applied Physiology* 48, no. 2 (1980): 218–224.

Hautala, A. J., A. M. Kiviniemi, T. H. Makikallio, H. Kinnunen, S. Nissila, H. V. Huikuri, and M. P. Tulppo. "Individual Differences in the Responses to Endurance and Resistance Training." *European Journal of Applied Physiology* 96, no. 5 (2006): 535–542.

Kiely, J. "Periodization Paradigms in the 21st Century: Evidence-Led or Tradition-Driven?" *International Journal of Sports Physiology and Performance* 7, no. 3 (2012): 242–250.

Morton, R. H. "Modeling Training and Overtraining." *Journal of Sports Science* 15, no. 3 (1997): 335–340.

Paton, C. D., and W. G. Hopkins. "Seasonal Changes in Power of Competitive Cyclists: Implications for Monitoring Performance." *Journal of Science and Medicine in Sport* 8, no. 4 (2005): 375–381.

Swain, D. P., J. R. Coast, P. S. Clifford, M. C. Milliken, and J. Stray-Gundersen. "Influence of Body Size on Oxygen Consumption During Bicycling." *Journal of Applied Physiology* 62, no. 2 (1987): 668–672.

Chapter 8

Banister, E. W., R. H. Morton, and J. Fitz-Clarke. "Dose/Response Effects of Exercise Modeled from Training: Physical and Biochemical Measures." *Annals of Physiology and Anthropology* 11, no. 3 (1992): 345–356.

Busso, T., R. Candau, and J. R. Lacour. "Fatigue and Fitness Modelled from the Effects of Training on Performance." *European Journal of Applied Physiology and Occupational Physiology* 69, no. 1 (1994): 50–54.

Costill, D. L., R. Thomas, R. A. Robergs, D. Pascoe, C. Lambert, S. Barr, and W. J. Fink. "Adaptations to Swimming Training: Influence of Training Volume." *Medicine and Science in Sports and Exercise* 23, no. 3 (1991): 371–377.

Esteve-Lanao, J., C. Foster, S. Seiler, and A. Lucía. "Impact of Training Intensity Distribution on Performance in Endurance Athletes." *Journal of Strength and Conditioning Research* 21, no. 3 (2007): 943–949.

Fitz-Clarke, J. R., R. H. Morton, and E. W. Banister. "Optimizing Athletic Performance by Influence Curves." *Journal of Applied Physiology* 71, no. 3 (1991): 1151–1158.

Gaskill, S. E., R. C. Serfass, D. W. Bacharach, and J. M. Kelly. "Responses to Training in Cross-Country Skiers." *Medicine and Science in Sports and Exercise* 31, no 8 (1999): 1211–1217.

Gomes, P. S., and Y. Bhambhani. "Time Course Changes and Dissociation in VO_2max at Maximum and Submaximum Exercise Levels as a Result of Training in Males." *Medicine and Science in Sports and Exercise* 28, no. 5 (1996): S81.

Hautala, A. J., A. M. Kiviniemi, T. H. Mäkikallio, H. Kinnunen, S. Nissilä, H. V. Huikuri, and M. P. Tulppo. "Individual Differences in the Responses to Endurance and Resistance Training." *European Journal of Applied Physiology* 96, no. 5 (2006): 535–542.

Helgerud, J., K. Høydal, E. Wang, T. Karlsen, P. Berg, M. Bjerkaas, T. Simonsen, et al. "Aerobic High-Intensity Intervals Improve VO_2max More Than Moderate Training." *Medicine and Science in Sports and Exercise* 39, no. 4 (2007): 665–671.

Houmard, J. A. "Impact of Reduced Training on Performance in Endurance Athletes." *Sports Medicine* 12, no. 6 (1991): 380–393.

Laursen, P. B. "Training for Intense Exercise Performance: High-Intensity or High-Volume Training?" Supplement, *Scandinavian Journal of Medicine and Science in Sports* 20, no. S2 (2010): 1–10.

Laursen, P. B., and D. G. Jenkins. "The Scientific Basis for High-Intensity Interval Training: Optimising Training Programmes and Maximising Performance in Highly Trained Endurance Athletes." *Sports Medicine* 32, no. 1 (2002): 53–73.

Millet, G. P., A. Groslambert, B. Barbier, J. D. Rouillon, and R. B. Cantan. "Modeling the Relationships Between Training, Anxiety, and Fatigue in Elite Athletes." *International Journal of Sports Medicine* 26, no. 6 (2005): 492–498.

Morton, R. H. "Modeling Training and Overtraining." *Journal of Sports Science* 15, no. 3 (1997): 335–340.

Morton, R. H., J. R. Fitz-Clarke, and E. W. Banister. "Modeling Human Performance in Running." *Journal of Applied Physiology* 69, no. 3 (1990): 1171–1177.

Mujika, I., A. Goya, S. Padilla, A. Grijalba, E. Gorostiaga, and J. Ibañez. "Physiological Responses to a 6-d Taper in Middle-Distance Runners: Influence of Training Intensity and Volume." *Medicine and Science in Sports and Exercise* 32, no. 2 (2000): 511–517.

Seiler, S. "What Is Best Practice for Training Intensity and Duration Distribution in Endurance Athletes?" *International Journal of Sports, Physiology, and Performance* 5, no. 3 (2010): 276–291.

Seiler, S., and E. Tonnessen. "Intervals, Thresholds, and Long Slow Distance: The Role of Intensity and Duration in Endurance Training." *Sport Science* 13 (2009): 32–53.

Shepley, B., J. D. MacDougall, N. Cipriano, J. R. Sutton, M. A. Tarnopolsky, and G. Coates. "Physiological Effects of Tapering in Highly Trained Athletes." *Journal of Applied Physiology* 72, no. 2 (1992): 706–711.

Taha, T., and S. G. Thomas. "Systems Modelling of the Relationship Between Training and Performance." *Sports Medicine* 33, no. 14 (2003): 1061–1073.

Thomas, L., I. Mujika, and T. Busso. "Computer Simulations Assessing the Potential Performance Benefit of a Final Increase in Training During Pre-Event Taper." *Journal of Strength and Conditioning Research* 23, no. 6 (2009): 1729–1736.

Chapter 9

Bosquet, L., J. Montpetit, D. Arvisais, and I. Mujika. "Effects of Tapering on Performance: A Meta-Analysis." *Medicine and Science in Sports and Exercise* 39, no. 8 (2007): 1358–1365.

Breil, F. S., S. N. Weber, S. Koller, H. Hoppeler, and M. Vogt. "Block Training Periodization in Alpine Skiing: Effects of 11-Day HIT on VO_2max and Performance." *European Journal of Applied Physiology* 109, no. 6 (2010): 1077–1086.

Buchheit, M., and Laursen, P. B. "High-Intensity Interval Training: Solutions to the Programming Puzzle. Part II: Anaerobic Energy, Neuromuscular Load and Practical Applications." *Sports Medicine* 43, no. 10 (2013): 927–954.

Fleck, S. J. "Non-Linear Periodization for General Fitness and Athletes." *Journal of Human Kinetics* 29A (2011): 41–45.

García-Pallarés, J., M. García-Fernández, L. Sánchez-Medina, and M. Izquierdo. "Performance Changes in World-Class Kayakers Following Two Different Training Periodization Models." *European Journal of Applied Physiology* 110, no. 1 (2010): 99–107.

García-Pallarés, J., L. Sánchez-Medina, L. Carrasco, A. Diaz, and M. Izquierdo. "Endurance and Neuromuscular Changes in World-Class Level Kayakers During a Periodized Training Cycle." *European Journal of Applied Physiology* 106, no. 4 (2009): 629–638.

Hartmann, H., K. Wirth, M. Keiner, C. Mickel, A. Sander, and E. Szilvas. "Short-Term Periodization Models: Effects on Strength and Speed-Strength Performance." *Sports Medicine* 45, no. 10 (2015): 1373–1386.

Issurin, V. B. "Block Periodization Versus Traditional Training Theory: A Review." *Journal of Sports Medicine and Physical Fitness* 48, no. 1 (2008): 65–75.

———. "New Horizons for the Methodology and Physiology of Training Periodization." *Sports Medicine* 40, no. 3 (2010): 189–206.

———. "Training Transfer: Scientific Background and Insights for Practical Application." *Sports Medicine* 43, no. 8 (2013): 675–694.

Jeukendrup, A. E., M. K. Hesselink, A. C. Snyder, H. Kuipers, and H. A. Keizer. "Physiological Changes in Male Competitive Cyclists After Two Weeks of Intensified Training." *International Journal of Sports Medicine* 13, no. 7 (1992): 534–541.

Kibler, W. B., and T. J. Chandler. "Sport-Specific Conditioning." *American Journal of Sports Medicine* 22, no. 3 (1994): 424–432.

Kiely, J. "Periodization Paradigms in the 21st Century: Evidence-Led or Tradition-Driven?" *International Journal of Sports Physiology and Performance* 7, no. 3 (2012): 242–250.

Kirwan, J. P., D. L. Costill, M. G. Flynn, J. B. Mitchell, W. J. Fink, P. D. Neufer, and J. A. Houmard. "Physiological Responses to Successive Days of Intense Training in Competitive Swimmers." *Medicine and Science in Sports and Exercise* 20, no. 3 (1988): 255–259.

Lehmann, M., P. Baumgartl, C. Wiesenack, A. Seidel, H. Baumann, S. Fischer, U. Spöri, et al. "Training-Overtraining: Influence of a Defined Increase in Training Volume vs. Training Intensity on Performance, Catecholamines and Some Metabolic Parameters in Experienced Middle- and Long-Distance Runners." *European Journal of Applied Physiology and Occupational Physiology* 64, no. 2 (1992): 169–177.

Lehmann, M., H. Wieland, and U. Gastmann. "Influence of an Unaccustomed Increase in Training Volume vs. Intensity on Performance, Hematological and Blood-Chemical Parameters in Distance Runners." *Journal of Sports Medicine and Physical Fitness* 37, no. 2 (1997): 110–116.

Rhea, M. R., S. D. Ball, W. T. Phillips, and L. N. Burkett. "A Comparison of Linear and Daily Undulating Periodized Programs with Equated Volume and Intensity for Strength." *Journal of Strength and Conditioning Research* 16, no. 2 (2002): 250–255.

Rhea, M. R., W. T. Phillips, L. N. Burkett, W. J. Stone, S. D. Ball, B. A. Alvar, and A. B. Thomas. "A Comparison of Linear and Daily Undulating Periodized Programs with Equated Volume and Intensity for Local Muscular Endurance." *Journal of Strength and Conditioning Research* 17, no. 1 (2003): 82–87.

Rønnestad, B. R., S. Ellefsen, H. Nygaard, E. E. Zacharoff, O. Vikmoen, J. Hansen, and J. Hallén. "Effects of 12 Weeks of Block Periodization on Performance and Performance Indices in Well-Trained Cyclists." *Scandinavian Journal of Medicine and Science in Sports* 24, no. 2 (2014): 327–335.

Rønnestad, B. R., J. Hansen, and S. Ellefsen. "Block Periodization of High-Intensity Aerobic Intervals Provides Superior Training Effects in Trained Cyclists." *Scandinavian Journal of Medicine and Science in Sports* 24, no. 1 (2014): 34–42.

Rønnestad, B. R., J. Hansen, V. Thyli, T. A. Bakken, and Ø. Sandbakk. "5-Week Block Periodization Increases Aerobic Power in Elite Cross-Country Skiers." *Scandinavian Journal of Medicine and Science in Sports* 26, no. 2 (2016): 140–146.

Szabo, S., Y. Tache, and A. Somogyi. "The Legacy of Hans Selye and the Origins of Stress Research: A Retrospective 75 Years After His Landmark Brief 'Letter' to the Editor of Nature." *Stress* 15, no. 5 (2012): 472–478.

Tønnessen, E., Ø. Sylta, T. A. Haugen, E. Hem, I. S. Svendsen, and S. Seiler. "The Road to Gold: Training and Peaking Characteristics in the Year Prior to a Gold Medal Endurance Performance." *PLoS One* 9, no. 7 (2014): e101796.

Chapter 10

Aubry, A., C. Hausswirth, J. Louis, A. J. Coutts, and Y. Le Meur. "Functional Overreaching: The Key to Peak Performance During the Taper?" *Medicine and Science in Sports and Exercise* 46, no. 9 (2014): 1769–1777.

Hausswirth, C., J. Louis, A. Aubry, G. Bonnet, R. Duffield, and Y. Le Meur. "Evidence of Disturbed Sleep and Increased Illness in Overreached Endurance Athletes." *Medicine and Science in Sports and Exercise* 46, no. 5 (2014): 1036–1045.

Lehmann, M., U. Gastmann, K. G. Peterson, N. Bachl, A. Seidel, A. N. Khalaf, S. Fischer, et al. "Training-Overtraining: Performance, and Hormone Levels, After a Defined Increase in Training Volume Versus Intensity in Experienced Middle- and Long-Distance Runners." *British Journal of Sports Medicine* 26, no. 4 (1992): 233–242.

Lehmann, M., H. Wieland, and U. Gastmann. "Influence of an Unaccustomed Increase in Training Volume vs. Intensity on Performance, Hematological and Blood-Chemical Parameters in Distance Runners." *Journal of Sports Medicine and Physical Fitness* 37, no. 2 (1997): 110–116.

Le Meur, Y., A. Pichon, K. Schaal, L. Schmitt, J. Louis, J. Gueneron, P. P. Vidal, and C. Hausswirth. "Evidence of Parasympathetic Hyperactivity in Functionally Overreached Athletes." *Medicine and Science in Sports and Exercise* 45, no. 11 (2013): 2061–2071.

Meeusen, R., M. Duclos, C. Foster, A. Fry, M. Gleeson, D. Nieman, J. Raglin, et al. "Prevention, Diagnosis, and Treatment of the Overtraining Syndrome: Joint Consensus Statement of the European College of Sport Science and the American College of Sports Medicine." *Medicine and Science in Sports and Exercise* 45, no. 1 (2013): 186–205.

Vesterinen, V., K. Häkkinen, T. Laine, E. Hynynen, J. Mikkola, and A. Nummela. "Predictors of Individual Adaptation to High-Volume or High-Intensity Endurance Training in Recreational Endurance Runners." *Scandinavian Journal of Medicine and Science in Sports* 26, no. 8 (2016): 885–893.

Chapter 11

Barnett, A. "Using Recovery Modalities Between Training Sessions in Elite Athletes: Does It Help?" *Sports Medicine* 36, no. 9 (2006): 781–796.

Bellenger, C. R., R. L. Thomson, E. Y. Robertson, K. Davison, M. J. Nelson, L. Karavirta, and J. D. Buckley. "The Effect of Functional Overreaching on Parameters of Autonomic Heart Rate Regulation." *European Journal of Applied Physiology* 117, no. 3 (2017): 541–550.

Bishop, P. A., E. Jones, and A. K. Woods. "Recovery from Training: A Brief Review." *Journal of Strength and Conditioning Research* 22, no. 3 (2008): 1015–1024.

Born, J., S. Muths, and H. L. Fehm. "The Significance of Sleep Onset and Slow Wave Sleep for Nocturnal Release of Growth Hormone (GH) and Cortisol." *Psychoneuroendocrinology* 13, no. 3 (1988): 233–243.

Bosquet, L., S. Merkari, D. Arvisais, and A. E. Aubert. "Is Heart Rate a Convenient Tool to Monitor Overreaching?: A Systematic Review of the Literature." *British Journal of Sports Medicine* 42, no. 9 (2008): 709–714.

Brummitt, J. "The Role of Massage in Sports Performance and Rehabilitation: Current Evidence and Future Direction." *North American Journal of Sports Physical Therapy* 3, no. 1 (2008): 7–21.

Busso, T., R. Candau, and J. R. Lacour. "Fatigue and Fitness Modelled from the Effects of Training on Performance." *European Journal of Applied Physiology and Occupational Physiology* 69, no. 1 (1994): 50–54.

Costill, D. L., R. Bowers, G. Branam, and K. Sparks. "Muscle Glycogen Utilization During Prolonged Exercise on Successive Days." *Journal of Applied Physiology* 31, no. 6 (1971): 834–838.

Dedering, A., G. Németh, and K. Harms-Ringdahl. "Correlation Between Electromyographic Spectral Changes and Subjective Assessment of Lumbar Muscle Fatigue in Subjects Without Pain from the Lower Back." *Clinical Biomechanics* 14, no. 2 (1999): 103–111.

Depauw, K., B. DeGeus, B. Roelands, F. Lauwens, J. Verschueren, E. Heyman, and R. R. Meeusen. "Effect of Five Different Recovery Methods on Repeated Cycle Performance." *Medicine and Science in Sports and Exercise* 43, no. 5 (2011): 890–897.

Etheridge, T., A. Philip, and P. W. Watt. "A Single Protein Meal Increases Recovery of Muscle Function Following an Acute Eccentric Exercise Bout." *Applied Physiology and Nutritional Metabolism* 33, no. 3 (2008): 483–488.

Halson, S. L. "Monitoring Training Load to Understand Fatigue in Athletes." *Supplement, Sports Medicine* 44, no. S2 (2014): S139–S147.

Hemmings, B., M. Smith, J. Graydon, and R. Dyson. "Effects of Massage on Physiological Restoration, Perceived Recovery, and Repeated Sports Performance." *British Journal of Sports Medicine* 34, no. 2 (2000): 109–114.

Hill, J., G. Howatson, K. van Someren, J. Leeder, and C. Pedlar. "Compression Garments and Recovery from Exercise-Induced Muscle Damage: A Meta-Analysis." *British Journal of Sports Medicine* 48, no. 18 (2014): 1340–1346.

Jajtner, A. R., J. R. Hoffman, A. M. Gonzalez, P. R. Worts, M. S. Fragala, and J. R. Stout. "Comparison of the Effects of Electrical Stimulation and Cold-Water Immersion on Muscle Soreness After Resistance Exercise." *Journal of Sport Rehabilitation* 24, no. 2 (2015): 99–108.

Kaikkonen, P., E. Hynynen, T. Mann, H. Rusko, and A. Nummela. "Can HRV Be Used to Evaluate Training Load in Constant Load Exercises?" *European Journal of Applied Physiology* 108, no. 3 (2010): 435–442.

Kaikkonen, P., H. Rusko, and K. Martinmäki. "Post-Exercise Heart Rate Variability of Endurance Athletes After Different High-Intensity Exercise Interventions." *Scandinavian Journal of Medicine and Science in Sports* 18, no. 4 (2008): 511–519.

Mackey, A. L. "Does an NSAID a Day Keep Satellite Cells at Bay?" *Journal of Applied Physiology* 115, no. 6 (2013): 900–908.

Maughan, R. J. "Nutritional Ergogenic Aids and Exercise Performance." *Nutrition Research Review* 12, no. 2 (1999): 255–280.

Maughan, R. J., D. S. King, and T. Lea. "Dietary Supplements." *Journal of Sports Science* 22, no. 1 (2004): 95–113.

McAinch, A. J., M. A. Febbraio, J. M. Parkin, S. Zhao, K. Tangalakis, L. Stojanovska, and M. F. Carey. "Effect of Active Versus Passive Recovery on Metabolism and Performance During Subsequent Exercise." *International Journal of Sport Nutrition and Exercise Metabolism* 14, no. 2 (2004): 185–196.

Meeusen, R., M. Duclos, C. Foster, A. Fry, M. Gleeson, D. Nieman, J. Raglin, et al. "Prevention, Diagnosis, and Treatment of the Overtraining Syndrome: Joint Consensus Statement of the European College of Sport Science and the American College of Sports Medicine." *Medicine and Science in Sports and Exercise* 45, no. 1 (2013): 186–205.

Mika, A., P. Mika, B. Fernhall, and V. B. Unnithan. "Comparison of Recovery Strategies on Muscle Performance After Fatiguing Exercise." *American Journal of Physical Medicine and Rehabilitation* 86, no. 6 (2007): 474–481.

Morrison, D., J. Hughes, P. A. Della Gatta, S. Mason, S. Lamon, A. P. Russell, and G. D. Wadley. "Vitamin C and E Supplementation Prevents Some of the Cellular Adaptations to Endurance-Training in Humans." *Free Radical Biology and Medicine* 89 (2015): 852–862.

Pasiakos, S. M., H. R. Lieberman, and T. M. McLellan. "Effects of Protein Supplements on Muscle Damage, Soreness and Recovery of Muscle Function and Physical Performance: A Systematic Review." *Sports Medicine* 44, no. 5 (2014): 655–670.

Paulsen, G., K. T. Cumming, G. Holden, J. Hallén, B. R. Rønnestad, O. Sveen, A. Skaug, et al. "Vitamin C and E Supplementation Hampers Cellular Adaptation to Endurance Training in Humans: A Double-Blind, Randomised, Controlled Trial." *Journal of Physiology* 592, no. 8 (2014): 1887–1901.

Peake, J. M., and S. C. Gandevia. "Replace, Restore, Revive: The Keys to Recovery After Exercise." *Journal of Applied Physiology* 122, no. 3 (2017): 531–532.

Pearcey, G. E., D. J. Bradbury-Squires, J. E. Kawamoto, E. J. Drinkwater, D. G. Behm, and D. C. Button. "Foam Rolling for Delayed-Onset Muscle Soreness and Recovery of Dynamic Performance Measures." *Journal of Athletic Training* 50, no. 1 (2015): 5–13.

Phillips, S. M., K. D. Tipton, A. Aarsland, S. E. Wolf, and R. R. Wolfe. "Mixed Muscle Protein Synthesis and Breakdown After Resistance Exercise in Humans." *American Journal of Physiology* 273, no. 1, part 1 (1997): E99–107.

Sands, W. A., J. R. McNeal, S. R. Murray, and M. H. Stone. "Dynamic Compression Enhances Pressure-to-Pain Threshold in Elite Athlete Recovery: Exploratory Study." *Journal of Strength and Conditioning Research* 29, no. 5 (2015): 1263–1272.

Schoenfeld, B. J. "The Use of Nonsteroidal Anti-Inflammatory Drugs for Exercise-Induced Muscle Damage: Implications for Skeletal Muscle Development." *Sports Medicine* 42, no. 12 (2012): 1017–1028.

Ten Haaf, T., S. van Staveren, E. Oudenhoven, M. F. Piacentini, R. Meeusen, B. Roelands, L. Koenderman, et al. "Prediction of Functional Overreaching from Subjective Fatigue and Readiness to Train After Only 3 Days of Cycling." *Supplement, International Journal of Sports Physiology and Performance* 12, no. S2 (2017): S287–S294.

Thiriet, P., D. Gozal, D. Wouassi, T. Oumarou, H. Gelas, and J. R. Lacour. "The Effect of Various Recovery Modalities on Subsequent Performance in Supramaximal Exercise." *Journal of Sports Medicine and Physical Fitness* 33, no. 2 (1993): 118–129.

Thorpe, R. T., A. J. Strudwick, M. Buchheit, G. Atkinson, B. Drust, and W. Gregson. "Sensitivity of Morning-Measured Fatigue Variables in Elite Soccer Players." Supplement, *International Journal of Sports Physiology and Performance* 12, no. S2 (2017): S2107–S2113.

Tiidus, P. M. "Manual Massage and Recovery of Muscle Function Following Exercise: A Literature Review." *Journal of Orthopedic Sports Physical Therapy* 25, no. 2 (1997): 107–112.

Tiidus, P. M., and J. K. Shoemaker. "Effleurage Massage, Muscle Blood Flow and Long-Term Post-Exercise Strength Recovery." *International Journal of Sports Medicine* 16, no. 7 (1995): 478–483.

Tomlin, D. L., and H. A. Wenger. "The Relationship Between Fitness and Recovery from High Intensity Intermittent Exercise." *Sports Medicine* 31, no. 1 (2001): 1–11.

Tseng, C. Y., J. P. Lee, Y. S. Tsai, S. D. Lee, C. L. Kao, T. C. Liu, C. Lai, et al. "Topical Cooling (Icing) Delays Recovery from Eccentric Exercise-Induced Muscle Damage." *Journal of Strength and Conditioning Research* 27, no. 5 (2013): 1354–1361.

Tucker, T. J., D. R. Slivka, J. S. Cuddy, W. S. Hailes, and B. C. Ruby. "Effect of Local Cold Application on Glycogen Recovery." *Journal of Sports Medicine and Physical Fitness* 52, no. 2 (2012): 158–164.

Weerapong, P., P. A. Hume, and G. S. Kolt. "The Mechanisms of Massage and Effects on Performance, Muscle Recovery and Injury Prevention." *Sports Medicine* 35, no. 3 (2005): 235–256.

Ziltener, J. L., S. Leal, and P. E. Fournier. "Non-Steroidal Anti-Inflammatory Drugs for Athletes: An Update." *Annals of Physical and Rehabilitation Medicine* 53, no. 4 (2010): 278–288.

Chapter 12

Baum, B. "Lower Extremity Muscle Activities During Cycling Are Influenced by Load and Frequency." *Journal of Electromyography and Kinesiology* 13, no. 2 (2003): 181–190.

Behm, D. G., D. Cappa, and G. A. Power. "Trunk Muscle Activation During Moderate and High-Intensity Running." *Applied Physiology, Nutrition and Metabolism* 34, no. 6 (2009): 1008–1016.

Behm, D. G., and D. G. Sale. "Intended Rather Than Actual Movement Velocity Determines Velocity-Specific Training Response." *Journal of Applied Physiology* 74, no. 1 (1993): 359–368.

Bijker, K., G. Groot, and A. Hollander. "Differences in Leg Muscle Activity During Running and Cycling in Humans." *European Journal of Applied Physiology* 87, no. 6 (2002): 556–561.

Byrne, C., C. Faure, D. J. Keene, and S. E. Lamb. "Aging, Muscle Power and Physical Function: A Systematic Review and Implications for Pragmatic Training Interventions." *Sports Medicine* 46, no. 9 (2016): 1311–1332.

Carroll, T. J., S. Riek, and R. G. Carson. "Neural Adaptations to Resistance Training." *Sports Medicine* 31, no. 12 (2001): 829–840.

Cormie, P., M. R. McGuigan, and R. U. Newton. "Developing Maximal Neuromuscular Power: Part 1—Biological Basis of Maximal Power Production." *Sports Medicine* 41, no. 1 (2011): 17–38.

———. "Developing Maximal Neuromuscular Power: Part 2—Training Considerations for Improving Maximal Power Production." *Sports Medicine* 41, no. 2 (2011): 125–146.

Craig, B. W., R. Brown, and J. Everhart. "Effects of Progressive Resistance Training on Growth Hormone and Testosterone Levels in Young and Elderly Subjects." *Mechanisms of Ageing and Development* 49, no. 2 (1989): 159–169.

Davies, T., R. Orr, M. Halaki, and D. Hackett. "Effect of Training Leading to Repetition Failure on Muscular Strength: A Systematic Review and Meta-Analysis." *Sports Medicine* 46, no. 4 (2016): 487–502.

Ebben, W. P., M. L. Fauth, L. R. Garceau, and E. J. Petrushek. "Kinetic Quantification of Plyometric Exercise Intensity." *Journal of Strength and Conditioning Research* 25, no. 12 (2011): 3288–3298.

Ebben, W. P., A. G. Kindler, K. A. Chirdon, N. C. Jenkins, A. J. Polichnowski, and A. V. Ng. "The Effect of High-Load vs. High-Repetition Training on Endurance Performance." *Journal of Strength and Conditioning Research* 18, no. 3 (2004): 513–517.

Fisher, J., J. Steele, and D. Smith. "High- and Low-Load Resistance Training: Interpretation and Practical Application of Current Research Findings." *Sports Medicine* 47, no. 3 (2017): 393–400.

Goto, K., M. Nagasawa, O. Yanagisawa, T. Kizuka, N. Ishii, and K. Takamatsu. "Muscular Adaptations to Combinations of High- and Low-Intensity Resistance Exercises." *Journal of Strength and Conditioning Research* 18, no. 4 (2004): 730–737.

Hakkinen, K., A. Pakarinen, M. Alen, H. Kauhanen, and P. V. Komi. "Neuromuscular and Hormonal Adaptations in Athletes to Strength Training in Two Years." *Journal of Applied Physiology* 65, no. 6 (1988): 2406–2412.

Hug, F., and S. Dorel. "Electromyographic Analysis of Pedaling: A Review." *Journal of Electromyography and Kinesiology* 19, no. 2 (2009): 182–198.

Jakobsen, M. D., E. Sundstrup, C. H. Andersen, P. Aagaard, and L. L. Andersen. "Muscle Activity During Leg Strengthening Exercise Using Free Weights and Elastic Resistance: Effects of Ballistic vs. Controlled Contractions." *Human Movement Science* 32, no. 1 (2013): 65–78.

Jorge, M., and M. Hull. "Analysis of EMG Measuring During Bicycle Pedaling." *Journal of Biomechanics* 19, no. 9 (1986): 683–694.

Kokkonen, J., A. G. Nelson, and A. Cornwell. "Acute Muscle Stretching Inhibits Maximal Strength Performance." *Research Quarterly in Exercise and Sport* 69, no. 4 (1998): 411–415.

Kraemer, W. J., R. S. Staron, F. C. Hagerman, R. S. Hikida, A. C. Fry, S. E. Gordon, B. C. Nidl, et al. "The Effects of Short-Term Resistance Training on Endocrine Function in Men and Women." *European Journal of Applied Physiology* 78, no. 1 (1998): 69–76.

Lee, B., and S. McGill. "The Effect of Short-Term Isometric Training on Core/Torso Stiffness." *Journal of Sports Science* 26 (2016): 1–10.

Lee, B. C., and S. M. McGill. "Effect of Long-Term Isometric Training on Core/Torso Stiffness." *Journal of Strength and Conditioning Research* 29, no. 6 (2015): 1515–1526.

Levenhagen, D. K., J. D. Gresham, M. G. Carlson, D. J. Maron, M. J. Borel, and P. J. Flakoll. "Postexercise Nutrient Intake Timing in Humans Is Critical to Recovery of Leg Glucose and Protein Homeostasis." *American Journal of Physiology, Endocrinology and Metabolism* 280, no. 6 (2001): E982–993.

Markovic, G., I. Jukic, D. Milanovic, and D. Metikos. "Effects of Sprint and Plyometric Training on Muscle Function and Athletic Performance." *Journal of Strength and Conditioning Research* 21, no. 2 (2007): 543–549.

McCall, G. E., W. C. Byrnes, S. J. Fleck, A. Dickinson, and W. J. Kraemer. "Acute and Chronic Hormonal Responses to Resistance Training Designed to Promote Muscle Hypertrophy." *Canadian Journal of Applied Physiology* 24, no. 1 (1999): 96–107.

McDaniel, J., A. Subudhi, and J. C. Martin. "Torso Stabilization Reduces the Metabolic Cost of Producing Cycling Power." *Canadian Journal of Applied Physiology* 30, no. 4 (2005): 433–441.

Mitchell, C. J., T. A. Churchward-Venne, D. W. West, N. A. Burd, L. Breen, S. K. Baker, and S. M. Phillips. "Resistance Exercise Load Does Not Determine Training-Mediated Hypertrophic Gains in Young Men." *Journal of Applied Physiology* 113, no. 1 (2012): 71–77.

Phillips, S. M. "A Brief Review of Critical Processes in Exercise-Induced Muscular Hypertrophy." *Supplement, Sports Medicine* 44, no. S1 (2014): S71–S77.

Rasmussen, B. B., K. D. Tipton, S. L. Miller, S. E. Wolf, and R. R. Wolfe. "An Oral Essential Amino Acid-Carbohydrate Supplement Enhances Muscle Protein Anabolism After Resistance Exercise." *Journal of Applied Physiology* 88, no. 2 (2000): 386–392.

Rønnestad, B. R., E. A. Hansen, and T. Raastad. "In-Season Strength Maintenance Training Increases Well-Trained Cyclists' Performance." *European Journal of Applied Physiology* 110, no. 6 (2010): 1269–1282.

Rumpf, M. C., R. G. Lockie, J. B. Cronin, and F. Jalilvand. "The Effect of Different Sprint Training Methods on Sprint Performance Over Various Distances: A Brief Review." *Journal of Strength and Conditioning Research* 30, no. 6 (2016): 1767–1785.

Schoenfeld, B. J. "Is There a Minimum Intensity Threshold for Resistance Training-Induced Hypertrophic Adaptations?" *Sports Medicine* 43, no. 12 (2013): 1279–1288.

Schoenfeld, B. J., J. M. Wilson, R. P. Lowery, and J. W. Krieger. "Muscular Adaptations in Low- Versus High-Load Resistance Training: A Meta-Analysis." *European Journal of Sport Science* 16, no. 1 (2016): 1–10.

Seger, J. Y., B. Arvidsson, and A. Thorstensson. "Specific Effects of Eccentric and Concentric Training on Muscle Strength and Morphology in Humans." *European Journal of Applied Physiology and Occupational Physiology* 79, no. 1 (1998): 49–57.

Sforzo, G. A., and P. R. Touey. "Manipulating Exercise Order Affects Muscular Performance During a Resistance Exercise Training Session." *Journal of Strength and Conditioning Research* 10, no. 1 (1996): 20–24.

Simão, R., B. F. de Salles, T. Figueiredo, I. Dias, and J. M. Willardson. "Exercise Order in Resistance Training." *Sports Medicine* 42, no. 3 (2012): 251–265.

Staron, R. S., D. L. Karapondo, W. J. Kraemer, A. C. Fry, S. E. Gordon, J. E. Falkel, F. C. Hagerman, and R. S. Hikida. "Skeletal Muscle Adaptations During Early Phase of Heavy-Resistance Training in Men and Women." *Journal of Applied Physiology* 76, no. 3 (1994): 1247–1255.

Sunde, A., O. Støren, M. Bjerkaas, M. H. Larsen, J. Hoff, and J. Helgerud. "Maximal Strength Training Improves Cycling Economy in Competitive Cyclists." *Journal of Strength and Conditioning Research* 24, no. 8 (2010): 2157–2165.

Tipton, K. D., B. B. Rasmussen, S. L. Miller, S. E. Wolf, S. K. Owens-Stovall, B. E. Petrini, and R. R. Wolfe. "Timing of Amino Acid-Carbohydrate Ingestion Alters Anabolic Response of Muscle to Resistance Exercise." *American Journal of Physiology, Endocrinology and Metabolism* 281, no. 2 (2001): E197–206.

Vikmoen, O., B. R. Rønnestad, S. Ellefsen, and T. Raastad. "Heavy Strength Training Improves Running and Cycling Performance Following Prolonged Submaximal Work in Well-Trained Female Athletes." *Physiological Reports* 5, no. 5 (2017): e13149.

Willardson, J. M. "A Brief Review: Factors Affecting the Length of the Rest Interval Between Resistance Exercise Sets." *Journal of Strength and Conditioning Research* 20, no. 4 (2006): 978–984.

Chapter 13

Banister, E. W., J. B. Carter, and P. C. Zarkadas. "Training Theory and Taper: Validation in Triathlon Athletes." *European Journal of Applied Physiology and Occupational Physiology* 79, no. 2 (1999): 182–191.

Houmard, J. A. "Impact of Reduced Training on Performance in Endurance Athletes." *Sports Medicine* 12, no. 6 (1991): 380–393.

Mujika, I., A. Goya, S. Padilla, A. Grijalba, E. Gorostiaga, and J. Ibañez. "Physiological Responses to a 6-d Taper in Middle-Distance Runners: Influence of Training Intensity and Volume." *Medicine and Science in Sports and Exercise* 32, no. 2 (2000): 511–517.

Mujika, I., and S. Padilla. "Scientific Bases for Precompetition Tapering Strategies." *Medicine and Science in Sports and Exercise* 35, no. 7 (2003): 1182–1187.

Mujika, I., B. R. Rønnestad, and D. T. Martin. "Effects of Increased Muscle Strength and Muscle Mass on Endurance-Cycling Performance." *International Journal of Sports Physiology and Performance* 11, no. 3 (2016): 283–289.

Shepley, B., J. D. MacDougall, N. Cipriano, J. R. Sutton, M. A. Tarnopolsky, and G. Coates. "Physiological Effects of Tapering in Highly Trained Athletes." *Journal of Applied Physiology* 72, no. 2 (1992): 706–711.

Thomas, L., I. Mujika, T. Busso. "Computer Simulations Assessing the Potential Performance Benefit of a Final Increase in Training During Pre-Event Taper." *Journal of Strength and Conditioning Research* 23, no. 6 (2009): 1729–1736.

Chapter 14

Atkinson, G., O. Peacock, and L. Passfield. "Variable Versus Constant Power Strategies During Cycling Time-Trials: Prediction of Time Savings Using an Up-to-Date Mathematical Model." *Journal of Sports Science* 25, no. 9 (2007): 1001–1009.

Cherry, P. W., H. K. Lakomy, M. E. Nevill, and R. J. Fletcher. "Constant External Work Cycle Exercise: The Performance and Metabolic Effects of All-Out and Even-Paced Strategies." *European Journal of Applied Physiology and Occupational Physiology* 75, no. 1 (1997): 22–27.

Foster, C., A. C. Snyder, N. N. Thompson, M. A. Green, M. Foley, and M. Schrager. "Effect of Pacing Strategy on Cycle Time Trial Performance." *Medicine and Science in Sports and Exercise* 25, no. 3 (1993): 383–388.

González-Alonso, J., C. Teller, S. L. Andersen, F. B. Jensen, T. Hyldig, and B. Nielsen. "Influence of Body Temperature on the Development of Fatigue During Prolonged Exercise in the Heat." *Journal of Applied Physiology* 86, no. 3 (1999): 1032–1039.

Piacentini, M. F., and R. Meeusen. "An Online Training-Monitoring System to Prevent Nonfunctional Overreaching." *International Journal of Sports Physiology and Performance* 10, no. 4 (2015): 524–527.

Swain, D. P. "A Model for Optimizing Cycling Performance by Varying Power on Hills and in Wind." *Medicine and Science in Sports and Exercise* 29, no. 8 (1997): 1104–1108.

INDEX

Italicized page numbers indicate a figure, table, or illustration.

Power
about, 195–197
-based training, 254
-duration curves, 17–18
zones, 50–52
Power cleans, 218–219, 226
The Power Meter Handbook (Friel), 53, 69, 99, 254
Power meters
about, xii, 43
for experienced cyclists, 31
for field tests, 67–68, 266–267
fitness and, 36, 65–66
necessity for training, 58–59, 69
for workouts, 222, 260, 263–265
zones and, 50–51
Power-to-weight ratios, 18
Preparation periods, 92–93, 103, 106, 116–117, 122, 130, 221, *224*
Principles, training
of individuality, 30, 33–34, 38, 146
of progressive overload, 28, 38, 145
of reversibility, 29–30, 38, 145–146, 174
of specificity, 28–29, 38, 145
Progressive overload, principle of, 28, 38, 145
Protein-rich foods, 203–204
Purposeful training, 20–21, 55, 61
Pyramid intervals (AnE3), 264–265

Q
Quadriceps muscles, 212

R
Race periods
duration of, *103*
linear periodization and, *92*, 147
tapering and, 230–231, 233–236
weight lifting and, 120–121
workouts in, 124
Race readiness, 34–35, 53, 229–230, 247
Races
fitness and results of, 35, 37
planning for first important, 92–93

planning for secondary, 93–95
prioritizing, 100–102
Race week recovery, 189
Racing Tactics for Cyclists (Prehn), 132
Random training, 147
Rating of Perceived Exertion (RPE), 42–43, 45, 50, 53, 75, 225
Rear derailleurs, 58
Recovery
active, *103*, 174, 180, 191, 233
adaptation and, 61, 178–181
aids, 182–186
anaerobic endurance workouts and, 80–81
in base and build periods, 125, 188–189
breakthrough workouts and, 133
on demand, 90, 190
before field testing, 49, 67
fitness and, 29, 34, 173
form and, 39
individuality of, 174
long-term, xiii
between mesocycles, 103–105
natural, 181–182
overreaching and, 167, 169
overtraining and, 65, 167, 170
passive, 110, 174, 180
post-race, 93
prior to B-races, 102, 107
progressive overload and, 28
race week, 189
short-term, xiii
slow, *103*, 104–105, 147–150, 187
stage racing and, 132–133
strategic, 186–191
tapering and, 231–232, 235
training diary and, 247
during transition period, 120, 124, 189–190
weight lifting and, 199, 202
Recovery workout (AE1), 259
Reps, weight lifting, 198–199
Responders, fast and slow, 19
Rest
at end of base and build weeks, 125
fitness and, 29
overreaching and, 169

ABOUT THE AUTHOR

Joe Friel is a lifelong athlete and holds a master's degree in exercise science. He has trained and conferred with amateur and professional endurance athletes from a wide variety of sports since 1980. His coaching experience and research led him to cofound TrainingPeaks.com in 1999 with son Dirk Friel and friend Gear Fisher.

Friel is currently retired from one-on-one coaching and now updates emerging top-level coaches from several sports on best practices for preparing endurance athletes for competition, work that regularly takes him to coaching seminars around the world. He also consults with corporations in the sports and fitness industry and with national Olympic governing bodies worldwide. His Training Bible books for road cyclists, mountain bikers, and triathletes are used by several national sports federations to train their coaches.

Friel's philosophy and methodology for training athletes was developed over more than 30 years and is based on his strong interest in sports science research and his experience training hundreds of athletes with a wide range of abilities. His views on matters related to training for endurance sports are widely sought and have been featured in such publications as *VeloNews, Bicycling, Outside, Runner's World, Women's Sports & Fitness, Men's Fitness, Men's Health, American Health, Masters Sports*, the *New York Times, Triathlete*, and many more.

For more information on training and for personal contact, go to his blog at joefrielsblog.com and follow him on Twitter at @jfriel.

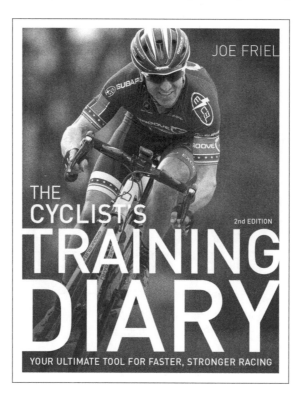

37 Jade Street
Walla Walla, WA 99362